THE
LITTLE
BOOK
OF
GENIUS

DR KEITH SOUTER

ILLUSTRATED BY FIONA MCDONALD

The
History
Press

For Nik, one of my oldest friends, who first introduced me to
the concept of heuristics

First published 2011

The History Press
The Mill, Brimscombe Port
Stroud, Gloucestershire, GL5 2QG
www.thehistorypress.co.uk

British Library Cataloguing in Publication Data.
A catalogue record for this book is available from the British Library.

ISBN 978 0 7524 5868 7

Typesetting and origination by The History Press
Printed in Great Britain
Manufacturing managed by Jellyfish Print Solutions Ltd

CONTENTS

ACKNOWLEDGEMENTS

This book began in the Galleria dell'Accademia in Florence. Not the actual writing, you understand, simply the idea. I was there to see the statue of David by Michelangelo. Unfortunately, I couldn't get as close as I wanted, because there was a large chap lying on his back with a cushion under his head. He was staring up at the statue and nodding his head.

'You need to view him from the ground,' he explained as he rose to his feet. 'Look, the head and the hands are out of proportion. Michelangelo meant for it to be mounted on the cathedral roofline. If you look up you will see how he meant it to be seen.'

I was impressed. That little snippet of information dropped into conversation would make one sound really knowledgeable about sculpture. From that simple idea the book developed.

And now it is done, I would like to thank some special people. First of all, I thank Dr Nik Chmiel for our many long and interesting discussions about all sorts of things when we were students.

I am grateful to Isabel Atherton, my wonderful agent at Creative Authors, whose advice on the manuscript was of great help.

Thanks to Simon Hamlet who was the Senior Commissioning Editor at The History Press and who accepted the book and started it on its road.

A huge thank you to Fiona McDonald, my talented artist and friend, who skilfully interpreted my text to make the book such a visually appealing work.

And finally, many thanks to my editor, Abbie Wood, for polishing the book, and to Lindsey Smith for help with the wonderful cover.

It has been a pleasure to work with you all.

INTRODUCTION

It is a fact that few people can truly claim to be called genius. The thing is that you don't have to be a genius to get by. There is nothing wrong in being one of the crowd, but, equally, there is nothing wrong in wanting to stand out – to shine.

If you pass a degree then you are assumed to have a significant knowledge about a subject. Yet you may have only scraped through with 50 per cent of the knowledge required to pass the syllabus for that degree. And that is a selected syllabus, rather than the whole subject. Then if you take a higher degree, that does not mean that you study more and more about the subject. Usually it means that you study more about a smaller area. Thus, an expert is actually someone who knows a great deal about less and less. If you get him or her off that small area then you may seem to be just as expert, because it is easy to get yourself up to the level of 'less.' If you do it with good humour then you will be seen as a pleasant dilettante, and that is a good reputation to have.

The premise that I am using in this book is that **'less is more.'** That may seem trite, but in fact you can use heuristics, or rules of thumb, to appear very knowledgeable through a whole range of subjects and topics. And the nature of heuristics is that you can do this very quickly, with just basic knowledge.

Do you remember people at school, college or university who seemed to goof around, yet who always did well at exams? They may even have been a source of irritation to others who had covered the whole subject and spent far longer in studying it. It may have seemed unfair that they were so successful with so little effort. Well, they were probably lucky to an extent, but they also probably used heuristics, or rules of thumb, to get quick results.

At parties or meetings, have you ever felt as if you are part of the furniture, unable to contribute because you know nothing about the topic of conversation? There are others who you know will have even less knowledge, yet they can hold forth and hold their own. You can learn to do that and you can be the one whose knowledge people admire.

This book will show you how.

PART 1

THE SEEDS OF GENIUS

YOU DON'T HAVE TO BE A GENIUS

Genius is 1 per cent inspiration and 99 per cent perspiration.

Thomas Alva Edison
Inventor and genius

It must be pretty amazing being a genius, don't you think? To be able to develop an idea that is so mind-bogglingly clever that you alter the very way that people think. The French philosopher, mathematician and physicist René Descartes did just that in 1637 when he wrote '*cogito ergo sum*,' meaning 'I think, therefore I am.' In that simple aphorism, which tells you that you prove your existence merely by the act of thinking about it, he literally raised the consciousness of western civilisation. Accordingly, he was rightly hailed as the 'Father of Modern Philosophy.'

And how marvellous it must be to unravel the nature of the mysterious force of gravity, or reveal the way that the solar system works, and then invent a whole new branch of mathematics in order to

Leonardo da Vinci

have the tools to delve where no mind had delved before. Sir Isaac Newton did all that and much more in the closing years of the seventeenth century.

Living and working in Italy during the Renaissance, Leonardo da Vinci was hundreds of years ahead of his time in too many areas to cover. He was the greatest representational artist of all time, an inventor, anatomist and engineer, and he pushed back the frontiers in all of those areas.

William Shakespeare, England's great Tudor playwright, left us plays that make us laugh, weep, think and wonder. The characters that he created are wonderfully formed psychological studies of emotions which are equal to anything that was written by Freud, Jung or Adler almost 400 years later.

Wolfgang Amadeus Mozart was a virtuoso on the keyboard and violin, and was able to compose music at the age of 5. When he died at the tragically young age of 36 he had written over 600 pieces of music and enriched the world.

Charles Darwin, the great English naturalist, wrote *On the Origin of Species* in 1859. Undoubtedly this is one of the most influential scientific books of all time, outlining his theory that all species of life on Earth have descended from common ancestors, in a branching, evolving manner that he called 'natural selection.'

Thomas Alva Edison was the most prolific inventor in history, holding well over 1,000 patents on various inventions. And what inventions they were: things like the light bulb, the phonograph and the film projector.

And, of course, Albert Einstein, that epitome of genius, gave us the special and general theories of relativity which have transformed the world of physics, our whole view of reality and the nature of the universe and time.

All of these great men deserve to be called genius, although by his own admission Thomas Edison felt that much of his genius was down to sheer hard work. And this rather begs the question, 'what is a genius?' It is a question that we must look at quickly, if only to get it out of the way.

SO WHAT IS A GENIUS?

This is a word that is bandied about a lot these days. That is understandable, since our modern world is dominated by celebrity culture. The use of superlatives has become second nature to people. We describe qualities or inadequacies as being hyper- or ultra-, to emphasise that they are well beyond the norm, even when they patently are not. Some people, who were at one time proclaimed to be stars in their particular walk of life, would nowadays be referred to as super-stars or even mega-stars. Similarly, people who would once have been called 'talented' after making some modest contribution to art or knowledge will these days be accorded the title of 'genius.'

This is a step too far, in my opinion. A genius is a unique character. To be a genius requires far more than merely being intelligent, or attaining a certain rating in an intelligence test. It is having the ability not merely to push back frontiers, but to create new ones that no one else believed to be possible. It is the ability to conceptualise the previously inconceivable and express it in terms comprehensible to lesser brains.

On that basis, I think I would have reservations about including Edison in the select little group that I started with, and would place him in the lower realm of ordinary mortals, where most of us belong. That is not to lessen his gargantuan achievements, for he undoubtedly belongs within the upper echelons of the intelligentsia, along with your common-or-garden Nobel Prize-winner. And what is wrong with that? It is still a level to which most of us can only aspire.

Yet being a genius probably makes life difficult. How do you get a partner, for one thing? If you are brighter than everyone else around it must make for a pretty lonely existence. Of course, this presupposes that a genius is a genius in all areas of their life or in everything that they think. There is actually no reason to suppose that to be the case.

William Shakespeare may have been a dab hand at writing plays, but could he play the ukulele? Similarly, could Mozart work out the reason for the anatomy of a sea-whelk or the behaviour of a barnacle? We know that Isaac Newton could be preoccupied to the point of rudeness, forgetting that he had dinner guests, or that he had even had dinner on occasions. There is possibly a price to pay for genius.

I am being slightly facetious here. While one can laud genius, admire it and strive hard to understand it, if you were handed it on a plate, would you really want it? I suspect you would, but remember, gentle reader, the downside. There is the weight of expectation. You have to use that genius. You have to show that you are able to fathom the unfathomable; you must be brave enough to visit realms unthought of, to pose a question then answer it in a highly creative manner that is beyond that of your fellows. You risk ridicule, envy and, worse, self-loathing if you under-achieve what only you are capable of believing to be possible.

BUT YOU DON'T HAVE TO BE A GENIUS

The chances are that you are not a genius! OK, I've said it. You have read it and you can either gnash your teeth, throw the book into a corner, or accept it and get on with life.

Once again, there is a serious point here. Just imagine that you are sitting round a dinner table with one or other of these geniuses, or are having a drink with a group of them in the pub: would they fill the air with words, would their wit scintillate you and would their contributions to the discussion leave everyone in their wake?

We do not know, of course, but just because they exhibited genius in one area does not mean that they did so in all that they ever thought or did. A genius out of his or her particular environment might be nothing but a dullard and a bore.

On the other hand, there may be others at the table or standing by the bar who positively glitter, and they may have no actual genius for anything. Yet at that particular gathering they may appear to be the genius in your midst.

Now, if you already are that type of person who everyone listens to, then this book will have little appeal. However, if you are a genuine genius, but, despite your genius, you sometimes come across as a dullard or a bore, then maybe you will reap the rewards that may be gained by reading the whole lot. And if you are one of the crowd who would just like to be listened to, then read on.

DO YOU WANT TO SHINE?

This is really the crux of the matter. If you are the sort of person who hovers in the background and hopes that no one is going to ask for your opinion, then this book is for you. You may not be as confident as the chap who will expound on anything, even if you are just as bright as or more intelligent than him. Some people even find themselves agreeing with others when they actually totally disagree, so dented is their confidence to stand up for their own point of view. If that describes you, then read on. There may be help for you in this book.

Does it gall you when you seem to get beaten in arguments all the time, when no one listens to your point of view, or when your point of view is ruthlessly swept aside? Why is that, you may ask? Is it because you are ignorant of a subject? Do you simply not have the confidence to stand your ground? On the other hand, could it be that you actually are less able than those around you?

Don't even go there. You can be the person that people listen to. It can be your argument that wins the day. And it can be your knowledge that people admire. The simple truth is that you don't have to be a reservoir of information. You can get by with heuristic knowledge. You can win arguments by practising the art of sophistry. And you can use various techniques to shine and impress people in all sorts of social and professional situations.

They may even think that, in a way, you are a bit of a genius.

That is what this book is about. And that is what I am going to show you.

FIRST OF ALL FORGET ALL THAT IQ NONSENSE

That's right – forget it!

People may hold their hands up in horror at this suggestion, but don't worry about them. They are either psychologists who have a vested interest in setting IQ tests or people who have high IQs and believe that this makes them more intelligent than other people. That is nonsense. All that an IQ demonstrates is an aptitude to do IQ tests.

What a ridiculous thing an IQ score is. It is a bit like having a golf handicap, only in reverse. A good golfer is someone with a low handicap; a good IQ puzzle-solver has a high IQ. A low golf handicap shows that you have an aptitude for knocking a golf ball around a field in fewer shots than other folk, but it doesn't indicate that you are especially good at anything else. True, in golf clubs you will go to the top of the pecking order, you will belong to that part of the membership who describe themselves as 'tigers,' whereas the poor golfer possessed of a high handicap will have to play with others of his ilk, and be derided as a 'rabbit' by the tiger group.

The same thing goes for the IQ brigade. They love knowing that they have higher IQ scores than the riff-raff. To them, that score officially means that they are members of the intelligentsia, the cognoscenti, the boffins' club. The higher the score the more are they apt to think that they have or are not far short of genius.

Well, stuff and nonsense. Don't for a minute allow yourself to be brow-beaten by a high scoring IQ puzzle-solver. Don't imagine that their score means anything in the real world.

No, none of it matters. Your own IQ is a total irrelevance. What we are talking about here in this book is how to make the best of yourself to win arguments, get your point across, make good decisions and appear to know what you are talking about. Generally, to be more confident in life.

And you can learn to do all this by understanding a bit about how the mind works, developing strategies to apply and use in arguments, and how to use basic knowledge to hold your own in any discussion. If you understand heuristics, or rules of thumb, which I shall come to later in the book, then you will appreciate the concept that 'less is more.'

Confidence may be one of the issues that you have, especially in social settings. Your confidence can be built up if you equip yourself with techniques to 'shine.' And here is how we are going to do it.

YOU CAN LOSE AN ARGUMENT
BEFORE YOU OPEN YOUR MOUTH

That is perfectly true. You may expect to lose and may even tend to avoid arguments and discussions because of your poor history in arguments or debates. Yet you may watch politicians in the news or on TV panel programmes spout utter nonsense, only to give a counter-argument on a later occasion or after there has been a change in party policy. You may form the opinion that politicians are dishonest bounders who change their minds and their opinions more often than you change your socks. If you think that, you risk missing the point. Politicians tend to be brilliant arguers. They don't lose; they win arguments, even when they should lose. They know how to argue or debate.

And you can do this as well. It is a matter of knowing some simple techniques. That is what politicians do. They do not all enter the world with innate tough skins, bulldog tenacity and hyper-intelligence.

Let us stick with politicians for a moment and look at a single example of how they win arguments. They don't answer the question asked of them.

It is as simple as that. Watch them on the news and you will see. They will not answer a question immediately, unless they really know their onions. More usually they will be evasive for a while. They will go off on a little diatribe during which they will refer to the political credo of their party, then they will eventually give a round-about answer that more or less answers the question, but which no one notices because they have diverted you from the original and you are either left marvelling at their intelligence or cursing their audacity. But they will have had their say.

The political answer is only one of several manoeuvres that you need to spot and understand. If you can see what other people are doing in a debate, then you can understand and apply the appropriate measures that can undermine their arguments. Arm yourself with, say, half a dozen of these little techniques and your confidence in such matters may soar. We will look at this in the chapter on the Lost Art of Sophistry.

UNDERSTAND HOW
PEOPLE MAKE DECISIONS

I am sure you will have marvelled at the wisdom of some people. And at the same time cringed and cursed the incompetence and rank stupidity of others. Decision-making is a fascinating study in itself. Whether it is a world leader making an unbelievably important and far-reaching decision, a top banker deciding how to handle his bank's finances or a general ordering a hazardous mission, all of them think that they are making a balanced, bias-free decision. Yet they probably are not. When it comes down to it, a decision may seem multi-faceted, complex and based on massive data, yet ultimately it will be stripped of all of these complexities and data to become a simple final choice one way or the other.

If you can understand basic decision-making you may make life a bit easier for yourself.

CULTIVATE A SENSE OF HUMOUR
AND CONSIDER TELLING THE ODD JOKE

Well, don't you envy those joke-tellers? It really is a useful thing to be able to do. Especially if you can drop in a quick-witted quip or an appropriate anecdote that isn't going to bore everyone or make them cringe.

I don't mean that you have to aim at doing a stand-up routine suitable for the Comedy Club, but you can learn ways of delivering a good wheeze to get them chuckling.

CULTIVATE YOUR MEMORY

There is nothing worse than having to excuse yourself for not remembering someone, forgetting their name or what they do. People will recognise you, recall your name and oddities, so why can't you?

Well of course you can. It is lazy not to and it is arrogant to think that you don't need to. If you want to shine, lick that memory into shape.

As we shall see, it is not that difficult.

KNOW THYSELF

All of this is working towards better awareness of yourself, your strengths, your weaknesses and your emotional tendencies. If you can understand yourself better then you can interact with others more effectively. And if you can understand other people then you are on your way to the most useful type of communication with them. This is what life is about.

BASIC KNOWLEDGE OF EVERYTHING

That might sound a tall order, but really it is not difficult to pick up the rudiments of anything. You may shy away from some areas in the belief that you know nothing about a subject. Take mathematics as an example. Many people struggle with elementary mental arithmetic and positively shudder at the mention of anything as rarefied as trigonometry or differential calculus.

But you don't need to be a maths whiz to get by. Everyone can learn a few basic mental arithmetic techniques to shine. And if you just brush up on a few facts then you will be surprised at how well you can hold your own at dinner parties.

Three Facts Are Generally All You Need

It is true: if you just know about three facts on a subject, such as you will find in the chapters of Part 2, then you can, by dropping them into a conversation, or expounding on them, really appear to know your onions – or your physics, Latin or mathematics.

In the second part of this book we are going to look at all sorts of things, from art to Zen, from poetry, philosophy and economics to science, sport and cooking. None of these chapters will be enough to get you a degree, but they will cover sufficient points to help you get by.

So, you may not be a genius, but you can still shine.

2

HEURISTICS AND RULES OF THUMB

A heuristic can make you smart,
And a rule of thumb can too.
Whether it be science or art,
These things will work for you.

Professor Phineas J. Stackpool
Phrenologist and mesmerist

Judgement is difficult. No one ever really teaches you how to do it. Parents may drum their code of morals into you, teachers may tell you what society expects, but when it comes down to it, you end up making your own decisions for good or ill. You may think that your teachers, professors and all the people who occupy positions of trust and responsibility have a special handle on judgement, but the truth is that they don't. Even geniuses don't always get it right. So what hope is there for mere heads of government? They are as much in the dark as you and I. Yet it need not be as gloomy as that, if you understand a little about how we think. If you can do that then you are on your way to making mental short-cuts. And that will help you see what this book is all about.

WAS KING SOLOMON REALLY ALL THAT WISE?

Judgement is a highly complex thought process. In an ideal world, judgement would be a matter of pure logic, wherein following a sequence of steps would lead to a correct solution. Yet experience teaches us that judgement can be extremely difficult, whether it is a straightforward decision between two options or selecting one item from many, all of which have both positive and negative factors to consider.

Good judgement is generally thought to be related to wisdom, as illustrated by the Biblical tale of the Wisdom of Solomon. The story goes that two harlots went to King Solomon, both claiming to be the rightful mother of a child. One claimed that her own baby had been swapped for the other's dead baby during the night. The other denied it vigorously. Solomon asked for a sword and offered to have the baby cut in two, with one half to be given to each mother. The rightful mother pleaded for this not to happen and for the baby to be given to the other mother. Solomon judged that she must be the true mother.

Now, is that not an example of good, clear, clinically detached judgement? I leave you to make up your own mind. But, on the other hand, ancient writers acknowledged that decision-making could be flawed by personal desires that had no relationship to logic or wisdom, as in Homer's account of the Judgement of Paris. This comes from the *Iliad*.

At the nuptials of Thetis and Peleus all the gods had been invited except for Eris, the Goddess of Discord. This peeved her no end, so she tossed an apple into the hall with the inscription, 'for the fairest.' Hera, Athena and Aphrodite all claimed it. Wise god that he was, Zeus declined to make the judgement but gave the task to a mortal, Paris, son of King Priam of Troy. All three goddesses attempted to bribe him: Hera with power and riches; Athena with victory in battle and Aphrodite with the love of the most beautiful of mortal women, Helen, the wife of King Menelaus of Sparta (usually known as Helen of Troy). Paris succumbed to Aphrodite's bribery, awarded her the apple and gained Helen – and the consequence was the Trojan War.

What do you think of that? Was it a good decision or a faulty one?

The point is that people have to make decisions and judgements every day in every walk in life. The decisions may be good, fair or bad, and the consequences have to be lived with. In many instances, judgement may be skewed because the person making the judgement may approach the situation with a particular emotional viewpoint, or he or she may be swayed by an argument in a particular manner. In other words, bias may be introduced.

In complex systems involving the selection of one option from a great range of possibilities judgement can be extremely difficult. It seems that when faced with a great number of options people try to trim the number down to manageable proportions, and then further subdivide until the best fit is obtained. It is not always done in a mathematically precise or even a logical order. What seems to happen is that we use rules of thumb, or heuristics, to help us.

ALGORITHMS AND HEURISTICS

I am not going to get bogged down with the concept of what 'thought' is. That is one of the toughest of philosophical questions. Let us just accept that you do a lot of thinking and that you are a really intelligent human being. You can be assured that you are, since you are reading this book and following everything so far.

Let us take it a step further and suppose that you understand what thought is and that you want to build a thinking machine. People do this for a living, you know. Not just in the realms of science fiction but in the lab.

Scientists working in the field of cybernetics strive to create computer programmes that will think and ultimately feel and function in a manner akin to a living system. The goal of producing Artificial Intelligence (AI) is a daunting one, yet much headway is being made, at least in some ways. For example, computers have been designed to perform 'high-level' skills, such as playing chess at grandmaster level. On the other hand, 'low-level' skills, such as recognition of a face, are proving almost impossible to achieve. In other words, the machine is not yet ready to take over.

There are two basic types of process that are programmed into AI machines: algorithms and heuristics.

Algorithms are named after the Iranian mathematician Al-Khawarizmi (AD 790–840). This man was a genius. He invented the subject of algebra, the name of which has been derived from his book *Al-Jabr wa-al-Muqabilah*. He explained the use of zero, developed the decimal system and had the term algorithm named after him.

An algorithm refers to a detailed sequence of actions which have to be performed in a finite number of steps in order to accomplish a task or solve a problem. In a cybernetic sense it is logical thought involving a purely mechanical, logical sequence of steps. Any computer programme is by this token an algorithm.

Heuristics are rules of thumb that are also integrated into AI programs. They are defined as being rules that are sometimes useful. They basically reduce or limit the search for solutions in areas that are difficult, complex or poorly understood. But a heuristic is not necessarily logical. While an algorithm will always deliver a logical answer, a heuristic may not always do so.

Yet another meaning of heuristic is that it is 'learning by experience' or 'finding out for oneself.'

In a computer programme for playing expert chess, for example, this mix may be advantageous. Chess-playing is a mixture of cold logic, which is algorithmic, and non-logic, which is heuristic.

ALGORITHMS MAY BE SLOW, HEURISTICS ARE FAST

In mathematics the application of algorithms should lead to a logical answer, although it may take a long time to arrive at the solution. Heuristics can also be applied, and can shorten the working of a problem, to produce an answer that is usually fairly accurate, although it may not be so. Suppose you need to set aside an amount of money to pay your tax. You go to an accountant and ask him the question. He may not want to give you an answer, because he wants to go through all of your books and finances and do the calculations in order to give you an accurate figure. That is, he wants to go through an algorithmic routine. Yet that may not be what you want. You want a quick ball-park figure so that you can plan. You want an estimate, or a guesstimate. You want a heuristically chosen figure.

HEURISTICS ARE UNCONSCIOUS RULES OF THUMB

The term heuristic is of Greek origin, meaning 'serving to find out or discover.' The word was introduced into the English language in the early 1800s, at which time it meant 'a useful, even indispensable thought process for solving problems that cannot be handled by logic and probability theory.'

Albert Einstein used it in 1905 in the title of a paper on theoretical physics: 'On a heuristic point of view concerning the generation and transformation of light.' In this paper Einstein used the word to mean an approach to a problem that is necessarily incomplete given the knowledge available, and hence unavoidably false, but which is useful nonetheless for guiding thinking in appropriate directions.

Essentially, a heuristic is a thought process that we tend to use if not in place of logic, at least as a short-cut or rule of thumb. And the bulk of evidence shows that people working in complex situations of uncertainty tend to operate heuristically.

In general there are three situations or types of problem where they seem to be particularly suited. These are: where the problem is 'fuzzy' or not easily definable; where the problem is complex and not easily broken down; and where the problem is large, and there is limited time to solve it.

THE 'SATISFICING' HEURISTIC

Herbert A. Simon introduced the term 'satisficing' in 1957. His concept was that in difficult situations one may strive to obtain an outcome that is 'good enough.' It is essentially a corner-cutting process that people often opt for when time is running out, or when they have used up their available time without reaching a decision.

Rational theories of decision-making would propose that one chooses the best option available from all the alternatives on offer. Simon argued that people are more likely to *satisfice*, that is to achieve a good enough result, even though it is not necessarily the best. They effectively choose the first option that meets their minimum criteria, thereby using the minimum amount of mental energy.

JUDGEMENT HEURISTICS

Following on from Simon's work, Daniel Kahneman and Amos Tversky in the 1970s introduced their 'heuristics and bias' approach. Their work drew attention to the unconscious mental processes that are used to make complex decisions manageable. As a result, an individual can arrive at both accurate but also biased decisions.

The basic concept that they introduced was that judgement in an uncertain setting is often based on a limited number of heuristics, rather than formal logical processes.

They identified three general judgement heuristics:

Firstly, the *representativeness heuristic*. This heuristic involves judging the likelihood of an event or situation, based on similarity between that event and existing knowledge about past similar situations. Essentially, judgements influenced by what is typical in a situation. For example, if you are shown two bottles of wine, one costing twice as much as the other, which will you choose to cook with? And if you were to taste them the chances are that you would find the more expensive one tastier and of a better quality. This has been fully researched by giving people the same wine with different labels. One is swayed by the representation heuristic.

Secondly, the *availability heuristic*. This heuristic refers to the way in which probability or frequency judgements are influenced by the ease with which past examples are recalled. Essentially, judgements are based on what comes easily to mind. It is available knowledge that you have from your past experience. For example, if you walk along a beach and you see a round smooth rock you are likely to think that it has been worn smooth by the action of the sea, rather than imagine it to be a meteor that had been worn smooth through its fiery descent from the skies. A sea-worn rock is commoner than a meteorite in your experience.

Thirdly, the *anchoring and adjustment heuristic*. This heuristic refers to the tendency to make a judgement that is biased towards a certain value. We anchor on that value and then adjust up or down to arrive at the ultimate result. Essentially, judgements relying on what comes first. Let us go back to your accountant and his wish to work everything out algorithmically, whereas you want him to guesstimate. So, on the basis of very approximate data, he anchors at a gross figure, and then adjusts up and down to allow for extra factors both ways. It is likely that his guesstimate will be close to his meticulously worked-out figuring. And that is what you wanted in the first place.

OTHER HEURISTICS

There is, in fact, a whole host of these which we operate in decision-making.

The *affect heuristic*. This has everything to do with how we feel about something. Affect, you see, refers to mood or feeling. Thought is never emotionless. The effect of the emotion is very relevant for it produces this rule of thumb by which we unconsciously tag factors as being good or bad. We do this in art, in music, in history, in sport. We empathise and we tag.

The *elimination heuristic*. This is a process wherein, when faced with a choice of one of a number of things, we tend to categorise them, then produce a factor that can be applied to eliminate a largish number of the contending things. For example, you want a romantic novel to read on holiday. Most people will eliminate those novels that seem to have been written by men. The elimination heuristic here is that only women can write effective romance.

The *recognition heuristic*. This is a very simple heuristic that can be operated to produce a fast answer or result. It is simply the 'one good reason' heuristic. The smack-in-the-face, glaringly obvious factor that supersedes and disregards all other factors. Love at first sight! The right candidate for the post! Exactly the right chair for that corner in the sitting room!

A characteristic of the recognition heuristic is that if one of two objects is recognised, then there is a tendency to tag that object with a higher value. And an interesting phenomenon follows it, and that is something that is at the very heart of this book. Read on gentle reader, read on!

LESS IS MORE

This really is curious, but there are many situations when the less one knows, the greater is the chance of success. In the introduction to this book I suggested that you may have known people who seemed to do the minimum amount of work yet always did well in exams. Rather than learning the whole syllabus they were selective and took a gamble at spotting the likeliest topics to come up in the examination. It can go badly wrong, but it can also be amazingly successful. Not that I am advocating this as an approach for anything as important as examinations, you understand. I would not be so irresponsible; yet in other areas of life it can bear amazing fruit.

Suppose a group of English people were asked to compare the populations of Edinburgh and another city in the UK – Bradford, for example. And suppose that a group of French people of similar age were also asked that question. Which group do you suppose would be correct? It may surprise you, but in similar tests to this the non-resident group would on average be more likely to get the right answer. This is an example of the less is more phenomenon, in that all of the English people would be likely to have heard of both cities, whereas all of the French people would be likely to have heard of Edinburgh, but many would not have heard of Bradford (which has a smaller population). They would unconsciously apply the recognition heuristic and achieve a collective greater score. This is the less is more phenomenon, which implies that making a choice with less knowledge, when recognition is likely, usually leads to success.

And that is what this book is about. It is going to equip you with enough knowledge to shine on many subjects, without having to be an expert.

RULES OF THUMB

So far we have been talking about unconscious heuristics, which are essentially unconscious rules of thumb. Now I am going to talk about conscious rules of thumb or little tricks and short cuts that we can use to work things out simply without having to go through the algorithmic process of logic.

There are several theories about the origin of the term, and some of them are quite colourful. Judge Sir Francis Buller (1746–1800) was caricatured as 'Judge Thumb' by the artist James Gillray in 1782 for reportedly saying that a man could beat his wife, provided that the stick used was no thicker than his thumb. For many years it was believed that the 'Rule of Thumb' was really accepted under English Common Law. This is actually just an urban myth.

In fact, the term was in use earlier than that and is thought to have been part of fencing lore. It is referred to in Sir William Hope's book *The Compleat Fencing-master*, which was published in 1692: 'What he doth by rule of Thumb, and not by Art.'

It is considered likely that it was also a reference to measurement, since the middle phalanx of the thumb, between the two knuckle joints, is approximately 1 inch. In traditional Chinese medicine, the width of the thumb is known as 1 'cun,' and is used to locate the position of acupuncture points. Artists also use a rule of thumb, in raising their thumb to assess size and perspective.

RULES OF THUMB IN PHYSICS

You may well find yourself chatting about rules of thumb and heuristics at a party or at the bar. You can give a neat little demonstration of how rules of thumb can enable one to work out the direction of various things in electromagnetics, instead of having to do complex mathematics. You may never have use for any of these tips, but they illustrate the principle and they will make you sound very knowledgeable.

Fleming's left-hand rule: this is also known as the 'motor rule' and is a way that you can work out the direction of a force, or the thrust on a current-carrying conductor, a coil, when it is placed in a magnetic field.

Raise your left hand and position your thumb, forefinger and middle finger so that they are all at right angles to each other. If the forefinger ('f' for forefinger) is pointing in the direction (North to South) of the magnetic field (and 'f' for 'field'), and the middle finger is in the direction of the current, then the thumb ('th' for thumb) will show you the direction of the 'thrust' or force on the conductor.

Fleming's left-hand rule

Fleming's right-hand rule: this is the 'generator rule.' It helps you to work out the direction of induced current flow in a conductor placed in an electric field.

Raise your right hand and position your thumb, forefinger and middle finger so that they are at right angles to one another. If the first finger is pointing in the direction of the magnetic field and the thumb is in the direction of motion of the conductor, then the middle finger will show you the direction of the induced current.

Fleming's right-hand rule

Biot-Savart Law: this is a rather complex inverse square law (you don't need to know any more than that), which is used to calculate magnetic fields due to currents.

Here you use your right hand with the thumb up, as if you were giving a thumbs-up sign. When the thumb is in the direction of the current in the wire, the fingers will point in the direction of the lines of force of the field.

Biot-Savart rule

NOW SHOW THEM *THE* RULE OF THUMB

You may find that you have fascinated everyone with that little description of rules of thumb, or made them all go glassy eyed. In either case it is no bad thing to do this little trick to end your physics genius routine.

Tell them to place their right hands on a flat table surface. Bend the middle finger underneath with the knuckle resting on the table, but keep all the other fingers and the thumb straight out on the table. Now, since you have been talking about rules of thumb, see if they can lift their thumbs. No problem, everyone can do that. Tell them to put it down again. Then tell them to lift their forefingers. Again, no problem, so they can put that down. Now ask them to lift the little finger. It is so simple, isn't it?

Then tell them to put it back and now lift the fourth or the ring finger. Wow! Most people cannot do it.

Tell them that there is an old legend that says that the wedding finger, the ring finger, tells all about how a relationship will be for someone. If you can't raise that finger, you will always be under your partner's thumb.

Now that's a real rule of thumb!

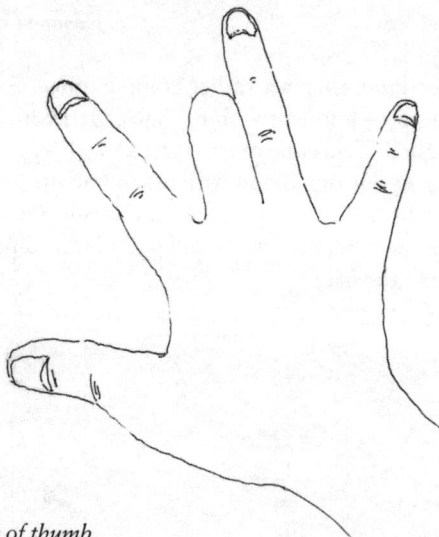

The real rule of thumb

Rules of thumb everywhere

You will have grown up hearing proverbs, aphorisms and, nowadays, sound-bites. They all represent little nuggets of wisdom, rules of thumb to be applied in all walks of life. Here are a few, culled from the centuries:

> One drink is enough, two is too many,
> three is not half enough

> Breakfast like a king, lunch like a prince,
> supper like a pauper

> Early to bed, early to rise, makes a man healthy,
> wealthy and wise

The important thing is that you will now have an idea of the unconscious heuristics that you operate when you make decisions. And that goes for world leaders, bankers and philosophers as well. Don't imagine that they have a better brain than you do. They make their decisions by whittling everything down until it is a single choice. And they make that decision for good or ill. It may seem to be the Wisdom of Solomon, but more likely it will be the Judgement of Paris.

3

A MATTER OF CHARACTER

Know thyself

The Delphic Oracle
(Inscribed in the forecourt of the Temple of Apollo at Delphi)

The study of character is as old as human inquiry. People have always wanted to have a system by which they can understand not only their character, but that of their fellows. There are undoubted advantages in being able to do so, for one could tell one's friends from one's enemies, those one could trust with one's life and those who one would not even trust to look after one's football boots. I know this to my cost, as I lost a good pair when I was 16 and I vowed that I would never be as poor a judge of character again.

FIRST IMPRESSIONS

Do you go on first impressions? Most people do and many a candidate has failed at a job interview because they didn't project the right image, or they didn't manage to gel with their interviewer. Never mind the fact that the interviewer thinks he or she is sitting with a list of questions and topics that they want to cover and score so that they can make a logical and objective decision. In fact, as we saw in the last chapter, judgement eventually comes down to a choice between two options. If the interviewer is a poor judge of character there is a good chance that he or she will make a duff decision.

And this happens in many of the different arenas of life. It happens in finance, in relationships, in the law courts. Oh yes, even there. Why on earth should one imagine that judges are actually any good at making decisions? Are they really wise? Are they really adept at assessing whether or not someone is guilty? Are they truly objective or are they subject to being swayed because they have unconsciously used a biased heuristic? Well, far be it for me to suggest such a thing. There is no such thing as a miscarriage of justice, after all.

Or is there?

WE ARE ALL DIFFERENT, AREN'T WE?

You would think that this question was hardly worth answering. People come in all shapes and sizes; they have different attitudes, different values and widely differing beliefs. No two people are exactly alike. There are no doppelgangers. So why is it that we strive to categorise people's characters? Why can't we just accept people as we find them and take it from there?

Well, in a perfect world we would do that, but society is a rat-race. It is a question of survival and it is natural to try and get a handle on people, to try to read them so that one can anticipate their thoughts and moods and behaviour. If you can judge character well, then you can get on with someone and possibly persuade them to your way of thinking and thence to your advantage.

That might sound cynical, yet it is realistic. We are social creatures, just as ants and bees are, and we are just as capable of wanting to work our way up the social pyramid as any drone or worker ant.

The interesting thing is that everyone unconsciously tries to assess other people. We tag whether we like them or not by using the affect heuristic that I told you about in the last chapter. And people tend to devise their own criteria according to the things that interest them. Those folk who are interested in astrology are convinced that they can assess character by someone's star sign. Golfers gauge people on a sort of handicap, using the anchor and adjustment heuristic. Gamblers may … well, gamblers are people who like to take risks.

I hope that you have understood my point. We try to assess the character of our fellows in order to understand how to interact with them. The trouble is that many so-called character-reading methods just fall down flat and we still make poor judgements. On the other hand, if you are good at character judgement then you are well on your way to shining in any company, because you know how to react to get the best out of a situation, whether that is meeting your girlfriend's parents for the first time, applying for a loan or a job, or just sitting at a dinner party.

So now I am going to look at an early type of character and personality analysis, and then I shall look at a little history of the subject. After that I will show you how to use a rule of thumb method. And then I am going to tell you about cold reading, which should help you to shine at those parties.

Would you like that?

Good, then read on.

PHRENOLOGY:
THE ART OF READING HEADS

You may have noticed the quote about heuristics and rules of thumb at the start of the last chapter. Did you wonder who Professor Phineas J. Stackpool was? Clearly he knew his onions well enough to pronounce about heuristics and rules of thumb. In fact, he knew more about lumps and bumps on the head, for he was a professor of phrenology and a mesmerist extraordinaire. At least, that is how he described himself.

I know Phineas J. Stackpool rather well, ever since he tapped on my head and introduced himself. Before I needlessly divulge more about his character let me explain: Professor Phineas J. Stackpool is a figment of my imagination, a character in a novel that I have penned. Having said that, I have the greatest of respect for him, for he knows all that there is to know about phrenology, which, in case you did not know, was a revolutionary system of character and human potential analysis.

Four-times Prime Minister of Great Britain William Gladstone had a high opinion of it. He said: 'I declare that the phrenological system of mental philosophy is as much better than all other systems as the electric light is better than the tallow dip.' The great inventor Thomas Alva Edison said: 'I never knew I had an inventive talent until phrenology told me so. I was a stranger to myself until then.' And even Professor Alfred Russel Wallace, the explorer, geographer, naturalist, anthropologist and biologist, the contemporary of Charles Darwin whose own work on natural selection made Darwin rush his *Origin of Species* into print, said: 'The phrenologist has shown that he is able to read character like an open book, and to lay bare the hidden springs of conduct with an accuracy that the most intimate friends cannot approach.'

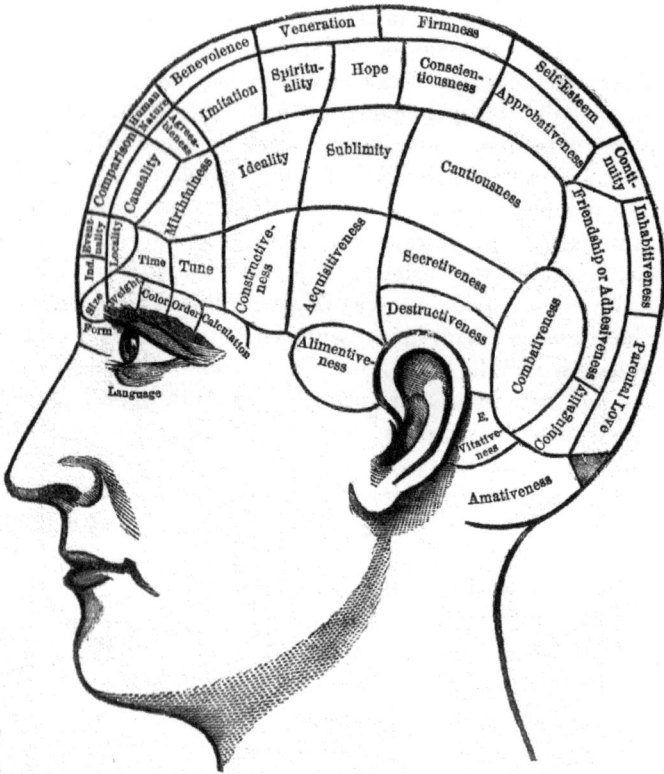

The phrenological faculties

Those are pretty impressive testimonials are they not? So what was this great discipline? Well, essentially it was a system devised by Dr Franz Joseph Gall at the end of the eighteenth century, which proposed that the shape of the skull mirrored the convolutions of the brain. From extensive anatomical studies and empirical observation he had concluded that the brain was made up of organs or faculties, each of which represented the temperaments, the emotions, the mental abilities and the controlling functions of the body. By assessing the shape of the skull, the size of its prominences, its lumps and bumps, he came to believe that it was possible to predict an individual's strengths and weaknesses, their potentials and their failings.

In the Victorian era professional phrenologists set up in consulting rooms like any medical specialist or general practitioner and made good livings. People flocked to them to have their heads read, to see what they should be doing with their lives, and to gain answers in matters of love, business and life in general. Children were taken to see what path of life they should be groomed for. And some practitioners would offer treatments with phreno-mesmerism, coupling their readings with hypnosis, to try to enhance faculties that seemed in need of a boost.

I confess to having a fascination with this subject and have built up a section in my library with first editions of many of these fabulous works. In my research I have seen how and why this discipline came to be so readily accepted. Anthropologists were looking at skulls, anatomists were recording the structure of the brain, and it all seemed to fit.

More importantly, at a practical level phrenologists seemed able to read characters exceedingly well. People were very satisfied with the things that the phrenologists could tell them. Why, just imagine what sort of a world we would be living in if Thomas Ala Edison had not wandered into a phrenologist's consulting room and found out that he had a talent for invention. No electric light bulb, no phonograph and no motion-picture camera. We could still be wandering about by candlelight and probably wearing top hats and tails when we went to the theatre.

You see, they knew what they were talking about and the science that they practised was so very plausible. So surely that fellow Dr Gall must have been a genius to discover it all?

THE ADVANCE OF SCIENCE

Sadly, although some people may once have regarded Dr Gall as a genius, he was to disappear into the ranks of nearly men.

As the years went on scientific advances touched all areas of medicine. It was realised that the brain was a far more complex organ than had been supposed by Gall and his followers and that there was virtually no correlation between it and the shape of the skull in terms of function. Gradually, phrenology was discredited because it no longer had any claim to plausibility. Effectively, it went the way of the dodo. That is at least in an actual professional sense. It persists in the consulting parlours of mystics and clairvoyants, and people still listen and marvel in awe at its accuracy, or rather at the skill of the phrenological 'reader' at fairs and parties.

BUT IT WON'T DIE AWAY!

Despite the oceans of vitriol, derision and contempt that have been poured upon it, the phrenological head remains as a kind of icon of the mind. No one practises phrenology seriously any more, but you will find the phrenological head reproduced in all manner of quasi-medical and bona fide psychological texts. It implies the complexity of the mind and people are happy to have the image printed in their papers and books, for it looks as if it should have something to do with the brain and the mind.

Is that not a curious paradox?

THE ANCIENT GREEKS KNEW A THING OR TWO ABOUT CHARACTER

As with most aspects of intellectual endeavour, we find that the ancient Greeks had been there first. They were probably the first culture to attempt to predict character. They did so in a typically clever manner, by linking it with medicine and the predisposition that people seemed to have to different types of ailments.

Hippocrates (460–370 BC), the 'Father of Medicine,' taught that the four elements – air, water, earth and fire – when acted upon by a 'vital force' became activated in living creatures to become the four 'vital fluids' or humours. Thus, air became absorbed by the lungs to form blood; water taken in through the mouth and the bowel would become phlegm; earth (as solid food) would become black bile; and heat and fire would be absorbed to become yellow bile.

Claudius Galen (AD 131–201), a second-century physician, further refined this theory by linking these 'vital fluids' with the temperaments of people, to define four basic characters: sanguine, phlegmatic, melancholic and choleric.

Incredibly, using nothing more than this, you can get a good handle on people's basic personality. Have a look at Table 1 and you will get the gist.

JUNG'S TYPOLOGY

Carl Jung (1875–1961) is, of course, one of the most famous names in psychology. He was an associate of Sigmund Freud for many years until he broke away and founded his own discipline of analytical psychology. He conjectured that people's personalities or characters are based on four main functions: feeling, thinking, intuition and sensing.

He also introduced the concept of introversion and extraversion. Introverted people tend to focus internally and be more concerned with thoughts and feelings. Extraverts tend to be more outgoing, more concerned with outward interactions. There are, of course, degrees and shades of the two.

SHELDON'S SOMATOTYPES

William Sheldon (1899–1977) produced a system of personality typing based upon body builds, which he referred to as somatotypes. There are three basic ones, each associated with various temperaments. These are: *endomorph* – pear-shaped types; *mesomorphs* – the athletes; and *ectomorphs* – the slim, bookish types. Please see Table 2 to get the flavour.

Again, it is not a clear-cut system, but you can in fact work out a balance for people. If you imagine measuring each type on a scale of 1 to 7, then you could say that Stan Laurel, the famous comedy actor, could be 1-1-7, which would be an ectomorph, whereas Oliver Hardy would be 7-1-1. And Superman would be 1-7-1, a mesomorph.

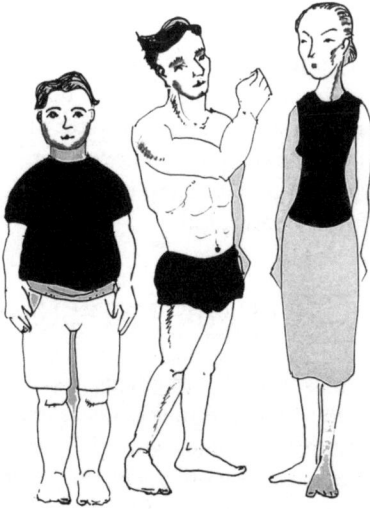

The somatotypes

A RULE OF THUMB FOR CHARACTER

You will find, if you are stimulated to delve deeper into personality psychology, that there are many other systems that have been developed. The Myers-Briggs Indicator, for example, was developed from Jung's typology. And of course Jung and all the rest owe everything to the ancient Greeks and the humoral theory.

I leave it to you to follow this up if you wish, but now I want to just show you how to get a handle on character analysis in a practical way in your day-to-day dealings with people.

All you have to do is think two, three, four.

That means extract the essence of the methods.

Two: is the person you are focused on an introvert or an extravert? They will give themselves away almost immediately.

Three: are they a jolly endomorph, an assertive, sporty mesomorph or a quiet, thoughtful ectomorph?

Four: the Greeks really had it taped, in my opinion. It won't take long to work out their humour and their temperament.

It is as simple as that. This little heuristic method will cut through all of the questionnaires and give you an inkling of what sort of person someone is. OK, by definition a heuristic may be biased and it may not give a strictly accurate picture, but most times it will. And you can then anticipate how you are going to interact with that person, work out what sort of strategy you may need to adopt in an interview, or in a discussion.

But, of course, it is a good thing to start at home. What sort are you? Remember – two, three, four.

THOSE LUMPS AND BUMPS

Let us return to the study of phrenology. You can, of course, see for yourself whether you can make this system work. All you need to do is familiarise yourself with the positions of the four main groups of mental 'organs' as in the diagram, according to phrenology theory. The front of the head is associated with the intellectual faculties associated with observing, thinking, reasoning and planning. The back is associated with domestic and social affections – love of the home and family, or children, animals and friends. The sides of the head indicate the so-called 'animal propensities.' These are also described as the 'selfish or self-preserving and commercial organs,' which give energy, force, executiveness, courage, prudence and so forth. Finally, the top of the head was associated with the moral sentiments.

Now please understand that I am in no way advocating phrenology as a way of seriously determining character or personality. Yet I draw your attention back to some of the testimonials that it gathered over the years. It actually was a movement that enjoyed great credibility for more than 100 years. It seemed utterly plausible, and it seemed very effective at predicting. How do we account for this? Were its practitioners duping people?

I think not. I think that they were for the most part genuine folk who muddled along with a system that seemed to have a scientific basis. But they became good at guessing what people wanted to hear. I rather imagine that practitioners became adept in assessing character, rather like the rule of thumb method I have outlined here. In addition I suspect that they became very skilled in a method called cold reading.

COLD READING

This is the name given to the type of rule of thumb analysis that is used by psychics, clairvoyants, fortune-tellers and current-day magicians, to 'psychically' give information about people. Essentially, it enables the 'reader' to seemingly derive information about someone that you could not actually know, and then deliver it to them as if derived from a mysterious source.

Tarot-readers, tea-cup fortune-tellers, psychics and magicians determine aspects of the individual's personality, couple it with areas that an individual is likely to hold dear and then deliver it as a reading. This can be a reading of the individual's personality or of their future.

The system that the person is using, be that tarot cards, tea leaves, palms or heads, is a distraction. The person who attends for a reading has probably already opened up their gullibility door and will accept the positive affirmations that are given, happily swallowing the flattering, the optimistic and even the cautionary notes that are being given to them via the skilled reading of the practitioner.

To do this in an entertainment setting, you

A consulting phrenologist in action

first have to demonstrate some knowledge and profess a skill in a particular subject. Say it is phrenology. You would start by suggesting that science is rediscovering that phrenologists were right, but perhaps for the wrong reasons. Nonetheless, having studied the method you have acquired skill and that you are willing to demonstrate, if you could borrow a head!

Imagine that you are at a party and that you planted this seed earlier on. Now phrenology comes up again and a head volunteers itself. You have already gone through your two, three, four system and have an idea about the person. If they have volunteered themselves then you are pretty sure that they are fairly extravert. You have assessed their somatotype and their conversation may have revealed what temperament they have.

Body language tells you a lot about people. So, too, do the words they use. You will find that people often talk about feelings: they preface statements with 'I feel ...', or they ask, 'don't you feel ...', or they ask for an opinion, 'how would you feel?' On the other hand, some people are more thinkers. They say 'I think ...' Or they ask, 'do you think ...', or they express an opinion, 'well, I would think ...'

Do you see what I mean?

Clothing tells you a lot. Colour, colour combinations, the state of dress, shoes, hairstyle, care of the fingernails and so on will all help you to build up this picture.

Their age will guide you into things that are likely to concern them. Young adults are probably interested in fun, or they are anxious about first steps in career. Thirty-somethings are probably building or reassessing. Middle-aged people are perhaps starting to think and worry about health, elderly relatives and career. Peri-retirement folk are possibly getting demob fever from the workplace, or starting to plan or worry about maturity.

All of these things you take into account. And they help you to locate the appropriate lumps and bumps. And the way you talk about a characteristic will give you feedback:

'Ah yes, this area, which is associated with benevolence, is interesting.'

'Tell me more,' your head's owner says enthusiastically.

'It is well developed; there is great potential here for benevolence.'

'That's funny; I just gave my husband a watch for our anniversary.'

And so on.

THE BARNUM EFFECT

Phineas T. Barnum (1810–91) was an American showman, circus supremo, businessman and entertainer. He was the world's first showbusiness millionaire and his philosophy could be encapsulated in his famous saying, 'There is a sucker born every minute.'

The Barnum effect is the name given to the psychological tendency that people have to accept vague statements or characterisations as being pertinent to themselves. This is especially the case if you are discussing qualities and pleasing characteristics.

The use of plenty of Barnum statements, which sound good, but which can have two meanings, will help you to build up the picture of your head's personality. They will feed the answers that they want to believe in back to you.

For example, 'you project a controlled image, but inside there is a deeper picture coming out.' Who can resist having a deeper inside? Expect some information being volunteered.

Or, 'a lot of the time you seem to be outgoing, yet there is uncertainty that you cover up well.'

And so forth. You will soon gain a reputation, perhaps as a bit of a genius, but certainly as someone with special ability. My one piece of advice, however, is this: don't let people think that you do this as anything more than a party-piece. Do not claim any special powers. Keep your head on your shoulders.

Oh, and as for Professor Phineas J. Stackpool – now you can see where I got at least part of his name, together with his showmanship.

Table 1: the four temperaments and the humoral theory

TEMPERAMENT	CHARACTER	HUMOUR	ELEMENT
Sanguine	Optimistic Impulsive Impressionable	Blood	Air
Phlegmatic	Calm Practical Hates limelight	Phlegm	Water
Melancholic	Cautious Serious Solitary	Black bile	Earth
Choleric	Irritable Fiery Confident	Yellow bile	Fire

Table 2: Sheldon's somatotypes

SOMATOTYPE	CHARACTER	BUILD
Endomorph	Jolly Sociable Relaxed Likes creature comforts	Chubby Soft and doughy Pear shaped
Mesomorph	Assertive Action-type Sporty Combative	Muscular Firm Wide shoulders
Ectomorph	Quiet Dainty Fragile Sensitive	Slim Delicate Weak

4

CREATIVITY

Imagination is the beginning of creation. You imagine what you
desire, you will what you imagine and at last you create what you
will.

George Bernard Shaw
Playwright, critic and Nobel Prize-winner (1925)

At what point does someone become a genius? Are they conceived
as a genius, their brain being merely the receptacle for a divine
gift? Or are they born a genius, even though their brain has yet
to develop? Then again, are they a genius even when no one
knows it, when they just seem like your average mischief-making
youngster? Will a genius always rise to the surface, as does the
cream on milk?

*Imagine how you
could think up a
theory about gravity*

I suspect that there are many geniuses around. People born in countries all over the world, who for some reason or another are not given the opportunities needed, who are capable of incredible intellectual feats or of producing amazing concepts, yet who fail to have their genius recognised.

Perhaps that is the crux of the matter. A genius is someone who produces something amazing. Until that amazing concept, piece of work or earth-shattering idea is revealed they may simply be regarded as someone with a very high IQ. A smart person, that's all.

And can anyone be a genius? Is every human brain capable of making those amazing quantum leaps forward that will enrich (or potentially destroy) our planet and our species? That is an interesting thought, don't you think? If only we could reach the genius within.

Well perhaps you can and perhaps you can't. One thing would seem to be necessary before you can hope to claim genius and that is to demonstrate creativity. And this is something that you can achieve. OK, perhaps not creativity of genius proportions, but perhaps enough to feel good about yourself. Who knows, with just a little creativity research you may just open up a new sphere of interest for yourself.

THE PROCESS OF THOUGHT

There are several disciplines which consider the process of thought. In philosophy, for example, the very nature of the mind has occupied centre-stage for literally over two millennia. We will meet some of the great thinkers who have pondered on such matters when we come to the chapter about philosophy.

Nowadays there is a fashionable neurobiological postulate that the mind is a mere product of brain chemistry and neuro-electricity. That is a pretty dismal thought in itself, but when all is said and done, that is merely an opinion. It cannot be proven.

The fact is that although we have discovered a great deal over the years about the way in which the brain works and the way in which we seem to think, we are still barely scratching the surface of the mysteries of the mind and thought.

Studies in biology and medicine indicate that the human mind was not, as Descartes would have averred, actually designed by God, but was evolved by nature. The fact that so much of our neuro-circuitry is 'twisted and crosses over' is actually evidence for this evolution. The cross-over effect, in which one side of the brain controls the other side of the body, is not logical, but arises, it would seem, because we have two eyes, each of which contains a lens. Now this is complicated, but it is worth thinking about, so bear with me.

Consider an object moving from left to right. Because of our lenses, the retinal images move from right to left. Therefore, in order to track an object, the eye needs to swivel to the right, requiring a contraction of muscles on the right side of the body. Yet the stimulus for this is on the left side of the retina, so the neural pathways need to go from the left side of the eye to the right side of the body. This twisting over is not logical, but is something that has evolved. And that may be why we have two hemispheres in the brain.

The way that those hemispheres work can have a lot to do with creativity and ultimately with genius.

RIGHT AND LEFT BRAIN FUNCTIONS

Certain functions of the mind seem to be associated with the right and left hemispheres of the brain. This has become known as the right brain v left brain theory of mind. It was based on the work of psycho-biologist Robert Sperry (1913–94), for which he received a Nobel Prize in 1981.

It had actually been known since the time of the ancient Egyptians that the right hemisphere of the brain seemed to control the left side of the body and the left hemisphere controlled the body's right side. Other than that not a lot was known until the twentieth century.

Sperry's work actually gave us some very good insight into the brain-mind connection and delineated functions that seem more associated with one hemisphere than the other. It does not mean that they are exclusively associated in that way, for other work indicates that in many ways the brain is holographic, in that all parts of the brain have the potential to operate the mind, so that if there is injury to the organ, other parts may be able to take over function. So it is more an order of pre-eminence of associations rather than exclusive association.

Table 3: right and left hemisphere associations

RIGHT HEMISPHERE	LEFT HEMISPHERE
Visual	Verbal
Intuitive	Logical
Creative	Analytical
Artistic	Scientific
Musical	Mathematical
Pattern recognition – see pictures	Item recognition – see links
Lateral thinking	Linear thinking
Emotions	Clinical
Physically expressive	Verbally expressive
Hears nuances	Hears sounds
Poor time sense or awareness	Good time sense and awareness
Poor organisation	Good organisation

Its significance is that some people seem to be more one-sided than the other. In other words, their brains and minds seem to operate with a prominence more of one hemisphere. Thus we talk about right-hemisphere dominance or left-hemisphere dominance. Once again, it is important to appreciate that this does not mean that only one side works, but that the functions of one side seem to be more to the fore in the way that someone thinks and lives.

In terms of the mind of a genius, the right hemisphere seems to be very important for the conception of an idea, the creativity function. Imagine something so wonderfully original that it will change the world, whether it is a scientific concept, a mathematical principle or a work of art or literature. The germ of the idea probably begins in the right-hemisphere function. The trick is to have sufficiently well developed a left-hemisphere function to then transcribe it in language, in mathematics, or in the chosen medium. We can all do that to an extent, but it seems that geniuses are those people capable of the greatest creative thoughts, that is a right-brain function, but also have the ability to describe it as a left-brain function. The communication between their hemisphere functions may be what marks them out.

But don't worry if your acts of creativity don't reach genius level. Just try to get the creative juices going. And so let's have a go. I hope that in some of the later chapters of this book you will find little snippets that will help you to seem smart. In the chapter on poetry, for example, you will learn enough to start writing clerihew poetry. Later in this chapter I am going to give you some ideas to get your creativity going so that you can plot a novel.

That's right, I said plot a novel!

Who knows, it may be that first push you need to begin your literary career. You may be on your way to unlocking the Shakespeare within you.

CREATIVE THINKING

There are two basic types of creative thinking, accidental and deliberate. Accidental creative thinking occurs when a chance observation leads to a train of thought that results in the production of something new that had not been thought of before. There are numerous examples of geniuses who have been stimulated by such chance observations.

History tells us of King Hieron of Syracuse who had a crown made by a jeweller from a block of gold. A suspicious fellow was King Hieron, for even though the crown weighed the same as the block of gold, he was doubtful as to whether the jeweller had used all of the gold, or whether he had substituted some silver. He handed the problem to Archimedes.

Archimedes (287–212 BC) was initially unable to come up with an answer, until one day he got into his bath and the solution presented itself to him. Or rather, he observed that when he got in the bath a great deal of water got out. In that moment his mind perceived the answer and he dashed off out of his house and down the street, naked as the day he was born, crying, '*Eureka*' ('I have found it')!

What he had discovered, of course, was to become known as Archimedes' Principle. This states that, 'any object, wholly or partially immersed in a fluid, is buoyed up by a force equal to the weight of the fluid displaced by the object.'

King Hieron was delighted with the result. Not so the jeweller!

Isaac Newton (1642–1727) also had an accidental piece of creative thinking. In 1666 he was sitting in his orchard at Woolsthorpe Manor when he saw an apple fall to the ground. Some say that it fell on his head, but that is pure conjecture. At any rate, it resulted in him thinking up the theory of gravity.

James Watt (1736–1813) was watching a kettle boil and was inspired by seeing the power of the steam raise the lid of the kettle. He set about harnessing that power, the result being the steam engine which was to transform the face of the world and speeded up the pace of the Industrial Revolution.

All three of these men and their insights were great acts of creative genius. Yet would they have occurred if circumstances had been different? If Archimedes had been having a shower would he have discovered his buoyancy principle? Would Isaac Newton have come up with another discovery if he had been sitting under a pear tree? Perhaps he would have come up with a recipe for pear compote instead of discovering gravity and mankind would long since have floated off to the moon. And if James Watt had been watching an egg boil rather than waiting to brew a cup of tea, perhaps his great invention would have been an egg timer and we would all still be riding about on horses and revelling in the joy of regular softly boiled eggs.

No, of course not! It is not as simple as that. Innumerable other people over the course of time had witnessed the same phenomena, yet they did not think of these great innovations. The truth is that these chance observations were simply catalysts for the mental reactions that were already simmering away in the crucibles of their great minds. The germ of the idea has to be there to begin with.

Deliberate creative thinking occurs when people go out of their way consciously to think up an invention, a work of art or a new theory. Leonardo da Vinci (1452–1519) did it with his countless war machines, helicopter plans and unbelievable works of art; Dr William Harvey (1578–1657) did it with his theory of the circulation of blood and Albert Einstein (1879–1955) did it with his theory of relativity.

The point is this: you can sit around waiting for a chance observation to stimulate your ground-breaking idea, but you will probably wait in vain unless you have the germ of the idea in the right hemisphere of your brain already, or you can deliberately try to stimulate it by getting your left hemisphere to start the process. And maybe it will talk to your right hemisphere to produce your great work.

It is worth trying.

DO YOU HAVE AN INVENTION IN YOU?

Thomas Alva Edison did not hang about waiting for inspiration; he got on and tried to produce things. And what things he made. At one time he had over 1,000 patents registered in the USA and many more in the UK, France and Germany.

You can invent something as well; you just start with the idea.

OK, so how do you get that idea? Well you might start with the area of your life that is most important to you. It may be sport, or it may be health. If the former, how could you improve your sport? And if the latter, what device or thing could help your health or that of someone you are concerned about?

Let us suppose your favourite sport is a ball game. With just a little thought you are bound to see something glaringly obvious that is silly about the game. It may be the rules, it may be the ball, it may be the number of players or the course, court, pitch or table that it is played on. Just get your mind thinking and you will be able to come up with a new variation on it. You could expand it, miniaturise it, add another dimension, or remove one, or just simplify the whole thing. Change the shape of some aspect of it.

The finished product might not be sufficiently good to persuade fans of the game that they should adopt your new version, but who knows? Perhaps you can create a board game that is analogous to this sport and which you could market as something that people could play on long journeys. Just get your mind thinking.

If it was a health concern, what aid could you invent that would help? A gadget that would help Aunt Flora shell peas with her arthritic fingers? A suction device that she could use to turn the pages of her knitting magazine? Or a cushion with pedals that Uncle Bob could use to exercise in bed? They might sound flippant, but one man's flippancy is another's creativity.

Then again you might consider how your new version of a sport could be adapted for someone who may have mobility problems. Would they like a miniaturised version, or a card- or board- or computer-game version? The initial idea is the starting point.

Or you could consider how you could harness the energy used in a sporting activity to power something else. Could you power a generator from an exercise bike, or power a gymnasium from the energy expended by the people who use it? Think ecologically and try to come up with something really innovative.

And if you haven't got a clear idea of what you would like to invent then just write down the name of a subject – say house-cleaning – then jot down a few random words. For example, jam jar, pogo stick and clothes horse. Think of how you could link those up in some way, perhaps adding others, in a way that they could help in house-cleaning. You may well conjure up some sort of Heath Robinson gadget, but that is great. It is a creation and you are on your way to becoming an inventor.

You should now have the idea. It is all about deliberately stimulating your creative juices.

CREATIVE WRITING

This is an area close to my heart. Millions of people want to write, but either never put pen to paper, figuratively speaking, since everyone seems to write on a computer these days, or they try but get discouraged after a few attempts. Well if you want to write, my advice is simple: write!

We are talking about creative writing here. That means virtually any original writing, whether it is a short story, a novel, poetry, play-writing, biography or non-fiction. Poetry is covered in a later chapter. Let us just consider fiction here.

CHILDREN'S STORIES

I started writing 300- to 500-word children's stories for women's magazines when I was a student at university. I found it broke the tedium of learning anatomy and biochemistry if I could take my mind somewhere else for a while. It actually paid to do so; not a lot, I admit, but it was paid so I considered it a sub-profession. Curiously, the diversion helped me to learn my anatomy because I was coming back fresh having stimulated and satisfied my creativity. I suspect that what I had also done was to stimulate my right hemisphere, the creative side, which is also the pattern-recognition side. That helped me to visualise anatomical structures in 3D.

The basic structure that I used for those stories for tiny tots, and I am talking about stories for the under-5s, was incredibly simple. I wrote a beginning, a middle and an end. It is the formula that I have adopted when I write novels as well.

I suspect that you will not think that to be a particularly good insight into story-telling. It is not, if that was all there was to it, yet it is the very essence of all good stories, whether they are six-word stories or epic novels. You just have to adapt them and add in little bits.

To tell a story I transform the three parts a bit. The beginning has to be interesting. It is a scene-setter, introducing your hero. The middle is all about conflict. That means you set your hero some sort of problem, possibly a dangerous situation. The end shows how he resolves it to reach that satisfying finish. The titles of some of my published children's stories hint at the tales they tell: *The Wasted Spells*, *The Frog that Couldn't Sing*, *The Duck that Couldn't Swim*. They all work because they tell a story.

FLASH FICTION

Ernest Hemingway once wrote a six-word story, which he regarded as one of his finest pieces of work. I entered a competition for a six-word story and used the basic structure of beginning, middle and end, and my story received a commendation. Six words are not a lot, but to stand out those six words have to tell a story.

I will let you search out Hemingway's story for yourself if you have a mind to. It is worth the effort.

If you want to write then I suggest that you begin with flash fiction, the name given to very short fiction. You will find many competitions on the internet and with various publishers and magazines which are great fun to enter. The following story is twenty-six words long and won first prize in a competition for an A to Z story. That is, a story written using every letter of the alphabet in order from A to Z. It was a play on words of the film *Lost in Translation*. Since I am a doctor it inevitably had a medical theme and so I changed the title.

Lost in Transplantation – a case of rejection

Aorta burst causing deadly exsanguination!
Foreign gutter headlines implied jealousy killing, leaving mistress needing oxygen. Police questioned rival surgeon's technique.
'"Unaccepted vessel was xenograft," yammered Zurginski.'

This is actually a good little exercise for you. Try writing a twenty-six-word A to Z story. Mine was medically based, but try one set in your walk of life. Allow some leeway with X and Z, but try to work a story into the strict format. It makes you search for words.

The next story won the 2006 Fish One-page Historical Prize. It is 300 words long. I started with an old proverb about two towns, created a 'hero,' a likeable rogue, and put him in a situation which he had to get out of through his wit. Note the twist ending that is essential to the tale.

A Villain's Tale

'From Hell, Hull and Halifax, Good Lord, deliver us!'
My old father used to recite that to me. 'Hell because there be'nt no redemption from there, Hull because of that fast-flowing river that drowns so many, and Halifax because they'll cut your head off for thirteen pence.'

The old man must have suspected that I would lose my head one day. And all because that verger's juicy wife said that two shillings was the price to lie with her.

Two shillings! The reddleman I robbed had only thirteen pence on him, so I had to try for another coach on the Halifax road. But they were waiting for me, the vermin! The magistrate laughed when he said they were going to crop my Adam's apple.

I was not a happy villain in that stinking cell with its rotting straw and pestilential rats. And then they sent that sanctimonious priest to harvest my soul before the morrow.

'I can save you, my son,' he says.

'How's that, master priest?' asks I.

'I can absolve your soul if you repent.'

'In that case I won't be troubling you, priest. I've already made a rare bargain with Old Nick. Look,' says I, showing him the birthmark on my bum, 'he sealed the deal with his kiss. When they lop off my head he gets my soul and also the souls of the last five men that I talk to.' I grinned at him as I lay back on the straw.

A Villain's Tale

'Now my lips are sealed forever.'

A superstitious rogue that priest. Just like the turnkey, his two lads and that wolfshead of a magistrate. And so here I am at six o'clock on my beheading day, with a flask of beer and three shillings in my purse, on my way to Hull. Neither Hell nor Halifax want me yet.

I wonder if that verger's wife would settle for a shilling?

PLOTTING AND WRITING A NOVEL

Here is how I do it, for what it is worth. I write westerns, historical novels and crime novels and I use the same method for them all. I have a top hat that I call my ideas hat. I then get a set of small cards.

I begin with a theme. *Murder Solstice*, a crime novel, for example, had the theme of cults. So I wrote cults on one card and threw it in the hat. That made me think of new age cults and beliefs, so I thought of Stonehenge. My novel is set on the fictitious Outer Hebridean island of West Uist, so I created a stone circle there called the Hoolish Stones. That went onto a card and into the hat it went.

Then I started to make cards for characters. I label these CHARACTER and use one for each person. These characters may be based on people I pass, meet or know vaguely. They are not direct copies, but go in fleshed out a bit. They have characteristics that I exaggerate. And in they go.

Then I have cards for VICTIMS – but I may leave that blank or I may have the idea early on. In they go, for there are usually several victims in my novels.

I have cards with MOTIVE on them. And I think of lots of potential motives, since some will be red herrings.

There are cards for CURIOSITIES. This can be for strange facts that may spice things up.

Then TWIST cards, THINGS PAST cards, SITUATION cards, SCENE cards. And then most importantly CLUE cards and definite RED HERRING cards.

All of them go into the hat until I have a lot. It can take weeks. I add to them every day, some notes on the cards being longish and others just a few words. But at least I am writing every day, so I am keeping the creativity going.

When I am ready I take them out, mix them up, then spread them out. This is where the creative right hemisphere comes in. A pattern will start to manifest itself. And at that stage I may prune some cards out, or add others. I then create a sort of flow chart so that I visually see the novel's structure.

Then I sketch out the number of chapters – usually about twelve, each of which will be broken up into around half a dozen scenes. The first murder will at the very latest be discovered in a cliff-hanging third chapter. Why this chapter? Simply because you have to have built up your story (and I may have implied another murder earlier on), and most editors will want to see the first three chapters. A reader has to be gripped and held. Your novel has to keep him or her reading.

Then I start writing.

And that is it; usually three months later, the novel is completed. Now, if you feel the urge, get an ideas hat or an ideas box and get writing.

This is an unashamedly heuristic way of doing it, but it works for me.

5

THE LOST ART
OF SOPHISTRY

A man heated in talk, and eager of victory, takes advantage of the
mistakes or ignorance of his adversary, lays hold of concessions
to which he has no right, and urges proofs likely to prevail on his
opponent, though he knows himself that they have no force.

> The Adventurer, 1753
> Samuel Johnson
> Essayist, lexicographer and poet

The ancient Greeks loved to debate. Just like the Irish and the
Scots, they especially loved a good argument over a drink or two.

Alcohol is often seen as a catalyst for discussion. A little loosens
the tongue and allows a pleasant exchange of views. A bit more
drops the defences and permits for the flaring of tempers. Liberal
amounts remove all inhibitions, slurs the speech, disengages the

A symposium

brain from the mouth to cause utter balderdash to gush from it. Feelings can be crushed, friendships may be broken and reputations smashed into smithereens forever. All this the Greeks knew. Indeed, they invented the symposium, or the drinking party to facilitate philosophical discussion.

The great philosopher Plato (428–347 BC), to whom we shall return in the chapter on philosophy, wrote a book entitled *The Symposium* in about 385 BC. It is all about one of these Greek drinking parties where a group of intellectuals including Socrates meet to gently discuss and debate the meaning, nature and purpose of love. It is a book that I would highly recommend that you read and it is one of Plato's easiest books to begin with. I mention it because he effectively gave the idea of the symposium to the academic world. Academics should therefore be aware that their spiritual beginnings belong more in the pub than in the lecture hall.

Plato was a follower of the philosopher Socrates (469–399 BC), who believed that there was one effective manner of argument, called dialectic. This takes the form of a discussion between two people holding opposing views who attempt through dialogue to persuade each other that their view is correct. This is what most people view as being the nature of argument. Indeed, it is the main method of argument that has dominated western thought since those days. Plato's writings, in which he places Socrates centre-stage as the debater *par excellence*, effectively gave us the blueprint for our discussions, arguments and legal tussles right down to today.

Logical discussion and balance were the main weapons used in Plato's writings. He held intellect to be all-important, and thought that arguments and discussions, as indeed life in general, should be governed by a code of ethics. That is, that you should fight fair.

THE SOPHISTS

Athens in the fifth and fourth centuries BC was an amazing place. The beginnings of democracy started there. Philosophy, literature, art and medicine were all blossoming and developing in the balmy intellectual atmosphere that was a consequence of the Greeks' domination of the ancient world. They had the luxury of time, leisure and wealth. The power of the mind seemed capable of opening up the mysteries of life and the universe. All problems were potentially solvable and those people who could persuade others were held in tremendous esteem.

The sophists were a group of teachers of philosophy and rhetoric. The word comes from the Greek words '*sophos*,' meaning 'wise,' and '*sophia*,' meaning 'wisdom.' Our word 'sophistication' comes from this root. They were often hired to represent people in court and were effectively the first lawyers. For a long time they were held in high regard as people of intellectual distinction, but in time their reputation plummeted, as people started to see them as the legal fat cats of their day. Rather than merely being driven by logic, they were driven by success. Arguments were to be won by any means and from any angle. They charged high fees to win legal and social arguments for people and to teach others how to do so themselves.

Understandably, Plato and his band of ethical philosophers felt such practices to be both unethical and downright bad. And he rubbished sophistry in one of his later books, *The Sophist*.

THE ART OF SOPHISTRY

Everyone wants to win an argument, yet many people shy away from all confrontations because they doubt their ability in the cut and thrust of intellectual debate. They may have had a bad experience in the past, have been humiliated by someone in a pub and made to feel intellectually inferior. Or they may have simply lost an argument because they let someone brow-beat them with a mixture of bombasticism, bad temper and dogmatism.

Can you relate to any of that? Do you feel the intellectual equivalent of the 7-stone weakling who gets sand kicked in their face while the burly beefcake gets the girl and the ice cream? If so, help is at hand. All you need to do is understand some of the rudiments of the lost art of sophistry.

Understand this very first point, that most people do not argue or discuss things logically. They tend to get hemmed in by their personality or character. That is where the last chapter on character may be useful. Expect an extroverted mesomorph to argue forcefully. Anticipate that a classic ectomorph will be pedantic and nit-pick on little things. Be surprised if a jolly endomorph doesn't get all whimsical and try to use sarcasm or humour to lessen your point of view and take the mickey out of your argument.

And appreciate that most people tend not to escape from their way of thinking and will always argue in the same old way. I liken this to a tennis player who has one very good shot, perhaps a top-hand forehand. It is very effective in a lot of situations, but they may have such a weak backhand that they run a long way to get into position to always play their forehand. It is also similar to a golfer who always slices the ball. While he may be able to reach a certain handicap or level of competence because he has a repeatable shot, he is never going to reach the top levels because much of the time a sliced shot will land him in danger and make certain shots decidedly risky.

The point is that if you are going to go into an argument you really need to have multiple strategies to hand so that you can adapt your game plan to any opponent. To use the tennis analogy, you play on the backhand, don't give him time to run into position to use his favoured forehand, and you play in an unpredictable manner.

That is the art of sophistry.

FALLACIES CAN TRIP YOU UP, BUT SMART FOLK DON'T FALL

One of the best things that you can do to start winning arguments is to be aware of various fallacious arguments that people use. If you can spot them, then you can punch a hole in them. And of course, the art of sophistry is to make use of them yourself. The trick is to present it in such a manner that your opponent or the other parties in the discussion do not recognise it for the fallacy that it is.

If you spot a fallacy in your opponent's argument you can immediately score a point by giving its Latin name. That impresses others involved in the argument, and will probably intimidate your opponent in the process. On the other hand, if you are using such an argument yourself you obviously keep quiet!

Let us go through a few of these fallacies.

ARGUMENTUM AD ANTIQUITATEM

This is the argument of tradition. It is the old 'we've always done it this way and found that it works' argument. It sounds right, but just because it has always been done that way does not mean that it is the best way, the most efficient way or even the ethically correct way.

If you have decided to use this argument then be prepared to back up why it is a good thing. For example, many moons ago, when I was a house surgeon, I was second assistant during an abdominal operation. My boss, the consultant surgeon, performed the actual operation. The first assistant, the surgical registrar, used forceps and retractors to give him the best possible view of the surgical field and did some of the surgery when permitted to do so by the boss. My function as the second assistant was to hold basins and cut stitches when told. My boss was an irascible fellow who was somewhat set in his ways and always used a particular type of surgical suture material for tying off blood vessels. No other surgeon in the hospital was still using it.

'Have you ever considered using one of the new suture materials, sir?' the registrar asked.

'Used this for 30 years and it works,' the great man replied. Then nodding at me, 'Cut!'

I cut as directed and the registrar opened up the field for the boss to continue. 'But the latest research shows that complication rates are lowest with ...'

The boss looked up slowly, his eyes like gimlets above his surgical mask.

'Check medical records to find out who has the lowest complication rate in the hospital.'

The boss's opener about having used this material was an *argumentum ad antiquitatem*. Just because he had used it for a long time did not mean anything. The published research suggested that other materials carried less risk. But the boss strengthened his argument by being able to claim the lowest complication risk. The registrar did not argue further, because he needed a reference from the boss, but he could have countered that his rates could have been lower because he was a luckier or a better surgeon than his colleagues.

But you see the point, I hope.

ARGUMENTUM AD HOMINEM

This is an argument against the person. It is when one makes it personal and discredits the other person or the authority. You can attack the credibility of your opponent or of your opponent's reference. For example, if one person says that his favourite writer proclaims a particular view then his opponent could claim that the view was valueless because the writer had no clue, or that they could not be listened to because they were of a particular political persuasion, or a member of some group of another, or they had a vested interest.

ARGUMENTUM AD IGNORANTIAM

This is the argument of ignorance. Don't mistake that to mean that this is a stupid argument. It can be handled with great effect. It is when it is assumed that something is true just because it has not been proven to be false.

For example, you could say that there are no such thing as ghosts because every attempt to photograph them has failed, or has been shown to be a hoax.

That does not mean that ghosts do not exist; it just means that attempts have not proven their existence.

ARGUMENTUM AD LOGICAM

This is the argument to logic. It is when something is assumed to be false just because a supporting theory has been disproved or discredited. There may well be different, more effective theories that would support the case.

Arguments about religion and belief frequently revolve around such a fallacy. Just because scientists have proposed the Big Bang Theory and discovered various particles and recorded energetic disturbances that seem to support the Big Bang Theory, it may suggest that the Old Testament version of the Creation is unlikely, but it does not mean that God did not create everything.

ARGUMENTUM AD MISERICORDIAM

Don't you love the sound of this one? A misericord or 'mercy seat' is a folding seat in a church placed in position to provide some ease for someone who has to stand during long periods of prayer. An *argumentum ad misericordiam* is an argument of mercy or pity. It is when one party makes a statement which will arouse feelings of pity or humanity in the other party, so that they cannot argue against for fear of seeming cruel or pitiless.

'How can we let people starve in this day and age? You have to send them food.'

This can be a good argument to invoke. We are all susceptible to this, but it may not be the correct answer just to send food. Perhaps you need to change the social situation that is responsible for people not having enough food. Perhaps you could send resources such as education that will teach people how to provide for themselves. Or perhaps practical help like giving people fishing rods or nets so that they could catch fish and become self-sufficient rather than just receiving food packages.

ARGUMENTUM AD NAUSEAM

This is the argument to the point of nausea, or repetition of the argument until you bludgeon your opponent into submission. This is the bully-boy argument style, which I am sure you will have come across. It is often delivered with increasing volume and often a good deal of intimidating finger-prodding. The point you can make against it, however, is merely to tell the person that it matters not a jot how many times the argument is repeated, the act of repetition will not make it more or less true. Tell them that *argumentum ad nauseam* is the refuge of the arguer who has no evidence to back up his or her argument.

Try to say this diplomatically rather than telling them that they are making you feel sick.

ARGUMENTUM AD NUMERUM

This is the argument by numbers. It is a little of the lies, damned lies and statistics. It is actually one of the most compelling arguments that can be given, because we tend to come to decisions heuristically. That is, when we hear that large proportions of people think in a particular way or respond in some manner, we tend to tag this as good or bad. The larger the number the more convinced we will be.

For example, if you hear that 80 per cent of the population support the right to protect your property against intruders with whatever force is necessary, then you might conclude that if a burglar is maimed when attempting to burgle a house that the householder should be immune from prosecution.

The thing is that just because a large proportion of people believe something does not in itself make that thing right.

In a discussion involving several people, if you are successful in persuading the majority to your proposal that may mean that you win the argument, but it doesn't mean that your proposal was the correct one. But then, that is the aim in sophistry.

ARGUMENTUM AD VERECUNDIAM

This is the argument to authority. It is when an authority is quoted. This can be very effective, because we all tend to be in awe of authorities. If you are able to quote Aristotle, Shakespeare or Einstein then you may gain the upper hand.

It is a fallacy, however, if the authority has no real claim to special expertise in the area that you are discussing. For example, you may be arguing about the reasons that murderers commit their crimes. You may recite a speech from Othello, thereby invoking the authority of Shakespeare who is believed by many to have had a remarkable insight into the workings of the mind. Yet as far as we know he never killed anyone himself, his ideas about jealousy and hate being purely speculative.

Nevertheless, if you know that your opponent is fond of a particular author or authority and you can work in a quotation or cite their authority, then you have a good chance of persuading them to your view.

Some people actually make up authorities or deliberately misquote or even put words into the mouths of their authorities. If you hear someone using vaguely plausible yet not well-known authorities, such as Fitzsimons Compendium of Bar Games, or Werner's Encyclopaedia of Flower Names, then you may well have not just a fallacy, but a downright fib. You can legitimately ask for this authority to be checked, an easy matter in these days of the Internet.

Be careful if you are the perpetrator of this scam yourself. You may be caught out and risk never being believed again.

DICTO SIMPLICITER

This means the sweeping generalisation. You can pull this off if you are able to state it quickly and move on. On the other hand if you find that your opponent has made such a fallacy, go for the kill.

An example would be, women have only been playing competitive chess for a few decades, so how could they possibly hope to play as well as men?

NON SEQUITUR

This means it doesn't follow. It is when one makes a statement then draws a conclusion that is not valid. You can often spot them when you hear the word 'so' or 'therefore.' There may be a case for the argument, but usually there is a mental step or two that is missing.

For example, battery farming is cruel so you shouldn't eat eggs.

THE THIN END OF THE WEDGE

This is also called the slippery slope argument or the creeping syndrome. It is implied that once a little alteration in a situation or an opportunity is given, it will lead to a whole succession of changes.

The counter-argument is that this is not necessarily the case and that it requires to be demonstrated. Also, the thin end of the wedge is actually the most powerful opportunity, because if you control the opening then you potentially control the whole process of change.

POLITICIAN'S ANSWER

This is the technique of evasion and irrelevance used in answering a question. The individual keeps talking around the subject while they think of how best to make their point. Effectively, rather than answering the question asked they answer the question that they want to answer or make a mini-speech on a subject that is close to but not actually the one asked about.

Just listen to any politician when they are asked a question and see how adroitly they side-step it.

If you know that you are likely to be involved in a particular argument, then have a think about subjects close to the topic and prepare a couple of mini-speeches or diatribes.

A few tips for argument's sake

When you are arguing there are a few things that you should aim at:

Try to assess your opponent's character as indicated in the chapter on 'A Matter of Character'

Be calm: whoever loses their temper loses the argument

Try to be factual: if you have real facts and statistics to back you up, then use them

Be logical: most of the fallacy arguments that I have referred to are logical fallacies, in that they are based on faulty logic; good logic is harder to argue against

Be a good listener: show your opponent that you are listening to their argument and not just over-riding them or attempting to sweep their argument aside

Be sporting and accept good points, but be ready with a riposte or ready to start a new thread
Use persuader words: these are words like 'surely,' 'truly,' 'clearly' and 'obviously'

OK, GENIUS, YOU TELL ME

When you hear this line, you know that you have won. All you have to do is take a deep breath and then explain cogently and carefully. Try not to be condescending, since that is ill-mannered and no one likes being talked down to. You are being given the opportunity to summarise your thoughts and close the argument down.

Do it gracefully.

6

IMPROVE YOUR MEMORY

Memory is the mother of all wisdom.

Aeschylus (525–455 BC)
Playwright and soldier

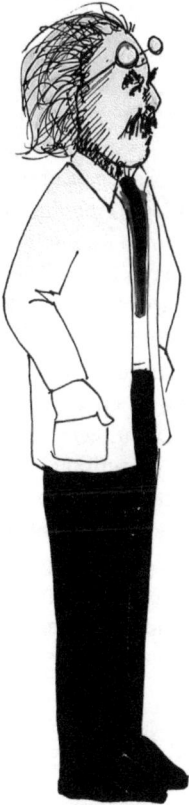

Don't you think it would be great to be a genius and be able to remember all sort of facts and figures? Just think of Albert Einstein, for example. Able to figure out many of the mysteries of the universe, he must have had a brilliant memory for numbers. You would think so, wouldn't you? In fact, he did not. Apparently he couldn't remember phone numbers or car registrations. It was not so much that he couldn't, but that he decided not to. He consciously chose not to clutter his mind with things that were not important so that he could allow it room to work freely. It was a bit like keeping a clean blackboard so that he could chalk away happily to discover the sort of things that geniuses are expected to find.

I personally used to have a pathetic memory for such numbers. And I blamed Einstein. Or, rather, having heard his view I thought that if it was good enough for him then it was good enough for me and I took a certain pride in being like Einstein. I realised eventually, when

'Now, where did I put my glasses?'

I had failed to come up with a ground-breaking mathematical theory, that having a poor memory for numbers was a most inconvenient thing, so I decided to do something about it. And that I want to impart to you now.

GET RID OF THE NEGATIVE THOUGHT

What negative thought, you may ask? Why, the thought that you can't remember things, of course. This is very important and very basic, because as long as you imagine that you have a poor memory, you will find that to be the case. Negative thoughts are self-fulfilling.

Do you ever say to yourself, 'Oh, I am hopeless with numbers,' or, 'I just can't remember names,' or even, 'I just have a poor memory for faces.'

If you do, then you are simply reinforcing that negative thought in your mind and you will find that you are not proficient in these areas. The truth is that your brain is capable of remembering numbers, names and faces, provided you allow it to do so. But if you tell it that you can't, it will close the door and shut out the facility.

So the very first thing you should do in striving to improve your memory is to tell yourself that you have a good memory. That your memory is like a sponge, it soaks up everything. In fact, say this little aphorism to yourself every morning when you wash your face and then look in the mirror and brush your teeth:

'My memory is like a sponge. I can remember everything.'

You can do it at night as well. The reason that you do it as you look in the mirror after doing your ablutions is to reinforce the idea of the sponge. You don't actually need to use a sponge, but if you have one for washing, so much the better. The mental association will work and you will open up that unconscious door to the memory banks in your brain.

DO YOU BELIEVE THAT?

I mean, do you believe that you can actually improve your memory? A lot of people give up at the first post because they refuse to believe that something they have lived with all their lives, meaning a poor memory, can be improved.

Well of course it can. It is estimated that we only ever use up to a tenth of the potential of the human brain. Geniuses like Einstein probably used up to about 20 per cent of theirs. That means that there is a great deal of potential in the brain to use up on functions like memory. And the simple thought of making your brain more like a sponge will start the process.

BRAIN EXERCISES AND HEURISTICS

This is really common sense. If you want to get better at something you need to practise. Whether that is playing a musical instrument, baking bread or playing snooker, the more you practise the better you will get.

Doing puzzles, sudoku, crosswords and playing chess are all activities that help you to exercise the brain. Although they are problem-solving functions, the more you do them, the more you will also stimulate memory function.

You will recall from Chapter 2 that heuristics are short-cuts that we use in making decisions and in making judgements. The mathematician George Pólya popularised the term in 1945 in his landmark book *How to Solve It*. This looks at heuristics as a means of discovering, inventing and problem-solving. His premise is that practice at different types of problems will result in heuristic production. It is not learning by rote, but learning to solve by application. Repetition of puzzle-solving will spin off to enhance all sorts of brain activity, including memory. This is because you will stimulate unconscious heuristic activity.

IMPROVE YOUR MEMORY FOR FACES

Have you ever had to excuse yourself and admit that you did not recognise someone? I am sure that you felt embarrassed. And really, so you should. If you fail to recognise someone they will probably feel quite slighted. After all, we all have egos and like to think that we make an impression on other people. If you fail to recognise them you are effectively saying that they failed to make an impression on you. On the other hand, if you recognise someone they will warm to you. And if you can remember things about them then you will shine.

Memory for faces is a visual memory skill. It is about recognising patterns, the way that the face is made up, and remembering mannerisms, the way that people act and move. And it is also assisted by sound memory, in that you may remember the timbre and accent of their voice.

You can enhance your visual memory by practice. At the end of every day just run through in your mind the people you met, bringing their image to mind. It is also worth getting an exercise book and trying to describe them.

Get into the habit of trying to 'tag' them. By this I mean choose a word that describes something that they volunteer about themselves. Perhaps they have told you about hockey, or golf. Tag that word with them and associate it with the image and, most importantly, with their name. Thus Bill and hockey, or Sandra and golf.

And make that an exercise any time you meet someone new. In the process of the meeting, imprint their image in your sponge-like mind along with their name – which you should make a real effort to remember. Add the tag of hockey, cooking, painting, or whatever seems the suitable and memorable thing they have talked about.

If you simply do this at the end of the day, especially when you have met new people, then your memory for faces will get better straight away.

MNEMONICS:
THE HEURISTICS OF MEMORY

These are memory prompts or rules of thumb for remembering things. The word is derived from Greek legend. Mnemosyne was a Titaness, who ruled over memory. Zeus, the king of the gods, seduced her and she gave birth to the nine creative muses. All of them are, of course, based on memory.

There are various mnemonic systems that you can use to help you learn a foreign language, recall complexes of numbers, facts, things and people. Some of these are very old, going back to antiquity.

'Now, which daughter are you?'

Take the *method of loci*, or *the memory palace*, for example. This was used by the Greeks and the Romans. The Latin word *locus* means place (*loci* is the plural). To remember a number of things you simply use a palace or a mansion, or even your own home, and picture it in your mind. You walk through the building in a set order, visiting the rooms one by one. In each room you place an item, or an action, whatever it is you are trying to recall, whether it is the components of a jet engine or just the shopping list that you have no paper and pencil available to jot down. It is very effective as long as you haven't moved into a new house! In that case an alternative would be to use the holes of your local golf course if you are a golfer.

Three hundred years ago Johann Just Winkelmann (1620–99), writing as Stanislaus Mink von Wennshein, devised a method for remembering numbers which became known as *the major system*. It is based on remembering each number by associating it with various consonants. Complex numbers can thereby be phonetically remembered as words by adding vowels. It is an incredibly good system, the description of which is outwith the scope or the needs of this chapter, but you may like to follow up on it yourself.

A shorter method, *the mnemonic dominic system*, was devised by Dominic O'Brien, a British mnemonist who can memorise a pack of cards, and who has been world memory champion on eight occasions. If such a feat is your ambition then again feel free to explore further. Alternatively, read to the end of the chapter when I will show you a mnemonic to do a great trick with a pack of cards.

But now let's look at some rules of thumb to help you improve your memory.

INITIAL LETTER SENTENCES MAKE SENSE

You probably know this one: Richard Of York Gave Battle In Vain. The initial letter of each word gives R-O-Y-G-B-I-V. These stand for the order of the colours of the rainbow: red, orange, yellow, green, blue, indigo and violet.

I personally think that this is a great system for recollecting the order of things, often very complex things. Indeed, when I was a young medical student I truly wondered if I would have the memory ability to learn anatomy. It is no mean task knowing the name, position, relationship, blood and nerve supply of every organ and tissue in the body. The textbooks are huge, the names are all in Latin and the examinations that you have to pass are enough to make your head spin. When you start you imagine that you have to be a genius to remember it all.

The truth is that you have to find a system that works. I found a perfect little book that I could slip into a pocket and which cost me a few pence. It was called Irving's *Anatomy Mnemonics*, and I still have it and still refer to it. It was first published in 1939 and it has been the saviour of generations of medical students, many of whom have the book to thank for helping them with their surgical careers. It is a book crammed with initial letter sentence mnemonics.

Let me give you an example. The sentence reads straight down and the item you need to remember is to the right.

Do	Diaphragmatic
Petting	Pleural
Parties	Pericardial
In	Inferior vena cava
Private	Peritoneal
Harm	Hepatic
Anyone?	Adrenal

These are the branches of the phrenic nerve. Unless you plan on becoming a doctor there is no need to know more than that. The point is that you can easily make up your own initial letter sentence if you have to remember complex items in a set order. And if the sentence is quirky or even a bit risqué, then you will probably remember it all the easier.

INITIAL LETTER WORDS

These are also very handy for remembering those things that slip the memory. Again, there are lots of these in *Irving's Anatomy Mnemonics*. For example:

S	Skin
C	Close connective tissue and cutaneous vessels and nerves
A	Aponeurosis
L	Loose connective tissue
P	Pericranium

These are the layers of the scalp.

If you have difficulty with those early Greek philosophers, then the word SPA might help you remember the order in which Socrates, Plato and Aristotle appeared and bamboozled us with their genius.

Or you might like a geography one: HOMES for the Great Lakes of America – Huron, Ontario, Michigan, Erie and Superior.

THE PEGWORD MNEMONIC SYSTEM

This is a very good method for remembering a list of items. You memorise a number of words that you can easily associate with numbers. This can be one to ten, which is going to be enough for most purposes, but if you want to show off you can remember up to twenty, fifty or even a hundred. These are your pegs and you then just visualise pegging the items you need to remember to them.

One	Bun
Two	Shoe
Three	Tree
Four	Door
Five	Hive
Six	Sticks (bundle of sticks)
Seven	Heaven
Eight	Gate
Nine	Line (washing line)
Ten	Hen

Suppose that you have ten items to remember, in a set order, such as: 1) hammer, 2) radio, 3) horse, 4) drum, 5) clarinet, 6) drawing pin, 7) cake, 8) golf ball, 9) book, 10) pencil.

You then associate each with the peg word and imagine the image. Thus, think of a bun containing a hammer, a radio inside a shoe, a horse in a tree and so on.

If you want to go beyond ten, then picture other appropriate words. For example:

Eleven	Elf
Twelve	Shelf
Thirteen	Thirsty
Fourteen	Forking
Fifteen	Fighting

Just find the pegwords that you are comfortable with and commit them to memory; the rest is easy.

REMEMBERING A DECK OF CARDS

These two little mnemonics can be used to stack a deck of cards so that they look completely random:

Eight kings threatened to save ninety-five queens from one sick knave
8-K-3-10-2-7-9-5-Q-4-A-6-Knave (jack)

And for the suits, use the word CHaSeD: clubs, hearts, spades, diamonds.

To set the deck up you lay the cards face up in order, thus: 8 of clubs, king of hearts, 3 of spades, 10 of diamonds, 2 of clubs, 7 of hearts and so on.

Knowing the sequence allows you to know where every card is. For example, if you lay the prepared deck down on the table and cut the deck and look at the exposed card (suppose it is the 7 of spades), you know that it is followed by a 9, and that diamond follows spades, so the card left on top of the pile is the 9 of diamonds.

The deck can be cut as many times as you want, the top pile being put on the bottom of the deck each time, without altering the sequence. You can make a false shuffle of the deck by just repeatedly cutting, and you can immediately identify the card that someone cuts to by looking at the bottom card of the top cut. Do it subtly, of course.

Rather than cutting, fan the deck and get someone to select a card. As they pull it from the deck you separate the fan and then gain a sight of the card that was above it. If this is a single trick (and repetition of card tricks is never a good idea, because someone will remark about you not shuffling properly) then you can get them to look at the card, show it to others then return it to the deck. Then you shuffle, think and riffle through the deck, asking distracting questions as you do so, until you reveal the card.

So, you see, you can remember a deck of cards, you genius.

A DIFFERENT WAY OF CHECKING A DECK

This is a neat little curio that you can use to check a deck. Instead of counting the cards one by one, you can check a fifty-two-card deck (that is, a deck without jokers in it) by spelling out the names of the cards. Before you start, riffle through the deck and bring the king of diamonds to the bottom. Then, with the deck held in one hand, all face down, place one card on the table and call out 'A,' then toss the next card on top and call out 'C,' then the next and call out 'E.' So you have spelled 'Ace;' then go through the entire deck, with 'T,' then 'W,' then 'O,' and keep going through the cards and carry on spelling until you do the king. And as you reach the final card, just ask the audience which of the four kings went to war? Let them guess, then you toss down the king of diamonds face up, explaining that you can always tell it was him, for he was the one who lost an eye. And if they would like to check, they will find that it is true.

Just remember that you spell jack, rather than knave!

7

COMIC GENIUS
(OR HOW TO TELL A JOKE)

My way of joking is to tell the truth. It is the funniest joke in the world.

George Bernard Shaw
Playwright, critic and Nobel Prize-winner, 1925

Some people are absolute geniuses at telling jokes while others just could not raise a titter even if their lives depended upon it. A lot has to do with the way the joke is told.

'Did I tell you the one about the Two Gentlemen of Verona?'

Now I cannot instantly turn a non-joker into a comic genius. I am not even going to tell you any jokes in this chapter. You can find your own. There are millions of joke books and the internet is littered with them. What I am going to do is talk about a few of the things that may help you to deliver a joke that makes people laugh.

So first of all, what is a joke? Well, it is basically something that makes people laugh. It can be a pun, a play on words, a humorous story or an anecdote. If you drop one into the conversation or into a speech at the appropriate time you can have your audience eating out of your hand.

DO YOU HAVE A SENSE OF HUMOUR?

That is a serious question. Do you? And, if so, what sort of thing tickles your fancy? Do you like irony, sarcasm, smut or even good old-fashioned slap-stick? Do jokes make you guffaw, bend double, chuckle, titter or just raise a slight smile? It is worth analysing, because if you don't find jokes amusing then you are going to have a hard job amusing others with your attempts.

So the first thing is to start developing that sense of humour. Get some joke books, read a few comic novels, watch sit-coms on TV, see some comedy films and maybe go to see some stand-up comics in action. And here is the important point: see the humour and let your hair down, allow the laughter to bubble up and feel the tears of joy roll down your cheeks.

ACT

That's right, when you tell a joke you do need to act a little. Get into the role of a joke-teller, believe in yourself and deliver it like a good actor. For instance, you can embellish aspects of the joke. If you are talking about a film, introduce where you first saw it, perhaps in a flea-pit cinema where even the fleas didn't want to sit in the front row ('and where did I end up seeing it – in the front row!'). Use voices and accents for the different characters if your joke involves them. Be careful, however, of using accents that are poorly done. If you can't do it properly, it will not work.

ACT is also a first letter mnemonic for the three most important guidelines about telling a joke. The letters stand for Audience, Confidence and Timing.

Audience

First, know your audience. This can be your family, your friends down the pub or the good folk at the church jumble sale. You have to know what sort of joke is appropriate for your audience and you have to have some sort of idea of their sense of humour.

Confidence

Many people fail to tell a good joke, or even a bad joke, because they are not confident that they can deliver it. Worse, they often preface the joke by telling their audience that they can't tell jokes. Then they stutter and stumble through it, smile nervously as they approach the punch line and then deliver it in a whisper so that no one can hear it properly.

A joke has to be delivered confidently. You have to believe in your ability to make it work and you have to commit to it. You have to tell it without bumbling, hesitating or giggling.

Timing

This is all important. A joke read out of a joke book will probably get a laugh if it is funny. If it is read out well, with suitable emphasis on certain words, a bit of acting, building of the tension within the joke, and the right amount of distraction, it will seem even funnier. The trick is to build it up so that the twist at the end is well timed, so that it hits the audience like a custard pie in the face. That is, it should be unexpected. If it does that you will make your audience laugh at the joke.

Emphasis on certain words will help. One of the best things you can do is to watch and listen to professional comedians. See how they act and behave. Some dash about the stage using their whole body to portray and magnify a character. Others stand still and deliver in a dead pan manner. Both can be hilariously funny provided the timing is right.

Listen to the way they use emphasis on certain words to produce a dramatic effect. And have no doubts, each of those little jokes is a vignette, a little work of drama that they are acting out as best they can for you to enjoy.

Watch how they use *the pause*. This is one of the most important things to remember in telling a joke. There should be two pauses in the joke: one just before the punch-line and one just after it. More than that can give it a stumbling, bumbling effect. Get those pauses right and you are on your way to developing good timing.

That second pause gives your audience the opportunity to get the joke. What you mustn't do is to laugh yourself. That ruins it, because you don't laugh at your own jokes. Don't make the pause too long or it looks as if you are waiting for them to laugh. You then go crisply on with the rest of your conversation or speech.

REPERTOIRE

I am not suggesting that your aim should be to build a stand-up comedy act, but even if you only want to amuse your friends or colleagues, then you should try to assemble some material and build up your repertoire.

You are going to succeed best with your joke if you actually use funny material. If you do not find your joke funny then how do you expect anyone else to? It won't be funny, not unless you really are a comic genius and can deliver it in a unique way. You can make your own jokes, of course. You have read the chapter on creativity, so you just need to use the brainstorming technique. Take a couple of words or people and put them in a situation and ask questions about them. What funny thought comes? What punch line can you come up with? When you have it, work backwards, until you are able to set the scene for the joke. Remember that the punch-line is a twist; the audience should not expect it to be the ending. That surprise is what makes them laugh.

If you are going to start making up your own material then start observing the world, people and the news. Material is everywhere: you just have to give it a humorous spin.

PRACTICE

Every new skill demands practice. The art of telling jokes is no different. The mirror is therefore one of your best friends, because it will show you if you are grinning or smirking as you approach the punch-line. It will show your fidgets, your unnecessary mannerisms, or alternatively it will show if you have a wooden aspect.

Telling a joke has to be done crisply. There is no room for umming and ahing as you struggle to recall what bit comes next. You almost need to be able to tell a joke verbatim. Of course, the more adept you become and the larger your repertoire – and you should aim at building a repertoire, so that you literally will have a potential joke for all occasions, and appropriate for all audiences – then you can change jokes. Add different endings, add ever more comic twists. Get a book and start writing them down. That is precisely what professional comics do. A joker needs his or her own joke book.

If you have a video facility you might try recording yourself telling a joke. Perhaps get a friend to record you on a camera or, if the joke is short, on their mobile phone. This has the advantage of not just seeing how you tell a joke, but hearing yourself. Did you make yourself laugh? Of course, you should choose a friend who is going to be faithful, not someone who is immediately going to post your faltering effort on YouTube for the world to fall apart with laughter. The problem is that they may end up laughing at you, not at the joke. So, leave the internet alone until you are ready to let the world see you for the comic genius that you feel you are.

Yet telling a joke to a mirror and even a camera are not real situations. It is a good idea telling it to a 3D live audience. Your cat or your dog perhaps. I would advise against parrots and budgies, since they have a tendency to learn your punch-lines and drive everyone berserk with them, even you. The point of telling them your jokes is that it gives you a focus, if not a great deal of applause, laughter or critical acclaim.

Then it is family and friends time. Go ahead, tell it and then ask them what they think. You are looking for a bit of criticism here. When you go out into the real world, of the pub, club or church hall, the last thing you think of doing is asking your audience what they think of your jokes. One of the great comic Eric Morecombe's punch-lines, usually delivered via a ventriloquist's doll or other prop, was 'rubbish!' You don't want to hear some wag cry that at you.

SOME HUMOUR ELEMENTS

A study of professionals will reveal that they use a variety of elements in their joke-telling. Some adopt one that becomes their comedic signature. With the late, great Tommy Cooper it was incompetence and bemusement. When telling a tale or performing a magic trick you just knew that it was going to go drastically wrong. It was all an illusion. He peppered his act with one-liners and his timing was masterful. It is not an approach that many have the skill to use, so unless you are a consummate actor, best avoid this. You want to appear in control and seem smart.

Mimicry is very good if you can pull it off. It demands a good ear and practice, practice, practice. Get the voice right, but also get the accent and the nuances off to a tee. It can be a lot of work if you are just telling a single joke, so you want to aim at having a few in store. That way you will have a surprise for the times when someone asks you to tell that old Benny Hill joke.

Walter Mitty jokes. These are ones where you can indulge your acting talents. 'The Secret Life of Walter Mitty' was a short story by the American humourist James Thurber, about a mild-mannered chap with an immense fantasy life as every kind of genius and hero. Any joke in which you have yourself as a character can be a Walter Mitty-esque tale in which you can demonstrate your pantomimic karate skills, your fencing, your linguistic ability (or not). The one thing about this approach is that you have to be able to laugh at yourself, and at your fantasy figures. After all, your aim is to get your audience laughing.

Puns are mini-jokes. They are a play on words. They can come off very well when dropped into ordinary conversation, just as long as you don't do it all the time. That can get boring and irritating. Be judicious in their use, but be observational and creative as you try to build up a repertoire of them.

Double-entendres are statements with two meanings. One way is the right, correct meaning; the other way is the banal, silly, joke meaning. Very often these are risqué, usually sexually explicit jokes dropped as one-liners. Be very careful of your audience here.

In the chapter on literature you will find a little piece about Spoonerisms and Malapropisms. These and other plays on words are good drop-in jokes which can gain you a reputation as a wit.

You can develop a skill for making them quite quickly; it is just a matter of juxtaposing and substituting words. Experiment with words and see how you can change one for another to alter the meaning of a sentence. And as you do this, all the time compiling examples in the joke book that you are compiling, so you will find opportunities for bringing them out in conversations.

Exaggeration is a well-used technique. It can be used to create a shaggy dog story of the Baron von Munchausen's variety, where the exploits get more and more bizarre, or it can be used in the short one-liners that you can use for a joke within a joke. For example, if telling a story about a journey to see someone, you get out your bicycle: 'Now my bicycle is pretty old. My granddad gave it to me. It's a penny-farthing.' And there is the opportunity to do a little acting, demonstrating the imaginary bicycle and the difficulty of getting on it. 'Not only that, but it was invented before they discovered oil.' Time then for a noisy metal grating noise, and away you go with the rest of the joke.

QUIT WHILE YOU ARE AHEAD

This is fundamental. There is nothing worse than trying to milk a situation. People tend not to like long-winded jokes, because they may lose the thread and they may start to get bored. Be pithy, be crisp and be funny. Then stop.

PART 2

OMNI-SCIENCE

8

SCIENCE

Louis Pasteur's theory of germs is ridiculous fiction.

Pierre Pachet
Professor of Physiology, 1872

This boy will never amount to much.

Albert Einstein's primary school teacher

Science is cool. I have always thought that since the day I first saw Patrick Moore on *The Sky at Night* when I was a youngster. I was fascinated by outer space, strange planets and rockets. Like most kids I wanted to be a spaceman and I wanted to meet aliens.

On *The Sky at Night*, Patrick Moore (now Sir Patrick) interviewed famous scientists, told you all about the wonders of space and the possibilities for the future. He brought science into the living room and propelled me into a quasi-world of science and medicine. For that, I am eternally grateful to him.

Yet there are many people who are baffled by science, who somehow have a mental block about all of the sciences and who find themselves sidelined whenever science comes up in conversation. So here is a potpourri of some of the main scientific advances that you should know about and a few explanations of some of the more curious everyday phenomena that make life so interesting.

THE BIG BANG

Where did it all start? That is one of the fundamental questions that everyone asks. Every culture has produced an answer, most of which are based upon the belief system or religion that is current in that culture. The ancients believed and taught that gods had created everything. Some modern religions still teach that there was a divine origin to the universe. Indeed, no one can prove that this was not the case.

Scientists have walked an uneasy path through the quagmire of the creation. In days gone by brave souls have faced excommunication from their Church, burning at the stake or even worse. Even the great Galileo Galilei was threatened with torture and then had to endure years of house arrest for daring to publish data supporting the Copernican view that the sun rather than the earth was at the centre of the known universe. Had he challenged the Church's view of the creation he would almost certainly have faced death for heresy.

The Big Bang

Yet scientific observations of the universe have shown us that while a divine origin may have been the case, it is not likely. What does seem credible is the concept of a big bang, a single event that created everything we know about, including all of the forces and all of the particles that make up the universe today. Even time itself was created at that single event, or that singularity, which occurred about 13.7 billion years ago.

In the 1920s Edwin Hubble, an American astronomer, working at the Mount Wilson Observatory in California, observed that galaxies in the Milky Way are moving away from us. Not only that, but the further galaxies are away from us the faster they seem to be moving. His brilliant conclusion, his eureka moment, one might say, was that the universe is expanding. From this he worked out that the entire universe must have come from a single point.

This theory was not accepted by all scientists, including the famous English astronomer Sir Fred Hoyle. In 1948 he and a couple of other scientists put forward the *steady-state theory of the universe*. Basically this postulated that the universe had always existed but that new matter could be added to it. He did not agree with Hubble's concept of the universe suddenly bursting into existence from a single point. Somewhat derisively, he coined the term 'the big bang' on a radio show in 1950.

In 1963 two astronomers, Arno Penzias and Robert Wilson, discovered a sort of cosmic 'afterglow' which was called the *cosmic microwave background*, or CMB for short. The significance of this was that it demonstrated that the universe was once a lot hotter than it is today. Effectively, it was strong evidence for a big bang from a 'singularity.'

The questions that everyone asks, and most people find hard to comprehend, are: what was there before the big bang? And what is beyond the universe? The idea of nothing is hard to accept and our experience of everything is that it has to have some limit.

The whole point about the big bang theory is that there was nothing to begin with. Space itself was created by the big bang. And so was time.

You can demonstrate the cosmic microwave background yourself
Every time you switch off a television set or retune a channel you will see black and white static. About 1 per cent of this comes from the CMB

THE BIG CRUNCH

If we accept the concept that the universe is expanding, rather than being a steady state, then you have to ask a basic question: when will it stop expanding and what will happen then? Well, it all depends upon the average density of the universe. This is denoted in science by the Greek letter omega, Ω. If Ω is greater than 1, then gravity will remain the dominant force in the universe. When the galaxies have run out of power, out of momentum, then gravity will haul them all back and everything will end in the *big crunch*.

It is estimated that this would be in about 80 billion years from now. If Ω is equal to 1, then the universe will slow down in its expansion, but it will never stop. This is called the *flat universe*. Finally, if Ω is less than 1, then the universe will continue forever. More than that, it will continue to expand and accelerate, because expansion will be dominant over all of the gravitational forces in the universe.

DARK MATTER AND DARK ENERGY

We really know incredibly little about the universe. It is currently thought that all of the known matter in the universe, the atoms, molecules and particles that make up you and me, the planets, the stars and the galaxies, only accounts for about 4 per cent of it; 23 per cent is thought to be dark matter and 73 per cent is dark energy. What exactly those are is currently pure speculation.

Dark matter

BLACK HOLES, WORMHOLES AND TIME TRAVEL

Firstly, understand that at the time of the big bang there was nothing, then space and time came into being. This accounts for the four known dimensions: the three directions and the fourth dimension of time. Although you cannot see time, we understand it as the space-time continuum. Effectively, this tells you the 'where-when' of whatever you are looking at.

A black hole is the result of the collapse of a giant star. Inside it the laws of physics go haywire. Its gravitational pull is such that not even light can escape from it and it can distort the space-time continuum or the where-when of anything that is too close to it. Indeed, because black holes do not give out any light or radiation it is purely because they produce distortion in other objects' movement that we are even aware of their existence.

Wormholes are a fascinating phenomenon that may exist, although we are not sure whether they are fact or pure science fiction. They are, however, predicted by Einstein's theory of relativity, which we will come to in a moment. They are potential hidden short-cuts through space-time that could come about if two massive bodies, like black holes, warped space sufficiently to create a tunnel through space between them. Passing through such a tunnel would permit fast space travel in an almost impossibly short period of time. And, of course, if you think about it, it would also be possible to travel back in time!

It is thought that the Large Hadron Collider at CERN in Switzerland may be able to create miniature black holes and miniature wormholes as a consequence. They would be quite transient and would disappear almost immediately.

Which all brings us to the subject of time travel. According to scientists such as Professor Stephen Hawking, time travel is theoretically possible, possibly via wormholes. Artificially creating one would, however, demand machinery so large that it would be impossible to build.

At least until a genius comes up with a way to do it.

ANTI-MATTER AND TIME

Our universe is made up of matter. It is well established that atoms are made up of a whole series of subatomic particles, such as *neutrons*, *positrons* and *electrons*. Modern particle physics recognises a whole range of other particles which are basically divided into two families, the *bosons* and the *fermions*. The hunt goes on at CERN in Switzerland with the Large Hadron Collider for an elusive particle that is called the *Higgs boson*, or 'the God particle', which would solve many of the inconsistencies in modern physics.

Anti-matter is the opposite of matter. Every particle in matter has a counterpart in anti-matter, which has an opposite charge. Thus in matter there is a negatively charged electron (and electricity is a flow of electrons), so in anti-matter there is a positively charged positron. The interesting thing is that the two are incompatible, so if a matter particle meets its equivalent anti-matter particle they annihilate each other and all that is left is gamma radiation.

This creates a curious conundrum, since physical laws would expect symmetry. That is an equal amount of matter and anti-matter. Yet in the universe there is very little anti-matter. Some scientists say that at the big bang, matter and anti-matter particles were created, but that there was an excess of matter particles so that the majority of the anti-matter was annihilated, leaving the residue of matter particles to form the matter of the universe.

Yet the laws of physics also show another curious anomaly. This is simply that unlike the three directional dimensions of space, time seems to be only directed forwards into the future. That is, it moves away from the past.

Consider the positron, the anti-matter equivalent of the electron. The 1965 Nobel Prize-winner Richard Feynman proposed that it was like an electron that is moving backwards in time. That is, it moves backwards along the space-time continuum.

Richard Gott III, Professor of Astrophysics at Princeton University, has developed several cosmological models over the years and has written about time travel. One of his models is the *three-universe big bang cosmology*. This would account for the deficit of anti-matter in the universe. Instead of the big bang creating all of the matter and anti-matter particles, the ensuing annihilation of most of the anti-matter particles and then the development of the universe, which is bound by the speed of light (meaning that nothing can travel faster than light), he proposed that three simultaneous universes were created and exist.

First, our matter universe which moves forward into the future and is cooling from the big bang. Second, an anti-matter universe which is moving backwards into the past and getting hotter as it approaches a big crunch. And thirdly, a tachyon* universe where everything is travelling faster than the speed of light. It is all perfectly logical, since at the instant of the big bang the tachyons would have escaped because they move so fast. The tachyon universe would therefore be segregated from the matter and anti-matter universes by space. The matter and anti-matter universes would be separated from each other by time.

THE THEORY OF EVERYTHING

Up until the 1990s most theoretical physicists agreed that all matter was made up of atoms and sub-atomic particles, which were held together by four fundamental forces.

First was the *gravitational force*, which keeps our feet on the earth, stops the sun from exploding and the galaxies from scattering. Second was the *electro-magnetic force*, which we harness to power our lights, our homes and our cities. Third was the *weak nuclear force*, which is responsible for radioactive decay. This we use in nuclear medicine, in the use of radioactive tracers in our highly sophisticated diagnostic scanners. Fourth was the *strong nuclear force*, which is demonstrated by the power of the sun, the power within the atom. In 1979 Sheldon Lee Glashow, Steven Weinberg and Abdus Salam were awarded the Nobel Prize for Physics for their work in showing that the weak nuclear force and the electromagnetic force were manifestations of a single force, called the *electroweak force*.

The way in which these three fundamental forces operate is of monumental importance in science. But just what is their

---

* A tachyon is a particle that travels at a velocity greater than the speed of light

connection? Indeed, can they all be unified into a single super-force?

There are two main theories, which have each partially explained the nature of these forces. One is the *quantum theory* as outlined by Niels Bohr and the other is *general relativity* as formulated by Albert Einstein. They deal with opposite ends of the spectrum, however, because quantum theory deals with the realm of the subatomic world, effectively particle physics, while general relativity explains the macrocosm, the nature of the big bang, galaxies and black holes, or cosmology.

Quantum theory explains forces as packets or quanta of energy, whereas general relativity explains forces as deformations of space-time. Interestingly, you can take either one and derive all of the laws of physics and chemistry from it. You can build the whole of science from one of the theories – but not from both!

This was the great problem that Albert Einstein pursued over the last thirty years of his life. He was looking for a solution to what he proposed to call the *unified field theory*. Effectively, it was to be a 'theory of everything.' It is the holy grail of physics to this day.

STRING THEORY

In the 1970s and 1980s it looked as if a possible solution had presented itself with the development of *superstring theory*. The basis of this theory was that all matter is composed of superstrings, which occupy a single point in space-time at any one time. This seemed compatible with both quantum theory and general relativity, except that it could only work if there were ten dimensions!

It was conjectured that just before the big bang, there was an empty, but unstable, ten-dimensional universe. This split into two fragments, our known four-dimensional universe and a six-dimensional universe. The universe made the quantum leap to another universe, causing the six-dimensions to curl up and the four-dimensional universe to expand. This rapid expansion at some point caused the big bang. Current thinking is that rather than this being the creation of everything, it was in fact an aftershock of the collapse of the ten-dimensional universe.

There have been five 'string' theories to date, culminating in the unification of them into a single *M-theory* in 1994. However, M-theory only holds true if there are eleven dimensions. Indeed, theoretical physicists are now talking about the possibility of a twelfth dimension.

THE HIGGS BOSON

In 1964 Peter Higgs of the University of Edinburgh proposed that there was a particle that could give mass to particles. It is predicted by string theory and if it is found in experiments in CERN with the Large Hadron Collider it will put the seal of approval on string theory.

CHARLES DARWIN AND THE ORIGIN OF SPECIES

In 1859 the naturalist Charles Darwin published a small book entitled *On the Origin of Species through Natural Selection*. It is one of the most important books ever written on science for it carefully explained Darwin's theory about evolution. Inevitably, it was highly controversial when it appeared for it flew in the face of creationism.

Charles Darwin's grandfather Erasmus Darwin had done early work on common descent and the acquisition of 'new parts.' Undoubtedly, Charles was deeply influenced by this. His father, Robert Darwin, was a doctor. Initially, Charles started training in medicine, but devoted much of his time and interest into the study of natural history. His father then enrolled him for a Bachelor of Arts degree at Cambridge, hoping that he would become a clergyman. But instead the young Charles was again distracted, this time by the collection of beetles. After he graduated, thanks to his professor of botany, the Reverend John Henslow, he obtained an unpaid post as naturalist and companion to the captain of HMS *Beagle*. It was on this five-year-long voyage that he collected a vast amount of data that helped him to formulate his theory of evolution.

Darwin worked on his theory for twenty-odd years, eventually rushing into print with the ground-breaking book after he became aware of the explorer and naturalist Alfred Russel Wallace's independent theory of evolution by natural selection. The result was that Darwin went down in history as the discoverer of evolution.

There are five key points to Darwin's theory:

1) Species have great fertility and produce more offspring than can grow to adulthood
2) Populations tend to remain about the same size, with modest fluctuations
3) Food resources are limited, but are relatively constant most of the time

As a result of the above points there will be a struggle for survival between individuals or a species

4) In sexually reproducing species, generally no two individuals are identical; variation is rampant and hence mates can be selected
5) Much of this variation is inheritable

THE GAIA HYPOTHESIS

In the 1960s Dr James Lovelock, a biochemist doing work for NASA on methods of determining whether there was life on Mars, came to the conclusion that looking for actual organisms was less likely to yield results than would a search for changes in the chemistry of the Martian atmosphere that only life would produce. From this he formulated an hypothesis, which he named after Gaia, the Greek nature goddess, about the self-regulating function of the Earth. He started publishing papers about this in the early 1970s, culminating in 1979 with his book *Gaia: a New Look at Life on Earth*.

The essence of the hypothesis is that the biomass of the planet, life as a whole, controls and regulates the conditions on the planet to sustain and maintain life. Thus the temperature, acidity, composition of the seas and the balance of gases in the atmosphere are all kept within an optimum range. These changes are not what one would expect, since the temperature of the sun has risen by about 30 per cent since life first appeared on Earth, yet the average temperature of the biosphere has never varied by more than a few degrees. Also, the saline content of the sea seems to be kept in a state of equilibrium, whereas it would be expected to become more concentrated. Indeed, it is amazing that it is has been kept at the level that is compatible with marine life.

The hypothesis has many supporters and many detractors. It seems utterly plausible and may well link up with the changes that we are seeing occur as a result of climate change. It seems as if Gaia is hitting back at mankind's interference with the system. The system is likely to overcome the changes that mankind is making, although the re-balancing that Gaia will make may not be to the benefit of humankind. Perhaps it will be time for another species to rise to dominance in the struggle for survival.

One can see how the Gaia hypothesis could be regarded as a quasi-religion. This is something that Lovelock would probably not wish to see.

GERM THEORY AND A FEW MISCONCEPTIONS

Over the centuries people have come up with various ideas to account for the festering of wounds, the feverish illnesses, plagues and epidemics that have caused so much death and misery throughout history. The *germ theory* changed all that and for the first time ever gave doctors a means of altering the pattern of morbidity and mortality in society. It was based on good science and proposed that many illnesses were caused by infection by various microbial organisms.

Louis Pasteur, a French chemist and scientist, was one of the founding fathers of microbiology. He was not the originator of the germ theory, but he was one of the most significant advocates of it. He demonstrated in the laboratory that beers, wine, milk and food went bad through bacterial contamination and the growth of these organisms. He went on to discover rabies and anthrax vaccines, did important work on cholera and introduced the process of pasteurisation (named after him, of course), which stops milk, cheese and wine from going off.

The discovery of penicillin by Alexander Fleming in 1928 and its introduction as an antibiotic some years later led to a belief that we had discovered a group of drugs that could be used as 'silver bullets' to target the bacteria that caused illness. Indeed, antibiotics have been incredibly successful, but now we are running into problems because so many bacteria have become resistant to them. We are now faced with bacteria like Methicillin-resistant staphylococcus aureus (MRSA), which are very difficult to eradicate. The problem is that we overuse antibiotics in medicine and have pumped them into the food chain, with dire consequences.

At the turn of the century people were concerned about the so-called 'millennium bug.' This was a fear of a potential technological glitch that could occur in all of the digital clocks if they failed to convert to the new millennium. The prophets of doom prophesied a complete shut-down of all technology. It did not happen.

The real millennium bug is still working away. The problem is that in the microbial world a decade is like a millennium. They are evolving and adapting to the adverse antibiotic world that we are subjecting them to. This is pure Darwinism. The microbial population is changing, and mankind is stimulating their evolution, to our detriment.

If you find yourself in a discussion about bacteria and the wonders of modern medicine and antibiotics, arm yourself with these facts:

- Only 10 per cent of the cells in the body are human, the rest are microbes (mainly in the bowel)
- We know very little about the microbial world and base our knowledge on the 1 per cent of microbes that we can

culture in the laboratory. As a result we do not know about the other 99 per cent
- Although we now know about the make-up of the human genome and expect it to answer all our questions about disease, in fact it will only tell us about 10 per cent of the cells that make up the body mass

THE CORIOLIS EFFECT

This is a good one to chat about at parties. Why do sinks and toilets drain clockwise in the northern hemisphere and anti-clockwise south of the equator?

You should do some experiments yourself first of all to see whether or not you think it is true. If you find that it seems to work according to which hemisphere you are in, then the following information may help to make you shine.

This curious phenomenon is said to come about because of the Coriolis force, which was first described in 1835 by Gustave de Coriolis (1792–1843), a French mathematician and engineer. It is all to do with rotating reference frames. Effectively, the Earth is a sphere rotating about its axis, so a point on the equator is moving much faster than points to the north and the south. At the equator the earth is moving at a speed of about 1,670 kilometres per hour, but at the poles it is a gentle, very slow spin. The air above is travelling at the same speed, but if it is moving northwards it will slow down and curve to the right. If it is travelling south it will curve to the left.

This seems to account for storms, which turn clockwise in the northern hemisphere and anti-clockwise south of the equator. Seems logical.

9

MATHEMATICS

I am ill at these numbers.

> *Hamlet*, Act II, Scene 2
> William Shakespeare

Arithmetic, algebra, geometry and trigonometry. Do they make you feel queasy even now? If they do then you are in illustrious company. Numbers and reckoning made poor old Prince Hamlet sink into fits of melancholy, according to William Shakespeare.

Mathematics is a blind area for many people. They shy away from numbers and find the very mention of equations, formulae and statistics enough to make them adopt avoidance behaviour. Bad teaching at school is probably the likeliest cause of such a phobia, since mathematics can literally open up the world to you.

Well, fear not, since you will find nothing to churn your stomach in this chapter. What you will find are a few rules of thumb to help you build up your confidence with mental arithmetic. You will possibly even find this fun! And then we shall focus on a few of the major mathematicians and some of the mathematics topics that you may come across at parties or meetings. Knowing about them will make you feel more confident and may make you seem to be more numerate than you are.

MENTAL ARITHMETIC IS JUST ABOUT LEARNING A FEW RULES OF THUMB

One of the reasons that people fear arithmetic is because they let themselves think that it is hard. Well, it isn't really. Anyone can learn a few heuristics or rules of thumb to make them seem more mentally agile. The Hungarian mathematician George Polya (1887–1985) was a great advocate of the use of heuristics in mathematical education. In 1957 he wrote a book entitled *How to Solve It*, which is regarded as one of the best ever guides to the art of mathematics. He believed that to develop mathematical skill you had to practise, and that you learned by recognition and experience of problems. So don't shy away, but look at the rules of thumb that I am going to outline and give them a go.

You might also care to look through the chapter on heuristics and rules of thumb again to get the concept of heuristics in your mind. In particular, you will find that the following heuristics or rules of thumb are used again and again in mental arithmetic: the *recognition heuristic*, the *availability heuristic* and the *anchoring and adjustment heuristic*. If you realise this, then you are halfway along the road to developing an insight into the mathematical mind.

There is nothing to be afraid of. Honest.

YOUR TEN-DIGIT COMPUTER

Probably everyone learned to count on their fingers. Eight fingers and two thumbs make them ideal for doing any counting in tens. And if you slip your shoes and socks off, there you are, you can go all the way up to twenty.

Now then, it may interest you to know that those ten digits make your hands a natural computer for working out – the nine times table.

Impressed? Well try this out, because other folk will like it. You can literally show them the nine times table on your hands. We'll do it in steps:

1) Hold your hands out in front of you, palms up, and think of multiplying any number from 1 to 10
2) Picture the numbers, e.g. 7 × 9
3) From the left thumb count to the seventh digit and bend it down
4) Your remaining digits will give you the answer. The number of digits to the left of the depressed finger gives you the tens, and the number of digits to the right gives you the units. You will find that you have six digits to the left and three to the right, making sixty-three

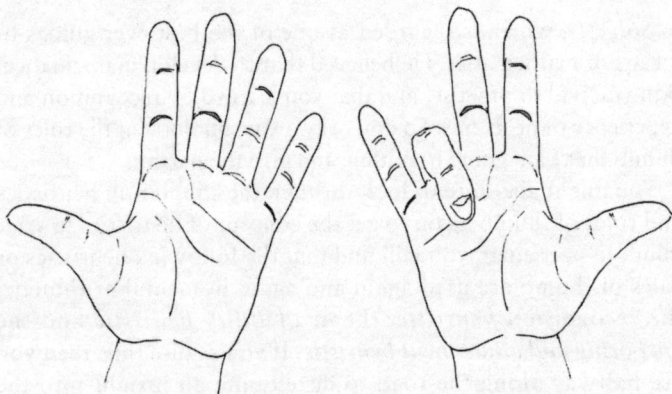

An easy way to figure out your 9s – in this case, 63!

BIGGER 9S

Dead simple, really. Just imagine that you are multiplying by ten. Add a zero as usual, then subtract the number you are multiplying by nine. And you do it with any sized number. Take 578 × 9, for example:

578 × 9 is the same as (578 × 10) – 578
Becomes 5,780 – 578 = 5,202

Multiplying by 99, or 999, is the same principle. Just add the appropriate number of zeros, then take away the number you are multiplying by. For example, 423 × 999:

423 × 999
Becomes 423,000 – 423 = 422,577

MULTIPLYING BY 11

This is fun, too. When you multiply by ten all you do is add a zero to the number. Well, multiplying by eleven is pretty easy too. Again, in steps:

1) For a single digit, just repeat it. Thus, $7 \times 11 = 77$. Easy, yes? And for 10×11, well that is just 11×10 so you add a 0 to get 110.

2) For two-digit numbers, separate the two digits, add them together and put that total between the others. Thus, with 63×11:

6 [6 + 3] 3 = 693

And if your middle number totals more than nine, just insert the second number, and then add the first to the number on the left. Thus, with 49×11:

4 [4 + 9] 9
becomes
4 [13] 9
becomes
[4 + 1] 3 9 = 539

3) For any three-digit number, it is a similar principle. Just keep the two end numbers, then to the right of the first one put the total of the first and second numbers. Then the total of the second and third numbers. Then put the third number down on the right side. For example, with 632×11:

6 [6 + 3] [3 + 2] 2
becomes
6 [9] [5] 2 = 6,952

Of course, if your totals are greater than nine, then you write down the number on the right and carry the other and add it to the left. For example, 897:

8 [8 + 9] [9 + 7] 7
becomes
8 [17] [16] 7
becomes
[8 + 1] [7 +1] 6 7 = 9,867

4) For any four-digit number, the principle holds. You just do the same as with a three-digit number, but instead of two numbers in the middle, you have three. And if you need to carry to the left you do so. For example, 6,279 × 11:

6 [6+2] [2+7] [7 + 9] 9
becomes
6 [8] [9] [16] 9
becomes
6 [8] [9 + 1] 6 9
becomes
6 9 0 6 9 = 69,069

Just run through them a few times and you will soon be very adept at it. It helps to run through them from right to left.

PERCENTAGES

Curiously, these stump a lot of folk. They shouldn't because they are just a simple fraction. To work out a percentage of something just divide it by 100 to get 1 per cent, then multiply to get the number of per cent you want. For example, 40 per cent of 584:

584 ÷ 100 = 1% = 5.84
so 40% = 5.84 × 40
which is 58.4 × 4
= 233.6

MULTIPLYING BY 5

This is a snip with little numbers, but with two-, three- or four-figure numbers people often get lost. But all you have to do is think of multiplying by five as being like multiplying by ten, which is easy, then halving.

So, all you do is divide by two, then, if you have a whole-number answer, add a zero to the end. If you end up with a fraction ignore it and add a five. For example, 879 × 5:

becomes 879 ÷ 2 = 439.5
this has a fraction, so ignore the 0.5 and add 5 to the end
thus 4,395

MULTIPLYING HARDER NUMBERS

You can often simplify these. For example, if you have two large numbers to multiply and one of them is even, then you can simplify, like this:

48 × 93
is the same as 24 × 186
is the same as 12 × 372
is the same as 2 × 2,232
all of which = 4,464

If you have to multiply a number by, say, seventeen, simplify it by multiplying it by seven, then add ten times the original number to it. And if you are multiplying by, say, forty-seven, simplify it to multiply by fifty, and then take three times the original number from the total.

MULTIPLYING BY ANY NUMBER THAT IS A MULTIPLE OF 2

Basically, if you have to multiply by four, eight, sixteen, thirty-two, etc., you just have to multiply the number by two and do it however many times it is a multiple, and add them up. For example, to multiply by four, just double a number then add the total to itself. Thus 4 × 87:

becomes
[2 × 87] + [2 × 87]
becomes 174 + 174 = 348

And so on.

SOME FAMOUS MATHEMATICIANS

You may not be a genius and you may not be a maths wizard, but if you know a few of these famous mathematicians and what they achieved, you can certainly hold your own.

Archimedes (287–212 BC) was truly a genius. He made major contributions to the understanding of geometry and proto-science. He is well known for inventing the Archimedean screw and for his discovery of Archimedes' Principle. For those interested, the principle is as follows:

Any object, wholly or partially immersed in a fluid, is buoyed up by a force equal to the weight of the fluid displaced by the object.

It is said that he rushed naked through the streets upon making this discovery, crying 'Eureka!', meaning, 'I have found it!' Tragically, he was murdered by an angry Roman soldier.

Pythagoras (*c.* 570–495 BC) was a Greek philosopher. He taught that mathematics was of fundamental importance in understanding the world and the universe. He is famous for his theorem:

In a right-angled triangle, the square on the hypotenuse is equal to the sum of the squares on the other two sides.

Fibonacci (*c.* 1170–1250) was an Italian merchant whose real name was Leonardo of Pisa. It was he who introduced the Hindu-Arabic numerals that we use to this day instead of Roman numerals. He wrote widely about geometry, equations and introduced the famous Fibonacci sequence, which we shall discuss later in this chapter.

Isaac Newton (1642–1727) was an English mathematician who became the Lucasian Professor of Mathematics at the University of Cambridge at the age of twenty-seven. He developed a gravitational theory, which he published in his famous three-volume *Philosophia Naturalis Mathematica Principia*

(*Mathematical Principles of Natural Philosophy*) in 1687. It is usually just referred to as *Principia*. He invented calculus and was involved in a long dispute with Gottfried Leibniz (1646–1716), another mathematical genius, who also had a claim to be the inventor of calculus.

Leonhard Euler (1707–1783) was a Swiss mathematician and physicist who introduced many of the famous mathematical symbols that we use to this day, including π, e, I and Σ.

Pierre de Fermat (1601–65) was a French lawyer and amateur mathematician famous for his work on the theory of numbers. He is famous in mathematics for 'Fermat's Little Theorem,' but perhaps even more so for what has come to be called 'Fermat's Last Theorem,' which we shall briefly consider later in this chapter.

Stephen Hawking (1942–) is a British mathematician who was, like Newton three centuries before him, the Lucasian Professor of Mathematics at Cambridge University. He wrote the bestselling *A Brief History of Time*, and has made many outstanding contributions, among them his work on black holes.

Andrew John Wiles (1953–) is a British mathematician who proved Fermat's Last Theorem in 1995.

FIBONACCI SEQUENCE

This is an utterly fascinating thing that is worth knowing about, because it demonstrates, perhaps more than any other formula or sequence, just how mathematics can explain things about the way the world works.

A Fibonacci sequence is a series of numbers in the following sequence:

0, 1, 1, 2, 3, 5, 8, 13, 21, 34, 55, 89, 144, 233 ...

The first two numbers are 0 and 1, and all the others are formed by the addition of the two preceding ones. We don't need to go a lot further with calculations than this in order to gain an insight into this remarkable sequence.

Fibonacci first devised this sequence when he was demonstrating the solution of a problem that he had posed in his famous book *Liber Abaci*. This was a problem relating to the population of rabbits that would be produced from a pair of rabbits, if all pairs reproduced at the rate of one new pair every month, but only becoming fertile from the second month. It was assumed that no rabbits died.

Interestingly, when you look at a sequence consisting of the ratios of one Fibonacci number to the previous one, you reach a limit which equates with the *golden ratio*, which is designated by the Greek letter ϕ (known as Phi):

1/1, 2/1, 3/2, 5/3, 8/5, 13/8, 21/13, 34/21 ...

This comes to approximately 1.618.

This ratio has been known since ancient days and was considered of especial aesthetic significance by the ancient Egyptians and the Greeks. Architects have used this ratio in producing great buildings like the great Pyramid of Giza, the Parthenon and Notre Dame Cathedral in Paris. Artists like Leonardo da Vinci used it to create the ideal proportions of beauty in paintings like that of the Mona Lisa.

A *golden rectangle* is considered to be the most pleasing shape for a rectangle. It is one where the ratio of the length to the width is the golden ratio: 1/1.618. If you remove a square from a golden rectangle you will produce a smaller rectangle with the same proportions as the first.

If you describe this graphically, you can start with a small square of *I* unit by *I* unit. Add another beside it, then beneath that add a larger square whose sides are equal in length to the length of the preceding rectangle that you had created. Keep adding squares of this increasing size and you will find that you are creating a Fibonacci sequence: 1, 1, 2, 3, 5, 8 ...

If you draw a quarter circle in each square, starting with the first, you will produce a Fibonacci spiral, as in Figure 17:

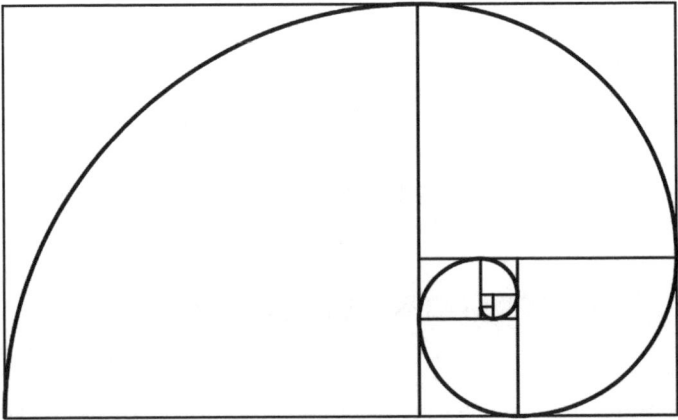

Fibonacci spiral

The golden ratio is also known as the *golden mean* and the *divine proportion*. But, fascinatingly, it seems to recur throughout nature. Let me give you a few examples.

Plants grow in a Fibonacci manner. They spiral, produce petals and seeds in sequences. They literally show Fibonacci numbers. For example, lilies and irises have three petals on their flowers, buttercups have five, delphiniums have eight, corn marigolds have thirteen, asters have twenty-one, while daisies may have thirty-four, fifty-five or eighty-nine. These are not haphazard numbers, they are all Fibonacci numbers. You can, of course, get other numbers, but this sequencing is remarkable. And, by contrast, how often have you found a four-leafed clover? Not often, I suspect. The reason is that four is not a Fibonacci number.

In botany the study of the order of leaves on stems is called phyllotaxis. This Fibonacci spiral pattern recurs again and again. Look at the spiral of rose petals. And also look at pine cones, pineapples and conical-shaped fruits like strawberries. You will see that they have two spirals of segments, one going right and one going left.

You can study this yourself and before long you will see Fibonacci spirals all about you. The animal kingdom also exhibits Fibonacci numbers. Look at a nautilus shell, a snail shell, a starfish.

Finally look at your own hands. If you measure and compare the lengths of the bones of your hand from the finger tips you will find that they proportionately increase in length in Fibonacci sequence. Not only that, but you have eight fingers, five digits on each hand, three phalanges (bones) on each finger, two bones in one thumb and one thumb on each hand: a Fibonacci sequence (with a little shenanigans for argument's sake!).

FERMAT'S LAST THEOREM

This is really a conundrum. As mentioned earlier, Pierre de Fermat was a lawyer and amateur mathematician who was fascinated by number theory. In the margin of a book that he was studying (a translation of Diophantos' *Arithmetica*) he made a note that he had found a marvellous proof to the problem of solving all solutions to the equations of Pythagoras' Theorem. He then inconveniently died before writing down his theorem. His son, however, went ahead and had the book published, including Fermat senior's note in the margin. From that moment onwards, the greatest mathematical brains in the world had tried in vain to prove Fermat's Last Theorem.

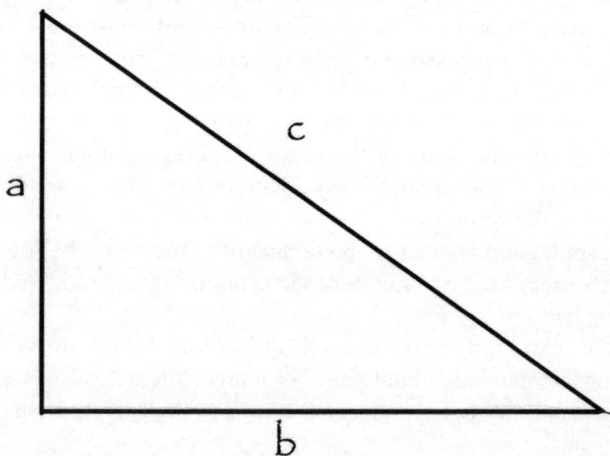

So what was this puzzle that was to be solved? In a nutshell, Fermat's Last Theorem states that:

No three positive integers a, b and c can satisfy the equation $a^n + b^n = c^n$ for any integer value of n greater than 2

Does that sound complex? To get a whiff of it let's go back to Pythagoras' Theorem, which we looked at earlier. It will help to look at the right-angled triangle on p. 108:

And, as you know, $a^2 + b^2 = c^2$. So, in this case, where n = 2, you can work it out. But as Fermat would conjecture, if n is greater than 2 it is not possible. Thus, if n = 3, for example:

$$a^3 + b^3 = c^3$$

It will not work. As your old maths teacher would say, prove this!

The proof is no easy matter. As I indicated, it took over 300 years for it to be proved. And that involved trips into a multiplicity of mathematical disciplines.

I leave you to puzzle this over. All that you need to know is what it was all about, and two other things. Firstly, it is of no use whatsoever. And secondly, no one knows whether Fermat actually had worked it out all those years ago.

A FEW CURIOUS NUMBERS

It is worth having an awareness of these curious numbers. Mathematicians delight in them.

π Good old pi. For any circle, the length of the circumference divided by the diameter is the same, a figure called π. It is approximately $^{22}/_7$ or $3\ ^1/_7$, but more accurately 3.142 to three decimal places, or 3.14159 to five decimal places, or 3.14159265 35897932384626433832795028841971 ... until you get bored!

i This is difficult to understand. In a complex number, which is a number in the form of bi, b is a non-zero *real* number and I (defined as $i2 = -1$) is the imaginary unit. Thus an imaginary number could be $3i$, where $I = \sqrt{-1}$. These numbers seem impossible, but they have great use in electrical engineering, for example. And now you know.

φ Known as Phi, the golden ratio; we have already talked about this, and you know that it is 1.61803 ...

0 or *nothing*. Believe it or not, this has been one of the hardest numbers to conceptualise. Huge tomes have been written about it, but that is up to you if you want to tie your cerebral neurones in knots about nothing very much.

∞ or *infinity*. This is the concept of a quantity that has no end. Fathom that out, genius.

Graham's number. This is not easy to comprehend either. Graham's number is named after Ronald Graham, an American mathematician. It is a number that is unimaginably large and which would take up the entire space of the universe to write it down, and still not have enough room. It relates to a branch of mathematics called Ramsey Theory, which is all to do with the conditions under which order must appear.

It has to be a real number, since it is cited in the *Guinness Book of Records*.

And that is enough maths for now. My brain is hurting even if yours isn't.

10

HISTORY

History is bunk.

Henry Ford
Founder of the Ford Motor Company

History is written by the victors.

Sir Winston Churchill
Soldier, statesman, historian and writer
Winner of the Nobel Prize for Literature

The two quotations above express different views about history. Henry Ford did not have a great deal of time for it as a subject, as expressed in his gung-ho opinion. He meant that all that has happened doesn't really matter and that we make our own history. He was a determined man with a mission to get his own way. This he did by giving the great American public an affordable motor car, the epitome of mass production. As for choice, he famously also said, 'People can have the Model-T in any colour – so long as it is black.'

As Britain's prime minister during the Second World War, Sir Winston Churchill was well aware that he was going to go down in history. Although he had won the war, he was also conscious that when the historians came to scrutinise his plans, his decisions and his overall leadership they might not be as kind as he felt they should be. Accordingly, he also said: 'History will be kind to me for I intend to write it.'

Ask yourself what you think of history. Is it a worthwhile study? Do we learn the lessons of history? What are the lessons of history?

I personally think that history is very important. We can see some of the mistakes that have been made and hopefully we will not make the same errors. Equally, it is to be hoped that we may adopt the behaviour that has been shown to have been successful in the past.

Yet it is never that simple. Churchill was quite right: the victors do write the history. And the writers may be biased.

HISTORIOGRAPHY

This is basically the study of how history is written. It is a fascinating subject and I want to dwell on it a little, because it can be important to you if you get into a discussion about anything in history.

First let me give you a couple of anecdotes and then I want to tell you about my credentials for writing about history. I received a substantial part of my early education in Scotland. I remember vividly being taught about the 1745 Rising, when Prince Charles Edward Stuart arrived in Scotland with the Seven Men of Moidart and set up his standard at Glenfinnin. It was an ill-fated adventure from the start that ended in the catastrophic Battle of Culloden Moor on 16 April 1746, after which Bonnie Prince Charlie was spirited away to Skye and thence to the Outer Hebrides by Flora MacDonald, disguised as an Irish serving girl. It was taught as a romantic adventure of the first order, extolling the bravery of the highlanders and the loyalty of the islanders.

Shortly after this our family moved to England where I was taught the history of 1745 all over again. Only this time I was told that instead of a Rising of the Clans it was a 'rebellion' against the King. And far from being a romantic figure, Bonnie Prince Charlie was described as an incompetent leader and a coward who ran away from the battlefield.

Effectively, I was taught the history of the Jacobite cause from both sides. My two teachers had given me my first lesson in historiography. At first, as a Scot I saw only the bias of the English teacher, but with some study over the years I see that they were both biased and that the truth, or as much truth as you can discover in such matters, probably lay somewhere between the two.

Over the years I have been fascinated to discover that the history I had been taught was flawed and biased. For example, the Glencoe Massacre in 1692, which led to a bitter rivalry between the Scottish clans of Campbell and MacDonald, was in fact a government ordered 'lesson' that used the Campbell clan as a scapegoat.

The English Civil War (which was in fact not one war, but three) was depicted as being between the fun-loving Royalist cavaliers and the puritanical, fun-despising Parliamentarian roundheads. It makes a fabulous historiographical study, for the history has been told and retold in different forms with differing biases over the years. The same can be said of the American Civil War, the Indian Mutiny, the French Revolution and so on.

Historians should not be biased. They should look at the evidence and be as objective as possible. Yet it never happens. No one is ever truly objective, since bias will creep into any assessment. The quality of evidence that is looked at is also important, since the ideal is to look at primary sources. That is, first-hand accounts. Yet this is obviously difficult since the further back one goes, the fewer people were able to write, so the documents are only from those who could get things down on paper, parchment, vellum or papyrus. Very often sources are secondary sources. That is, they are accounts based on those of others. And when you get to tertiary accounts, well they are like the accounts of a match that you might get from a friend of a friend who saw something and told it to a man in a pub.

> Historians probably unwittingly use the affect heuristic when they write history. We, the consumers, also use the affect heuristic as we digest the history that is fed to us (see Chapter 2).

So, after all that, what are my credentials for writing about history? Not great, I have to admit. I enjoy history and I write about history. That is, I write historical novels, so in a sense I am guilty of historiographic bias. Although I try to get historical facts right in my novels, I am a bender of the truth at times. That is inevitable when you write fiction. But that is my point: much of history is biased and some of it is undoubtedly fiction. Take the case of William Shakespeare and Richard III, for example.

Well, that is too good an example to gloss over. Let's consider it for a while, since it is a discussion that you may get involved in at some stage.

THE WICKED UNCLE
AND THE PRINCES IN THE TOWER

I am sure you remember from your history lessons that King Richard III was the most evil English monarch who ever ruled. While he was the Duke of Gloucester he colluded with his brother King Edward IV to have King Henry VI murdered (that's right, for a while England actually had two crowned kings at the same time),

The Princes in the Tower

and arranged for their brother the Duke of Clarence to be drowned in a butt of malmsey wine. Then, after Edward IV died, Richard usurped the throne from his son, Edward V, and had Edward and his brother Richard, Duke of York, imprisoned in the Tower of London. In July 1483 the two princes mysteriously disappeared and were presumed to have been smothered in their bedchamber by three assassins working on the orders of Richard III.

That is the history that most people know. And in fact it is mainly from the quill pen of William Shakespeare that we know this. In turn, Shakespeare wrote his play *The Tragedy of Richard III* in the 1590s using the book *The History of King Richard the Third* by Thomas More. More was executed by Henry VIII in 1535 and his book was not published until 1557. Understandably, it was biased towards the House of Tudor, for Henry VIII's father, Henry VII, gained the throne from Richard III by right of conquest (not through having a better claim to the throne) at the Battle of Bosworth Field in 1485. William Shakespeare was writing during the reign of Henry VIII's daughter, Queen Elizabeth I, and inevitably the bias grew in the telling.

Now, it has to be admitted that we do not know whether or not Richard III was in any way responsible for the mysterious disappearance of the two Princes in the Tower. Yet he may have been. The skeletons of two young boys were found by workmen in the Tower in 1647 and the bones were moved to Westminster Abbey and interred there. Queen Elizabeth II has not given permission to have their tombs opened in order for DNA analysis to be made.

This remains one of the great English history mysteries and it may never be resolved. The point is that we have had a very coloured picture from the way the tale has been told. William Shakespeare, true genius that he was, may have done the finest hatchet job in historiography.

SOME HOT HISTORICAL TOPICS

The following are subjects that often come up for discussion. They do not have any absolute answers and you can have fun with them.

We are all descended from a female in Africa: some would say that, with DNA analysis, it is proven. No, it isn't. It is merely a possibility.

All civilisations eventually crumble: look at the ancient Egyptians, the Greeks, the Romans, the Hapsburgs – they all crumbled into the dust. Well they declined, but they were really absorbed into others. And most of them lasted a long time. The Egyptian civilisation lasted about 4,000 years, the Hapsburgs almost a millennium.

All civilisations crumble

Dynasties, however, are another matter. While some Egyptian and Persian dynasties lasted for many generations, others petered out very quickly. The Qin dynasty, named after the first emperor of China (the name of which was derived from Qin), was predicted to last for 10,000 years. It lasted a mere fifteen years before it was deposed.

You can argue that inbreeding always leads to weakening of a strain, whether you are talking about garden peas, armadillos or royal families. Sexual diversity is the best hope for a strong dynasty.

Wars never settle anything: look at all the lives that are lost. Then, after a few years, people forget and play football with each other.

Wars do settle things, albeit only temporarily. It takes a long time to overcome resentment and the enmity that war brings. Peaceful settlement is always more desirable, but when one is faced with atrocities, genocide and possible world domination by a morally corrupt regime under the rule of a vicious warlord, then surely war is inevitable.

Edmund Burke (1729–97), an Irish political philosopher, said that 'All that is necessary for the triumph of evil is that good men do nothing. Do not allow evil to triumph. Do not sit and do nothing.'

We never learn the lessons of history: after all, we go to war, we allow idiots to govern us, we see ourselves as having a more enlightened view than other countries, systems, etc.

Do we? What lessons does history try to teach? Is history a sentient thing, a teacher? Are the situations the same?

You can always argue from the other side.

KNOW A FEW HISTORIANS

As I mentioned in Chapter 5 on the Lost Art of Sophistry, it is very effective to use *argumentum ad verecundiam*, or the argument to authority. This can be particularly effective in a historical argument. People are generally in awe of authorities and knowing them may sway the discussion your way.

It is perhaps surprising, but in most casual discussions people tend to be more impressed when the authorities used are old.

Modern authorities are still speculative, no matter how erudite they seem on programmes on television. On the other hand, if you quote the old masters then you will sound educated, the sort of person who is at home thumbing through dusty old tomes or who likes nothing better than fiddling with ancient manuscripts.

Herodotus (484–425 BC): a Greek historian, born in Halicarnassus. He is regarded as the 'father of history.' He wrote about the origins of the Graeco-Persian Wars, but also recounts his travels throughout the then-known world.

Thucydides (460–400 BC): the definitive historian of the Peloponnesian War, the great conflict between Athens and Sparta.

Pliny the Elder (AD 23–79): influential Roman writer and governor. He died of suffocation in AD 79 while making observations of the eruption of Mount Vesuvius, which destroyed Pompeii.

The Venerable Bede (672–735): a monk at St Paul's Monastery in Jarrow, Sunderland. In 731 he completed his great work, the *Historia Ecclesiastica Gentis Anglorum* (*Ecclesiastical History of the English People*).

William of Malmesbury (*c.* 1080–1143): a monk at Malmesbury Abbey in Wiltshire. An admirer of the Venerable Bede, in 1120 he wrote *Gesta Regum Anglorum* (*Deeds of the Kings of the English People*), covering the period from AD 449–1120.

Geoffrey of Monmouth (1100–55): a monk at an abbey somewhere in Wales. His chronicle *Historia Regum Britanniae* (*History of the Kings of Britain*) gives an account of the early kings of Britain, including King Arthur, his Round Table and the magician Merlin.

Edward Gibbon (1737–94): an English historian who wrote a six-volume work, *The History of the Decline and Fall of the Roman Empire*.

A.J.P. Taylor (1906–90): one of the foremost historians of the twentieth century, and an authority on the causes and events of the First and Second World Wars.

A FEW PAPYRI

This will always make you sound knowledgeable.

The *Westcar Papyrus* from 1500 BC, now in the Berlin Museum, tells tales of magic and conjuring, performed at the court of King Khufu, the builder of the Great Pyramid.

The *Ebers Papyrus* in the University of Leipzig Library; written about 1550 BC, it tells of Egyptian medical practices.

The *Edwin Smith Papyrus*, now in the New York Academy of Medicine, was written at about the same time, and outlines surgical techniques in those far-off days.

The *Amherst Papyrus*, now held in the Musée d'arts in Brussels, is an interesting papyrus devoted to the investigation of crimes.

The *Judicial Papyrus of Turin* from the twelfth century BC tells of the Harem conspiracy against Rameses III.

A FEW SIGNIFICANT ASSASSINATIONS

This may seem a gruesome topic, but some of these events have literally changed the world.

44 BC, Julius Caesar: stabbed to death by several senators of Rome, led by Brutus and Cassius. Shakespeare has the dying Caesar say, '*Et tu, Brute?*' This means, 'Even you, Brutus?' It is the ultimate betrayal.

AD 1170, Thomas Becket: the Archbishop of Canterbury was murdered by four knights in Canterbury Cathedral. Becket had been in dispute with King Henry II about Church rights and the knights, acting on their own, assassinated him in the belief that it was the king's wish. They were not arrested or punished by the king, although they were excommunicated by the Pope.

1793, Jean Marat: a Swiss-born scientist, physician and journalist and a leading member of the French Revolution. He helped establish the Reign of Terror and compiled death lists of aristocrats. He was stabbed in his bath (he had a skin disease and found ease by bathing for hours) by Charlotte Cordet, a young royalist who had been granted an interview with him. *The Death of Marat*, a famous painting by Jaques-Louis David, depicts the scene.

1865, Abraham Lincoln: the sixteenth President of the United States of America who led the Union through the Civil War, opposed slavery and delivered the famous Gettysburg Address, was shot by John Wilkes Booth, an actor, while watching a play. Booth leapt onto the stage from the box where Lincoln had been sitting, breaking a bone in his leg. Subsequently, Dr Samuel Mudd, a physician, splinted Booth's leg, and was charged with being a conspirator. He was found guilty and sentenced to life imprisonment, but was later pardoned. He eventually became a politician. The expression 'your name is mud' is thought to refer to Mudd.

1914, Archduke Franz Ferdinand: the Crown Prince of the Austrian Empire was assassinated in Sarajevo. This is the famous 'shot that was heard round the world,' which precipitated the First World War.

1916, Grigori Rasputin: the so-called 'mad monk', a faith healer who gained great influence over the Romanov family when he managed to stop Alexei, the son of Tsar Nicolas II and his wife Alexandra, from haemorrhaging from haemophilia. A group of aristocrats led by Prince Felix attempted to murder him by poison, then by shooting, stabbing and bludgeoning and then finally by drowning in the Neva River. The tsar was furious and banished the prince. Yet Rasputin's hold over the Romanovs had strengthened the hatred of the Bolshevics and the Russian Revolution began soon afterwards. It would have fatal consequences for the Romanovs.

1940, Leon Trotsky: the Bolshevik revolutionary, former minister under Lenin and organiser of the Red Army was assassinated with an ice-pick by Stalin's agents in Mexico. He did not die instantly, but was hospitalised and operated upon, only to die a day later from his wound and brain damage.

1948, Mohandras Gandhi: known as Mahatma ('great soul') Gandhi, he was assassinated by a fanatical Hindu gunman in a crowd because he had preached peace to Muslims. Gandhi had taught peaceful, non-violent disobedience, the result being that India had gained her independence from Britain in 1947.

1963, John Fitzgerald Kennedy: known as JFK, the thirty-fifth President of the United States of America was assassinated by a sniper, Lee Harvey Oswald, in Dallas, Texas. Kennedy had dealt with the Cuban Missile Crisis in 1962. Numerous conspiracy theories have surrounded the assassination, although the official verdict is that Oswald (who was himself assassinated by another gunman, Jack Ruby) was acting alone.

1968, Martin Luther King, Jr: a clergyman, civil-rights leader and Nobel Peace Prize-winner, he was assassinated on a hotel balcony in Memphis, Tennessee, by James Earl Ray. Martin Luther King was one of the world's greatest orators.

1979, Lord Mountbatten of Burma: a British Admiral of the Fleet, a statesman and the last Viceroy of India before Indian Independence, he was assassinated by a bomb planted on his sailing boat in the Republic of Ireland by the Provisional Irish Republican Army.

1984, Indira Gandhi: the granddaughter of Motilal Nehru was assassinated by her Sikh bodyguards in revenge for the storming of the Golden Temple at Amritsar, which she had ordered the army to carry out after Sikh extremists had barricaded themselves inside.

2007, Benazir Bhutto: the former prime minister of Pakistan was assassinated in Rawalpindi in a gun attack and a suicide bomb explosion, when she was campaigning for a return to power.

THE SIX WIVES OF HENRY VIII

This is one of those topics that comes up again and again. King Henry was a fascinating monarch, who established the navy which gave Britain the ability to become a major world force. His marital history, as he sought to sire a son and heir, led to a bitter dispute with the Pope, resulting in Henry's excommunication. As a result he ordered the Dissolution of the Monasteries in 1536, which allowed him to plunder their wealth for his own benefit. A gangster with homicidal tendencies he certainly was, yet history being history, the England that we now have is in no small measure down to Henry.

Henry married six wives, the order of their fates being remembered by the following little heuristic: divorced, beheaded, died. Divorced, beheaded, survived.

The wives were: Catherine of Aragon, Anne Boleyn, Jane Seymour, Anne of Cleves, Catherine Howard and Catherine Parr.

11

LITERATURE

To learn to read is to light a fire; every syllable that is spelled out is a spark.

Victor Hugo
Poet, dramatist and novelist

How dark the world would be without books and stories.

The very fact that you have just read that sentence probably means one of two things. Either you are an avid reader and you just devour words. If that is the case, then I respect you. In picking up this book you have demonstrated that you obviously have good taste in your choice of authors.

Alternatively, you know next to nothing about literature and drama and you hope that I am going to give you enough dope so that you can bluff your way. And if that is the case, I also respect you. You are a person after my own heart.

So let's get on. In order to hold your own in most conversations about literature and drama, you just need to know a bit about some of the classic books and plays that have shaped the world. So here is an ultra-condensed read of some of the most influential books, both fiction and non-fiction, ever written.

Treasure Island

THE GREAT RELIGIOUS BOOKS

These are the main religious texts of the world. There are others, but these are the works of the most prominent religions.

The *Bible*: it has two main sections, the Old Testament and the New Testament. The Old Testament is the original Hebrew Bible, the sacred scriptures of the Jewish faith, written over 1,000 years BC. The New Testament books were written by Christians in the first century AD. The King James Bible was published in 1611.

The *Qur'an*: the central religious text of Islam. Islam teaches that the message of the Qur'an was revealed from Allah to the Prophet Muhammad through the angel Gabriel over a period of approximately 23 years, 610–32 AD.

The *Vedas*: the ancient religious texts for Hindus. Hindus believe that the word of God was given directly to scholars and then transmitted verbally to succeeding generations. They were written around 3500 BC.

Tao Te Ching or *Lao-tzu*: this is the main book of Taoism, which was compiled around the third century BC. It is also known as 'The Way and Its Power,' and is said to have been written by Lao-tzu.

The *Torah*: this is the first part of the Jewish bible. It is believed to have been dictated by God to Moses on Mount Sinai during the exodus from Egypt. The *Talmud* is the written version of the Jewish oral laws, originating in the second century AD.

PARDIGM-SHIFTING BOOKS

These are books that have brought about a major change in the way that people think or in the way that we understand life, the universe and our place in the scheme of things.

De Humani Corporis Fabrica (*The Fabric of the Human Body*) by Andreas Vesalius was published in 1543. This was the first major book about anatomy. It set medical science on its way and dispelled many of the myths about the body.

The Revolution of the Heavenly Orbs by Nicolaus Copernicus was also published in 1543 and established that the sun was at the centre of the heavens, rather than the earth. This heralded the Scientific Revolution.

Philosophia Naturalis Mathematica Principia (*Mathematical Principles of Natural Philosophy*) by Sir Isaac Newton was published in 1687. A three-volume work, it is usually just referred to as *Principia*. It is one of the greatest pieces of scientific work ever produced and includes Newton's laws of motion, which formed the basis for mechanics and, most importantly, his law of universal gravitation.

On the Origin of Species by Charles Darwin was first published in 1859, under the title *On the Origin of Species by Means of Natural Selection, or the Preservation of Favoured Races in the Struggle for Life*. The title was reduced to the simpler, more familiar one with the sixth edition in 1872. This presents Darwin's ground-breaking theory of evolution.

The Interpretation of Dreams by Sigmund Freud was published in 1899. In it, Freud sets out the theories that were to form the basis for psychoanalysis.

CLASSIC FICTION

These are a few of the most influential books of fiction that have been produced over the centuries. You will find this to be an eclectic selection, probably missing out many people's favourites. But if you already know the ones I missed out then that is great, since I don't need to tell you about them.

The Canterbury Tales by Geoffrey Chaucer was the first book printed by William Caxton in 1483. It is a collection of tales recounted by pilgrims on their way to Canterbury to see the shrine of St Thomas Becket.

Don Quixote by Miguel de Cervantes was published in two parts in 1605 and 1615. It tells of Alonso Quixano of La Mancha and his faithful Sancho Panza as the chivalry-obsessed gentleman embarks on an eccentric, hair-brained quest.

Le Morte d'Arthur by Sir Thomas Malory was published by William Caxton in 1485. It is all about King Arthur and the Knights of the Round Table.

Robinson Crusoe by Daniel Defoe was published in 1719. It is a fictional autobiography of a castaway who spends 28 years marooned on an island near Venezuela.

Gulliver's Travels by Jonathan Swift was published in 1626. It is a fictionalised travel book detailing the adventures of Lemuel Gulliver in strange lands where he meets the miniature Lilliputians and the giants of Brobdignag and others. It is a clever political satire.

Fanny Hill by John Cleland was published in 1749. It is the most famous erotic novel in English.

Pride and Prejudice by Jane Austen. It tells of the Bennett family and the social prejudices and pride among the classes that could hinder and keep lovers apart.

Frankenstein by Mary Shelley was published in 1818. The original tale of the man-like creature built from body parts by a Swiss scientist and philosopher and re-animated. The character has transcended the original tale in numerous film adaptations.

The Hunchback of Notre Dame by Victor Hugo was published in 1831. Set in fifteenth-century Paris it is a complex tragic tale of love, deceit and murder. Quasimodo the hunchbacked bell-ringer falls in love with the beautiful gypsy Esmeralda.

Oliver Twist by Charles Dickens was published in 1838. The classic tale of an orphan, his early life in the workhouse, his escape to meet the Artful Dodger and through him Fagin's criminal gang of thieves and pickpockets. Tragedy ensues when Nancy, a warm-hearted prostitute, is murdered by bully-boy Bill Sykes.

The Three Musketeers by Alexandre Dumas was published in 1844. Set during the reign of King Louis XIV, the young D'Artagnan from Gascony arrives in Paris determined to become a musketeer. He inadvertedly offends three musketeers and is challenged to duels by all of them. It is the ultimate swashbuckler.

Wuthering Heights by Emily Brontë was published in 1847. It is a brooding tale of passion and obsessive love between Catherine and Heathcliff, set in the remote wastelands of Yorkshire.

Wuthering Heights

Great Expectations by Charles Dickens was published in 1861. It tells of the young boy Pip's meeting in a graveyard with an escaped convict, Abel Magwitch; his subsequent meetings with a bitter, jilted recluse, Miss Havisham, and of his love for the beautiful Estella. Pip mysteriously receives an inheritance and determines to become a gentleman. But who is his benefactor? (Magwitch!)

Alice's Adventures in Wonderland by Lewis Carroll was published in 1865. It is a strange tale about Alice, a small girl who falls down a rabbit hole and finds herself in a fantasy world with living playing cards and anthropomorphic characters. Carroll followed it up in 1871 with *Through the Looking Glass*.

Crime and Punishment by Fyodor Dostoevsky was published in 1866. It is a great book about guilt, detailing why Raskolnikov commits a double murder.

Journey to the Centre of the Earth by Jules Verne was published in 1866. It is one of the first science fiction stories. It is in fact a descent into hell.

War and Peace by Leo Tolstoy was published in 1869. It is the epic story set during Napoleon's invasion of Russia as told through the effect it has on several aristocratic Russian families.

Treasure Island by Robert Louis Stevenson was published in 1883. It is the classic pirate adventure, complete with curses, buried treasure, the duplicitous one-legged sea-cook Long John Silver and the heroic cabin boy Jim Hawkins.

The Adventures of Huckleberry Finn by Mark Twain was published in 1885. It is the great American tale of a life along the Mississippi as young Huck flees from his drunken, violent father with escaped slave Jim.

The Strange Case of Dr Jekyll and Mr Hyde by Robert Louis Stevenson was published in 1886. It is the great gothic story of Dr Henry Jekyll's experiments, which result in him unleashing his own darker side, his other personality of Mr Hyde. It has spawned a whole genre of its own.

A Study in Scarlet by Sir Arthur Conan Doyle was published in *Beeton's Christmas Annual* in 1887. Doyle wrote this novel in just three weeks and in doing so introduces the consulting detective Sherlock Holmes and his companion Dr John Watson to the world.

The Picture of Dorian Gray by Oscar Wilde was published in 1891. It tells of how socialite Dorian Gray leads a life of dissolution and cruelty, yet remains ever youthful – while the portrait of himself that he keeps secret ages and shows the moral decay that reflects what he has become.

Dracula by Bram Stoker was published in 1897. It is the immortal tale of the vampire, Count Dracula from Transylvania, and his adversary Dr Van Helsing.

The Invisible Man by H.G. Wells was published in 1897. This is the wonderful tragic tale of Griffin, a chemist who discovers a formula that makes him invisible.

The Ragged-Trousered Philanthropists by Robert Tressell was published in 1914. It is an Edwardian working-class novel critical of capitalism.

Tarzan of the Apes by Edgar Rice Burroughs was published in 1914. Although it is not brilliantly written, it introduced the character of Tarzan, the boy who is taken in by a family of apes after his parents' plane crashes in the jungle. He becomes king of the jungle. Like Sherlock Holmes and Frankenstein, his character has transcended the original tale.

The Thirty-Nine Steps by John Buchan was published in 1916. It recounts the story of Richard Hannay, who is framed for the murder of a spy, and his adventures in the moors of Scotland as he seeks to stay one step ahead of his enemies and the police in order to get a secret diary to the authorities. It is a short novel, but it is the blueprint for all spy-chase stories.

Ulysses by James Joyce was published in 1922. It is a large novel set in Dublin and told in the space of a single day (16 June 1904, which was the day that Joyce first dated his future wife) about the adventures of two characters, Stephen Dedalus and Leopold Bloom.

The Great Gatsby by F. Scott Fitzgerald was published in 1925. It is a great American novel about the tragic rise and fall over a summer of self-made millionaire Jay Gatsby.

The Murder of Roger Ackroyd by Agatha Christie was published in 1926. It is regarded as Christie's tour de force, a detective novel with such a twist that it is almost good enough to fool its hero, the little Belgian detective Hercule Poirot.

Lady Chatterley's Lover by D.H. Lawrence was first published in 1928 in Florence, but not in England until 1960, due to the UK's strict obscenity laws. It is a classic erotic novel.

Brave New World by Aldous Huxley was published in 1932. Set far in the future, the 'world controllers' have created a brave new world, a state of dystopia.

The Grapes of Wrath by John Steinbeck was published in 1939. It is set in the Great Depression in the 1930s and follows the Joads, a farming family from Oklahoma, as they go west to California in the forlorn hope of a better life.

Animal Farm by George Orwell was published in 1945. It is a satirical novel or a modern fable about the animals who take over Manor Farm. They manage to run it for a while, until corruption and tyranny take over. It is in fact a critique of communist totalitarianism.

Age of Reason by Jean-Paul Sartre was published in 1945. It is the first of a trilogy of novels collectively known as the 'Roads to Freedom.' They set out his concepts of existentialism.

Brideshead Revisited by Evelyn Waugh was published in 1945. It follows the fortunes of various members of the aristocratic Flyte family, especially the charismatic, gay, hard-drinking Sebastian as he sinks into alcoholism and dissipation. It is narrated by his friend Charles Ryder, who meets Sebastian at Oxford University.

The Diary of a Young Girl by Anne Frank was published in 1947. This is not a novel, but is one of the most important books of the twentieth century, in my opinion. It is the diary of Anne Frank, a Dutch Jewish teenager, written over two years while she was in hiding in a secret flat above and behind the family business beside one of Amsterdam's canals. Beautifully written, it is a testament to life under persecution, and her death in the concentration camp of Bergen-Belsen makes this book a poignant symbol of the Holocaust.

Nineteen Eighty-Four by George Orwell was published in 1949. It is a futuristic warning against totalitarianism. In it, Orwell describes a society ruled by the omniscient, all-seeing cameras of the leader, Big Brother. No one is permitted to rebel and all must conform. 'Thoughtcrime' or rebellious thoughts are illegal and he introduces the concept of Room 101, where one has to face one's deepest fears.

The Catcher in the Rye by J.D. Salinger was published in 1951. It is a *Bildungsroman* (see the box of expressions after this section) about Holden Caulfield, an American teenager. It is a great picture of teenage rebellion, angst and sexuality.

Foundation by Isaac Asimov was published in 1951. This is the first in what was to become a series of science fiction books about the far future, when humans have colonised the galaxy and are ruled under a vast empire. A brilliant mathematician and scientist called Hari Seldon has developed a mathematical tool called psycho-history, which can foretell future trends, if not the future itself. To prevent human decline he gathers a group of scientists and their families on a remote planet to form the Foundation, a group of encyclopaedists to preserve humankind's knowledge.

Casino Royale by Ian Fleming was published in 1953. It introduces the secret agent James Bond 007 and his licence to kill.

Lord of the Flies by William Golding was published in 1954. It is a gruesome tale of right and wrong, survival of the fittest when a group of schoolboys are marooned on a tropical island after their plane is shot down during the war.

Lord of the Rings by J.R.R. Tolkien was published between 1954 and 1956. It is a trilogy of books: *The Fellowship of the Ring*, *The Two Towers* and *The Return of the King*. It is set in Middle Earth and is about the fight between the forces of good and the power of evil. A power ring has been lost for many years and falls into the hands of a hobbit (recounted in an earlier book *The Hobbit*, published in 1937) and a fellowship is formed consisting of hobbits, elves, dwarves and men to destroy the ring rather than allow it to be reclaimed by an evil warlord. It is the fantasy novel that set the trend.

Catch-22 by Joseph Heller was published in 1961. It is a satire on war and bureaucracy. It is set on an American air base in the Mediterranean during World War II. It introduced the term 'catch-22' into common parlance.

One Hundred Years of Solitude by Gabriel García Márquez was published in 1967. It is by one of the greatest writers of the twentieth century (who won the Nobel Prize for Literature in 1982). It is set in a fictional Colombian town called Macondo and follows the fate of the founding Buendía family.

The Godfather by Mario Puzo was published in 1969. It is set in New York and follows the story of the Corleone family. It is the ultimate Mafia novel.

Trainspotting by Irvine Welsh was published in 1993. It is a gritty novel about drug culture in Leith.

Atonement by Ian McEwan was published in 2001. The novel starts in 1935. Thirteen-year-old Briony has literary aspirations and an active imagination. Later she wrongly declares that a man had sexually attacked her cousin, resulting in her sister's boyfriend being arrested and imprisoned, wrecking both his and her sister's future life together. Atonement has to be made.

The Curious Incident of the Dog in the Night-time by Mark Haddon was published in 2003. It gives a remarkable insight into the literal working of the mind of someone with Asperger's Syndrome.

Some literary expressions you should know about:

Spoonerism: this is the unconscious (or deliberate) transposition of the first two or three letters of a word in a sentence with those of a subsequent word. The result is to change the meaning of the sentence, often hilariously. For example:
'a well-boiled icicle,' instead of 'a well-oiled bicycle'
'go and shake a tower,' instead of 'go and take a shower'
The term is named after the Reverend William Archibald Spooner, Warden of New College, Oxford, who seemed prone to such utterances.
Another term for a Spoonerism is a *Marrowsky*, after a Polish count who had the same speech impediment.

Malapropism: this is the inappropriate use of one word when a similar-sounding, more apposite word is meant. The term is named after Mrs Malaprop, a character in the comedy play *The Rivals* written by Richard Brinsley Sheridan in 1775:
MRS MALAPROP: I would have her instructed in geometry, that she might know something of the contagious countries (i.e., should have been geography and contiguous).
Another term for a malapropism is a *Dogberryism*, after Constable Dogberry, a character in *Much Ado About Nothing* by William Shakespeare:
CONSTABLE DOGBERRY: Our watch, sir, have indeed comprehended two auspicious persons (i.e., should have been apprehended and suspicious).

Bowdlerism: this is the name given to the process of removing improper or offensive language. It is named after

Dr Thomas Bowdler, who published an expurgated edition of Shakespeare in 1818, removing all terms that could be misconstrued.

For example, in *Henry V* the character Pistol, instead of having 'a brace of balls' has 'two bullets in his gun.' Also, instead of 'cocking his weapon,' he is said to 'prime his piece.'

Bildungsroman: the name for a novel that follows one individual and their personal and social development. Several of the novels cited in this chapter belong to this genre: *Great Expectations*, *The Catcher in the Rye*, *Oliver Twist*.

12

DRAMA

All the world's a stage, and all the men and women merely players: they have their exits and their entrances; and one man in his time plays many parts, his acts being seven ages.

William Shakespeare

Drama is fiction in performance. It is an art form that goes back to the days of the ancient Greeks. Indeed the word comes from the Greek and means 'action.'

'Action'

In Athens in the fifth century BC there were three types of play that were regularly performed. These were tragedy, comedy and the satyr plays. The satyr plays were a sort of mix of tragedy and comedy, which were played in a kind of pantomimic manner, with depictions of drunkenness, sexuality and slap-stick humour. Gradually they became developed into regular competitions, with playwrights producing new works and citizens paying for a 'chorus' – effectively paying the cast of the play. These competitions tended to be held as festivals to celebrate the god Dionysus, the patron deity of wine, carnivals and festivities.

The universal symbols of the theatre today are the comedy and drama masks which were worn by ancient Greek actors to depict different emotions. They were made from clay, with a facial expression painted on them and with wigs to cover the head of the actor and a large mouth through which he or she could speak. The two masks, one smiling to represent comedy and the other sorrowful to depict tragedy, also represent the two faces of Dionysus, for he could change his nature as quickly as winking. In addition, they show the two faces of wine, one side being merry and the other melancholic in hangover.

ANCIENT GREEK PLAYWRIGHTS

Aeschylus, Sophocles and Euripides were tragedians. Their plays are rarely performed these days, but it is worth knowing that Sophocles wrote several plays about Oedipus, who killed his father and married his mother, without knowing that they were his parents. As a result his family was doomed by the gods for three generations. Sigmund Freud draws on this legend in building up his concept of the Oedipal Complex.

Aristophanes and Menander wrote comedies. Aristophanes is well worth a read. His play *The Wasps* is set in Athens in the fifth century BC and is a hilarious romp about the generation gap and the silliness of the law.

ROMAN PLAYWRIGHTS

The Romans were great conquerors and absorbers of the customs and traditions of other cultures. They adopted the Greek theatre and Roman playwrights often based their works on that of the earlier Greek writers.

Titus Maccius Plautus, known as Plautus, and Publius Terentius Afer, known as Terence, were two of the finest Roman comedy playwrights.

Plautus wrote several farces, upon which Stephen Sondheim, Burt Shevelove and Larry Gelbart based a highly successful musical. *A Funny Thing Happened on the Way to the Forum* is a bawdy story of a slave named Pseudolus and his attempts to win his freedom by helping his young master seduce the girl next door. The BBC also used his plays as the basis for a long-running comedy series called *Up Pompeii*, starring the late comedian Frankie Howerd as the slave Lurcio.

Terence (Publius Terentius Afer) had actually come from Africa as a slave, hence his name, Afer, it being common to name slaves after their place of origin. All six of his comedies survive. He was accused of plagiarising the Greek dramatist Menander, to which he replied that 'nothing has ever been said that has not been said before.'

ELIZABETHAN AND JACOBEAN PLAYWRIGHTS

This was the time of a great flowering of theatrical talent. Plays were much in demand as one of the main forms of entertainment by the masses.

The main playwrights of this time were William Shakespeare, Christopher (Kit) Marlowe, Thomas Middleton and Ben Jonson.

Kit Marlowe (1564–93) is a fascinating character himself. Some historians aver that he was a spy, a duelist, a tobacco user and a drunkard. Some even say that he probably wrote several of the plays attributed to Shakespeare. We do know that he was stabbed to death (possibly through the eye) in a tavern brawl after a dispute over the reckoning of the bill by Ingram Frizer, also reputed to be a spy.

His plays are interesting in that he pits his characters against the gods. You can see this in plays like *Tamburlaine the Great*, which he based on the great conqueror Timur. In this play he follows the fortunes of Tamburlaine as he rises from shepherd to emperor, and then has nothing left to conquer except death. In *The Tragical History of Doctor Faustus*, usually just referred to as *Doctor Faustus*, he has his main character sell his soul to the devil in order to be able to satiate his desire for knowledge.

Ben Johnson (1572–1637) was another fascinating character who found himself in trouble with the authorities on several occasions. In 1597 a play co-written with Thomas Nashe entitled *The Isle of Dogs* was suppressed because it was said to cause great offence. Both writers were arrested and sent to Marshalsea Prison, charged with 'Leude and mutynous behavior'. In 1598 he killed a fellow actor, Gabriel Spencer, in a duel and was sent to Newgate Prison. He was tried for manslaughter, to which he pleaded guilty. Thanks to a loophole called 'benefit of clergy,' by which one gained leniency by reciting a brief verse of the Bible in Latin, he was released upon forfeit of his 'goods and chattels.' He was also branded on his left thumb as a convicted criminal. His plays were predominantly comedies with a London setting.

THE GENIUS THAT WAS WILLIAM SHAKESPEARE (1564–1616)

Apart from the fact that William Shakespeare was the greatest literary figure who ever wrote in the English language, we know remarkably little about him.

The known facts are:

He was born in Stratford-upon-Avon in 1564, the son of John Shakespeare, a glover and a mayor of the town
He married Anne Hathaway when he was 18 years old and she was 23

Anne Hathaway was three months pregnant at the time of the marriage

Shakespeare's own family were all illiterate

It is thought that he left Stratford to avoid prosecution for poaching deer

By 1592 he was working in London as an actor and playwright

Between 1592 and 1613 he wrote at least thirty-seven plays and probably collaborated on several others

He wrote 154 sonnets, including several to and about the 'Dark Lady' (see the chapter on poetry)

We only have fourteen words written in Shakespeare's own hand: six signatures and 'by me' on his will

In his will, the only thing he specifies that should go to his wife is his 'second-best bed'

The unknown facts:

We do not know his exact birthdate; it is thought that he was born on St George's Day, 23 April, and that he died on his fifty-third birthday

We do not know his whereabouts for the years 1585–92; these are called the lost years

We do not know for sure what he looked like; there are several contending images of Shakespeare, including portraits, busts and an engraved image in the first folio of his works, published in 1623; it is currently thought that the Chandos portrait is a true likeness

We do not know the cause of his death; a death mask found in a ragpicker's shop in 1842 may be authentic; there is a theory that it could indicate that Shakespeare had a tumour of the eye socket

We are not exactly sure of the order in which he wrote the plays, since they have tended to be placed in three groups – the Comedies, the Histories and the Tragedies

We do not know whether or not a missing play – *Cardenio* – was written by Shakespeare; at the time of writing these notes, it is believed that the play has been found!

QUOTING SHAKESPEARE NEVER DOES ANY HARM

William Shakespeare seems to have had something to say about everything. He understood human emotions, he invented many words and gave us many expressions that we take for granted. Indeed, people often use Shakespearean expressions without knowing it.

A Midsummer Night's Dream

Shakespeare gave us these expressions:

bated breath
brevity is the soul of wit
foregone conclusion
foul play
hoist with his own petard
laughing stock
one fell swoop
own flesh and blood
wild goose chase
to thine own self be true
too much of a good thing

The following quotations can often be slipped into a conversation and are worth committing to your memory bank. They are all short and easily remembered.

There are more things in heaven and earth, Horatio,
Than are dreamt of in your philosophy
Hamlet, Act I, Scene 5

Fair is foul, and foul is fair.
Macbeth, Act I , Scene 1

This above all; to thine own self be true,
Hamlet , Act I, Scene 3

Lord, what fools these mortals be!
A Midsummer-Night's Dream, Act III, Scene 2

Now is the winter of our discontent
Made glorious summer by this sun of York;
Richard III, Act I, Scene 1

Friends, Romans, countrymen, lend me your ears;
I come to bury Caesar, not to praise him.
Julius Caesar, Act III, Scene 2

If you prick us, do we not bleed?
If you tickle us, do we not laugh?
If you poison us, do we not die?
And if you wrong us, shall we not revenge?
The Merchant of Venice, Act III, Scene 1

Oh Romeo, Romeo, wherefore art thou Romeo?
Romeo and Juliet, Act II, Scene 1

Parting is such sweet sorrow
that I shall say good-night till it be morrow.
Romeo and Juliet, Act II, Scene 2

To be, or not to be, that is the question …
Hamlet, Act III, Scene 1

The tears live in an onion that should water this sorrow.
Antony and Cleopatra, Act I, Scene 2

He doth indeed show some sparks that are like wit.
Much Ado About Nothing, Act II, Scene 3

Thy head is as full of quarrels as an egg is full of meat.
Romeo and Juliet, Act III, Scene 1

If music be the food of love, play on;
Twelfth Night, Act I, Scene 1

I can express no kinder sign of love
than this kind kiss
Henry VI, Part 2, Act I, Scene 1

The first thing we do, let's kill all the lawyers.
Henry VI, Part 2, Act IV, Scene 2

He hath eaten me out of house and home,
Henry IV, Part 2, Act II, Scene 1

The soul of this man is his clothes.
All's Well That Ends Well, Act II, Scene 5

Thou villain base,
Knowst me not by my clothes?
Cymbeline, Act IV, Scene 2

How bravely thou becomest thy bed! Fresh lily!
And whiter than the sheets!
Cymbeline, Act II, Scene 2

13

POETRY

Poetry is a subject that is capable of evoking all manner of emotions in people. Poetry lovers are forever reading poetry, seeing beauty in clouds, daffodils and bird droppings, and happily make up rhymes in their heads while they go about their daily toil. They are hooked and cannot go a day without their fix. On the other hand, poetry detesters can happily go a lifetime without hearing a single couplet. They loathe the very mention of a poem. It is curious. There is neither rhyme nor reason to it.

I suspect that if you are a poetry detester then you were taught to dislike poetry. That is, you were probably mis-taught in English lessons; forced to memorise the unmemorable verse of some long-forgotten minor poet, or humiliated in front of your class by some old fossil of a teacher because you didn't know the difference

"Cut out the poetry, Watson," said Holmes, severely.

between your alliteration and your assonance. If you can relate to that, then I would urge you to read on, because poetry can be immense fun. If you don't relate to this then read on anyway, as there is no need to be snooty.

The truth is that you do not have to be a genius to appreciate poetry. Indeed, if you can master a few of the rudiments, perhaps even make up a limerick, ode or clerihew yourself, then your eyes will not glaze over when the subject of poetry comes up at a social gathering. Indeed, you will relish it as much as you relished the gherkin and frog leg hors d'oeuvres that you washed down with a couple of schooners of dry sherry.

WHAT IS POETRY?

That is a tough question and whole books have been written to answer it. Curiously, a lot of the authors of such tomes give hosts of examples, but never come up with an adequate definition. So I am just going to say that it is a literary art form using language in an aesthetically pleasing manner. It can rhyme if you want it to, but that is not essential. Indeed, some performance poets today completely eschew rhyme and just spout out, challenging the audience to prove that their words are not poetic. So there you go, you can conform or you can challenge, it is up to you. There are no rights or wrongs, there are just guidelines. The listener or the reader can judge for him- or herself whether he or she feels it is a pleasing piece.

Poetry can be classified according to style and content. Some poets restrict themselves to one type or another, while others experiment and write whatever suits them.

NARRATIVE POETRY

These poems are all about story. It is the poetry of the bards, who would recite tales of derring-do in great halls or around camp fires. It is therefore probably the oldest form of poetry. The ancient ballads, lays and idylls are story poems, as are the longer epics. Here are a few examples that you ought to know about.

The *Iliad* and the *Odyssey*, by Homer (flourished around 850 BC). These are two epic poems. The *Iliad* is about the Trojan War and features King Agamemnon and Achilles. He followed it up with the *Odyssey*, which is about Odysseus and his journey home after the fall of Troy.

Beowulf was composed by an unknown Anglo-Saxon bard some time between the eighth and the eleventh centuries.

The Canterbury Tales, by Geoffrey Chaucer (1343–1400). This is a collection of narrative poems written in Middle English. The book was the first one to be printed by William Caxton in 1483. Each tale is a story related by a group of pilgrims as they make their way from the Tabard Inn in London's Southwark to the shrine of St Thomas Becket at Canterbury Cathedral. They are definitely worth reading.

Paradise Lost and *Paradise Regained*, by John Milton (1608–74). Milton was an academic and a civil servant who served under Oliver Cromwell. *Paradise Lost* is an epic poem about the fall of man, and covers the temptation of Adam and Eve by Satan and their expulsion from the Garden of Eden. *Paradise Regained* is a sequel epic poem concerning the temptation of Christ.

The Idylls of the King, by Alfred, Lord Tennyson (1809–92). This is all about King Arthur and the Knights of the Round Table.

LYRIC POETRY

This is not about story, but tends to be more personal. It is usually about feelings and perceptions. It is the commonest type written today. It is normally rhymed.

The Romantic poets were a group of poets who wrote about feelings and perception, almost using intuition instead of reason. It is said that they were reacting against the Enlightenment. The progenitor was Robert Burns (1759–96), Scotland's national poet. He wrote in the Scottish dialect and is one of the few poets in the world to have his own commemorative night. 'Burns' Night' is celebrated by Scots folk all over the world.

As a Scot, I am an ardent Robert Burns fan, having gained third place in the school's annual Burns' recitation competition at the age of 8 with my rendition of 'Tam o'Shanter.' If you have never heard it, then get a copy of Burns' poems and rectify the matter straight away. Know also that he wrote such classics as 'Auld Lang Syne,' 'A Red, Red Rose,' 'A Man's a Man for a' That,' 'To a Louse,' 'To a Mouse' and 'The Selkirk Grace.' The latter is worth knowing, since you can recite it at the start of any dinner party meal.

> Some hae meat and canna eat,
> And some wad eat that want it,
> But we hae meat and we can eat,
> Sae the Lord be thankit.

And this is the translation!

> Some have food and cannot eat,
> And some would eat that have none [food],
> But we have food and we can eat,
> So the Lord be thanked.

There are six main Romantic poets. Here they are with an example of their most famous poems:

William Blake (1757–1827), 'The Marriage of Heaven and Hell'
William Wordsworth (1770–1850), 'I wandered lonely as a cloud,' often called 'Daffodils'
Samuel Taylor Coleridge (1772–1834), 'The Rime of the Ancient Mariner'
George Gordon, Lord Byron (1788–1824), 'Don Juan'
Percy Bysshe Shelley (1792–1822), 'Ozymandias'
John Keats (1795–1821), 'Great Odes'

I personally love the poem 'Ozymandias,' which is about finding the monumental statue of a pharaoh (probably Rameses the Great) in the desert sand. It is about how even the mighty fall. Read it and revel in that glorious opening line:

I met a traveller from an antique land,
Who said: Two vast and trunkless legs of stone
Stand in the desert. Near them on the sand,
Half sunk, a shatter'd visage lies, whose frown
And wrinkled lip and sneer of cold command
Tell that its sculptor well those passions read
Which yet survive, stamp'd on these lifeless things,
The hand that mock'd them and the heart that fed;
And on the pedestal these words appear:
'My name is Ozymandias, king of kings:
Look on my works, ye Mighty, and despair!'
Nothing beside remains. Round the decay
Of that colossal wreck, boundless and bare,
The lone and level sands stretch far away.

DRAMATIC POETRY

This is drama written in verse. William Shakespeare is the most famous exponent, who we considered in the chapter on drama. We shall touch on him again in a few moments when we look at 'form.'

Ancient dramatic poets include Aeschylus and Sophocles.

SATIRICAL POETRY

This is poetry used to satirise. It is often done from a political background. John Dryden (1631–1700), the first Poet Laureate, was a famous satirical poet.

THE WAR POETS

Technically, this means any poets writing at the time of, or about, a war. More specifically, people think of the poets who wrote during or about the Great War (1914–18).

There is a memorial plaque in Poets' Corner in Westminster Abbey dedicated to sixteen accomplished poets of the Great War. These are: Richard Aldington, Laurence Binyon, Edmund

Blunden, Rupert Brooke, Wilfrid Gibson, Robert Graves, Julian Grenfell, Ivor Gurney, David Jones, Robert Nichols, Wilfred Owen, Herbert Read, Isaac Rosenberg, Siegfried Sassoon, Charles Sorley and Edward Thomas. Several of them tragically died or were killed during the war, notably Rupert Brooke, Isaac Rosenberg and Wilfred Owen.

You should appreciate that many of the poems in the early years of the war reflected an idealism about the conflict. This is epitomised in Rupert Brooke's collection, *1914 & Other Poems*. You may recall the famous lines:

> If I should die, think only this of me;
> That there's some corner of a foreign field
> That is forever England.

As the war went on, with increasing casualties, war poetry became more sombre and disparaging about the nature of war and the failure of those in authority.

Laurence Binyon penned the immortal poem 'For the Fallen,' which you will have heard and been moved by every Remembrance Day.

MODERN POETRY

This is a huge area and if you are smitten with the subject you will already know the names of some of the great poets of the twentieth and twenty-first centuries.

It is worth knowing that there were two important movements. Firstly modernist poetry, which was essentially a new type of poetry where poets sought new ways of writing, such as with free verse rather than the traditional forms (which we shall look at soon), and they explored different themes and subjects. Roughly, modernist poetry was developing between 1910 and 1940, so the Great War had an impact on it. The three great exponents of this were T.S. Eliot (1888–1965), T.E. Hulme (1888–1917) and Ezra Pound (1885–1972). More recently there has been a second movement, post-modernist poetry. And that is as much as you need to know, but feel free to delve deeper yourself.

The following poets are worth searching out and enjoying. I have merely given the name of one famous poem by each. I am sure that they will inspire you to love poetry. My apologies for missing out many great poets, but space is limited and, anyway, you will have enough to be going on with here. If you do find yourself smitten by the poetry muse then you will soon ferret out a whole army of bards, old and new.

T.S. Eliot (1888–1965), 'The Waste Land'
W.H. Auden (1907–73), 'The Age of Anxiety'
Dylan Thomas (1914–53), 'Under Milk Wood'
Philip Larkin (1922–85), 'This Be The Verse'
Ted Hughes (1930–98), 'Birthday Letters'

THE POET LAUREATE

This is one of two great positions in poetry. Correctly, it should be the Poet Laureate of the United Kingdom of Great Britain & Northern Ireland. It was until recently a post held for life, but since the last Poet Laureate, Andrew Motion, it has been changed to become a ten-year appointment. The position is effectively court poet to the monarch and was first created during the reign of King Charles II.

The current Poet Laureate is Carol Ann Duffy, whose poems you may enjoy. The Poet Laureate receives a small honorarium each year, together with a 'butt of sack.' In case you did not know this, it is a great deal of sherry.

THE OXFORD PROFESSOR OF POETRY

This is the second of the prestigious poetry posts. It was first created in 1708 in the University of Oxford. It is held for five years and is by election. Voters have to be graduates of the university. It also carries a small honorarium, but immense prestige. The current professor is Geoffrey Hill.

THE DIFFERENT FORMS

Now we get down to the nitty-gritty. As I have indicated, there is a trend to use free verse nowadays. That means it does not have to have structure or rhyme. You could argue that any old collection of words could be a poem.

But I am not going to argue any such thing. Instead, I want to run through a number of the traditional forms of poems, and then we shall have a look at how you can start writing your own poems straight away. You never know, this may just make people think that you are a genius.

Here are a few meanings, in the order you need to know, if not in importance:

Verse: a single line of a poem is a verse. A group of lines are often referred to as verses.

Stanza: the correct term for a group of lines.

Metre: refers to a measure of the rhythmical structure of verse or song.

Feet (singular, *foot*): the traditional verse of English poetry is based on regular patterns of unstressed or unaccented syllables and stressed or accented. The nature of the English language makes an *iambic* metre the easiest to use. That is, an unstressed syllable followed by a stressed one. *Iambic pentameter* is the traditional pattern of verse and verse drama. Shakespeare wrote using this.

Rhyme: the repetition of two or more words in a poem. A rhyme is also the name for a short poem, as in a nursery rhyme or a rhyming couplet. Indeed, rhyming couplets are the simplest form of poetry and can be built on effectively to produce a poem of epic proportions. Geoffrey Chaucer wrote *The Canterbury Tales* in rhyming couplets, as in this description of the Miller. It is written in Middle English, but is worth the effort of reading. If you want to read a bawdy tale, then 'The Miller's Tale' is for you.

> The Millere was a stout carl for the nones:
> Ful big he was of braw, and eek of bones.
> That proved wel, for over al ther he cam,
> At wrastlinge he wolde have alwey the ram.

Alliteration: the repetition of the same initial consonant, as in: six, sizzling sausages for sixpence.

Assonance: the use of similar-sounding words, such as musing, boozing. It is used to create internal rhyming.

Triplet: a group of three lines.

Quatrain: a group of four lines. The *Rubaiyat* of Omar Khyam, the great Persian poet (1048–1131), which were translated by Edward Fitzgerald in the mid-nineteenth century, are fine examples of quatrains.

Sestet: a group of six lines.

Octet: a group of eight lines.

RHYME SCHEME

This is perhaps the key to making sense of traditional poetry forms. It is the pattern of rhyme between lines of a poem. It is usually referred to by using letters to indicate which lines rhyme. For example, in 'The Selkirk Grace,' the pattern is A,B,A,B. In the rhyming couplets in *The Canterbury Tales* above, it is A,A,B,B.

So now let's look at a few of the classic forms.

SONNETS

This is the traditional form used in lyric poetry. The word comes from the Italian '*sonetto*,' meaning 'little song.' It was invented in the thirteenth century and its greatest early poet was Francesco Petrarch (1304–74).

There are two types of sonnet, both of which have fourteen lines. Firstly, there is the *Petrarchan* or *Italian sonnet*, which was the style used by Petrarch. It consists of an octet, an eight-lined stanza, followed by a six-lined sestet. The rhyming scheme is A,B,B,A,A,B,B,A, followed by C,D,E,C,D,E. But sometimes there is a variation in the sestet to C,D,C,D,C,D.

The sonnet was introduced into England in the sixteenth century. This was convenient because a genius by the name of William Shakespeare was around to modify it to his purpose. Thus, the second type of sonnet is known as the *Shakespearean sonnet*. It consists of three quatrains of the rhyming scheme A,B,A,B, C,D,C,D, E,F,E,F followed by a rhyming couplet G,G. And, as you already know, they were written in iambic pentameter.

Now you know the structure you can start to appreciate the sonnet's beauty. And if you like mysteries, then the sonnet is one place to start. We don't know a great deal about William Shakespeare, but he does reveal a lot about his feelings in his sonnets. In addition, he also leaves a set of tantalising mysteries. Let me tell you about them.

In addition to his marvellous body of plays, Shakespeare left 154 sonnets, which were published in 1609. In these he wrote about his love for two people. First there is a fair youth, whom he idolises. And then there is a married dark lady, a brunette, whom he lusts after and undoubtedly conducts a sexual affair with. If you are interested and want to do your own detective work, the sonnets about the Dark Lady (he never refers to her as this, it is the label that scholars have attached to her) are numbers 127–54.

Who the fair youth was is another of the Shakespearean mysteries, yet it is nothing compared to the identity of this dark lady with whom he had the illicit affair. Scholars have debated whether she was the Countess of Pembroke, Mary Fitton; one of Queen Elizabeth I's ladies in waiting; the landlady of an Oxford inn; a prostitute called Luce Morgan; or even a man, the Earl of Southampton.

The latest idea is that she was Emilia Bassano (1570–1654), wife of Alphonse Lanier, a court musician, and that she was the mistress of Henry Carey, Lord Hunsdon. He was the patron of Shakespeare's theatre company. And she was a beautiful, voluptuous brunette, skilled in music and wit. A fitting mistress

The Dark Lady

for England's finest Elizabethan mind! There is even a miniature portrait of her, apparently, tucked away in a corner of the Victoria & Albert Museum in London.

It is all good stuff, and if that doesn't whet your appetite for poetry …

THE KEATSIAN ODE

This is named after John Keats, one of the Romantic poets. The rhyming scheme is A,B,A,B,C,D,E,C,D,E. The famous one is 'Ode on a Grecian Urn.'

TERZA RIMA

This is the form used by Dante Alighieri (1265–1321) in his *Divina Commedia*. It uses three-lined stanzas in the rhyming scheme A,B,A, B,C,B, C,D,C, D,E,D.

THE LIMERICK

This was popularised by Edward Lear in 1846, in his *Book of Nonsense*. It is a humorous poem with the rhyming scheme A,A,B,B,A. The first line is usually about a person from somewhere, and the final line usually refers to that person again.

There was an Old Man on some rocks,
Who shut his wife in a box;
When she said, 'let me out!'
He exclaimed, 'Without a doubt,
'You will pass all your life in that box.'

Edward Lear

HOW TO BE A CLERIHEW POET

Clerihew poems are my favourites. I confess to being addicted to writing these. They may not be good, but they make me smile. The clerihew is a simple four-lined poem named after its inventor Edmund Clerihew Bentley (1875–1956). He was a fascinating character who wrote the celebrated crime novel *Trent's Last Case*.

The clerihew is a biographical poem with the rhyming scheme A,A,B,B. It does not have to have regular feet. You can write about historical characters, friends, relatives or acquaintances. Just take care, of course, since some people may be unduly sensitive, and you do not want to risk litigation!

Here are a couple to give you the idea:

Sigismund Schlomo Freud
believed all religion was void.

He said the woes of womankind
Were due to sex on mankind's mind.

This is in praise of Sigmund Freud, whose full name is contained in the poem. His theories of the mind make this clerihew an example of *Zeitgeist poetry*, in that it defines the spirit of an age. That, or just bad doggerel.

William Topaz McGonagall,
Dundee's poet of verse abominable.
He fancied himself a tragedian and thespian supreme,
until he was booed off stage in his final death scene.

The world's worst poet

No section on poetry could be complete without a mention of William Topaz McGonagall (1825–1902.) He was a Dundee mill-worker, amateur actor and self-styled tragedian. He wrote unutterably bad poetry and is said to have been the world's worst poet. If you want to appreciate poetry, then read some McGonagall first. It will have you in stitches and show you that the poetical bar was set pretty low by his muse. This clerihew refers to a famous incident in a play he was acting in when he took so long to die that he was pelted with eggs and vegetables and had to be dragged off the stage by his fellow actors.

Dr Joseph-Ignace Guillotin
Inventor of the decapitation machine.
History books say he was the first to be cropped,
but it was another Dr G whose head was lopped.

This refers to the belief that, during the French Revolution, Dr Joseph-Ignace Guillotin (1738–1814), invented the guillotine and was guillotined himself. This is a myth. He 'proposed' that such a machine should be used, but did not actually invent it. His name just became associated with it after his proposal. It was entirely a coincidence that another Dr Guillotin was executed during 'The Terror.'

So you see, the clerihew is not difficult. The first line is the person's name, the second line rhymes with the name. Then the third line tells something about them, usually something trivial, and the last line rhymes with it.

I recommend that you obtain a rhyming dictionary, which is all that you need to become a clerihew poet.

Adieu.

14

ART

Poor is the pupil who does not surpass his master.

Leonardo da Vinci

The only time I feel alive is when I am painting.

Vincent van Gogh

It is hard to define art. Let us just say that it is organising things in such a way that they produce an emotional response.

OK, I accept that almost anything you do could be called art by that definition. Yet what is wrong with that? Many people would say that fine art or contemporary art is just bunging a few bricks in a pile, scattering some paint about or actually having a go at painting something with some body fluid or another. All of those examples have been classified as art and they certainly seem to have induced an emotional response of one sort or another among people who have seen them in art galleries.

Art is about coming up with ideas and ways of portraying things to other people. The deliberate act of creating something to evoke a response seems to be what it is all about these days. For the purists among us this may seem nonsensical, since a rebellious toddler may do something to outrage his parents, yet is that art? Some would say that it could be.

Yet for many art has to be representational. It has to look like the thing that is being represented. A portrait should look like its subject, a statue should seem lifelike and a landscape should have more than a passing similarity to a place.

There is no shortage of opportunity for arguments about art and there are no right and wrong answers. Art nowadays seems capable of going in many directions. It is for each person to say whether they like something or not. All that the artist can do is produce something and hope that it strikes a chord in your heart or evokes a pleasing emotion. That is the way that you are most

*Why van Gogh
painted his boots*

likely to buy their work, which is of course one way that you could measure the worth of art.

But before this starts to look dangerously like an essay on art let us get down to the nitty-gritty. By that I mean let us cover some of the main schools of art that you may come across or that you should know about if you want to hold your own in a discussion.

ART NOUVEAU

You might think that this means modern art. The sort of stuff that artists are churning out now. Well it doesn't actually mean that. It is very specifically art produced in the period 1890–1910. It is really an approach to design that used bright colours, twisting, floral motifs and tapering figures. It was very much a reaction to the science and technology of the times and what artists thought to be pseudo-classical art.

Think of the work of the Czech Alphonse Mucha or the British artist and sculptor Charles Rennie Mackintosh.

RENAISSANCE ART

This is the art that flourished through the fifteenth and early sixteenth centuries. It is characterised by what one would describe as classical depictions of the mythological world. It is the art of Leonardo da Vinci (the Mona Lisa), Michaelangelo (the ceiling of the Sistine Chapel), Titian (Salome and paintings of women and men with flowing locks) and Raphael (the Deposition of Christ).

MANNERISM

This was a style that immediately followed the Renaissance period. It lasted from about 1520 to 1580, before the Baroque period. It is characterised by vivid colours and exaggerated and elongated figures.

Giorgio Vasari was an exponent of Mannerism.

BAROQUE

This is a grand style that flourished between the late sixteenth and early eighteenth centuries. These artists produced large paintings with exaggerated curves, voluptuousness and sometimes Biblical or legendary subjects.

Exponents were Tintoretto, El Greco, Rubens and Carravagio. People probably have never actually looked as dramatic or as good as these artists painted them.

THE DUTCH SCHOOL

This is the artistic tradition that blossomed in the Netherlands in the seventeenth century. Think of cavaliers, men with baggy trousers, tight stockings, majestic sweeping hats with curly feathers and with swords by their sides. Think also of taverns, men smoking long clay pipes and drinking appetising glasses of wine, and maidens pouring milk from pewter jugs. These artists managed to produce beautifully executed reproductions that were so exact that it is likely they used *camera obscuras* to do so.

Exponents include Rembrandt (The Anatomy Lesson of Dr Tulp and numerous self-portraits), Franz Hals (The Laughing Cavalier), and Vermeer (Girl with a Pearl Earring).

THE PRE-RAPHAELITES

The Pre-Raphaelites, or the Pre-Raphaelite Brotherhood as they are sometimes known, were a group of artists who wanted to recreate the spirit of art that flourished before Raphael. Rossetti, John Millais and William Hunt were the three founders who were joined by others to make up their brotherhood of seven artists. They aimed for a natural, realistic style.

THE IMPRESSIONISTS

This was a school formed by French artists in the mid-nineteenth century. Light and its effects were their main concerns.

Impressionism caught fire and Impressionist paintings by such artists as Edouard Manet, Claude Monet, Pierre Auguste Renoir, Edgar Degas and Mary Cassatt are immediately recognisable.

But later the Impressionist movement moved from simply light and its effects to look at experimenting with form and shape. This became known as Post-Impressionism and was practised by such luminaries as Paul Cezanne and Vincent Van Gogh.

CUBISM

This was an interesting movement that started in France in 1907. It sought to reduce objects to basic geometric shapes, such as cubes, cylinders and spheres. It was started by Pablo Picasso and George Braque.

DADAISM

This was a cultural movement that began in Zurich in Switzerland in 1916 and lasted until 1922. It was effectively a nihilistic reaction to culture. They were very much anti-war and aimed at portraying the meaninglessness of the modern world and the values and interests that had led to world war. It spread across Europe and America.

Duchamp epitomised Dadaism, and Modigliani and Kandinsky were notable dabblers.

SURREALISM

This is the art of the unconscious mind which developed out of Dadaism. That might sound rather esoteric, but you cannot see surrealist art without feeling that you are witnessing the bizarre world of dreams. It is a twentieth- and twenty-first-century art movement that aimed and aims to escape the fetters of the consciousness and show the symbolism of the unconscious mind.

Exponents of this form are André Breton, Salvador Dali and Man Ray.

CONTEMPORARY ART

We have briefly considered this at the start of the chapter. It is effectively any art that has been produced since the Second World War. As such, it encompasses a great variety of styles, techniques and approaches.

Damien Hirst is a famous British contemporary artist known for works which include dead animals, such as a shark, a sheep and a cow. The preserved shark piece that he called 'The Physical Impossibility of Death in the Mind of Someone Living' is regarded as an iconic artwork of the 1990s.

Tracey Emin is a British artist who won the 1992 Turner Prize for her piece entitled 'My Bed.' Another of her works is a tent entitled, 'Everyone I Have Ever Slept With, 1963–95.' Both of these works are bound to make an impact upon the viewer.

Personally, I think they are brilliant.

'It's called "Polar Bear in a Snowstorm"'
'Can't see it myself'

15

PHILOSOPHY

I know that I am intelligent, because I know that I know nothing.

Socrates

cogito, ergo sum – I think, therefore I am.

René Descartes
Discourse on Method, 1637

People often shy away from philosophical discussions because they may have heard that philosophy makes your brain hurt. That is a slight exaggeration, for there is nothing about philosophy that can hurt you, unless you get struck on the back of the head by a hefty philosophical tome when you are pulling out a book on philately.

Philosophical discussions can be fun. It doesn't take long to learn about some of the great philosophers of the past and the sort of thoughts that they dabbled in and peddled to the masses. You may even find that you agree with one or two of them.

WHAT IS IT ALL ABOUT?

That question pretty well sums philosophy up. It is the study of knowledge and the nature of reality. Accordingly, there are two main branches of philosophy. Firstly, epistemology, or the theory of knowledge. Secondly, metaphysics, or the investigation of the nature of reality. The first is about trying to understand what it is possible to know and the second is about trying to understand about existence.

You might sit and ponder that for a few minutes and conclude that you can't really know very much about either and decide that you have had enough of philosophy and go and enjoy yourself for the rest of your life, or you might ponder these matters for a lifetime without reaching an answer, but yet still think that philosophy is the coolest of endeavours. Whichever you decide is all right by me and who is to say which path you choose is right or wrong?

And that is part of the fun of philosophy. Let's look at some of the celebrated philosophers of the past and their philosophies.

ANCIENT GREECE

Inevitably, we turn back to the ancient Greeks, since they seem to have thought of everything vaguely useful first. Apart from golf and the Internet, of course.

It is easy to imagine that the Greeks were a race of geniuses who could turn their minds to anything. Mathematics, medicine, music and drama, they excelled in all of these and thereby sowed the seeds of western civilisation. Yet it was in their consideration of the nature of the mind, the self and the whole panoply of reality that they showed their true colours. They created the wonderfully mind-bending study of philosophy. The word comes from their word *philosophia*, meaning 'love of wisdom.'

Yet as we shall see there were quite a few different schools of thought, some devoted to epistemology and others to metaphysical concerns. It is customary to think about the pre-Socratic and post-Socratic philosophers. Socrates himself is bang in the middle as Socrates himself.

PRE-SOCRATIC PHILOSOPHERS

There are several clever chaps here that are worth knowing about. They were concerned about where everything came from and what it was made of.

Thales of Miletus (624–546 BC), the father of Greek philosophy, thought that everything came from water. He discovered static electricity when he found that if amber was rubbed with fur it would attract light objects, like straw or feathers. He assumed that it was similar to magnetism.

Anaximenes (585–525 BC) thought that everything came from air and that it could be thickened and altered to make fire, wind, clouds, water and earth.

Heraclitus of Ephesus (535–475 BC) thought that everything came from fire.

Empedocles of Agrigentum (490–430 BC) thought that there were in fact four elements that made up everything. These were earth, air, fire and water. Everything was made up of them, even man himself. The different combinations accounted for the huge array of different substances.

He taught that whenever they were given the opportunity to do so, the constituent elements would try to get back to their source. And he suggested that the sources had natural positions, such that earth was at the centre of the world, water covered it, and was in turn covered by air, which had above it fire from the sun.

Thus, when you burned wood, the flames would always rise upwards, as if trying to get back to the sun; the ash would crumble and try to get back to the earth; the smoke, being air, would try to get back to the sky, and any sap in the wood would run out and try to get back to the sea. Similarly, solid objects put in water, being mainly earth, would sink. Bubbles, being air, would rise in water, and rain would fall through the air to get back to water.

Socrates of Athens was mainly concerned with the branch of philosophy that studied ethics. He never actually wrote anything himself, but left an incredible legacy. What we know about him is entirely due to his follower, Plato.

He taught by using a question-and-answer technique, called Socratic dialectic. He also taught that once one acknowledged one's own ignorance, one was on the way towards wisdom. Isn't that a curious thought!

Sadly, he died by drinking hemlock after being sentenced to death for corrupting the minds of the youth of Athens. Apparently, his followers bribed his jailors so that he could flee the city to save himself, but he refused to go. He reasoned that if he went it would show that he was afraid of death, which no philosopher should be.

POST-SOCRATIC PHILOSOPHERS

There are two philosophers who came after Socrates who you should know about. People often know the names but forget the order they lived. Just use this mnemonic heuristic SPA. 'S' is of course Socrates, followed by Plato and then Aristotle.

Plato (428–347 BC) was one of the greatest writers of the ancient world. He wrote numerous books with Socrates centre stage.

He was interested in how the universe was made, and was the first philosopher to actually use the word 'elements' in reference to the building blocks of the world. He believed that everything had a soul and that the human soul resided in the brain. The soul operated the body through the brain, which produced seminal fluid which flowed down the spinal cord carrying its messages.

One of his most famous works is *The Republic*, in which he described the island of Atlantis, which existed for more than 9,000 years, but which vanished under the waves as a punishment from the gods when its people became corrupt and decadent.

Aristotle (384–322 BC) modified Plato's view somewhat, promoting the concept that there are three types of soul: the *vegetative soul* possessed by plants, which allows for growth and decay and which enjoys nourishment; the *animal soul*, which gives motion and sensation to animals; and the *rational soul*, the conscious

Plato

and intellectual soul that is peculiar to humans. He taught that happiness stemmed from human reason.

There were other ancient Greek schools of philosophy that you should have an awareness of:

The Cynics: this school of thought was founded by *Diogenes of Sinope* (412–323 BC). He had been a pupil of *Antisthenes*, who in turn had been a follower of Socrates. Upon Socrates' death Antisthenes rejected philosophy, thinking that it was useless quibbling and that man's sole concern should be to be good.

Diogenes adopted this life of austerity and lived in a barrel, like a dog. The word 'cynic' does not have its current meaning, but meant canine, or dog-like.

The Epicureans: this Athenian school of philosophy was based on the teachings of Epicurus (341–270 BC) who taught that the aim of life should be pleasure, achieved through peace, freedom from fear and the companionship of friends.

The Stoics: this was another Athenian school of philosophy that vied with the Epicureans. It was founded by *Zeno of Citium*. He taught that one should be self-controlled and that, since the gods had created everything, one should live a good life and accept one's destiny. They are named after the *Stoa Poikile*, the 'painted colonnade,' a part of Athens where Zeno set up his school.

MEDIEVAL EUROPE

We tend to think of the Middle Ages as being fairly static in terms of intellectual development. Yet there are a couple of philosophers that you should know about.

William of Ockham (1288–1348) was a young Franciscan monk who devised a tool of logic which came to be known as Occam's Razor. The principle states that the explanation of any phenomenon should make as few assumptions as possible and those that make no difference to the observed predictions should be eliminated, or cut away like using a razor. This is often expressed in Latin as *lex parsimoniae*, the law of parsimony, meaning succinctness. At its simplest form you can think of it as 'all things being equal, the simplest solution is the best.'

St Thomas Aquinas (1225–74) was an Italian priest who founded Thomism. He taught that truth is truth wherever it is found, and that no ideology has a unique right to it.

THE RENNAISSANCE

During this time there was a flourishing of intellectual opinion. There are a couple of notable philosophers that you should be aware of:

Niccolo Machiavelli (1467–1527) was an Italian statesman, philosopher and writer. He taught that all rulers should aim to improve the welfare of the state, using whatever means were necessary. His name has come to be a by-word for duplicity and cunning.

Sir Thomas More (1478–1535) was a lawyer, writer and statesman. He served under King Henry VIII until he fell out of favour with the monarch when he refused to recognise him as the Supreme Governor of the Church of England, the consequence being that he was beheaded for treason.

He wrote a history of King Richard III, a Tudor piece of propaganda that was used by Shakespeare to besmear the reputation of the last genuinely English monarch of England. More significantly, he wrote a book called *Utopia* in 1516, about an imaginary island and its idyllic political system.

MODERN PHILOSOPHY

It may seem stretching it a bit to describe the work of philosophers who have been dead for several hundred years as 'modern,' yet I do so for two reasons. Firstly, there are several other epochs that one

could subdivide this study into, which might risk boring the socks off your feet. And secondly, there was something of a quantum leap in philosophy during this time which has not really continued in a linear manner. It has just bobbled along, so to speak. We await the next genius, so get your thinking cap on.

René Descartes (1596–1650) was a French philosopher who is considered by many to be the 'Father of Modern Philosophy' and of a particular way of thought. He was the first scientist-philosopher to organise the process of thought and link it to the meaning of one's very existence. This is embodied in his famous argument *cogito ergo sum*: I think, therefore I am.

He is famous for developing the concept known as *Cartesian dualism*: the view that mind and body are separate, distinct substances. He believed that the tools of science and mathematics could be used to explain and predict events in the physical world. Reductionism, the belief that complex things can be reduced to simpler, more fundamental things, was a natural result.

David Hume (1711–76) was a Scottish philosopher who was opposed to rationalists like Descartes, instead teaching that man is governed by his beliefs rather than by his reason. In these days of religious fundamentalism one can see what he means.

Immanuel Kant (1724–1804) was a German philosopher and writer who taught about the philosophy of the mind, ethics and epistemology. Kantianism revolves around duty, suggesting that actions are performed according to acquired maxims and principles rather than because of emotions.

Friedrich Nietzsche (1844–1900) was a German philosopher who taught that the motivation for most human endeavours was the desire for power. He suffered a mental collapse in the year before his death, which has aroused much speculation as to his mental state when postulating his philosophy.

Karl Marx (1818–83) was a German philosopher, historian and writer whose ideas led to the development of socialism and communism. He wrote *The Communist Manifesto* in 1848. He is buried in Highgate Cemetery in London.

Bertrand Russell (1872–1971) was a mathematician, logician, philosopher, atheist and pacifist. He wrote the best-selling *History of Western Philosophy* in 1945. In 1950 he won the Nobel Prize for Literature. He is regarded as one of the founders of analytical philosophy.

Ludwig Wittgenstein (1889–1951) is regarded as one of the towering figures of twentieth-century philosophy. He studied under Bertrand Russell and did work on mathematics, logic and language. He served in the Austrian army during World War I and kept a notebook which became the basis for his single book *Tractatus*, which was to prove highly influential among philosophers. He believed that language could not be trusted, since it is imprecise and therefore nothing can be said or understood with precision and truth is hard to achieve. There are two distinct periods to his life and work, pre-*Tractatus* and post-*Tractatus*. The post period was in conflict with the pre period.

It shows what a dodgy subject philosophy can be.

Jean-Paul Sartre (1905–80) was a French existentialist philosopher, playwright, novelist, Marxist and literary critic. He was awarded the 1964 Nobel Prize for Literature but refused to accept it, as only a philosopher would.

Existentialism is about living in the here and now, or in the moment. Questions of the divine, of the future and of the past are of little import.

Sir Karl Popper (1902–94) was a philosopher of science. He taught that scientific theories are abstract in nature and can be tested only indirectly, whatever scientists actually think.

OTHER BRANCHES OF PHILOSOPHY

I said that there were two main questions in philosophy. Well, there are other branches that you should have an awareness of:

Aesthetics: the appreciation of art and art forms, the nature of beauty.

Ethics: the study of right and wrong and the principles of morality.

Philosophy of politics: the nature of justice and fairness within society and the rights and wrongs of the political systems that operate within societies.

Philosophy of science: the nature and methods of science and the logical basis for the scientific method.

16

MEDICINE AND THE BODY

Doctors are men who prescribe medicines of which they know
little, to cure diseases of which they know less, in human beings of
whom they know nothing.

Voltaire (1694–1778)

People have a fascination with medicine and the workings of the
body. At virtually any social gathering the topic of health will come
up and someone will volunteer information about some ailment
that they have, or about some part of their body that is playing
up. Someone else, usually someone with no medical knowledge
whatsoever, will hazard a diagnosis and then it will be a free for
all of remedies tried, trusted or read about in some magazine or
other while waiting to have the car tyres changed or for the dentist
to call you in. Often the most bizarre of ideas will be extolled and
expounded, betraying the greatest ignorance imaginable. The
truth is that most people don't know their acetabulum from their
zygoma.

You don't have to know a great deal in order to be able to chip
in and impress folk on such occasions. Just be armed with a little
rudimentary knowledge and a few odd facts. The odder the facts
the better, in fact.

LET'S TALK ABOUT BOWELS

Do you remember when you were a youngster and how fascinated
you were by your bowels? Oh don't shake your head, because you
know very well that it is true. You were fascinated at the way all
those brightly coloured foods went in, gurgled about for a few
hours, and then were transformed into stupendously noisy and
odiferous farts, followed later by strange brown poo. And later
on, if you did a course on psychology, you would have heard good

old Sigmund Freud's ideas about being anally fixated and all that jazz. But there is really no need to worry, because I assure you, everybody is fascinated with their bowels, their bowel habit and they secretly like the smell of their own farts.

Essentially, the digestive system is central to our whole being! When I say that I do not mean to be flippant, it is just that it actually is a central feature of our anatomy. In a sense, the digestive tract is a long tube, around which our various tissues and organs are arranged. The food we take in is passed along that tube, being altered by grinding, chemical reaction and enzymatic breakdown. We absorb nutrients from it and dispel unwanted products of digestion as it passes, finally getting rid of the waste matter with the passage of a bowel movement. And the amazing thing is that it is, like most of our body workings, an automatic and well-nigh continuous process.

If you look at an earthworm, or even a snake, then you get a fairly clear impression of the tubular nature of their digestive tracts. They seem to have very simple anatomies with literally straight digestive systems that run the length of their bodies. By contrast, the 9 metres of the digestive tract of the human being is convoluted and compressed into a relatively short body. This curious anatomy that we have makes conventional diagnosis of problems extremely difficult at times. I know, for as a doctor I have often scratched my head as I tried to work out what was going on inside someone's tummy.

Abdominal pain, for example, can arise from several organs, or from different parts of the digestive system, and the pain-sufferer may not be able to pinpoint where the pain is coming from. If we were simple long tubes, like the earthworm or snake, then you would probably have a clearer idea of the source of a pain. Don't let me mislead you, though. A tall, thin, stick-like person still has the same anatomy as a little round roly-poly.

WIND

Here are the fundamentals. Everyone strives not to fart in public; unless you are one of those adorable folk who is forever 12 years old. That being the case, don't you just hate those noises that occur inside you and which you can do nothing whatever to prevent or control. You might call them internal farts, but more correctly this is a *borborygmus*. It is simply gas and liquid in transit. Classically they start off at a low pitch and get gradually louder until they pop with a neat crescendo. Next time you are sitting on a settee with friends and one intrudes into the conversation, just explain that it is simply a borborygmus, and that your doctor is fascinated by your borborygmi. You will probably get oodles of sympathy and everyone but you will feel embarrassed.

Farts are fascinating, though. Many moons ago when I was a medical student I made a study of intestinal gas. And a fascinating subject it is too, although propriety prevents me from divulging the scientific details of the research methods. I would not wish to embarrass anyone, no matter how distinguished a physician or surgeon they may now be.

At any time the average person's bowel has about 250 millilitres, or about half a pint, of gas. At times when they feel gassy, this figure may rise to a couple of litres. The most abundant gas is nitrogen, which makes up 90 per cent of intestinal wind. The rest consists of carbon dioxide, hydrogen, methane and occasionally hydrogen sulphide. The latter is the one that creates the cushion-creeper farts that smell of bad eggs. A healthy young adult will probably pass 2 litres of assorted gases every day, in between fifteen to twenty-five farts.

There is a medical opinion that our modern, mainly indoor life has stopped people from passing wind as and when they need to. As a result of this people build up internal pressure and retain it for far longer than their rural ancestors, who could fart outdoors with abandon. This may be the cause of various intestinal ailments like diverticulosis and irritable bowel syndrome. Indeed, it was this thinking that induced a health publicity campaign in Holland in the early 1990s, which encouraged people to make sure that they passed wind at least fifteen times a day.

THIRTY INTERESTING FACTS ABOUT THE BODY

So here you are. Take your pick. There are bound to be a few that you can drop into conversation at least once a day.

1. The adult human body is made up of about 50 to 75 trillion cells.
2. All of the functioning cells in the body will be replaced over about a 10-year period.
3. The average stomach lining cell is replaced every 5 days, your red blood cells live for 120 days, your liver cells are replaced every 18 months and your bone cells are replaced every 10. years.
4. 15 billion blood cells are destroyed and the same number are produced every second.
5. Only 10 per cent of the total body mass is made up of human cells, the rest are microbes.
6. The brain is made up of about 100 billion cells.

7. The average taste bud lives for 10 days.
8. 80 per cent of the human body is made up of water.
9. Nerve impulses to and from the brain travel at speeds of up to 170 miles an hour.
10. The average human heart will beat 3,000 million times in its lifetime and pump 48 million gallons of blood.
11. The adult intestine is almost 9 metres long.
12. Cartilage (which lines joints) is 8 times slippier than ice.
13. The teeth are the only place in the body where bone naturally comes through skin.
14. At the age of 6 years most people have 48 teeth in their head (20 baby teeth and most of the developing 32 adult teeth).
15. Tooth enamel is the hardest tissue of any animal or plant.
16. When you are born you have over 300 assorted bones.
17. By adulthood many bones will have fused to leave 206.
18. The healthy human thigh bone is stronger than concrete.
19. Babies do not have knee-caps. The patella is a sesamoid bone, which means it develops inside a tendon. It only develops at about the age of 2.
20. The average human head weights 8 pounds.
21. The average human scalp has 100,000 hairs (even bald people, whose hairs are very thin, short and fine).
22. It takes 72 different muscles to produce speech.
23. Humans have internal tails.
24. Your fingerprints are unique to you.
25. The acid in your stomach could eat through wood.
26. Human ears may once have been pointed like a dog's. Charles Darwin, the scientist who discovered the theory of evolution, suggested this, and a vestigial flap at the top of the ear is still called Darwin's tubercle.
27. The view of the world is slightly different in each eye, thereby allowing you to perceive depth.
28. Your ears hear at different times, thereby allowing you to pinpoint the source of sounds.
29. Your two nostrils pick up different types of smells.
30. You use thirty muscles to smile.

BURKE AND HARE AND THE VILLAINOUS BODY-SNATCHERS

This is one for late at night, not round the dinner table.

In the early nineteenth century the teaching of anatomy occupied a major part of a medical education. The problem was that there was an insufficient supply of cadavers to the medical schools. As a result, the nefarious practice of body-snatching began. Unscrupulous rogues began digging up recently buried corpses and sold them illegally to medical schools. They became known as Resurrectionists.

In the West Port of Edinburgh in 1827 William Burke and his partner William Hare took matters a step further and committed a murder, then sold the body to Dr Robert Knox at the Edinburgh Medical School. He was an anatomist and the Conservator of the Museum at the Royal College of Surgeons of Edinburgh. Over the following year the gruesome twosome murdered and sold sixteen more bodies for anatomical dissection.

When they were finally brought to justice, Hare turned king's evidence and was spared, but Burke was sentenced to death by hanging followed by public dissection of his body by Professor Alexander Munro. A riot broke out during the execution and dissection in 1829 and somehow most of Burke' skin was stolen. Some weeks later, wallets and pocket books found their way onto

The Resurrectionists, Burke and Hare

the black market, purportedly made from the tanned skin of the murderer William Burke.

This horrible practice extended to many cities in Britain and seemed to have been going on for longer than the time that Burke and Hare had been active. A gang of body-snatchers called the London Burkers came to prominence in 1831 and were arrested. The press gave them the name, assuming that they were copy-cats of Burke and Hare, yet the gang leaders confessed that they had been operating around the Shoreditch area of the city for a dozen years, during which time they had stolen between 500 and 1,000 bodies. It is speculated that they had murdered several people, but a confession about one death led to a trip to the gallows and subsequent dissection for the gang leaders.

In 1832 the Anatomy Act was passed by Parliament. This allowed for the legal supply of bodies to the medical schools and so the grizzly trade of body-snatching died out.

17

RELIGION AND BELIEF

I can believe anything provided it is incredible.

Oscar Wilde

People throughout history have lived and died for their beliefs. That fact does not legitimise the belief that they died for; it merely demonstrates the conviction that the belief was held within the mind of the individual.

I state here and now that I am not suggesting in this little chapter that any one belief system is superior to any other, or indeed whether any one of them is based on truth or not. That is for theologians to debate and for you the reader to make up your own mind about.

Religion and belief are strong motivators for the way that people think and behave. A look through history right up until this day will illustrate that many conflicts and wars have their origins in religions and ideologies. At a more mundane level people argue about such matters at all sorts of occasions and it is worth just having a basic idea about the major religions and beliefs.

BELIEF SYSTEMS

Virtually everyone develops a belief system. That is, they develop a frame of reference upon which they base their life. This can be a religion, an ideology or a system that works for them.

At one time virtually all people believed in magic and the supernatural. The realms between this and religion became blurred, for most religions in their early development also had magical or supernatural aspects inherent in them. Nowadays, while the majority of people would claim that magic did not exist, superstition even among folk who would claim to be utterly rational still holds sway. How often, for example, do you touch wood, cross your fingers or throw salt over your shoulder? The point is that such beliefs are deeply rooted in most people, because a magical explanation of the universe is one of the first impressions that people develop as they begin to experience the world as children.

A frame of reference, whatever its nature, helps you to operate. It is the basis from which you can make decisions, make judgements and make comparisons between things that are acceptable to you and things that are not.

All that being the case, a word of caution is in order. If you get embroiled in discussion about belief and religion you should be mindful of the fact that you may be attacking another person's frame of reference, their most dearly held belief system. Undermining it may be detrimental to that person, for it could rob them of their raison d'etre. For that reason most people will feel threatened and when people feel threatened they usually fight back hard. Do you see what I mean about conflicts and wars?

Now let us just look at some of the main systems.

THEISM

This is the belief in at least one god. The word is derived from the Greek *theos*, meaning 'god.' *Monotheism* is belief in a single god and *polytheism* is belief in many gods. By contrast, *atheism* is the rejection of belief in the existence of any divine or supernatural agency. Epicurus of Athens, whom we met in the chapter on philosophy, was one of the first atheists.

Agnosticism refers to those people who are unsure whether there is a god or not.

Now, believe it or not, there are over 4,300 religions practised throughout the world. If I simply listed them that would take up more room than this chapter will allow, so more usefully we shall consider the five most influential religions, which are worshipped by more than 75 per cent of the population of the world. These are: Buddhism, Christianity, Hinduism, Islam and Judaism. Christianity is currently the most widely practised religion with 2.1 billion followers. Islam is next with 1.3 billion. Atheism or non-belief would be the third commonest if it was a religion.

Hinduism is the next with 900 million, then Buddhism with 376 million and Judaism with 14 million. I should just add that there are other religions which slot in between the big five in terms of followers, but the big five are chosen because they are older and perceived to be the most influential.

Christianity, Islam and Judaism are referred to as the three Abrahamic faiths, for all three can claim the prophet Abraham as part of their sacred history.

BUDDHISM

The Buddha

This is a philosophy rather than a religion. It was founded by an Indian prince, Siddhartha Gautama, known as the Buddha, 2,500 years ago. It centres on personal spiritual development rather than the worship of a deity. It teaches that the way to salvation or Nirvana is through discipline, meditation and good personal ethics. Buddhists believe in 'karma,' the universal law that you reap what you sow, or what goes around comes around. They also believe in reincarnation, wherein one is reborn to learn the lessons that we have failed to learn in previous incarnations, until ultimately we can achieve Nirvana.

CHRISTIANITY

This is the religion founded on the life and teachings of Jesus Christ, who lived and died by crucifixion just over 2,000 years ago.

All of this is recounted in the four Gospels of the New Testament of the Bible. These are: Matthew, Mark, Luke and John. The word 'gospel' is from Old English, meaning 'god-spell' or 'good tidings.'

The Gospels all tell the same story, albeit they were written at different times and they all have a slightly different approach.

Christians believe that Jesus Christ was the son of God and that he was sent by God to save mankind from its sins. He was crucified by the Romans on Good Friday and rose again from the dead on Easter Sunday.

Christmas celebrates the birth of Jesus Christ.

There are various sects and churches of Christianity.

HINDUISM

This is the last of the great polytheistic religions. The ancient Egyptians, the Greeks and the Romans all worshipped a pantheon of gods. That is, they had many gods, each of whom oversaw particular groups of people, activities or festivities.

Hinduism is the world's third-largest religion and it is extremely old. Its roots stretch back to about 3,500 BC, so it can claim to be the oldest living religion in the world. In India 80 per cent of the population is Hindu. There is no single prophet or teacher. Indeed, it is a religion with several traditions, all of which revere the sacred literature known as the Vedas.

Although there is a vast pantheon of gods, Hindus actually only worship one god, called Brahman. The deity takes three main forms, the divine trinity: Brahma, the creator of the universe; Vishnu, the preserver; and Siva, the destroyer. The lesser gods and divinities assist the divine trinity.

The concept of reincarnation, similar to that of Buddhism, is also accepted in Hinduism.

Diwali, or the Festival of Lights, takes place in about October and is a five-day-long celebration of the New Year.

ISLAM

This is the second-largest religion in the world. It was founded by the prophet Muhammad in AD 622, although a movement had been in existence for about 1,000 years before that. The word Islam means 'submission to god.'

According to Islam there is only one god, Allah, and he revealed the faith to various prophets. The final revelation was shown to Muhammad. The Qu'ran is the holy scripture of the words of Allah as revealed to Muhammad.

There are five pillars of Islam: the recitation of the *creed* (one must say with utter conviction that 'there is no god but Allah and Muhammad is his prophet'); the *salat*, the recitation of prayers five times a day; *zakat*, the giving of alms to the poor; the observation of the fast of *Ramadan*; and *hajj*, a pilgrimage once in one's life to the holy city of Mecca.

Predestination is a tenet of Islam. Effectively it means that all has already been written by Allah, although it does allow for personal choice in action.

Prayers are led by an imam, an Islamic scholar.

There are two main branches of Islam, the Sunnis and the Shiites. 80 per cent of Muslims are Sunnis. The difference has to do with the succession from Muhammad. The Sunnis believe that Abu Bakr, a friend of Muhammad, became his successor or caliph. The Shiites believe that the succession should have been through the bloodline, going directly to the fourth caliph.

JUDAISM

Judaism is the religion of the Jewish people. It is believed that God appointed the Jews to be his chosen people in order to set an example of morality to the rest of the world. The first prophet was Abraham and when Moses led the people out of Egypt in 1300 BC he was given the Ten Commandments by God. This was the beginning of Judaism.

The religion is based on the Old Testament and the Talmud.

In Judaism it is believed that each person can have a special relationship with God, and that there is a covenant relationship. This means that in exchange for God's favours and good deeds, the Jewish people will obey his laws and strive to maintain goodness in their lives.

Community is very important in Judaism and people worship in the synagogue. In Orthodox synagogues men and women worship separately, everyone covering their heads. The services are led by rabbis.

Rosh Hashanah is the Jewish New Year celebration of the Creation and lasts for two days.

Passover is the celebration of the Exodus from Egypt led by Moses. This lasts seven or eight days and during this time the house has to be cleansed.

Hanukkah or the Festival of Lights celebrates the victory of the Macabees over the Syrian Greeks. It often coincides with the Christian Christmas.

AND ...

You should know about these:

Sikhism: a relatively new religion founded by Guru Nanak in about AD 1500 in the Punjab. Sikhs worship God in an abstract form, without image or statue.

Shinto: a Japanese form of Buddhism with a strong emphasis on ancestors.

Voodoo: a curious amalgam of African beliefs and Roman Catholicism. It is prevalent on Haiti. Through the practice of Voodoo the spirits of the dead are said to be contactable to give advice and help when it is needed.

Zen Buddhism: a sect that was introduced to Japan in the sixth century from China. It utilises meditational practices.

Zoroastrianism: founded in about 1200 BC in Persia by the prophet Zoroaster. Morality is all important and can be summed up as 'good thoughts, good words, and good deeds.'

18

ECONOMICS AND FINANCE

If all the economists were laid end to end, they'd never reach a conclusion.

George Bernard Shaw
Playwright, critic and Nobel Prize-winner, 1925

No one truly understands economics. There do not seem to be any real geniuses here, despite the fact that a Nobel Prize for economics has been awarded with monotonous regularity since it was instituted in 1968. When things like credit crunches occur no one takes responsibility, there is much buck-passing (literally) and so-called experts glibly say they 'told you so.' My reason for saying that there seem to be no economic geniuses is simply that a genius in my book is someone who contributes something mind-bogglingly clever which enriches the world, not just themselves.

Having said that there are many people who do know how to make money. Millionaires were once the richest people, now they are ten a penny. Billionaires are the new rich and there are even a few trillionaires about. They have obviously done something right, haven't they?

So how do you become one?

Well, I haven't got a clue, to be honest. I suspect that you have to have a ruthless streak somewhere, because as sure as eggs are eggs, your increase in wealth will be made at the cost of someone else's prosperity. The simple truth is that not everyone prospers. Somebody ends up worse off and in a way it seems that the pursuit of wealth is a kind of survival of the fittest.

Let's have a look at some of the guiding principles in economics.

LAWS OF ECONOMICS

Well, some of these are called laws, but they are all just axioms or heuristics. That being the case, they are in keeping with the subject of this book, so let's have a look at some.

THE LAW OF DIMINISHING RETURNS

This is a principle in business. Essentially, if there are several factors needed to produce something, then an increase in one factor while the others are kept constant will eventually reach a stage where any further increase in that factor will result in a diminished production when compared to the previous increase.

ENGEL'S LAW

This was devised by Ernst Engel (1821–96), a German statistician and economist. It states that, with a given set of tastes and preferences, as income rises, the *proportion* of income spent on food falls, even if *actual* expenditure on food rises.

MALTHUSIAN THEORY

The Reverend Thomas Robert Malthus (1776–1834) was an English clergyman, scholar and economist. Between 1798 and 1826 he published six editions of a treatise, entitled *An Essay on the Principle of Population*. Each edition was an updated version of the one before. His theory of population was that populations tend to increase by geometric progression, whereas resources progress by arithmetical progression. If the population is allowed to rise in an uninhibited manner, it will run out of resources and difficulties will occur.

His *Rule of 70* is a neat little heuristic or rule of thumb about time periods involved in exponential growth. For example, if growth is measured annually, then a 1 per cent growth rate will result in a doubling every 70 years. A 2 per cent growth rate will result in a doubling every 35 years.

You can extrapolate his theory and apply it to other systems, perhaps not entirely legitimately, but if you do you will see an early form of the Gaia hypothesis.

MICAWBER'S PHILOSOPHY

Charles Dickens created the memorable character of Mr Wilkins Micawber in his novel *David Copperfield*. His philosophy was: 'Annual income of twenty pounds coupled with expenditure of only nineteen pounds nineteen shillings and six pence was, he mused, happiness itself. But spend say twenty pounds and six pence and it's misery.'

Essentially, live within your means.

PARETO'S PRINCIPLE

This is named after Vilfredo Pareto (1848–1923), an Italian philosopher, economist and industrialist, although he did not formulate it as such. It is sometimes called the 80-20 rule. It is that 80 per cent of the effects come from 20 per cent of the causes. It is actually a remarkable rule of thumb, in that you see it again and again. In business people get 80 per cent of their sales from 20 per cent of their clients. And globally the richest 20 per cent of the population controls about 80 per cent of the world's income.

PARKINSON'S LAW

Cyril Northcote Parkinson (1909–93), an English historian and writer, wrote a humorous essay in *The Economist* in 1955. He began: 'work expands to fill the time available for its completion.' He expanded his thinking in a bestseller called *Parkinson's Law: the Pursuit of Progress* in 1958.

LAW OF SUPPLY AND DEMAND

Effectively, increase in supply will lead to lower prices for that product. The prices will only start to rise when there is an increase in demand.

STOCK EXCHANGES AND INDEXES

A stock exchange is the name for a market of stocks and shares. There are many stock exchanges around the world. A stock-market index gives you an idea of how well the market is doing. Generally several of these are quoted. If you can't tell your footsie from your tootsies you probably aren't going to make a killing on the stock market.

'*Footsie:*' this is the popular name given to the FTSE 100 Economic Index. It is owned by the Financial Times and the London Stock Exchange and it is not an acronym. It is a share index of the 100 most highly capitalised UK companies listed on the London Stock Exchange. It is published every 15 seconds and gives a crude measure of business prosperity.

Dow Jones: this is the Dow Jones Industrial Average. It is the second-oldest market index in the USA and it is based on the thirty largest publicly owned companies based in the USA.

NASDAQ Composite: this is an index of the common stocks and securities that are listed on the NASDAQ (National Association of Securities Dealers and Quotations) stock exchange, which has over 3,000 components. Both US and non-US companies are listed.

Nikkei 225: this is the stock-market index of the Tokyo Stock Exchange. It is updated every 15 seconds and is a measure of the Japanese exchange.

A FEW SPECIAL ECONOMIC TERMS

You hear these in the news but may not be aware of what they are:

Bull market: investor confidence is high, so people are buying shares and hoping to make a profit when they sell.

Bear market: this is a general downward decline in stock.

Gnomes of Zurich: supposedly the Swiss bankers who influence world finance.

Inflation: when rising prices lead to a decrease in the spending power of money.

19

SPORT

Don't play too much golf. Two rounds a day are plenty.

Harry Vardon
Six-times Open golf champion

Sport is a fascinating but eccentric aspect of life. Its origins are fairly obscure, many sports are utterly banal and most have rules that make no sense in the real world. I mean, just consider how silly golf is. Hitting a small ball across varied terrain with an

I know it sounds silly, but the idea is to …

assortment of clubs, aiming to get it into a series of eighteen holes in as few shots as possible. Or football, a game that ignores the dexterous upper limbs, the very features that have propelled us up the evolutionary tree, demanding instead that we kick or head a ball about a field and get it into a net, past a goalkeeper, the only man on the field allowed to use his hands. Or tennis, a strange game that seems to have had its origins in French farmyards, in which you hit a ball back and forth across a net.

Why do we like sports? None of them make a great deal of sense. Yet they are played and watched with passion. In many people's minds they take priority over politics, philosophy, art or even sex. It is a mystery to the uninitiated.

If you tune in to any sports programme or even open the sports section of the newspaper you will not have to wait long before the word genius comes up. Is that not interesting? There seem to be more geniuses in sport than in the worlds of art or science put together. Yet what are the achievements that these geniuses are bestowing upon the world? Are they discovering things that make life better for us all? No, they are entertaining us and in many cases they are pushing back the frontiers of skill. And there is nothing wrong with that, is there?

If you are shaking your head and raising a doubtful eyebrow at this then you are probably in need of this chapter. You undoubtedly belong to the canaille of non-sporting folk who feel left out when the discussion comes round to sport. So let us cover a few basics and then consider a few odd facts that you can bring up to show that you know something about sport.

SOME GENIUSES WHO PLAYED SPORT

There is no reason that geniuses should not play sport. They usually gain fame from their activity in some egg-headed sphere, so presumably they just played for fun.

William Shakespeare, the world's greatest playwright, was a dab hand with a bow and arrow, according to the tales of his poaching skills.

George Gordon, Lord Byron, the poet, was a cricketer, boxer and swimmer.

Sigmund Freud, the founder of psychoanalysis, was a tennis player of some note.

Sir Arthur Conan Doyle, the creator of Sherlock Holmes, was a golfer, cricketer, balloonist, early aviator and English billiards champion. He also introduced Nordic skiing to Switzerland! It is he you have to thank for those Swiss ski holidays.

Niels Bohr, the quantum physicist, was an enthusiastic gunfighter. Well, perhaps not in the Wild West, but he did study the gunfighter phenomenon in which films always showed the goodie drawing second, yet always winning. In a series of mock gunfights with colleagues he always won.

AND SOME GENIUSES OF SPORT

Everyone has heard of modern exponents of sport, like Jack Nicklaus and Tiger Woods in golf, Roger Federer in tennis, Muhammed Ali in boxing, Cristiano Ronaldo, David Beckham, Lionel Messi and Wayne Rooney in football, all of whom are often cited as geniuses of their respective games, but some of the old guys also shook their worlds of sport. If you can drop their names into a sport discussion then you will show that you know your stuff.

Izaak Walton, a writer and fisherman, wrote *The Compleat Angler* in 1653. It was considered *the* book on fishing for centuries.

Gypsy Jem Mace (1831–1910) was the son of a Hungarian Gypsy and a Norfolk cabinet-maker. He was born in Swaffham and was the last of the great bare-knuckle fighters, as well as the first Heavyweight Boxing Champion of the World.

Old Tom Morris (1821–1908) was one of the pioneers of professional golf. He was born in St Andrews (as was I, but

thereafter there is no golfing similarity between us) and won the Open Championship on four occasions. He is recognisable in pictures by his long white beard.

Dr W.G. Grace (1848–1915) was a medical practitioner who became the face of modern cricket. In his long bushy beard he epitomised the Victorian sportsman and could claim to have been the greatest cricketer of all time. He was a good all-rounder and excelled at batting, bowling and fielding. He captained England, Gloucerstershire and several other teams. It is not so widely known that he was a master at gamesmanship. Also, he was a champion 440-yard hurdler, golfer and footballer.

Young Tom Morris (1851–75) was an even greater golfer than his father, Old Tom. He won the Open Championships of 1868, 1869, 1870 and 1872, only missing out on 1871 because it was not played that year. Tragically, his wife and child died in childbirth and he died of a broken heart on Christmas Day four months later.

Lottie Dodd (1871–1960) was one of the finest women athletes ever. She won the Wimbledon Ladies' Championship at tennis five times, played hockey for England, won the British Women's Golf Championship and was a skilled mountaineer, horse rider and skater.

Paavo Nurmi (1897–1973) was a middle- and long-distance runner, who became known as the Flying Finn. He won nine gold medals and three silvers over three Olympic Games. He is rightly regarded as one of the finest runners of all time.

Sir Stanley Matthews (1915–2000) was the only footballer to have been knighted while he was still playing the game. He was a vegetarian and a teetotaller and was still playing competitively at the age of 50.

THE PSYCHOLOGY OF SPORT

Just why do people play sport? Generally it is for fun, although very often it does not seem to be fun during the game. Indeed, many players vow after a bad game to give it up forever. Yet they rarely do. When the next game or match looms they get out their clubs, racquet, kit or whatever is needed in the particular sport and head off to the locker rooms with eager anticipation.

Sport spectators watch other people playing in order to give them support and to be entertained in turn. There again, they are often badly let down when their player or team gets thoroughly trounced.

The fact is that people play sport because human beings are competitive creatures. Everyone is competitive in some way, no matter what they may say. They may not like sport, yet they will have a competitive edge in some aspect of their life. It is the way that we are programmed. It is the way in which creatures evolve. Our bodies are designed to compete. When faced with a threatening situation we pump out adrenaline from the adrenal glands in order to fight or run away. This is the fight or flight reaction. It gives you that tingle to get stuck in or the fear that makes you want to run away. Most people in civilised societies do not actually have to fight or defend their lives, so we have created sport instead.

Sport is simply a substitute for combat. Instead of fighting each other, an unconscious mental mechanism called *sublimation* comes into action. This means that we transform a socially unacceptable behaviour into a lesser one that is acceptable. Instead of fighting we channel that aggressive drive into a game or sport.

Being thinking *homo sapiens*, we create rules for each sporting activity. Pick any sport or game and think about the rules. They are usually totally silly. From football to underwater hockey, from chess to tiddlywinks, they all have strictures that make the activity harder than it needs to be. Yet those rules reinforce the competitive edge. Playing within the rules are what people like in sport.

Watching sport is also about that aggressive urge and here again we use the unconscious mental mechanism of sublimation. In addition, we use another mental mechanism called *identification*. That is, we select one player in the game or one team as our favourite. It is no different from the Roman mob backing one gladiator, or the crowd at a medieval joust choosing a particular knight.

Different types of sports seem to have different types of crowd. At some football matches the crowd seems to degenerate into a mob. Tennis matches seem more genteel, and golf spectators seem to be almost too embarrassed to make any utterance – apart from the halfwits who scream out 'get in the hole' when someone is driving a ball at a hole over 500 metres away. The truth is that the same people may go to all three of those games and their behaviour will tend to conform to that of the crowd they are in at the time. Again, this is because of the identification mental mechanism.

You hear a lot about sports psychology these days. All of the top professional sports folk seem to have a sports psychologist in their back-up team. They can make a huge difference in getting a player motivated, and they can help them to channel drive, modify behaviour and develop a winning attitude.

Norman Triplett, the first sports psychologist

In 1898 he described the *social facilitation phenomenon*. Effectively he found that people performed better at activities if they did them alongside someone else, which he referred to as the *co-actor effect*, or if they were being watched, which he termed the *audience effect*. He actually did experiments with cyclists and found that they rode faster if they rode in pairs or more. He said that 'the bodily presence of another contestant participating simultaneously in the race serves to liberate latent energy not ordinarily available'.

FOOTBALL

This term covers several team games that are basically played with the feet. The aim is either to score a goal by hitting a ball into a net, or over H-shaped posts as in Gaelic football or rugby.

The word *soccer* is derived from *Association* football. Its first recorded use was in 1891. The Football League was formed in 1888. The Premiership was formed in 1992 consisting of the top twenty-two clubs. This left the Football League with three divisions. In 2004 the three divisions were named The Championship, League One and League Two respectively.

The offside rule

This causes many a heated debate among football fans. If you want to score a point in a discussion you can explain that this is technically Law XI of the Laws of the Game, which is published by FIFA. It states that, if a player is in an offside position when the ball is touched or played by a team mate, he may not become actively involved in the play. A player is in an offside position if he is closer to the opponent's goal line than both the ball and the second-to-last defender, but only if the player is on his opponent's half of the field (pitch). Interpretation of the term 'actively involved' has become the subject of complex debate.

You can add that if you modified this single rule you could dramatically increase the scores in football.

TENNIS

Tennis is played across a net and seems to be derived from a game called *jeu de paume*, which was played in France as long ago as the twelfth century. Originally it was played with a cork ball and the hands, then with gloves, then bats and finally racquets. It was an indoor game played in a court, rather like a farm courtyard, with protruding slanting roofs which the player could utilise.

There are four major tennis tournaments played by both male and female professional players. These are, in order throughout the year: Australian Open (hard court), French Open (clay court), Wimbledon (grass court) and US Open (hard court).

The main trivia you should know about tennis is the eccentric scoring. A tennis match is scored in points, games and sets. A match is usually played as the best of three sets, although five sets may be used in men's competitions. Both players start a game on zero points, which is called 'love'. Then if a player wins a point his score goes to 15, then with another he goes to 30, then 40. If he wins another then the game is won.

If both players reach 40, it is called 'deuce'. The game is won when one player wins by two clear points. One more point takes him to 'advantage', then a winning point gives him 'game'. If the opponent wins the point, however, they go back to deuce.

A set is won when one player gains six games, provided that he has a two game lead. If the score goes beyond the six games, the set will be won when one player has a two-game advantage. This used to be the way that all matches were played, but nowadays a tie-break comes into play at six games each and the set is decided by the winner of the tie-break, which is won when one player reaches seven points with a two-point lead. If the score goes to six each then they continue until a player has a two-shot lead.

Two possible origins of tennis scoring

No one knows this and these possibilities are speculation only. However, knowing them can be useful.

Firstly, love is thought to come from '*l'oeuf*', 'the egg', which is shaped like a zero. Some authorities think that it actually came from '*l'heure*', 'the hour', which would be in keeping with the clock theory for scoring.

The clock theory:

It is thought that a clock face was used in *jeu de paume* courts to determine the score for each player.

Originally, the first point gained a quarter turn to 15. A second point reached 30. A third reached 45 and a fourth was game when 60 was reached. Then the concept of winning by two clear points and 'deuce' came in. To accommodate this the scoring went 15, then 30, then 40 instead of 45. This then allowed one player to advance by 10, to their 'advantage'. If they won the next point it went to 60 or game. If they lost their advantage they both went back to 40, or deuce.

Jeu de paume:

As mentioned earlier, this is the name of the original game that is still played as real tennis in a special olde worlde court. There are still forty-seven such courts dotted around the world. It is thought by some that the scoring related to measurements on the court. The court measures 90 feet, each player having 45 feet on his side of the net. It is said that originally the server moved forward 15 feet if he won a point, then 30 feet, and then 10 more feet.

King Charles X of France died in 1316 after a strenuous game of *jeu de paume*.

King Henry VIII of England was a keen tennis player and had a court built at Hampton Court in 1528. Legend says that he was playing tennis there when he heard of the execution of Anne Boleyn.

CRICKET

Cricket is a bat-and-ball team game played by two sides of eleven men on a field between two wickets. The wickets are made of three stumps topped by two pieces of wood called bails. One team bats to accumulate as many runs as possible, while the other bowls and fields to get the batting side out.

The game is probably many centuries old, possibly even a Norman game, but the first reference is to a game of *creckett* in 1598. The origin of the name is thought to be from the old English 'crick', for staff or crutch.

The game is played in 'innings'. This is the time each team is allowed to score their runs. 'Overs' meaning six balls from a bowler are bowled from one end, then another bowler bowls from the other end at the other batsman. Up until 1889 there were four balls per over, but this was increased to five until 1900, when it became six.

There are two types of cricket, each with its own set of rules: *one-day cricket*, where each team only has one innings and it lasts up until the fiftieth over, and *test cricket*, where the teams each have two innings to score their runs. There is no limit to how long an innings can last. It could go on for five days.

Sir Jack Hobbs (1882–1963) was the first English cricketer to be knighted.

The Ashes myth

The Ashes are played every two years between England and Australia, since they are the two oldest test nations. They play for a trophy reputedly containing the ashes of a bail from a test match held at the Oval in 1882, when Australia beat England on their home turf for the first time. A mock obituary was printed in the *Sporting Times*, in which it was said that English cricket had died and that the body would be cremated and the ashes taken to Australia. This caught the public imagination and the next test match in Australia was heralded as an expedition to regain the Ashes. A small terracotta urn was presented to the England captain by a group of Melbourne women, containing ashes that may have been a bail or a lady's veil, but no one knows!

Although the Ashes are played for, it is not actually a trophy. It was regarded as a personal gift to the captain, the Honourable Ivo Bligh, and it was kept at his home until he died in 1927. His wife then bequeathed the urn to the Marylebone Cricket Club (MCC) at Lord's, where it remains to this day. A facsimile is often seen being presented, and a Waterford Glass crystal trophy is given to the winning team.

GOLF

Golf is a club-and-ball game played over varied terrain on a course consisting of eighteen holes. Each 'hole' consists of the ground between a tee where the ball is driven off and a green, a closely mown area where a hole is indicated by a flag. Various hazards have to be avoided or played from, such as bunkers, streams or ponds. The rules are surprisingly complex and there are various penalties.

The origin of golf is obscure, and there are various theories. The difficulty is that there are many games which involved striking a ball as far as possible with a club of some sort. The Romans played a game called *paganica* with a ball stuffed with feathers and a club. The Dutch played a game that may have been transported to the east coast of Scotland, where it was transformed into a game played across seaside 'links' terrain. Or it may genuinely be a Scottish invention. We will probably never know.

A hazardous game

King James II of Scotland banned the game of 'gowff' because it was interfering with the practice of archery, which was necessary for the defence of the realm. Indeed, in 1593 two golfers were imprisoned in Edinburgh because they played golf on the Leith links every Sabbath day instead of going to church to listen to a sermon.

Each hole has a designated par, which is usually 4. This means that you should get the ball into the hole from the tee in four shots. That is usually a drive, an iron shot to the green and two putts. Short holes have a par 3 and long holes a par 5.

Golf has a handicap system whereby anyone of any standard can play against an opponent and have a competitive game. A scratch player has a 0 handicap, whereas an 18 handicapper is given eighteen shots when he plays. A scratch player would have to play to par for the whole round and the eighteen handicapper would receive one stroke on each hole, so could take one over par on each hole. If two such players played together like this they would draw.

There are four major tournaments in the men's Professional Golf Association (PGA) tour. These are, in order of play throughout the year: The Masters, always played at Augusta, Georgia, in the USA; the Open, always played on a British seaside 'links' course; the US Open, played on an American course; and the PGA, also played on an American course.

In addition, there is a biennial tournament between the male professional golfers of America and the male professional golfers of Britain and Europe. This is the Ryder Cup, named after a seed merchant, Sam Ryder, from St Albans.

To be stymied

In the old days golf was played against a player, rather than against the card of the course. It was quite legitimate to put your ball between the hole and your opponent's ball. If he hit your ball he incurred a penalty. This was called a stymie. Players could 'loft a stymie,' which meant chip the ball over the other into the hole. It did not do a lot for the greens, so the rule was changed and players have to mark the spot where their ball is on the green so that the opponent can play over.

BOXING

Boxing is one of the sports included in the original Olympics in ancient Greece. Men in virtually every culture throughout history have fought with their fists and in many societies it was common to gamble on the outcome of such bare-knuckle fights.

The Marquis of Queensbury rules were formulated in 1858 and elevated pugilism into the 'noble art of boxing'. Up until then fights were barbaric affairs, which were effectively fought bare-fisted until one of the fighters was beaten into submission or knocked out. Some fights would go on for over a hundred rounds and fighters could be maimed. The Marquis of Queensberry Rules ensured that gloves were worn, that rounds were of 3 minutes each, that a bout should be fought in a 24-foot ring and that if a man was kneeling he could not be struck, and that a count of 10 when a man was down would indicate a knockout.

The Marquis of Queensberry did not draw up the rules; he merely allowed his name to be associated with them. A sports journalist called John Chambers actually thought them up. They were a great advance and were used until 1929, when they were updated. Queensberry is also famous because his son, Lord Alfred Douglas, had a homosexual affair with Oscar Wilde. Wilde sued Queensberry for libel, but lost the action and was sentenced to two years' hard labour in Reading jail.

Several weight divisions were established in 1920, but in professional boxing there are now seventeen. Mini-flyweight is the lightest, for fighters up to a weight of 105 lbs, and heavyweight is the heaviest, with a lower limit of 190 lbs and no upper limit.

There are four professional boxing organisations, each of which recognises world champions. These are the World Boxing Organisation (WBO); the World Boxing Council (WBC); the World Boxing Association (WBA); and the International Boxing Federation (IBF). For a boxer to claim to be the undisputed world champion at any weight level he has to be recognised by all of these organisations.

OTHER SPORTING TRIVIA

It is worth having a few odd facts that you can drop into chats at the pub or if you are invited to a clubhouse:

Toxophily: love of archery.

Leotard: a close-fitting costume named after Jules Leotard (1830–70), who also invented the flying trapeze.

The *blazer*: a sporting jacket was first worn by the Cricket Union of Mexico.

Fencing: there are three types of sword used: the foil, a thin, stabbing sword in which hits are scored on the trunk; the épée, a slightly larger duelling-type sword in which hits are scored on the entire body; and the sabre, a slashing sword such as used to be used by cavalrymen on horseback, in which hits are scored anywhere from the waist up.

Chess: an intellectual board game played by two people on a sixty-four-square playing board. It is representative of two armies and is fought either until one king is taken (checkmate) or until a draw is agreed (stalemate). In 1997 a computer called Deep Blue did the unimaginable and beat the reigning world champion Gary Kasparov.

20

A LITTLE LATIN

aut insanit homo, aut versus facit
(The fellow is either mad or he is composing verses)

Horace

Latin is supposed to be a dead language. Strange that, because it just won't lie down, but keeps popping up when you least expect it to. The truth is that this ancient Indo-European language is everywhere. You see snatches of it on old buildings, on mottos and it is actually in an awful lot of common speech. We just take it for granted. Of course, no one really speaks it these days except for the odd Latin teacher, which is why knowing the odd word or phrase can liven up a conversation and elicit awe in your fellow conversationalists.

Now I have a confession to make. Although I have written a book on doctors' Latin, I am neither a linguist nor a Latin scholar. I am a humble medical practitioner and it is through my years of medical practice that I have picked up a fair bit of both Latin and Greek. You see, about 90 per cent of medical terms are derived from these classic languages. Most anatomical terms and the scientific names of most micro-organisms are of Latin origin, whereas many pathological and medical terms come from Greek. The Greek terms reflect the knowledge and skills of the early classical Greek physicians, while the Latin terminology comes both from antiquity and from the Renaissance, when Latin became the language of science and medicine.

When we use the word 'Latin' we actually use a generic word encompassing several types of Latin. Classical Latin is the language of the educated people of Rome, the Latin of the great prose writers, Livy, Tacitus and Cicero, and of the great poets, Horace, Virgil and Ovid. Late Latin is the language of the Church and New Latin is the written language of science, as it was written in the days of the Renaissance. And since it is a 'dead' and therefore unchanging language, it is still the language used in scientific nomenclature.

Until very recently, Latin was commonly used by the legal profession, but that is dying out now (the Latin, not the legal profession, which is of course blossoming and showing signs of excellent health and wealth). Nonetheless, a few legal Latin phrases and words coolly dropped into conversation can make you shine.

It's obviously beyond the scope of a single chapter to teach you Latin, but you can pick up enough here to start using it. You may even be so smitten with it that you itch to start mugging up on Latin verbs.

ROMAN NUMERALS

This is a good place to start. You see dates on lots of ancient monuments and it makes sense to know just how old they are. And it is not that difficult. Just memorise these letters and numbers:

I	=	1
V	=	5
X	=	10
L	=	50
C	=	100
D	=	500
M	=	1000

When one, two or three Is are placed together, they make 1, 2 and 3 respectively.

When two Roman numerals are written next to each other you subtract the smaller from the larger, if it is on the left of the larger number. Thus IV means 1 to be subtracted from 5, making 4. And IX means 1 is to be subtracted from 10, making 9. If the smaller number is on the right of the larger number, then you add it. Thus VIII means 3 is added to 5 to make 8.

It is that simple. So, the year 1952 would be written MCMLII, the year 1998 would be written MCMXCVIII and the year 2010 would be written MMX.

COMMON GREETINGS

These can be useful little ice-breakers:

salve: this is used to say hello. It means 'greetings'. You only use it when talking to one person, since it is singular.

salvete: this is the word you use when greeting or saying goodbye to two or more folk.

vale: this means farewell, when you take your leave of one person.

valete: this is farewell to several people.

vale, lacerate: means 'see you later.'

pax tecum: this means 'peace be with you', when addressing one person.

pax vobiscum: is 'peace be with you', when addressing several folk.

THE CLASSICAL WRITERS

You may never feel inclined to read the words of these great writers, but knowing who they were may help you one day in a pub quiz, or at a dinner party.

The prose writers

Livy: Titus Livius (*c.* 64 BC – AD 17) was born in Patavium (modern-day Padua) in north-eastern Italy. He was one of the three great Roman historians. He wrote a monumental history of Rome from its founding in 753 BC, entitled *Ab Urbe Condita* ('From the Founding of the City' – Roman dates started with 1 AUC – *ab urbe condita*). Written in chronological order with a narrative style, it became a classic in his own lifetime and acted as a blueprint for historical texts down to the eighteenth century.

Tacitus: Gaius Cornelius Tacitus (AD 56–117), Roman orator, lawyer and senator, is considered one of antiquity's greatest historians. His major works, the *Annales* (Annals) and *Historiae* (Histories), covered the history of the Roman Empire's first century, from the accession of the Emperor Tiberius to the death of Domitian.

Cicero: Marcus Tullius Cicero (106?–43 BC) was an orator, lawyer, politician and statesman who lived in the tumultuous period that saw the decline and fall of the Roman Republic. At the end of his life he was declared an enemy of the state and forced to flee. He was caught and decapitated by his pursuers on 7 December 43 BC. His head and hands were displayed on the Rostra in the *Forum Romanum*. According to Plutarch, the wife of one of his enemies pulled out his tongue, repeatedly stabbing it with a hatpin, taking a final revenge against Cicero's power of speech.

The poets

Horace: Quintus Horatius Flaccus (65–8 BC) was a Latin poet famous for his four books of odes (known in Latin as *Carmina*), which contain over 100 individual poems. In one of these odes

Horace bragged that his poetry would live as long as Vestal Virgins climbed the Capitoline Hill in Rome. Interestingly, there are no longer any Vestal Virgins in modern Rome, but Horace's odes are still going strong!' Many of his Latin phrases are still in use today, such as '*carpe diem*,' ('seize the day').

Ovid: Publius Ovidius Naso (43 BC– AD 17) was a Roman poet who wrote on topics of love, abandoned women and mythology. His greatest work, the *Metamorphoses*, enjoyed huge popularity. He was banished to Tomis by the Black Sea by the Emperor Augustus, reportedly because Augustus was offended by his work *Ars Amatoria*, although it is more likely that it was because of an affair he had with a relative of the emperor. He died in exile.

Virgil: Publius Vergilius Maro (70–19 BC) was a Latin poet who wrote the *Eclogues*, the *Georgics* and the *Aeneid*. The *Aeneid*, an epic poem of twelve books, was deservingly considered to be the Roman Empire's national epic.

MEDICAL LATIN

You may have wondered about some of the strange writing and abbreviations that you see on a prescription from your doctor. They are all Latin instructions for the pharmacist to make up:

Prescription: the very word is from the Latin – *prae*, meaning before, and *scribere*, meaning to write.
Rx: short for *recipe*, which means 'take thou'.
Ad libitum: meaning 'take freely' or 'as necessary'.
B.i.d.: short for *bis in die*, meaning 'take twice daily'.
T.i.d.: short for *ter in die*, meaning 'take three times a day'.
Q.i.d.: short for *quater in die*, meaning 'take four times a day'.
Q.d.: short for *quaque die*, meaning 'take once each day'. Understandably, this is similar to q.i.d, so because of the risk of confusion, q.d. is rarely used these days.
P.r.n.: short for *pro re nata*, meaning 'take as needed'.

Some interesting little medical facts and a few phrases

You can drop these into conversations if you feel it is appropriate:

Abdomen: this is literally 'the cavity that hides the entrails' – from *abdere*, to hide and *omentum*, entrails.

ab imo pectore: meaning, 'from the bottom of the heart', or the bottom of the chest; it means to speak sincerely, and was attributed to Julius Caesar.

ab incunabulis: meaning 'from cradle to grave'.

cacoethes loquendi: meaning 'compulsive talking' – from the Greek *kakoethes*, meaning bad habit, and the Latin *loqui*, to speak.

cacoethes scribendi: meaning 'compulsive writing' – from the Greek *kakoethes*, meaning bad habit, and the Latin *scribere*, to write.

Testis: this, as I am sure you know, is the name for the male genital organ, of which there are two, contained in a scrotum. The word scrotum means 'leather pouch', such as Romans used to keep coins. The scrotum's precious contents, the testes, were also highly valuable to the Romans, since in Roman days only a man could 'testify' or bear witness in court. The word testis, therefore, was proof of being a man (women and eunuchs being excluded from testifying). And that is the origin of the term. The male organs are man's 'little witness', which is what it means.

Cadaver: this is the scientific word for a dead human being, as opposed to the more lurid word of corpse. Medical students study anatomy by dissection of a cadaver. This is one of the ways that people generously help when they leave their body to science. Organs and other tissues (such as corneas) may be removed from a cadaver and used for transplantation into live patients, if the deceased has expressed a wish to leave their body parts for organ donation.

Vagina: this is the female front passage that has the uterus or womb at its apex – from the Latin word *vagina*, meaning sheath. In Roman days a *gladius*, the name for a short sword, was a euphemism for a penis.

vaginae synoviales: these have nothing whatever to do with the female vagina, but are the lubricating sheaths that surround some of the tendons of the hands and feet.

valetudinarian: this means a sickly or weak person, who is always concerned about their health; a hypochondriac; from *valetudinarius*, itself from *valetudo*, state of health.

valetudinarium: this means a (Roman) hospital.

I testify!

LEGAL LATIN

These may be easier to work into conversations than medical Latin names and phrases:

in flagrante delicto: 'while the crime is blazing'; effectively, caught red-handed or caught in the act.

compos mentis: 'of sound mind.'

corpus delicti: 'the body of the crime.' At one time it meant the body in a murder, but latterly it referred to the main evidence in a case.

bona fide: 'in good faith.'

lex parsimoniae: the law of parsimony, meaning succinctness.

mea culpa: 'I am to blame.'

mea judice: 'I am the judge.'

ignorantia legis neminem excusat: 'ignorance of the law is no excuse.'

modus operandi: 'manner of working', the way it is done.

modus vivendi: 'the way of life', or lifestyle.

rigor mortis: 'the rigidness or stiffness of death.'

tabula rasa: 'a blank slate'. The Romans used to write on wax tablets, which were easy to erase. Literally, *tabula rasa* means a scraped (clean) slate.

SOME GENERAL PHRASES

These are all quite famous, so you may consider committing some to memory:

ab ovo usque ad mala: 'from start to finish.'

acta est fibula: 'it's all over.'

ad infinitum: 'without end.'

ad nauseum: 'to the point of sickness.'

alea iacta est: 'the die is cast.' This is attributed to Julius Caesar, when about to cross the Rubicon.

alter ego: closest friend. Literally, it is 'another I'.

ars longa, vita brevis: 'art is long, but life is short.' It is an abbreviated snippet from Hippocrates' famous first aphorism about medicine.

carpe diem: 'seize the day.'

caveat emptor: 'let the buyer beware.'

causa sine qua none: 'a necessary condition.'

consensus facit legem: 'consent makes law.'

deus ex machine: this literally means 'a god out of the machine'. It effectively means an unlikely but welcome happening.

et tu, Brute?: a famous quotation from *Julius Caesar* by William Shakespeare. It means 'you also, Brutus?' Effectively, 'so you are in it as well?'

gaudeamus igitur: 'let us rejoice.' Many people will recall this from student days.

hodie mihi, cras tibi: 'today me, tomorrow you.'

nil carborandum: 'don't let them grind you down.' This is a made-up piece of Latin, but it sounds good.

nil desperandum: 'never say die.'

oleo tranquillior: 'smoother than oil.'

pecunia obedient omnia: 'all things yield to money.' You can, if you wish, mix this and the one above!

quo vadis: 'who goes there?'

q.v. or *quod vide*: 'which see.' You use it in reference to something else in a text.

in vino veritas: 'in wine, the truth.'

And I leave you with the gladiator's salute to the emperor:

nos morituri te salutamus: 'we who are about to die salute you.'

21

COOKING OR CUISINE

Edible, adjective: Good to eat, and wholesome to digest, as a worm to a toad, a toad to a snake, a snake to a pig, a pig to a man, and a man to a worm.

Ambrose Bierce (1842–1913)
Journalist and writer

Exactly when mankind started cooking food is not known, although it is likely that it was soon after he had discovered fire. Depending upon your historical sources, that is sometime between 1.4 million and 500,000 years BC.

The chemistry of cooking is very interesting, and if you want to appear knowledgeable at the dining table then it is worth knowing about this reaction.

THE MAILLARD REACTION

You cannot have failed to notice that when many foods are cooked they turn brown or go golden. Meat, bread and all the things that you toast and grill change colour. It is not a burning process that does it, it is a specific chemical reaction called the Maillard reaction.

The Maillard reaction was first described by Louise-Camille Maillard in 1912, when he was trying to synthesise proteins. What he described is actually a series of chemical reactions that take place between sugars and the amino acids that make up some proteins. It happens when molecules containing an amine group ($-NH_2$), typically an amino acid, meets a sugar molecule like glucose in the presence of heat. A water molecule is then eliminated, thereby forming a compound called a Schiff base. This is rapidly changed into another compound, called an Amadori product. This then reacts with other molecules to produce a variety of ring-like or cyclical aromatic molecules. These produce the tantalising smell and flavour of cooked food.

It is an extremely complex process that may produce 200 or 300 of these aromatic chemicals during the cooking process. And that is where the skill of cooking comes in, when one knows how to cook the food to produce the right aromas and flavours.

The Maillard reaction only takes place at high temperatures, however. That is why cooks use fats or oils to baste food or to fry them in. When you do that you attain temperatures well above 100° C. That is what you need to produce a Maillard reaction. If you don't hit that temperature, you will not brown the meat or the food and you will not produce the range of aromatic compounds. That is why boiling food does not brown it.

Microwaves

In the 1940s Percy Spencer, a self-taught engineer, was working for a company building magnetrons for radar equipment. While working with an active machine he noticed that a peanut chocolate bar in his pocket had melted. Realising that microwaves from the machine must have been responsible he experimented and found that the microwaves could cook food. The first food he cooked was popcorn and the second was an egg, which exploded. In 1945 his company took out a patent for the microwave cooking process and in 1947 the first microwave oven was produced.

The microwave will not produce a Maillard reaction, because it works by causing the water in the food to boil. It will only boil at 100° C, which is too low to induce the Maillard reaction. Hence, microwavable food will not be crisp and will not smell as good or turn a beautiful golden brown.

VINEGAR

This really is one of the most useful household ingredients. We know that most ancient cultures used vinegar. A jar found in the Middle East dating back to 8,000 BC was used to contain vinegar, and Egyptian papyri from 3,000 BC tell of its use as an antiseptic in medicine as well as something that helps to flavour food. Indeed, according to legend, Queen Cleopatra dissolved pearls in vinegar to prove that she could consume a fortune in a single meal. Remember that one the next time you are tucking into your fish and chips. The Babylonians fermented date palm juice to produce vinegar to use as a preservative agent, which would have been of inestimable value in those hot, hazy days when food would go off so quickly. And the Chinese were also using it as long ago as 2,000 BC.

Salad dressings or vinaigrettes are a good example of the use of vinegar. A vinaigrette is an emulsion. That means it is a mixture of two immiscible or unblendable liquids which have been mixed together so well that one is dispersed in the other as tiny globules. To make a vinaigrette dressing for a salad you mix vinegar with oil, salt, pepper and a pinch of mustard. The mustard is the emulsifying agent that will turn the vinegar and oil into an emulsion. It is as simple as that.

THE STRANGE CASE OF ASPARAGUS

If you have ever eaten asparagus at a meal it is almost inevitable that someone will bring up the subject of the effect asparagus has

How asparagus can kill a first date

on the urine. If you are not aware of this, it makes the urine smell strange – rather like rotten or boiled cabbage. But the thing is that only about 50 per cent of people notice this effect. It really is an intriguing little mystery.

In fact, it has been known about for a long time. An eighteenth-century physician to the French royal family wrote a treatise about various types of food, and commented that when asparagus is eaten to excess it 'causes a filthy and disagreeable smell in the urine.'

Asparagus belongs to the lily family, along with garlic, onions and leeks. It was first cultivated about 2,500 years ago in Greece, and the name comes from the Greek word meaning stalk or shoot. The Greeks believed that it had important medicinal qualities, being of value in toothache and stopping bees and insects from stinging.

Asparagus contains a substance called *mercaptan* (which is also present in rotten eggs, onions and garlic), which is broken down by the digestive tract into a number of sulphur-containing by-products. The main one, *methyl mercaptan*, is responsible for the smell. It will be passed in the urine 15 to 30 minutes after eating a couple of asparagus stalks.

There have been several research studies done on this curious phenomenon. Most trials have found that about 50 per cent of people can smell this boiled cabbage odour in their urine, and 50 per cent cannot. This has caused debate among scientists as to whether it was due to the presence or absence of a particular enzyme that breaks down mercaptan.

But another research trial has found that when they analysed the urine of everyone in a study, it seemed that most people did actually produce the substance methyl mercaptan, but that only 50 per cent could smell it. Interestingly, those who could smell it in their own urine could also smell it in the urine samples of other people, even in those who could not smell it themselves. Thus, the mystery has been solved. There is a genetic inheritable pattern, but it is the ability to detect the smell of methyl mercaptan that is actually genetically determined.

You can suggest that you try an experiment after the meal – if you dare!

SOME FAMOUS CHEFS

It is always good to drop a few names into the conversation:

Apicius was a Roman gourmand who lived at the time of the Emperor Tiberius in the first century AD. He is sometimes associated with a ten-volume text on cooking called the *Cookery Book of Apicius*, but it was written three centuries after him.

Alexandre Dumas, the author of *The Three Musketeers*, *The Count of Monte Cristo* and *The Black Tulip*, was a gourmand and chef. He wrote *Grand dictionnaire de cuisine* (*Great Dictionary of Cuisine*), which was published posthumously in 1873. If you want to know about decadent cuisine, read this.

Antoine Beauvilliers (1754–1817) opened a restaurant in Paris in 1783 called the Grande Taverne just before the French Revolution of 1789. It stayed open during the whole Reign of Terror and he wrote a major text called *L'art de cuisiner*.

Marthe Distell was a journalist who launched a cooking magazine called *La Cuisinière Cordon Bleu*, which in 1895 became the School of Cordon Bleu Cuisine. Professional chefs taught the highest standard of cuisine. The school closed during the Second World War, but afterwards it was bought and developed so that there are now around thirty cordon bleu schools in seventeen countries.

AFTERWORD

In *The Hound of the Baskervilles*, the famous novel by Sir Arthur Conan Doyle, Dr Watson comes to a series of totally erroneous deductions about the ownership of a gentleman's cane that had been left in their rooms. Before enlightening him, Sherlock Holmes remarks:

> Really, Watson, you excel yourself ... Some people without possessing genius have a remarkable power of stimulating it. I confess, my dear fellow, that I am very much in your debt.

It is my fervent hope that within the pages of this modest little book you may have found one or two points of interest which have stimulated the genius within you. And if they haven't exactly done that, then I trust that you will at least have picked up a few rules of thumb to help you shine.

Visit our website and discover thousands of other
History Press books.

www.thehistorypress.co.uk

HANDBALL: A COMPLETE GUIDE

An incident from the French National League match
R. A. L. Bellére (Pau) v. R. S. Marca (Toulouse)

HANDBALL
A Complete Guide

B. J. ROWLAND

Chairman and Staff Coach, The British Handball Association.
Head of the Physical Education Department, The Holt
Comprehensive School, Liverpool.

Illustrated by Ronald Wright

FABER & FABER London

First published in 1970
by Faber and Faber Limited
24 Russell Square London WC1
Printed in Great Britain by
Latimer Trend & Co Ltd Plymouth
All rights reserved

ISBN 0 571 09373 6

This book is dedicated to
WOLF SCHNEGGENBURGER
of the West German Handball Federation for his
valuable help and technical assistance to
British Handball. His constant enthusiasm
for handball did much to help the formation
of the British Handball Association

FOREWORD

It has been both a pleasure and an honour to have been asked to write a foreword to this first book on handball to be published in Great Britain. I have been a member of the International Handball Federation since its formation in 1946 and it gives me great pleasure to witness handball gaining in popularity throughout the world, particularly in the English-speaking countries.

This excellent and much needed publication will help to promote even further the growth of this exciting game which can be played by all irrespective of ability.

Carl Filip Borgh, *Stockholm, May 1969*

PREFACE

This is the first book to be written on handball in this country. It is not intended to be a purely technical book dealing solely with the tactical aspects of the game. It has been my intention to make it of use to as many people as possible: the beginner, finding out about the game for the first time, the teacher, the coach and the various officials of the game. I have tried to show the attributes of this great sport as simply as possible, showing how it can be successfully introduced to beginners, and at the same time how it can be developed to a relatively high degree of skill.

B. J. Rowland, *Liverpool, 1970.*

ACKNOWLEDGEMENTS

I would like to thank the following people whose efforts have made the writing of this book possible.

Jean Guy Tetin of the French Handball Federation for his help and advice in the chapter on the tactics of the game.
M. Tetin Snr. and the R.A.L. Bellére Handball Club, Pau, for their help in procuring photographs for the book.
Hanns Apfel for providing five of the photographs.
Carl Filip Borgh, of the Swedish Handball Federation for kindly agreeing to write a foreword for the book.
Ken Watson of the British Handball Association for casting his critical eye over the later chapters and giving his approval.
Susan Newall of Deyes Lane School, Maghull, for her help in the chapter on handball for schools.
Doreen Schlechte, my colleague at Holt School, and the two senior girls who assisted her in the mammoth task of typing out the manuscript.
The boys of The Cardinal's Handball Club, Liverpool, for patiently posing for photographs, and Gerrard Barrow for his patience with the players whilst he took the photographs.
Ronald Wright for his excellent illustrations.
Sarah Gleadell of Faber and Faber for her help and encouragement.
    And last, but certainly not least, my wife Christine, an established international player in her own right, for her wonderful patience and practical help. To all these people I offer my most grateful thanks.

CONTENTS

ILLUSTRATIONS

DIAGRAMS

INTRODUCTION

The game of handball in its modern form can truthfully be described as a product of the twentieth century although if we read Carl Diem's *Universal History of Sport*, we will soon discover that some form of the game has been played since antiquity. The ancient Greeks had their version of handball in which a ball the size of an apple was thrown from hand to hand. Homer describes this game in the Odyssey in the following words:

'And Alkinoös called upon bold Halios alone/ To dance with Laodamas, for none dare venture with them./They took at once in their hands the lovely ball/ Which Polybus with cunning art had woven from purple wool./One cast this up to heaven to reach the sparkling clouds/ Bent hard back; the other then sprang high up in the air/ And caught it nimbly, ere his foot touched the ground again./And after they had tried to toss the ball on high I danced light as air upon the all nourishing earth/ In position often changed.'

During the Middle Ages also a form of handball was very popular amongst the Knights of Honour. The rules of this game called for a ball, often adorned with ribbons, to be thrown from hand to hand. This game was often referred to by the troubadours as the first game of spring.

Today there are two main forms of the game played throughout the world—eleven-a-side handball and handball for seven. In Britain there is a third form, handball for five. Before the Second World War eleven-a-side handball was the only competitive form of the game played. This game was played outdoors on a pitch of dimensions similar to those of a soccer pitch by two teams of eleven players.

After the war, however, a new form of the game was developed in Northern Europe which could be played indoors. This form of the game, which was played by teams of seven players and became known as handball for seven, spread rapidly and today it is the main form of the game that is played throughout the world. The reasons for the rapid progress of seven-a-side handball are self-evident. The game could be played irrespective of climatic conditions and it dispensed with the large playing area required for eleven-a-side handball. In addition to this, indoor handball has become, next to ice hockey, the fastest team game in the world.

Eleven-a-side handball is still played today, mainly in Central Europe. Elsewhere, with the exception of North America, it does not have a very big following.

Seven-a-side handball is the most popular form of the game played in Britain. However, many of our clubs and schools do not possess a large enough surface area indoors to play the game during the winter months and so were restricted to playing handball during the summer. The British Handball Association, the governing body for the sport in this country, was keenly aware of this fact and, after much careful thinking, developed handball for five. This version of the game takes into consideration the limited facilities available and, without detracting from the larger version of the game, has enabled clubs and schools in this country to play handball all year round. The rules for five-a-side are exactly the same as for seven-a-side except for the court dimensions, the rule governing the size of the team and the number of substitutes allowed.

Handball for seven is still, however, the main form of the game and this book has been written specifically with that form in mind. Most of what is said is also applicable to the smaller game, with the exception of the chapter on tactics, and it should be remembered, when reading the section on the rules of the game, that certain of the rules must be altered to suit the smaller game. However, the basic skills and the methods described in the chapter on introducing handball to beginners are applicable to both forms of the game.

The idea of handball is clear and the game itself is elegant and varied, combining all the advantages of a team sport. As its name suggests, hands play the most important role. That the hands are the deftest members of the body helps to explain the growing popularity of the game. When played at its highest level it is very demanding of its players. However, it is basically a very simple game that can be played and enjoyed by all, whatever their level of ability.

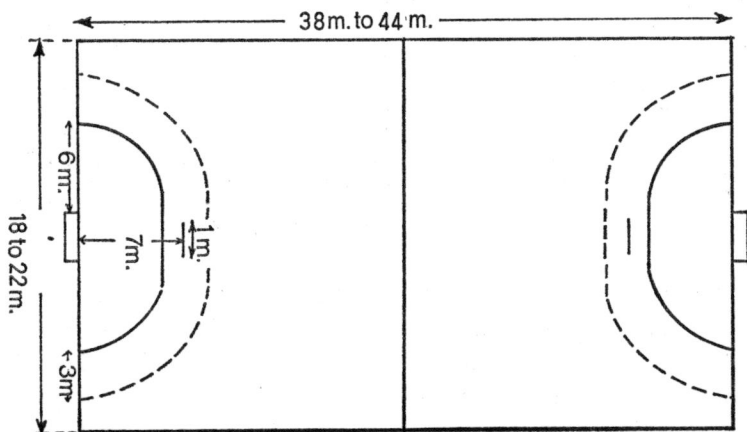

FIG. 1. The playing court

The aim of the game is to score goals by throwing the ball into the opponent's goal. The game is started by means of a throw off from the centre of the court after the referee has blown his whistle. The ball is then passed from player to player until a shot at goal has been made. Whilst the ball is in the possession of the attacking team, the defending team should line up in a defensive position in front of their goal until a goal has been scored or they come into possession of the ball. When possession has been obtained, they then become the attacking force and it is the turn of the other team to be on the defensive. Attack and defence, these are the most important aspects of the game; there is very little need or opportunity for play in the centre of the court.

At the beginning of the game the players of both teams line up as indicated in Fig. 2. The team who are in possession of the ball should have their forward players standing close to the centre line but in their own half of the court and the opposing

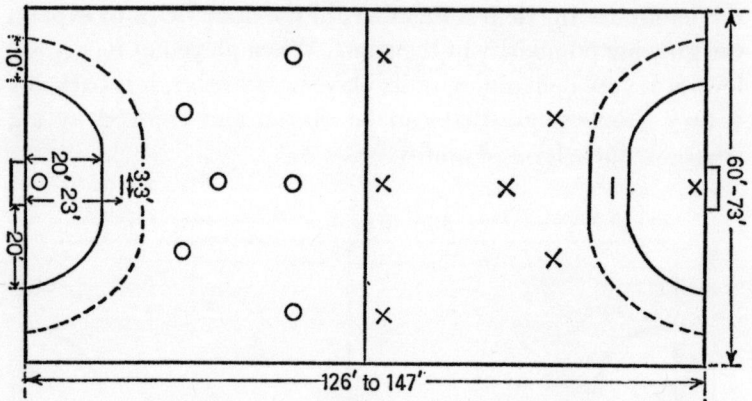

FIG. 2. Position of players at start of game

team players must be at least three metres (ten feet) away from the centre line. Although there are only seven players on court at any one time, a complete team consists of twelve players, five of whom are substitutes.

Unlike a lot of other sports where substitution of players is allowed, the rule governing substitution in the game is not a complicated one. Five substitutes are allowed in each team and substitution may take place at any stage of the game. There is no rule as to which player may substitute for another, though each substitution must be brought to the notice of the referee before it takes place. There is, however, a very strict rule regarding the substitution of the goalkeeper. One of the five substitutes must be a goalkeeper and he is not allowed to take up his position in the goal until the man he is substituting for has left the goal area. It is permitted for a court player to take the place of the goalkeeper but the goalkeeper is not allowed to substitute for a court player.

After each goal, the ball should be returned to the centre of the court where the team conceding the goal should restart the game with a throw off, both teams lining up in the manner described previously.

There has, in recent years, been growing interest and concern in this country, particularly in secondary schools, in the work of preparing young people to be able to spend their leisure time wisely. As the working day grows shorter the time for leisure increases and it is important that people are educated to use this time in a beneficial manner. In our schools preparation for this is now growing, particularly in the sphere of physical education. Activities hitherto undreamed of are beginning to appear in the more enlightened physical education programme. Physical educationists are working very hard indeed to make this country a nation of players rather than a nation of watchers. Obviously, it would be foolish to think of every individual as a potential sports player—there are many who prefer some other form of relaxation. However, I am of the opinion that the physical educationist should endeavour to reach as many individuals as he possibly can in some way or another.

Handball, I feel, can prove of immense value in this effort to provide leisure-time pursuits. Although, as we have seen, at is highest level it is the fastest team game played with a ball, it must be remembered that for every individual playing the game at this level there are many more who play for sheer enjoyment and relaxation. Compared with many other sports, handball is a 'natural game'. It requires only natural, innate skills to play. Many of the sports that are played in our schools today require specific skills which, although depending to a certain amount on natural ability, nevertheless have to be taught. In some cases, the specific skills are taught to the detriment of the natural ability of the player.

Handball requires of its players only natural ability. It requires that the performer is able to run, jump, throw and catch, all natural skills. In return it offers the players enjoyment and a feeling of achievement from having participated and contributed.

However, if the campaign to educate our future citizens to spend their leisure time wisely is to succeed it must not be left to the teacher alone. The teacher can play his part and this, if we look around, is certainly being done in excellent fashion. There must be help from the authorities that are expecting schools to do this work. They must be prepared to help by providing facilities that will be required and by sponsoring the sporting bodies of this country in a concrete way. The young individual, when leaving school, must not feel that all the preparation made in school was a waste of time because there is nowhere for him to carry on the activity he has chosen. There is a feeling of frustration amongst physical educationists over this problem of the lack of facilities and it is because of this that the country has lost the services of some potentially great sportsmen.

Handball, we have said, is a simple game, but it has another great advantage in that it is an inexpensive game, requires very little equipment and can easily be played with whatever facilities are available. There is only one basic necessity for a game of handball to be got under way and that is a ball. The only other equipment used are the goals and these can, if it is impossible to obtain the correct form, be chalked on to a wall or improvised in other ways. There are facilities in every town for the playing of handball out of doors. This is particularly so in the summer when the pitches which are used for soccer in winter are lying idle.

The game of handball can be useful in the youth club as well. Quite a lot of modern youth clubs have the facilities for the game to be played and if the demand is there they should endeavour to introduce the game into their programme of activities. I am sure they will find that there will soon be an enthusiastic response from other members once they have been introduced to the game. This certainly has been my experience with handball. Once it has been introduced in a proper way, its success at any level has been assured, such is the appeal of the game.

In Britain, handball still has a long way to go; it is still an emerging sport. However, there is no doubt in my mind that it is in time going to become a very popular sport. More and more teachers are showing interest and asking for more and more information. Once the development in the schools progresses, there will be a steady stream of players coming into handball and, as a result, there will be continuous development at the club level of the game.

Handball has again been included in the Olympic Games for 1972, in Munich, and this should do much to popularize the game in this country when it will be seen through the medium of television in many homes.

1 - THE HISTORY AND DEVELOPMENT OF HANDBALL

The game of handball that we know today originated in Germany at the end of the nineteenth century, when it was introduced to the world by a gymnastics master, Konrad Koch. However, the development of the game since its introduction has not been continuous. After it had been introduced by Koch, little was heard of the game until 1904, when it began to develop in Europe, with the rules of the game based on those of Association Football.

At first, handball was not recognized as a separate sport. It did not have its own governing body and it came under the jurisdiction of the International Amateur Athletic Federation, (I.A.A.F.), the body responsible for the organization of most of the minor sports in Europe at that time.

From 1904, handball developed steadily under the watchful eye of the I.A.A.F. Many more nations began to include handball in their list of sporting activities and international matches became more and more popular. In 1926, to keep pace with the progress of handball and other developing sports, the I.A.A.F. appointed a special committee, representing the countries where handball was played, to look into the possibility of producing a standardized set of rules for the game. The outcome of this was the birth of handball as a separate sport, and the setting up of an independent handball federation was made possible.

In 1928, eleven handball nations met in Amsterdam on the occasion of the Olympic Games and, as a result of this meeting, the International Amateur Handball Federation was formed. It is interesting to note that Avery Brundage, the President of the International Olympic Committee, was a member of the first committee of the new federation. One of the first tasks of

25

the International Amateur Handball Federation at Amsterdam in 1928 was to arrange demonstration matches at the Games. In 1931, just three years after the independence of handball, the sport was included in the programme of the Games by the International Olympic Committee.

The meeting in Amsterdam was attended by representatives from eleven nations and it is interesting to note that by 1934 the membership of the I.A.H.F. had risen to no fewer than twenty-five. Handball had indeed become a world-wide sport, and it was included in the Olympic Games in Berlin in 1936. Two years later, the first world championships were held to mark the tenth anniversary of the International Amateur Handball Federation.

The Second World War created many problems for handball, as indeed it did with many other sports, and very little handball was played. However, after the war, representatives from several handball nations met at an international congress in Copenhagen to endeavour to re-establish the sport. The result of this congress was the dissolution of the I.A.H.F. and the birth of the International Handball Federation, the present ruling body of the sport throughout the world. In 1956, the rules of the game were revised and accepted in their present form, apart from some minor later modifications.

Until the outbreak of the Second World War, there was only one form of handball, that of eleven-a-side, played outdoors on a pitch similar to a soccer pitch. However, after the war, radical changes began to take place. In Northern Europe, a new form of the game was emerging and becoming increasingly popular; this was indoor handball played by teams of seven players. This form of the game was eventually to revolutionize the whole sport. At first, many of the older, more established handball countries did not take the seven-a-side game seriously but, before long, even the die-hards had to admit that seven-a-side handball had become the prevailing form of the game throughout the world.

The new form of the game has done much to increase the world-wide popularity of handball. National coaches began to concentrate on the tactics of the seven-a-side game and the result of the research by these people has led to handball becoming the second fastest team sport in the world. Only ice hockey can be played faster.

The reasons for the rapid rise in popularity of indoor handball are reasonably self-evident. There is no difficulty with weather conditions and the size of playing area is smaller, a point which is important in this country as the need for urban development increases. Although handball for seven is always referred to as indoor handball, it is not limited to the sports hall, and can indeed be played outdoors as well.

The old form of handball, however, is still being played in Central Europe, although it is very much the minor form of the sport today.

In Great Britain, handball has been played to a limited extent for many years, but it was not until the formation of the British Handball Association that its values became widely known. Since the formation of the British Association, the popularity of the game has increased rapidly, particularly in schools and youth clubs, where those in charge of sport have realized how valuable the game can be when it is included in their programme. Many Colleges of Education are including handball in the curriculum, most of them running courses leading to the coaching award of the British Handball Association.

In Britain, while the prevailing form of the game is seven-a-side, during the winter months it was difficult for many schools and clubs to provide the amount of playing surface required for indoor handball to take place. With this in mind, the B.H.A. developed a smaller version of the game played by five players instead of seven and adapted the court measurements to give virtually every school and interested club a chance to play handball all year round. Because of this development, the main form of the game, that of seven-a-side handball, is played mainly during the part of the year that allows outdoor activities.

Organized handball began in Britain in the north-west and it has quickly spread throughout other parts of the country, although the original area has become established as the home of British handball. The headquarters of the Association in

Liverpool have become the nerve centre of the sport and contact with all handball enthusiasts begins here.

The most important milestone in the history of British handball was passed in 1968 when the author and Phil Holden, a member of the Executive Committee, attended the International Congress to apply for membership of the British Association to the International Federation. It was a proud occasion when the speech of application was applauded by the Congress, the first time this had happened, and when all the members of the Congress rose to their feet to show their unanimous approval of our application.

The results of this membership have been manifold. Friendship has been developed between the British Association and those of many other member nations, many of them seeking close ties with Britain through the medium of handball. In March, 1969, the first of these friendships bore fruit when the Italian national handball team came to England to play against the Great Britain team.

Handball is one of the world's great sports, played by over two and a half million people throughout the world. It has been an Olympic Sport since 1936 and it has been included in the programme for the Olympic Games in Munich in 1972.

2 - WHY PLAY HANDBALL?

This is a question I have frequently been asked when talking to people concerned with sport. What, they ask, has handball got to offer that other sports cannot? This is a valid question when one considers the full programme that schools and youth clubs already have. The handball enthusiast must be ready to answer these and other questions when trying to promote his sport.

Two of the most important reasons for playing handball, particularly at the school stage, are that it does not require, initially, a high level of skill and that it makes use of the most basic skills, namely running, jumping, throwing and catching. It is a game that can be played by all, whatever their ability. The rules of the game can be introduced gradually to enable new players to learn the game quickly.

Basically, handball is a simple game and not too technical, a point which hampers some of the games that are played in schools today. It has been found that handball has become very popular in schools for the mentally handicapped, and in some of these schools handball has reached a very high level due to the painstaking work of the teachers coaching the sport. In primary schools, too, the game can be most effective and can be instrumental in developing the basic skills of the individual.

The primary school very often suffers because little money is allowed for promoting sport, and handball is ideal in this sort of situation. The only equipment required to begin the game is a ball, and the only other equipment that will ever be necessary are the goals, although many people get by with chalking goals on walls or improvising in some other way.

Whilst one of the main values of handball is that people of all levels of ability can play the game, and this point alone makes it of great educational value, it is also a game which can be developed to a very high degree. When played to a high level, handball is faster than any other ball game played. It is so fast that the game cannot be played without regular substitution, and it demands a never failing concentration and the capability of adapting oneself to continuously changing situations.

Unlike other games that require use of the hands, body contact is not avoided and the throws of the game are extremely hard and fast. Handball is a hard but fair game.

One of the main aims of the handball coach, particularly in the early stages with young players, is to develop the personal qualities of each player. Physical fitness alone will not suffice, although it is certainly a quality a player must have if he wishes to contribute something to a game of handball. The Italian team coach, Egidio Capra, after the Great Britain v. Italy game in March, 1969, said that the British players were extremely fit and that he thought this was the main attribute of the British team. However, this did not help the British team to win the match. As well as fitness, the handball player will find his self-control, his sense of fairness and his courage often put to the test. He must try to do his best for his team mates and he must realize his dependence on them also if his team is to function properly. He must realize that handball is a fair game and he must be able to win and lose before he can consider himself a true handball player.

3 - INTRODUCING HANDBALL TO BEGINNERS

Handball is a particularly fine game for both boys and girls, men and women. Whatever the ability of the player the satisfaction and enjoyment derived from participation is high. This is a very important attribute; all physical educationists have enjoyment high on their list of priorities.

Enjoyment, however, is not enough. It must be followed by satisfaction. The player must be satisfied that he has attained sufficient skill to be able to contribute something to a game. With most school sports it is difficult to achieve an all-round satisfaction because of the large numbers in an average class and the wide range of ability that is to be found there. Too often the good performer feels that he is being held back because of others who are not quite so good, whilst at the other end of the scale the poorer performer is often conscious of inferiority and therefore does not always give his best.

This difficulty is largely eliminated in handball; the skills of running and jumping, catching and throwing which are basic to the game are natural ones and can be performed by all whatever their level of ability. There is no need for the good performer to be separated from the poorer one; they can work together for their common good, and both can derive pleasure and satisfaction. From this working together a higher degree of skill can be achieved and an interest in both the skill and the game sustained.

It is important when introducing the game to beginners that the correct size ball is used. The official sizes and weights of the ball are 58–60 cm. (23–24 in.) in circumference and 425–475 g. (15–17 oz.) in weight for youths and men, and 54–56 cm. (21–22 in.) and 325–400 g. (11½–14 oz.) for children and women. At first the weight of the ball does not matter quite so much but the circumference is most important. If a ball is used that is too big it will spoil the enjoyment of the game. The performer must be able to hold the ball in one hand to throw it, and this would be impossible with a ball any bigger than the official size. On the other hand, the ball should not be too small or it will fly through the air too quickly and cause the players to spend time wondering which way the ball has gone rather than what they themselves should be doing.

The important thing to remember when dealing with beginners is not to waste too much time teaching the basic skills. The need in the early stages is to stimulate interest and enjoyment and there is no doubt that these will soon be destroyed if the performer is made to learn skills which to him will seem no more than natural. Handball must be introduced to players by allowing them to play a game.

Any game that resembles handball will serve the purpose providing that it introduces the game quickly and does not alter the pattern too much. The coach must not allow himself too much time with players at this stage. He should want to bring them along as quickly as possible to reach a stage where the basic skills can be developed further.

Whatever game the coach may favour as his method of introduction it should resemble the main game as closely as possible. However, the rules should be relaxed a little or there will be too many interruptions in the flow of play and this will prove a burden to the coach in two ways. He will find himself continually having to expain why in his opinion an offence has been committed and, particularly if he is dealing with young people, the interest will wane and a lot of the values to be obtained in the later stages will be lost at the very beginning.

The game of benchball which I describe below is, I have found, a simple and effective way of introducing handball to people who have not played before, and it is useful in that it can be played by the whole of the group concerned irrespective of the numbers involved.

Two benches are placed, one at each end of the playing area, and the group is divided into two equal teams (Fig. 3). Each team appoints a goalkeeper who then takes his place on the

1. The correct way to catch the ball with two hands

2. The correct way to block an opponent

3. Catching a low ball

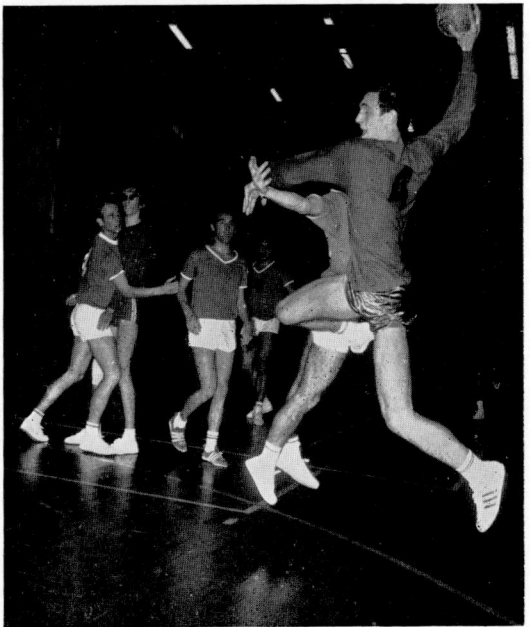

4. The jump shot from inside the goal area line

Photo: Louis Bachoue of 'Sud-Ouest'

opposite bench which his team is facing. By passing the ball quickly amongst themselves the aim is for each team to pass the ball to their goalkeeper who must catch it cleanly for a point to be scored. The team who are not in possession must guard their opponents' goalkeeper to try and gain possession and then start their own attack. The goalkeepers must not be touched or

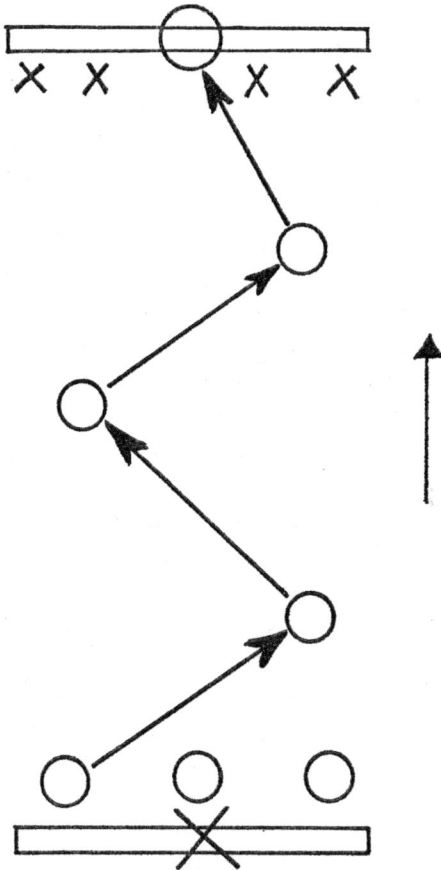

FIG. 3

Diagram showing the simple game of benchball which is a most effective way of introducing handball. Team O are attacking trying to get the ball into the hands of their goalkeeper. Team X are defending and attempting to gain possession in order to begin their own attack

pushed from their places or a penalty throw is awarded. The penalty throw can be taken in any manner the coach chooses.

Handball is a very fast game when played properly and consists mainly of attack and defence, very little mid-field play, and in a simple game such as benchball, the idea of being first on attack and then on defence is brought out most effectively. With quick, short, accurate passing the team in possession will realize how effective they can be in setting up the attacking movements, whilst on the other hand the defenders will quickly see how easy it is for points to be scored against them if they do not protect their goal quickly enough.

A game which can easily follow benchball is the well-known, time-honoured skittle ball (Fig. 4). For this the apparatus required is a ball, two skittles and a piece of chalk. The skittles are placed at each end of the playing area and a circle chalked around them large enough to accommodate a goalkeeper. The aim of the game is to knock over the skittle. As in the previous game passing is important, but we have introduced some other very important aspects of the main game.

Firstly, the idea of a goal area will be introduced to the players. Entry must be forbidden to all but the goalkeeper, which will serve as a useful introduction to the goal area on the the handball court. Skittles are, of course, close to the ground and therefore all shots at them will have to be aimed down, a point which will be shown later, when we look at the skill of shooting, to be most important. The most useful point however that should emerge from the game is that of the defending team lining the circle to keep out the attackers. In handball this is precisely what a defending team would be drilled to do.

It would be wise, during the skittle ball games, for the coach to begin to introduce some of the more basic rules of handball to his group. He could, for instance, stipulate the length of time a player can hold the ball before releasing it and allow him only one bounce and three steps, to prevent too much dribbling which, as we shall see in a later chapter, only serves to reduce the speed at which the game is played.

34

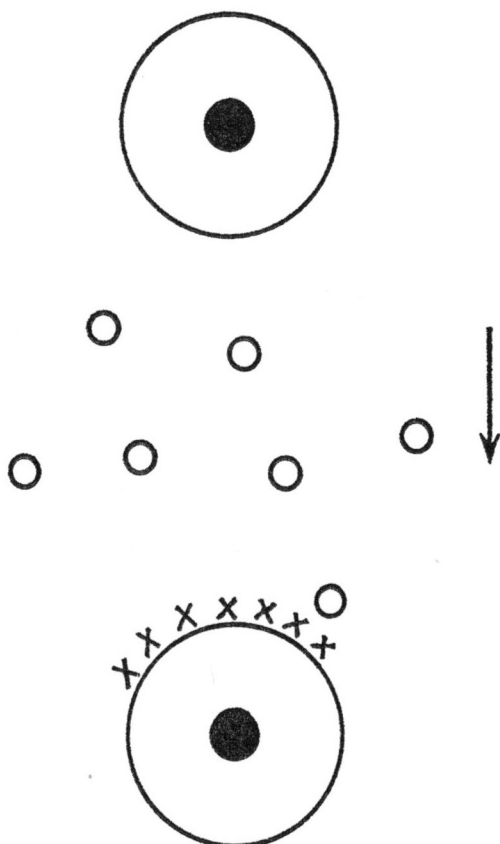

FIG. 4

Skittle ball. Team X are defending and have ringed their circle against the attacking team. Team O are attacking and must find a way to penetrate the circle and be ready to run back to defend their own goal if they lose possession

4 - THE BASIC SKILLS

Like basketball, handball consists mainly of one court play, all the action being concentrated around the defending team's goal area. As was pointed out in an earlier chapter, the attacking team are only in that position whilst they are in possession of the ball and once possession is lost they immediately become the defending team and must try to gain possession of the ball once more.

As the pace of the game is so fast, all court movement must be exercised with the minimum amount of thought. Teams should be so well drilled that all activity is virtually automatic and the coach must ensure that this is the case. Each individual must be able to start quickly and be a persevering runner; he must also be so co-ordinated that he can deceive his opponents by using his body; he must be able to change direction quickly, pick up the ball without hesitation, throw and catch with precision and be able to master numerous ways of throwing the ball.

Running

One of the most important aspects of court movement is running, and the coach should tackle this at his earliest opportunity, especially where young players are concerned. Running practice should, where possible, simulate the type of situation the player is likely to meet in a game, such as the need for quick acceleration from a standing position, body weaving and sudden changes in direction.

Relay practice is valuable for developing this type of skill. Each individual coach will, of course, develop his own type of activity in the course of his experience in dealing with players. There are, however, numerous types of relay activities which will easily fit into the coach's schedule, and I would like to mention two which I have found to be useful. The first (Fig. 5) deals purely and simply with quick starts and running, but the second (Fig. 6) also includes body weaving and direction changing, and is a favourite amongst continental coaches.

FIG. 5. Relay practice number one

The group is divided into equal teams and each team stands in line at one end of the relay course. On the command "Go" the first member of each team races to the opposite end of the course, turns round and runs back. The second runner must not move from the standing position until he has been touched by the returning member of his team.

37

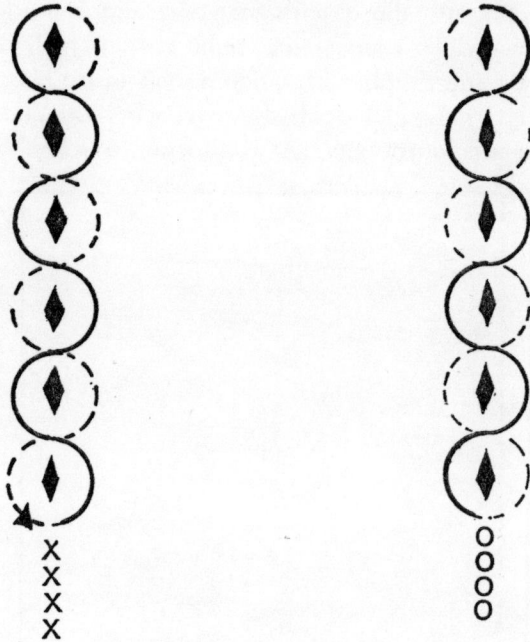

FIG. 6. Relay practice number two

Six skittles are placed as shown above and each team member must in turn make one circuit of the course and, on finishing, must touch the next member of the team before he is allowed to start.

Relays, the coach will find, are a simple way of making running interesting and enjoyable and with the introduction of competition a little more effort and enthusiasm will be put into the training.

Catching

We have seen how important running is within the game but we must not forget that in the end it is the team that has the better skill in ball manipulation that will eventually win the day. The player who can catch the ball cleanly, particularly at speed, will save his team much time and trouble.

To be absolutely safe, the ball must be caught with two hands and, when dealing with younger players, the coach must stress this point above all else. Although it is permitted in the rules to catch the ball in one hand, this should only be done when it is impossible to do so with two. Figs. 7, 8, 9, 10 and 11 show different ways in which a ball can be caught and held safely by a player. Fig. 7 shows how the hands are positioned around the ball when it is caught properly. The fingers are outstretched to cover as much of the ball as possible and the thumbs are positioned to form a line behind the ball. This will help to make sure that the ball, when caught, will remain in the hands and

FIG. 7. Catching the ball with two hands

FIG. 8. Catching the ball at chest height

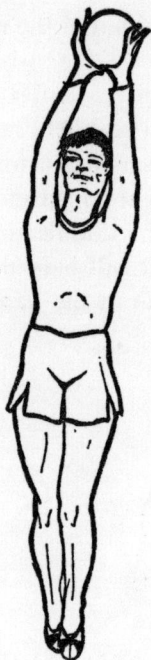

FIG. 9.
Catching a high ball

FIG. 10.
Catching the ball to the side

FIG. 11. Catching a low ball

not slip straight through as could happen if the whole of the hands are placed at the side.

This method of catching is adopted in catching the ball which is received at chest height (Fig. 8). In receiving this ball the head should be pushed slightly forward and the arms held to the front of the body, bent at the elbows. The feet must be positioned to give a firm base to the body. When catching a high ball above the head, the same position of the hands must be used. The body should form more or less a straight line, legs straight and arms above the head together (Fig. 9). When the ball is caught, it must be brought into the body as soon as possible. This will give the added protection the player will need to prevent opponents taking the ball away from him.

Fig. 10 shows how a ball to the side of the body should be held. The hands are still in the same position as before but the wrist is turned to meet the new situation that has arisen. In catching this ball the body weight is positioned over the leg nearest to the ball. Fig. 11 shows the position of the body, legs and hands when catching a low ball. Depending on the situation the player finds around him, the legs can be either bent, in a squatting position, or straight in order to allow the player to move away quickly. In both cases, the head and body are brought forward and the hands are turned down with the fingers pointing towards the ground.

When catching, the player should, if possible, ensure that his body is placed behind the ball to give extra cover in case he fails to hold the ball cleanly. When dealing with a high ball or one which is to the side, the ball should be brought into the body as quickly as possible. The arms outstretched are vulnerable to opposition players who will find it all too easy to knock the ball away. When the ball is close to the body it is much more difficult for a player of the opposite team to gain possession.

Passing and Throwing

The skills of passing, throwing and catching are inseparable, for between them they form the basis of the game of handball. In all practices concerning catching, throwing or passing is involved so the coach can easily teach these skills together although emphasis can be on catching rather than passing or vice versa.

During a game, it is important that possession of the ball is kept so that quick, short passes are of more use to a team than long passes which are less accurate and can easily be intercepted by defending players. The ball can be passed with one or two hands and players should keep close to one another to cut out the danger of interception.

The One-handed Shoulder Pass

The one-handed shoulder pass is the most used pass in handball because it is relatively simple to execute and it is by far the most accurate of passes. This is important when we realise that most passing is done amongst a team that is moving quickly and weaving in and out on their way to build up an attack. More controlled power is put behind the ball from this pass than any other, and we have already seen that the team which is attacking needs short, crisp passing to avoid the danger of interception by the defending team.

In making this pass, the whole of the body is brought into action (Fig. 12).

The ball is held at approximately shoulder height behind the

FIG. 12. The one-handed shoulder pass

body. The arm holding the ball is bent at the elbow and the body is arched slightly and more or less sideways on to the player for whom the pass is intended. The fingers of the throwing hand are outstretched to cover as much of the ball as possible. The index finger of the throwing hand is used to guide the ball when it is released.

When teaching this skill in the early stages, the coach will find it useful to tell the player to stretch out the non-throwing arm, in the direction the ball will travel, to act as a guide in directing the ball, as a cricketer would do when throwing in from the boundary. This will ensure that the eye is kept firmly on the target and show that the non-throwing arm has a purpose in the action.

The Two-handed Chest Pass

This pass is only made when the ball does not have far to travel, as it quickly loses its power. However, when it is made in the correct situation it can be very accurate and most dangerous.

When making the pass the ball should be held tightly with the hands placed behind it, fingers outstretched (Fig. 13).

FIG. 13. The chest pass

43

The arms are held in towards the body, the elbows slightly away and to the side. The ball is held underneath the chin at about chest height. When the pass is executed the arms are pushed forwards until they are straight and the ball is released from the hands. It is important that there is a follow-through with the hands and that the fingers remain outstretched, pointed in the direction of the flight of the ball.

The Reverse Pass

This pass (Fig. 14) is probably the least accurate pass in the game but it can be most effective if it reaches its objective. It is a pass that is relatively difficult to execute and is used mainly when a player wishes to surprise his opponents and trick them into going in the wrong direction.

A lot of practice is required on the part of the player before the coach allows him to use it during a game. If, when it is made, it does not reach its objective then the attacking movements of a team will be finished and they will be thrown back on the defensive.

For the reverse pass the ball is held in the hand between closed fingers and wrist, with the wrist cocked. The thumb is

FIG. 14. The reverse pass

held away from the fingers and across the ball. The arm is extended and slightly abducted from the body, the wrist being locked.

The pass is made by moving the arm slightly forward and swinging it backwards until it hits the side of the body. It is when this contact with the body is made that the ball is released and, as with the two-handed chest pass, the fingers point in the direction of the objective, although this time they are closed. The swing of the arm backwards and the jolt of the body contact will make the ball fly away quickly and the closed fingers will act as a chute to channel the ball in the right direction. The force with which the arm is moved against the body will determine how far the ball will travel through the air. If the pass is a short one a lot of force will not be required but if a long pass is required, then the force must be equal to the distance.

The reverse pass is, very often, made more difficult by the fact that the player making the pass is unable to look directly at the player receiving and must pass the ball by means of peripheral vision. It is at this stage that the coach can take the opportunity, particularly with young performers, of explaining and demonstrating how important peripheral vision can be and how it can be used on occasions to measure up a situation even though the main focus of attention might be some other aspect of the game.

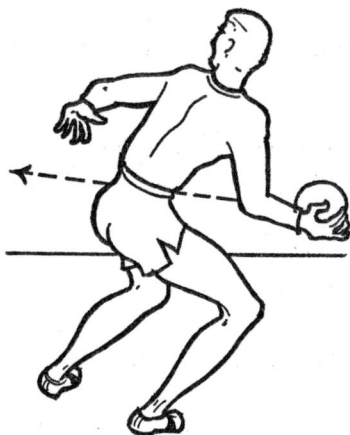

FIG. 15. The pass to the side across the front of the body

The Pass to the Side

The pass to the side across the front of the body (Fig. 15) is another attempt to force the opposition in the wrong direction, this time, however, with a feinting movement.

The ball is held with the hand underneath it, fingers outstretched to give maximum grip. The body is moved to the right (or left depending on the direction of the pass) with the body weight distributed over the right leg and the ball is then passed to the left across the front of the body.

This pass to the side gives the coach a wonderful chance to demonstrate how, by use of a feinting movement, a player can deceive the opposition without actually moving the feet or the ball. This is an aspect of play which can be important when a team is attacking and trying to score a goal against a strong defence.

The four passes that have been described in this chapter: the one-handed shoulder pass, the two-handed chest pass, the reverse pass, and the pass to the side are the main orthodox passes of the game. There are, of course, numerous other ways of passing the ball used in an actual game, many of these passes being peculiar to individual players and coaches. However, if one looks carefully at these other methods it can be seen that basically they are no more than variations of the orthodox passing methods. This being so, it is important that the coach assures himself that his players are proficient in the basic movements.

The Long Throw

The long throw (Fig. 16) is used mostly by strong backline players and its aim is to give a team a quick break away from defence into attack.

The action of the throw is similar to the shoulder pass; the ball is held in an open hand at about shoulder height. The leg furthest away from the throwing arm is placed slightly in front of the body and the weight is distributed over the other leg. Just as in the shoulder pass, the non-throwing arm is extended in the direction of the pass and the eyes are fixed on the receiving player. When the throw is made there is a follow through

46

FIG. 16. The long throw

of the throwing arm and the back leg is moved forwards to transfer the body weight to the front. When the movement is begun the body is arched backwards and when it is finished this position is reversed, the body leaning forwards.

Running with the Ball (Dribbling)

It is permitted by the rules of the game to run with the ball, bouncing it with the hands as in basketball (Fig. 17). However, the coach must be wary of introducing this too early to new or young players, or he will find that dribbling will dominate their minds. It is advisable, therefore, that running with the ball is not introduced until the players have perfected the skills of throwing, passing and catching, which will put them into a position to appreciate how too much dribbling slows down the game and reduces the effectiveness of a team.

Running with the ball brings once again to the coach's attention the use by the performer of both central and peripheral vision. The ball is bounced by using the tips of the fingers slightly in front of the moving player. The main focus of the

47

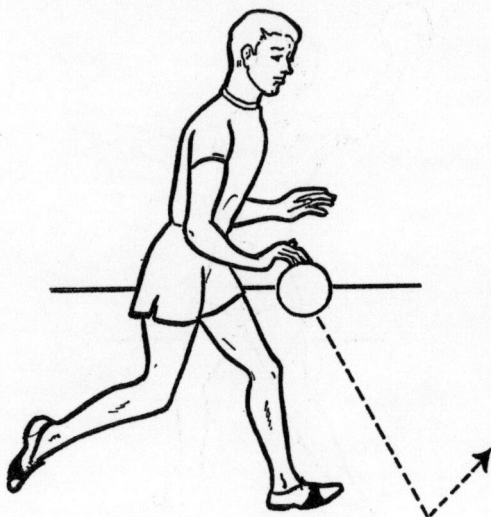

FIG. 17. Running with the ball

player's attention is on the direction in which he is moving and the game around him, the ball is watched by peripheral vision. This enables the player to assess the situation around him and to react quickly to any changes in the game which might involve him.

Shooting

The shot for goal is the climax of any attacking movement in handball. Goals are what handball is about. There are many different ways of throwing the ball at goal; many of these shots are peculiar to individual players and as such cannot be regarded as basic movements for coaching purposes.

We have already seen that handball is a game in which teams are mainly attacking or defending and how important possession of the ball is to the attacking team. Shots for goal, therefore, should not be taken lightly. Each attempt needs to be approached carefully because the shot must be regarded as the final movement of the attack and, if it is unsuccessful, the attacking team, unless they are very lucky, will have lost possession and be forced back on to defence.

48

Photo: Louis Bachoue of 'Sud-Ouest'

5. The falling shot from outside the goal area

Photo: Louis Bachoue of 'Sud-Ouest'

6. The falling shot showing a feinting movement. The player is falling one way and throwing the ball in the other direction in an effort to deceive the goalkeeper

7. The diving shot

Photo: Louis Bachoue of 'Sud-Ouest'

8. A diving shot skilfully made from the side of the goal round a defending player

Patience and quick reaction are required by an attacking team. They should be drilled by their coach in the tactics of mounting an attack, and shown that shots at goal are only made after skilful preparatory groundwork by the team as a whole.

In the early stages of the game the coach will find that he will have to work exceptionally hard to bring out this sense of awareness and teamwork from his players. Beginners will naturally enough want to shoot at every opportunity, whether or not there is a good chance of a goal being scored.

At first, during practice sessions, this will stand the player in good stead, for it will give practice at shooting and help him to co-ordinate the basic aspects of the skill. However, the coach must be careful not to let this go on too long. As soon as he feels that his players have mastered the individual skills involved he should then introduce the tactics involved in mounting an attack before shooting. He must impress on his players that it is team work not individuals that will eventually bring about a successful attack.

Peter Wardale, in his book *Volleyball: Skills and Tactics* (Faber), mentions the fact that all spectator sports reach a stage where the spectators leap from their seats in excitement. The game of handball is no exception to this rule, and this point is reached when the ball, after a successful attack, is finally on its way into the back of the net.

We will look at the tactics involved in shooting at a later stage and we will pause for the moment to study the basic skills and individual movements.

The Standing Throw Shot

The standing throw shot (Fig. 18) is the simplest way of shooting for goal and the coach will find that it serves as an excellent method of introducing the skill of shooting. However, as the name suggests, it is a slow action and the chances of its success are not very good. To make the throw, the performer must stand with both feet on the ground and at some stage of the action the ball is static, which gives the defence time to prepare themselves and block it. The action, however, used in this shot, is the principle for many of the other types of throw, so it is

FIG. 18. The standing throw shot

worthwhile if the coach spends time on the action, making sure that every detail is grasped by the performer.

In making this shot, the player stands sideways on to the goal with the non-throwing arm extended towards the goal. The eyes, too, must be focused in this direction. The method of holding the ball is the same as in the shoulder pass, the ball at about shoulder height, or slightly higher, behind the body, the fingers of the throwing hand being open. The action of the shot is also similar to that of the shoulder pass, the important difference being that the ball first travels downwards to bounce up off the floor. This action of keeping the ball low and, if possible, making it bounce, is probably the most important aspect of shooting for the coach to get over to his players. The low ball is more difficult for the goalkeeper to contend with than a ball thrown high, and with the added difficulty of the bounce the possibilities of scoring are almost doubled.

The Jump Shot

The action of the jump shot is basically the same but movement has now been introduced, which gives added difficulty to the defence and goalkeeper and more impetus to the ball.

The ball is held in the same way as in the previous shot and the action of the body, the arms and the eyes are also the same. The most important aspect of this shot is rhythm. The player must be able to receive a pass cleanly and move smoothly into his three permitted steps (five if the ball is taken whilst both feet are off the ground) before taking off into the air after the final step. In this final movement, the player must concentrate on getting as high as he possibly can in order to get the throwing arm over the defensive wall before releasing the ball (Fig. 19).

The whole of this movement should become second nature to the players. Once a player has committed himself to this action, he will not have time to change his mind. If he lands on the floor still holding the ball, the referee will have no hesitation in awarding a free throw to the defenders. It has been stated that a player may take five steps instead of the usual three if he takes the ball whilst both feet are off the ground. This is permitted because it is understood that the first two steps on landing form part of the landing and not the player's ground movement. This being so, a single player can easily cover a great distance before throwing and the jump shot becomes a very powerful weapon in the game. In teaching the jump shot, the coach should concentrate on three essentials—perfecting height, rhythm and distance.

Fig. 19. The jump shot

51

Why distance? We now move on to another important aspect of shooting. The attacking player, when shooting for goal, is permitted to shoot from inside the goal area, providing that both feet are off the floor whilst he is in possession of the ball. Naturally, the more distance a player can cover in his final leap, the nearer the goal he will get and the already harassed goalkeeper will have to contend with a moving body as the ball comes in his direction.

The Side Throw

This throw (Fig. 20) is made when an attacking player finds that any further forward movement is blocked by either a defender or a wall of defenders ringing the goal area line. Very

FIG. 20. The side throw

often it is preceded by a feinting movement to trick the opposition into moving in the wrong direction, leaving a gap wide enough for the ball to be thrown through. The aim of the throw is to get the ball round the defence by diving sideways or alternatively, if only a single defender is blocking the way, by lowering the body sufficiently to enable the throw to pass under the outstretched arms of the defender.

The action of the throw begins with the feinting movement. The player moves first of all on to his left foot and then on to the right. As soon as the right foot reaches the floor it is used to push the body sideways. The ball is held at shoulder height just behind the body and as soon as the performer is low enough it is released towards the goal, passing underneath the arms and between the legs of the defending players.

However, when there is only one player to be beaten there is often no need for a diving action. Lowering the trunk sideways and bending the knees, until the body position is low enough for the shot to be executed, may suffice. In this action the body weight is distributed over the leg nearest to the throwing action.

The Reverse Shot

Up to now we have looked at methods of shooting in which the player making the shot has been facing the goal. Handball is a game which lends itself to a variety of situations and often players will find themselves in positions from which it is impossible to shoot whilst facing the goal. There are some handball players who specialize in this type of action, and thoroughly enjoy the challenge of shooting with their backs to the goal. As with other skills many players invent their own movements, taking great delight in deceiving the opposition with their own trick shots.

There is, however, one method of shooting with the back to the goal which can be called the basis of all reverse shots. Once players have learned this, and how to use it in a game situation, the coach can allow them to experiment and devise their own methods of shooting.

In making the reverse shot (Fig. 21) the player stands with his back to the goal, both feet firmly placed on the floor. The ball is held in front of the body, and can for a brief period, before the action begins, be held in two hands. However, when the movement for the shot is started, the ball is passed into the throwing hand, the hand still being in front of the body. The fingers are open and facing away from the body, and the wrist, during the action, is cocked backwards. The arm is swung from the front of the body to the back, the ball being released on the way.

FIG. 21. The reverse shot

Dive and Fall Shots

Many handball players will endeavour to get as near to the goal as they possibly can before they shoot for goal to add to their chances of beating the goalkeeper. The jump shot as we have seen is one method of enabling the player to shoot from inside the area. There are two other methods which players sometimes use. These are the dive shot (Fig. 22) and the fall shot (Fig. 23). Of these two throws the diving shot is by far the most adventurous with the player diving towards the goal, his whole body lifted into the air. The action is a very quick one, the player often reacting immediately to the situation when it presents itself. When making the shot the player thrusts his body into the air as soon as he reaches the goal area line. The ball is held about level with the shoulders and slightly behind, the arm holding the ball being bent. The eyes should be kept on the part of the goal that the player intends the ball to reach. The non-throwing arm is thrown forward and the ball is released when the final point of the dive has been reached.

The fall shot is similar to the dive shot in that the whole of the body is at some time or other moving forwards. However, as its name suggests it is a throw that is made by the player falling rather than diving and at all times there is contact with the floor. The shot is often made when the player finds himself in a situation where a diving shot would be too difficult to execute. In making the throw the player stands with one foot on the ground, and lifts the other foot into the air away from the body. It will often be found that this raising of the leg will be automatic and will not have to be taught at all. The body can in the first instance be placed facing the goal, but the coach will often find that there is a natural tendency to turn the body sideways to the goal, with the non-throwing shoulder pointing inwards in the direction in which the ball will ultimately travel. This is quite acceptable and will often prove to be the best way to execute the throw as it will allow the player to add more power to the action. The ball should be held slightly away from the body by a bent arm and it should be held at about shoulder height or just a little bit higher. It must be released before the body touches the floor.

In making the first of these two shots a correct rhythm of movement is essential if it is to be executed correctly. The player must be able to move smoothly, making use of the amount of movement allowed by the rules of the game and he should, through coaching, be able to gain maximum impetus from the thrust of the leg that is to launch him into the air towards the goal. In a goal-scoring attempt the fall shot is not as potentially

FIG. 22. The dive shot

useful as the dive shot, although when it is executed correctly, at the right time, it can prove most effective. However, the player should realize fully its limitations when compared to the dive. The coach may find a tendency amongst some players to restrict themselves to the fall shot as there is less risk attached to it when landing. He must be aware of this and deal with it as soon as he can. He should spend time in making sure that players know how to land when they have finished the diving movement. An awkward landing could obviously lead to injury. The coach should stress the importance of a rolling movement when the body comes into contact with the floor, and he should point out the soft parts of the body, such as the deltoid muscle of the shoulder, on which it is much easier to land. If the player does this and immediately moves into a rolling action he will soon realize that there is very little risk attached to the dive.

The fall shot is an excellent throw to use when executing the penalty (seven-metre) throw. The penalty, when it is awarded, is taken from the seven-metre line drawn in front of the goal at

FIG. 23. The fall shot

a distance of seven metres from the goal line. The penalty throw can be taken in numerous ways providing that it conforms to the rules of the game relating to this type of throw. The rules state that the person executing the throw must have both feet behind the seven-metre line, and one foot must remain in contact with the floor all the time the throw is being executed. By employing the fall throw for this action the player gives himself an opportunity of getting closer to the goal before shooting, and by watching the actions of the goalkeeper he can use the throw to deceive him into moving in the wrong direction.

It will generally be found that during a game of handball one of these two throws will be most effective when the player finds himself at the side of the goal. They enable him to move sideways across the face of the goal and also make possible a shot round the body of the goalkeeper.

Blocking and Gaining Possession of the Ball

It is permitted by the rules of the game to block an opponent, whether or not he is in possession of the ball, by means of a body check. It is important, however, that the coach is sure that his players are fully conversant with the rules on this aspect and that they know the correct procedure. They must realize that it is used to impede a player's progress and must not be used illegally, for instance, to force a player into the goal area. The body check is made by the trunk only; the use of the arms and legs is strictly forbidden. A defender may stop a player by standing in front of him as he progresses or he may check a player who is waiting for the ball to be passed to him. In the latter case the defender stands behind the player he is marking with his arms outstretched away from the body.

When tackling another player, possession of the ball may be gained by knocking the ball away from the other's possession by means of the flat of the hand. Players must realize that this is the only method the referee will tolerate and any other method employed, such as snatching the ball, will be considered an infringement of the rules and a free throw will be awarded against the player committing the foul.

57

Goalkeeping

In handball the goalkeeper must be a very brave man indeed. He has to contend with a ball that is moving exceptionally fast and often the ball will be accompanied by a player hurtling towards him through the air. He must be prepared to accept this and more, and be prepared to stand his ground. He must also be able to react very quickly indeed.

To a large extent the goalkeeper will rely on the other members of his team to keep the attacking players at bay. If they can keep the opposition players from entering the goal area or can block a shot that is made they will enable the goalkeeper to have more time to prepare for the ball. However, this is not always possible and attacking players will be able to break through to shoot from inside the area. It is when this happens that the goalkeeper will need to have very sharp reactions. The ball will travel so fast on its way towards the goal that a cat-like action will be required on the part of the goalkeeper. Catching the ball is of course the safest way of dealing with it, particularly if the body can be placed behind the ball as well. However, it will be found that it is very often impossible to do this and the goalkeeper must rely on deflecting the ball round or over the goal. This can be done by using all or part of the body. The rules of the game permit the goalkeeper to use his feet to stop the ball whilst it is travelling towards the goal. If the ball is travelling fairly high then it is wiser to use the arms to deflect it away from the goal. The use of the legs is obviously the best way of dealing with low shots.

The basic stance of the goalkeeper (Fig. 24) should be such that he is able to give maximum coverage to his goal. He should stand in the middle of the goal, the arms and legs extending as far as possible outwards to cover the extremities. Obviously, it will not be possible for the player to remain in this position all the time, but it is an excellent way for the coach to show new players how this position will enable them to cover the goal in the fullest possible way. The position is, however, basic to many goalkeeping movements and the goalkeeper should try to use it when he can, whether he is on the goal line or moving to tackle an oncoming player of the opposition.

Unlike the goalkeeper in soccer, it is very difficult for the handball goalkeeper to move forward to narrow the angle of the shot at goal. Once the goalkeeper tries to do this, it is quite easy for the ball to be lobbed over his head into the goal. When he intends to meet an attacking player, he should move out quickly and try to gain contact with the player before he has time to release the ball. If the player jumps, he must be sure that he can match the height of the opponent and he must stretch out as shown in the basic stance in an effort to cover as much of the shooting area as possible. He should restrict his movements to his goal line when players are shooting from the side of from outside the goal area line. When the ball is on one side of the goal, he should position himself near the post on that side to cut down the attacker's view of the goal, thus making it more difficult for him to score. If the shot is coming from the centre, he should come a little way from the goal, making sure that he is not too far forward enabling the shot to be made over his head. He will find that there is no time for him to rectify his mistakes so he must be so well drilled that he can act instinctively.

FIG. 24. The goalkeeper. Basic stance

The goalkeeper is, of course, allowed to leave his area and become a court player. However, he must take care when doing so or it will lead to the scoring of a simple goal by the opposition. There is nothing in the rules of the game to prevent a goalkeeper scoring for his team if the opportunity arises and the goalkeeper can be used to good purpose if he is allowed to take any free throw that has been awarded to his team near their own goal. By bringing the goalkeeper out of his area for this purpose, the team will make maximum use of their court players and will be able to take up their positions on the field without having to wait for one of their number to first take the free throw.

5 - ELEMENTARY TACTICS

It must always be remembered that handball is essentially a team game and no matter how much natural ability and talent each individual player might possess it is team work that will eventually score goals and win matches. The handball coach must be able to blend the skills and abilities of his players until he has developed a team capable of playing together. He should begin this gradually in the early stages of the game leading each player to understand what he is doing and why. Each player should also be aware of his colleagues' movements during the game.

When dealing with beginners, particularly with young children, the coach should introduce his team work in such a way that tactical play is incorporated into the general pattern of the game. The game type activities mentioned in the chapter on Introducing Handball to Beginners are a good example of this. Handball is a one-court game and all play is situated around the goal area. The two games mentioned in the earlier chapter introduce this to players who have never played handball before. Obviously, these are simple practices and whilst they are valuable in the early stages, the coach must not spend too much time at this level.

The coach must encourage his team to establish a thinking game; it is here that he is likely to encounter difficulty. For many years, the attitude of British sportsmen has been against tactical development and this, in the past, has allowed continental opposition to overtake us in many fields of sport. Fortunately, this attitude is changing but the coach must realize that it has still to be overcome.

Peter Wardale, in his book *Volleyball: Skills and Tactics*, mentions the qualities that a coach should have. These are:

   (i) Personality.
  (ii) A sound technical knowledge of the game and ability to demonstrate skills.
 (iii) The ability to teach.
 (iv) Powers of observation.
  (v) The ability to draw logical conclusions from his observation.
 (vi) Organizing ability.
(vii) Patience.
(viii) Tact.
 (ix) Willingness to experiment.
  (x) Luck.

These qualities are basic, not only to volleyball but to any team sport.

Given that the coach is in possession of these qualities, how should he begin to introduce tactics to his handball players? It is not within the scope of this book to delve too deeply into the question of tactics, but in order that the game can be introduced effectively, it is essential to consider them briefly.

Basic Tactical Play

In handball, unlike most other sports, defensive formation is taught before attacking moves are developed. The tactics of the team mounting an attack are governed by the defensive formation used by their opponents. Once the basic form of defence has been established, it will be seen that the tactics of attack and defence become interrelated.

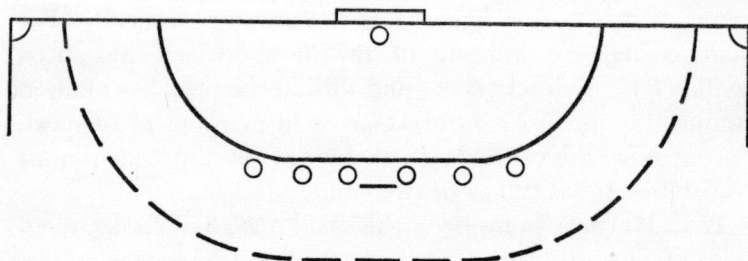

FIG. 25. 6–0 Defence formation

The most basic form of defence is known as six and nought, 6–0. Here all the defending players line up inside the free-throw area (Fig. 25).

Once this basic form of defence has been understood, the coach can begin to show his players what form of attack should be used to penetrate it (Fig. 26).

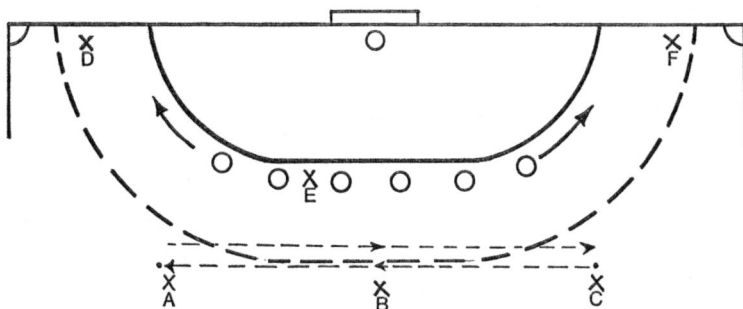

FIG. 26. Setting up an attack against a 6–0 defence

The defence, it will be seen, all line up inside the free-throw line. This means that it is very difficult for the attacking players to shoot from inside this area and it is therefore very important that they have strong back line players capable of shooting from a distance.

The defending players move from side to side as indicated by the arrows, in an attempt to cover the player in possession of the ball. This is the only type of movement allowed for in this form of defence.

The aim of the attacking players is to move the ball about as quickly as possible across the court in an effort to defeat the sideways movement of the defence. The main threat to the defence should come from the three back line players, A, B, C. The two wingmen, D and F, should move into the positions shown and remain there for the possibility of a quick pass which could lead to them being in a goal scoring situation.

The attacking player, E, should, immediately the attack has been set up, position himself inside the defensive wall to try and destroy the sideways movement of the defence.

The main onus on the attacking players is to keep possession of the ball until a goal-scoring opportunity arises. The best means of achieving this is by a jump shot from one of the back line players. The coach must ensure that his attacking players realize the importance of retaining possession of the ball, and when a shot has been made, they must be ready to retrieve the ball if it rebounds from the defensive wall.

The method of defence we have just studied is the main basis from which all other systems are developed. Six–nought, can in itself, be an excellent defensive formation but it can become rather limited; it does not allow for very much movement by the defensive players and it virtually eliminates any chance of the defending team making a counter-attack when they obtain possession of the ball. There is also the danger of the attacking team rendering it ineffective if their back line players are particularly good at shooting from a distance.

The six-nought system allows for free movement for the attackers when they are outside the free-throw line as they know that their opponents are not likely to intercept the ball. It is useful, however, in the first instance, for the defence to make use of this system as it will give them time to study their opponents and weigh up their potential strength or weaknesses. However, at the right time they should move into a more positive form of defensive cover which will give them more opportunity to gain possession of the ball.

A counteracting defensive formation that should be explored is that known as the five–one defence. Here the defence line-up is illustrated in Fig. 27. The defence cover is very similar to that

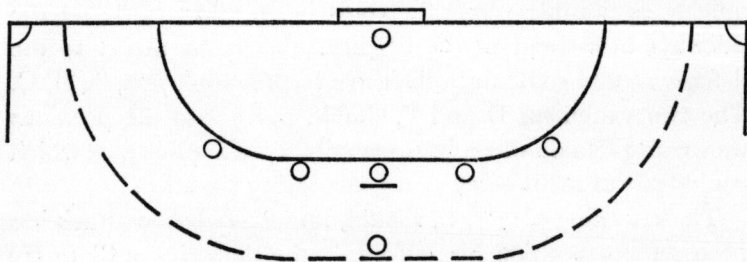

FIG. 27. The 5–1 defence formation

9. The penalty shot from the 7 metre line. The concentration on the player's face and the position of the body show something of the power behind the throw

Photo: Pierre Ducousso of 'La Republique'

10. The penalty shot, showing the position of the feet in relation to the 7 metre line

11. The handball goal-keeper. This photograph shows how the keeper must use the whole of his body in his attempts to save from attacking players

Photo: Pierre Ducousso of 'La Republique'

12a. Duell, the West German goalkeeper, demonstrates the use of hand and leg together to prevent the ball entering the goal

Photo: Hanns Apfel

12b. Showing the risk the goalkeeper runs if he comes too far forward. Here the ball is being thrown over his out-stretched arms in an attempt to score a goal

Photo: Pierre Ducousso of 'La Republique'

of the six–nought, but now we have introduced the idea of a member of the defence standing slightly in front of the rest of the team. This will have one immediate effect in that it will encourage the attacking team to be more careful in their passing movements because of the threat of interception. The attackers no longer have the freedom of the court in front of the free-throw line and they must alter their tactics to meet this new situation. There is little point now in shooting from a distance; the final shot for goal should be made from a point nearer to the goal. However, the final shooting moment should not arrive until the attackers know that there is a positive opportunity of a goal being scored. Again the coach must emphasize the importance of possession, particularly as there is now a direct threat to this in the form of the leading defence player. The defending team must not remain static and the leading defender does not always remain the same man; there is constantly an interchanging of positions in the defence. With the introduction of a defender outside the free-throw line, most of the attacking work will have to be done from a deeper position on the court and this will cancel any threat of shots from a distance. The attacking players must, therefore, try to penetrate the defence

The attacking movement in Fig. 28 is seen coming from the left-hand side of the goal. The player making his way towards goal has passed the defender and, by dribbling the ball, has made his way inside the free-throw area. When he reaches the goal line, he can do one of two things. He can either shoot for

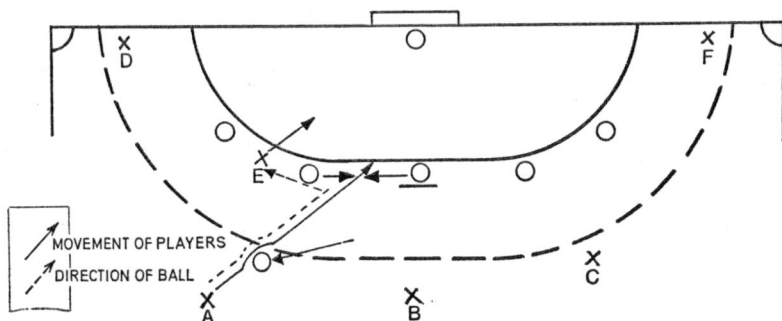

FIG. 28
An attacking move designed to defeat the 5–1 defence formation

goal or he can pass to player E. The extra pass will help to confuse the defenders and probably lead to a more likely goal-
scoring situation. It is important that the attacking players
realize that once inside the defence it will be difficult to pass the
ball in the usual way and it is wiser to make use of deceptive
passes such as the reverse pass.

We have now introduced to the defensive team the possibility
of attacking players coming into their midst. The coach must
make sure that the defence can function as one unit. One
mistake and the goal-scoring chance is presented. Co-ordinated
movement and team thinking is essential.

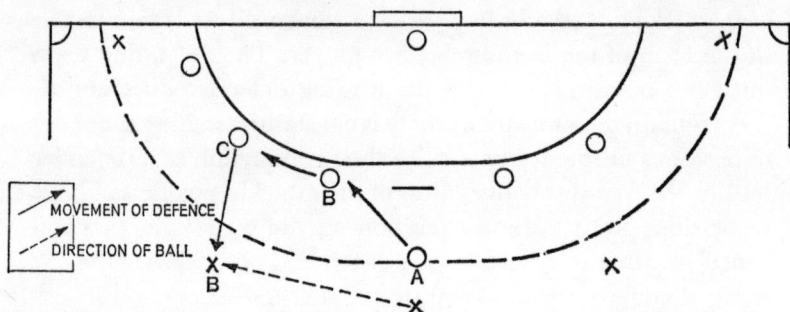

FIG. 29
Movement of defending players in a 5–1 defence formation

In Fig. 29 we see the ball in the possession of attacker A in the
centre of the court; the forward defender A is the centre man of
the defence. The ball is passed across the court to attacker B,
which should bring an immediate response from the defence to
meet this new situation. Defender C, who is nearest to the man
in possession of the ball, should move forward and become the
leading defender. This, of course, means that there will be a
gap in the defence which must be covered. Immediately C
moves forward, defender B moves sideways to take his place
and defender A moves backwards to fill the gap left by B.
The attacker will see that the way has now been blocked and
will probably pass the ball to the centre of the court again.
Should this happen then the movement of the defence is
reversed.

Movement has now been brought into the defensive situation and, when the coach is satisfied that his players know what is required of them, he should begin to explore the possibilities of making a counter-attack. This can be extremely dangerous, particularly as it can put the goalkeeper in a very vulnerable position. We have seen that by bringing a member of the defence forward there is a very good possibility of the ball being intercepted by the leading defender. Should this happen, then the defender will very likely find himself with a clear pathway to his opponents' goal. He will have three of the attacking players a long way behind him inside the free-throw line and the other three alongside, all facing the wrong way. When this situation presents itself the defender should be able to act instinctively and, by dribbling the ball away, he should move as quickly as possible towards the opponents' goal and try to score direct.

It is important, therefore, that when attacking against this form of defence all the passes made are accurate and hard. The soft pass can quickly be used by the defence to their own advantage.

Another form of defence that is often used in handball is the four–two formation (Fig. 30).

This form of defence is normally used when the opposition has very strong full-backs. As its name suggests, the defensive formation consists of four players in the back line inside the free-throw area and two defenders forward, inside the area. This formation will limit the threat posed by the attacking full-backs. However, it is important that the defence are well disciplined when operating this formation, as it means bigger gaps in the

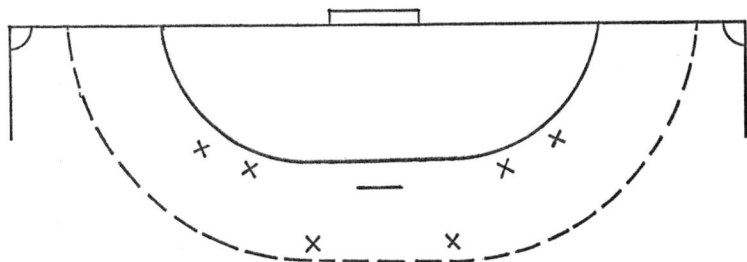

FIG. 30. The 4–2 defence formation

defensive wall behind the two forward players. The forward players must make sure that they are not too far in front of the free-throw line, thus weakening their effect on the attack.

When attacking players meet this form of defence, they must keep up a constantly moving form of opposition. However, they must be even more careful in their passing movements if they wish to avoid interception of the ball. There must be a constant interchanging of positions and quite a lot of reverse passing if they are to force the defence to make an error.

All passing between attacking players must be done at speed; the ball must be made to travel through the air very quickly indeed. Movement, too, must be continuous. There is no place now in the attack for stationary players. The attack must move until the opportunity for a shot occurs. The three diagrams show different ways of breaking through the four and two defence. Fig. 31(A) shows a direct way of moving the ball into the defence. Attacking player two passes the ball to number five on the wing and he in turn delivers the ball across the goal for number six to run in, collect the ball and shoot for goal. The method used for the shot in this case would most probably be a diving shot or a falling shot.

That would be a simple way of breaking the defensive pattern but, of course, it is very unlikely that it would be successful very often in the course of a game. Fig. 31(B) shows a more intricate move designed to outwit the defence. The attack begins in the same corner of the court. The ball is passed from attacker two to number three and on to number seven, who is positioned in the corner of the court. From number seven the ball is passed across the court for number five to run in and score with the type of shot used in the previous attack. Attacking player number six runs forward as the ball is passed by number seven in an attempt to prevent the player in front of him reaching number five before he can shoot.

Fig. 31(C) shows how effective the reverse pass can be when mounting an attack against the four–two defence. The first pass is made by number two to number three. Number three immediately moves with the ball inside the man who is marking him and, when his opposite number tries to follow, he quickly

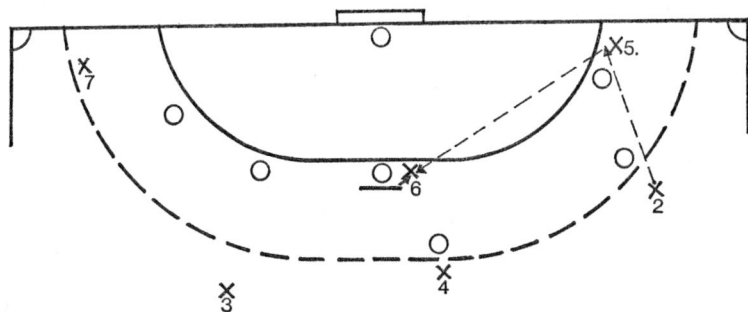

A

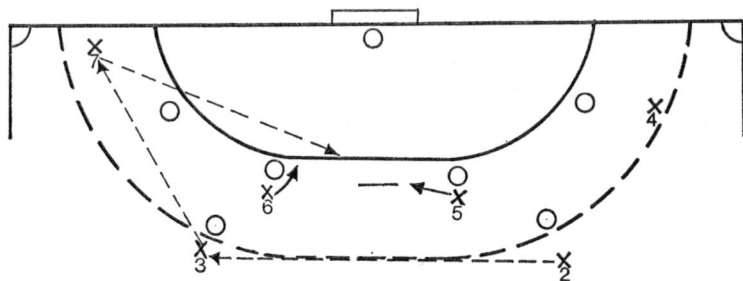

B

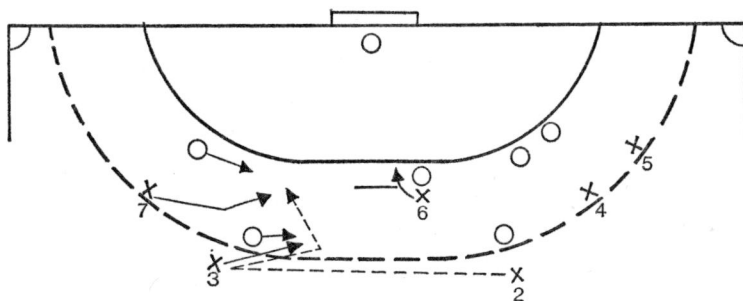

C

Figs. 31 (A), (B) and (C)
Three attacking movements designed to defeat the 4–2 defence

changes direction and passes the ball to number seven. This player, it will be seen, was originally placed to the left of the goal. Immediately the first movement was begun by number three, he began to run across the court to receive the ball. It will be seen that player number six has moved to prevent his opposite number moving forward to intercept.

It will be noticed that on all of these diagrams the defensive players are playing what is, in effect, a man to man marking system. This is important. The coach must always make sure that his players understand fully the task they have within the defence. If there is one weak link then the defence will fail. The same applies with attacking formations, particularly when playing against a five–one or four–two formation. The players should know where they are supposed to be in a given situation. It is important, however, that the coach makes sure that his coaching schedule, both on attacking and defensive movements, allows scope for individual expression and thinking. There can be no hard and fast rule as to what type of pass should be used by each player. The coach can advise, but his main function is to blend the individual differences in his players into an effective team.

I have described three methods of defensive tactics in this chapter and of these it will be found that the system known as five and one is the most effective. It is less tiring than the four and two method and it has several advantages over the six–nought defence. However, it must be understood that both the six–nought and four–two can play a very useful part in the game.

Six–nought is purely a defensive formation and is best used when playing against teams with weak shooting power from a distance. The use of all players on the defensive line will virtually rule out close shooting if the system functions properly. Another useful point in favour of the six–nought formation is that the coach can use it at the beginning of the game to give him time to look for the strength or weakness of the opposition. Once he has done this, he can then give the order to his team to keep the formation or change it to what he feels will be most beneficial to his team.

We have already seen that the six–nought defence allows for limited movement within the defence and that it allows the attacking team complete freedom outside the free-throw area. This is obviously not to the defending team's advantage and use of one of the other systems will allow the team a better chance to break down the attack and set their own in motion. When there is a chance of a counter-attack, it should be realized that it is not always wise to try and break away too quickly to try and score. This is where good coaching is essential. When a counter-attack is beginning there can often be too many attacking players round the player with the ball, so that the chances of a clean individual breakthrough are only slight. When a player finds himself in this position it is wiser for him to hang back with the ball. True, this will give the opposition more time to return to their own defence formation but at the same time it will give his own team more chance to collect themselves for a more positive attack. Should the player move too quickly and lose possession of the ball the result could be disastrous for his team. They will have started to break from their defensive formation and the way to a goal-scoring attempt by the opposition will have been laid wide open.

Until the coach is confident that his team are proficient in effecting a good five-one defence it would be unwise for him to expect them to attempt the four–two. Five and one means that there is less likelihood of gaps being made in the defence by the attacking team and any mistakes that do occur can more easily be covered. However, as I have already said, it does allow the possibility of interception and counter-attack and, most important, it stops the attacking team having sole possession of the outer court. The introduction of movement within the court obviously makes each individual player's task more difficult and the coach must work to see that the players understand these movements fully.

The team playing on court will depend on their coach to help them to read the game in which they are taking part. The coach must be able, through his observations from the bench, to instruct his team as to what sort of defence they should employ to counteract the movement of the opposing players. It is the coach who should realize where the strength or weakness of the opponents lies and act accordingly.

In the case of substitution, the team will rely entirely on the judgement of their coach. Handball is such an exacting game that a great deal of substitution of players is needed. The coach must make the decision when to substitute, but he must be sure that he does it at the right time and he must know why he is making the substitution. He must not allow key players to stay on the court until they are too tired and so become less effective.

It is perhaps relevant at this point to say something on the procedure of substitution, for if it is done incorrectly it can result in a foul being awarded against the substitute or, for a subsequent offence, a two-minute suspension. When the substitution is made, the player leaving the field should indicate this to the referee and he must have left the playing area before the player substituting enters, indicating the fact to the referee. The player entering the game must do so at the place where the other player left.

Suspension of a player can, of course, be caused through offences for other infringements of the rules besides faulty substitution and when this happens it is important that the weakened team keeps possession of the ball for as long as they possibly can during the period of the suspension.

Although I have described three methods of defensive movements in this chapter, there is one other form of defence that is sometimes used that should be mentioned. However, I do not propose to explain it in any detail as it is a complicated formation and is used by teams of the highest playing ability.

This is the defensive system known as three and three (Fig. 32). Here we have three men forward and three back. It is a highly technical form of defence and needs a great deal of preparation before it can be used. We have already seen the problems caused by the four–two system which, in effect, cuts the main defence down to four men. The three–three formation now means only three men are back and unless it can be executed very skilfully, there is little point in the coach adopting this method of play.

The coach is the deciding factor on the tactics that are to be used in the game by his team and it is he who must take most of the credit or otherwise for his team's performances. His is a lonely task in many ways, but it can also be rewarding. There can be no more pleasing experience for a coach, in my opinion, than to begin with a group of individuals with hardly any knowledge of the game and to watch them mould into a good, skilful unit through his efforts and experience. This is the greatest reward for any coach. Giving enjoyment to people who want to play handball is also a reward in itself. Not every player the coach deals with will want to become an expert; many will play handball purely and simply for relaxation and enjoyment. Here, handball is an ideal sport for, as we have seen, it can be played by anyone, whatever their level of skill and, most important, it can be enjoyed by all.

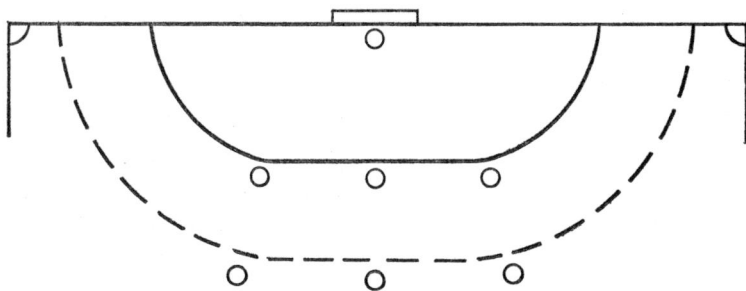

FIG. 32. Three-and-three defence formation

6 - HANDBALL IN SCHOOLS

In the past, much of the games interest in our schools has centred round the playing of the major sports of this country. However, there has in recent years been an awakening to the advantages of developing more of the minor games and introducing them into the physical education programme, though it must be admitted that there are still some schools who insist on having only one sport played to the exclusion of all others, very often without thought to the people who matter—the children.

Since the publication of the Newsom Report, there have been interesting efforts on the part of teachers, particularly those concerned with physical education, to promote the ideas advocated in the Report regarding education for leisure-time activities. There is, indeed, a great deal of dedicated work done by teachers today to ensure that their pupils derive benefit from their time in school and are able to leave the school environment with the ability to spend their leisure-time wisely.

Educating for leisure has become part of our school curriculum in one way or another and there can be no doubt as to its importance in helping the physical and mental development of the individual. To be successful in its aims, it must, however, be tackled in a serious and sensible manner. There must be a wide variety of choice for the child, in order that as many as possible can find something of interest to them. The extent of this choice and the type of activities to be included will ultimately depend on the teacher concerned with physical education and he, in turn, will obviously be influenced by the facilities available and the help he receives from his colleagues in the school.

Whether or not a particular sport is to be included in the physical education programme is a matter that should not be decided on lightly. The teacher concerned should ask himself the following questions:

74

(i) Why?

(ii) What are the aims of the activity; are these aims of value and can they be achieved?

(iii) Will the activity be acceptable to the type of child I am dealing with?

(iv) Will it be of help in his physical development?

(v) What are the mental attributes needed for the game?

(vi) Is there any correlation between this and any other activity included in the programme?

(vii) Will it give enjoyment and satisfaction to the majority?

(viii) Does it fit into the environment of the child when he is outside school?

(ix) Have I sufficient facilities to introduce the sport properly or can my existing facilities be utilized sufficiently?

(x) If the sport is to be carried on by the child after he has left school, will he be able to afford it or will it be too expensive? Are there facilities available outside school to allow the child to continue?

When the teacher is asked why he is organizing any particular activity, he must be able to give sound and acceptable reasons. If he can answer satisfactorily all or most of the questions set out above, then he need look no further for his explanations, providing that he really believes in what he is doing and his children are deriving maximum benefit from his efforts.

I firmly believe that handball is an activity which can be of immense value when it is included in the physical education programme, both from the point of view of playing the game for its own sake, and when using it as an aid to the development of other sports. The idea of the game is easy to understand; it is elegant and varied and it combines all the advantages of a team sport.

There is no doubt in my mind that handball is acceptable to children. The game is basically a simple one and can be played by any individual, irrespective of his ability. It is a game which quickly fires the imagination of the naturally gifted games player who is encouraged to use his hands to develop his ideas. At the other end of the scale, it gives the performer who is not quite so good, an opportunity to play a game in which he can feel that he has made a contribution and from which he has derived a sense of achievement. Even in practising the skills, the poorer performer does not feel that he is holding other players back because, the basic skills of the game being natural to his own movements, he is capable to a certain degree of doing what is expected of him.

Obviously, the game will help in the physical development of the child; the very nature of handball will ensure this. As handball is a fast game, it requires never-failing concentration and the ability to adapt oneself to countless changing situations and this must help the young performer mentally. He must realize that handball is a team game and therefore a thinking game. There is little point in being a brilliant performer when practising basic skills if he cannot learn to use his ability as a member of the team. One thing that handball will do for the young player is make him realize that there is no room for gamesmanship within the game. All too often nowadays, schoolboys try to emulate the bad example of their idols in the sporting world. How many times do we see youngsters playing in soccer matches running away with the ball after a foul has been awarded against them, or kicking the ball into touch as hard as they possibly can just to gain a few minutes of time in order that the opposition will not have a chance to equalize in the time available? When playing handball, the performer has to realize that if these things occur then the offender will be dismissed from the field for a period of suspension and that if he persists he can be dismissed from the game completely. Gamesmanship on the part of the handball player can only result in hardship for the rest of the people in the team who will have to carry the extra burden of responsibility whilst the offender is off the field. The rules of handball cover the field of gamesmanship completely. It is an offence to play the ball into touch and the penalty for arguing with the decision of the referee is instant dismissal.

As handball develops skills which are fundamental to the individual, there must be correlation with other sports. The game is based on the three athletic disciplines of running, throwing and jumping, and if we add to this the skill of catching, we will immediately see that it can be used to help in the development of other games. That handball gives enjoyment is without doubt. The simplicity of the game is pleasing to children. Each individual soon finds himself involved with the quickness of movement within the game and from this involvement it is inevitable that satisfaction will be derived.

There is no specific type of environment to which handball could be termed peculiar. Handball can be played anywhere. It is just as enjoyable to the down-town schoolboy as it is to children who are fortunate enough to live in a more pleasing environment. The only requirement for a game to be got under way and enjoyed is a ball. Where it is played does not matter providing the space is available. Two sets of coats will suffice for goals if the correct equipment is not available.

The provision of facilities for physical activities can sometimes be a headache to teachers. Not everyone has the facilities he would like and this can be a considerable problem in schools in the centre of large cities. The playing fields used by these schools are often a long way from the school premises and can only be reached by means of the school bus provided by the local authority at a certain time each day. Use of the field is not exclusive—it has to be used by other schools in a similar position and this can lead to a lack of continuity in teaching. Where a school is in this position, there is the problem of time lost through the journey and the loss of games through bad weather or other causes. All this, of course, only serves to hinder the work of the teacher concerned and he must of necessity look around for a game which will not be affected by these problems. The down-town school will feel the lack of facilities, particularly in the summer term when the teacher will want to have his children outside as much as possible when the weather is good. Handball can be a means of overcoming these difficulties when they arise. In winter the game can be played indoors and there is no need for lack of continuity through any of the reasons mentioned above. In the summer the school yard will be suitable for playing the seven-a-side game. Handball does not require a particularly large surface area for a game to be got under way and it does not require a great deal of organization causing loss of valuable time.

The question of facilities for any sport also arises when the individual leaves the school environment and looks around for somewhere to carry on the activity of his choice. A great number of children leaving school have developed their playing ability in various sports to a very high level only to find that there is virtually no opportunity outside school to improve their game or for regular participation. This, I know from my own experience, is particularly galling to teachers who, after spending a great deal of time with individual players, find that they are lost to the sport in which they excelled simply because of the lack of continuity when they have left school. There is, without doubt, a great deal of potential talent lost to British sport because of the seeming lack of interest on the part of people in authority in spending money on sport.

However, if we look closely at the question of facilities for sport after school, the picture may not always be so bleak. If the teacher is interested in seeing that his players are able to carry on, then the facilities can sometimes be made available. An ideal situation is to form a club at the school using the facilities available there. The club can be associated with the school and boys and girls in their final year at school encouraged to join as well as those who have already left. In this way, the club will be assured of a healthy membership and, most important of all, there will be opportunity for the game to be carried on after life at school is ended. If this form of club is introduced to the school-leavers there is no reason why it should be confined to them alone; members of the teaching staff in the school could be encouraged to become members. This will benefit the teacher concerned with the coaching in several ways. It will help in providing a mature leadership for the club and it will add to the number of teachers who are able to assist in the teaching of the game during school time.

For the enthusiastic boy wishing to take up handball in a more serious way, the expense involved will not be very high. On joining a handball club, he will find that he will have to pay a membership subscription and, in some cases, depending on the circumstances of the club, a small contribution to the club each week. It may be found that, where a club is using premises belonging to someone else, a small charge to the players is made to help keep down the expense to the club of such things as weekly payments to the caretaker and the cost of electric lighting, etc. However, teachers will find that, if they themselves organize an after-school club, in nearly every case the Education Committee concerned will pay the expenses I have just mentioned. Nevertheless, I am sure that a more responsible attitude, both towards the game and the club, will be developed if the young player knows that he himself is helping the growth of the handball club through his contributions however small they might be.

If we cast our minds back to the questions posed at the beginning of this chapter and apply them to the game of handball we will see that every one of them can be answered positively, in favour of including the game in the physical education programme. There is no rule as to when the game should be introduced, as it is a game that can be played by very young children and can be developed throughout the life of the individual at school.

Handball in the Primary School

Handball can make an important contribution to the physical education programme in the primary school. Primary school teachers concerned with the physical development of children are constantly looking for new activities and ideas which will be beneficial to their pupils. Primary school teachers that I know are very often conscious of the fact that many of the games played and enjoyed in the secondary school are not suitable for their children because the skills required are too difficult and the games are unsuited to the pattern of education in the primary school.

It must be remembered, too, that most primary school teachers are not physical education specialists and are not able to develop some games as much as they would like. However, these people feel that there is room for more activities and are constantly looking for new ideas.

The provision of facilities and of money often pose problems in the primary school. The primary school needs activities which will conform to their aims of education, make use of the facilities which exist, and take up very little money. Handball will meet all three of these basic necessities.

It is generally agreed that physical education in the primary school should be aimed at the general all-round physical development of the child. In the early stages, certainly, there should be no attempt at specialization; development should, where possible, be natural.

Handball will definitely be an aid in this development. What could be more natural to the child than running, throwing and jumping? These skills are the basis of handball and, at the same time, they are recognized as the three fundamental athletic principles. We often see toddlers on the beach, during the summer, deriving great enjoyment from a beach ball. They throw it, run with it and jump with it. That they are enjoying their activity is obvious to everyone, and their enjoyment has certainly come from a natural source. No one has had to teach them the skills they have utilized, they are all innate to the normal child.

Running, throwing, jumping: add to these catching and you have what handball is all about. In the early stages of the primary school this is all that is required, there is no need for the teacher to attempt to improve these skills artificially, they will develop naturally and unconsciously. The only thing that the individual performer will be conscious of is the enjoyment that he or she is deriving from participation in the game.

Handball, as a natural game, is of value to the primary school but there are other reasons for it being of value to the primary school teacher. There are, in the opinion of many teachers, not enough activities for the primary school and handball can provide an attractive alternative to the more usual team games that are at present part of the primary school curriculum. Existing facilities are usually sufficient for successful application of the game and it can be introduced by non-specialist physical education teachers.

Photo: Louis Bachoue of 'Sud-Ouest'

13a. Referee! How not to stop an opponent

13b. The 3–3 defensive formation, employed by Sweden against Rumania in the World Championship final in Prague

Photo: Hanns Apfel

13c. A 4–2 defensive formation used by West Germany in a match against Switzerland. A defensive error has allowed a Swiss attacker to penetrate the defence and shoot at goal

Handball in the Secondary School

It is at the secondary level of education, where the child is more likely to be taught by specialist teachers of physical education, that the development of handball from a purely natural game to that of a competitive sport will take place. Boys and girls at the senior end of the school who have developed handball as their particular choice of activity should, by this time, be emerging as good handball team players.

This, of course, does not mean that as soon as the boy enters the secondary school the teacher should expect him to begin right away to learn complicated skills and tactics. The process must be methodical and it must be achieved gradually. It is important to remember that the child, at the beginning of this new stage in his education, is still a very young individual.

The need for specialization is not required in the early stages of the secondary school programme on handball. It should be sufficient to centre the work done round the natural ability of the players, but with a more methodical approach than that used in the primary school. Tactics should at this stage be a word that is strictly taboo, this aspect of the game being incorporated in the general coaching that the teacher will give to his children. The teacher should show why it is important for each team to line up in a particular way to defend the goal and how, because of this way of defending, all the action of the game takes place at one end of the court. This is the only set type of play that should be found necessary in the first year. It should not be taught specifically: it must be developed within the game and the performers themselves should be able to see the reason for this type of play. They will soon realize that this is far better than for everyone to be charging all over the court at the same time trying to obtain possession of the ball.

The basic skills should be taught in a simple way if they are to be of interest and of benefit to the player. The teacher should not fall into the trap of separating the better performer from the poorer. It is much better to allow them to work together for their common good than to destroy the willingness to take part. One of the great joys of handball as an activity in schools is that

F 81

it allows the boy who is not blessed with a great amount of skill an opportunity to play his part side by side with the more able boy. This helps to stimulate an interest which in a lot of other sports quickly turns to disillusionment because they cater only for the child of good ability. Obviously, we do not mean to instil a false confidence into the poorer performer, nor indeed should we want to. Nevertheless, we are allowing him to take his place in the game with the knowledge that he is giving of his best and that his efforts are making a contribution which is of value.

The teacher should remember that when he is introducing the basic skills it is essential that they are taught in such a way that the child receiving the instruction understands what bearing the skill has to the game. Each skill that is taught must, as soon as possible, be put into a game situation to show its relevance. The teaching of isolated skills is in itself worthless.

Handball at the second year stage can be taken to a higher level of skill than in the first year, but the teacher must still be careful that he does not specialize too much. The children will, of course, have a basic knowledge of the game from their first-year course so that the teacher will not have to concern himself solely with promoting the natural side of the game, though it must still be in his mind that this is one of the reasons for including the game in the syllabus. More detailed work on the basic skills can now be undertaken, and, whilst there is no need for the tactics of the game to be uppermost in the mind of the teacher, he must now begin to develop these a little further. Again this can be done during the course of the game, but there will be cause for a little more detailed explanation as to why, in the teacher's opinion, this will help the players to enjoy the game even more.

There can be no doubt that children in the second year are the most receptive in the secondary school. They are keen to please and to learn and a great and important step forward can be made at this stage if the teacher introduces the game to them in a sensible manner. A knowledge of the more basic rules of handball will have been taught at the first-year stage. This should be developed further in the second year, when the playing of the game has greater importance in the mind of the child at this stage of his development. The knowledge of the rules need not be exhaustive but it should at least be sound and cover the main rules of the game. If handball is taught in a sensible way to second-year children its future success will be assured. The players themselves will see to this. Unconsciously they themselves will introduce the skills of team play and this will become more and more noticeable as their play develops.

By the third year in the secondary school, the rules of the game and their application should be fully understood by the players. Teaching can develop in a more formal manner and the development of more complicated tactics and skills can be begun. However, it must be remembered that the performers we are dealing with are still children and still very impressionable. The form of coaching used should not attempt to be too specific or there is the danger of loss of interest on the part of the children. The coaching should be aimed at the level of their ability and it must not be too involved.

Again, at this stage, there must not be too much emphasis laid on bringing the game down to the level of the poorer performer. If, in the previous year's work, this type of child has been made to see how he, too, can play an important part in the team, he will, by the time the third year has been reached, be waiting to improve the standard of his play. Obviously, by this time he will be aware of his limitations in the game, but nevertheless if we are to continue in our aim of giving him an interest we must realize that he too will want to play at a more advanced level.

Even so, the teacher must still be aware of the great range of ability within the class and all progress must take into account the speed of development of which the average performer is capable.

During the third year, the teacher may find himself faced with the great temptation of working with the abler children who have developed a strong interest in the game and are anxious to play at a higher level than can be catered for during the normal lesson time. This interest should be stimulated, but not at the cost of the other members of the class. Class work should be at a level which will give interest and stimulation to the majority. Work with the more able should be done outside the normal lesson, and when the teacher finds that interest has been stimulated in this way he should work towards the formation of a school handball club with meetings after school. When such a club is formed it is there that the teacher can feel free to stimulate the desire of the pupil to develop as a handball player. In the after-school club where there will be smaller numbers for the teacher to cater for the work can, of course, be directed towards the more tactical side of the game and to using skills which will aid the players to become in time valuable members of the school handball team. Certainly, if their talent is such, this is what they will want to become.

When the pupil reaches the fourth-year stage of the secondary school the basic skills should have become automatic. The time has arrived for a more technical approach to the game and this is what the pupils themselves will expect. After three years learning to be skilled handball players, they will want to put this practice to good use and become co-ordinated, thinking players. Again, however, it must be stressed that the teacher must not fall into the temptation of spending his lesson time solely for the benefit of the more able. The lesson must not become an extension of the after-school club. Whatever the theme of his lesson may be, it must still be within the capabilities of the whole range of the class.

It is with the fifteen plus age group that the work of education for leisure-time activities will begin to assume its place in the physical education programme. During the organized games period when, usually, more time is available to the physical educationist than in the ordinary lesson, the principle of options can be introduced. Options will allow the pupil, within reason, to choose which activity he would like to pursue. It is here that opportunities for the further development of the individual on a more personal level will present themselves. Group teaching is made possible and the teacher in charge of the activity will be working with receptive participants, taking part because it is the activity of their choice.

Part of the time with the option group should be spent in furthering this interest to enable them to continue with the sport after they have left school. The player should be told of the clubs in his area which would make him welcome and provide him with the facilities to take his interest further. Again I would mention the importance of having a club connected with the school to which interested pupils can belong, even before they have finished at school. This will provide continuity and familiar surroundings, where the boy (or girl) knows that he is welcome, and a contact with the place where an important part of his life has been spent.

It would be a mistake for handball, or any other activity, to be included in the physical education programme only to add another game or just to give the pupils something to do. It must be there because the teacher is convinced that the children are gaining something from its inclusion. He must ask himself the questions set at the beginning of this chapter and only when he is certain that they can be answered in the affirmative should he include any activity in his programme. That handball meets these requirements I have no doubt.

7 - THE HANDBALL CLUB

In the previous chapter, we discussed the development of the young handball player at school. We saw how, at the end of his or her life at school, it was important for the young player to find a handball club to which he could belong, a club where he could feel welcome and develop his handball skill further.

The handball clubs are, of course, the backbone of successful handball at the senior level of the game. It is important that the individual seeking membership to a club is assured that the club is run in the correct manner and will help him in his desire to progress as a handball player. He must be sure that membership will be an aid to his development along the lines he would wish and not just a means of playing handball for the sake of satisfying a few individuals.

It is imperative for the success of any club that there is some coaching available. If a club meets purely and simply to enable a few individuals to throw a ball around throughout the whole of the time available, there can be no doubt at all that there will be no future at all for the club. It will die a natural death as the participants become bored with their aimless wasting of time.

Obviously, the better the coaching, the more successful the club will become in the long run, always assuming that the players concerned realize the importance of coaching and respond favourably to their coach's efforts.

A friendly atmosphere within the club is of vital importance to its success, and there must be a warm welcome extended to newcomers. New members should be made to feel at their ease right from the start. They must not be made to feel that they have entered a closed shop during their first encounter with club members or they will never be seen again. First impressions are important, vital even. This is particularly so with young people leaving school, who will be looking for a club into which they can impart some of their personality. It must be remembered that these people will be leaving a world in which they have been, in effect, the senior and most prominent members, and are entering a life where they are very much junior partners. It is important and indeed of great value to them to feel happy and contented within the club.

The club welcome should obviously not be confined to younger members who have developed handball within the confines of their school. It must be prepared to welcome people who have never played before, both young and older people, who feel that they would like to be introduced to the game, and develop as players. The door must be open, too, to players who are not so good. These people should be encouraged to become active members of the club if they express a wish to do so. These people, whilst enjoying playing at their own level of ability, could perhaps be of great use to the club in an organizing or officiating capacity. However, whether or not this is the case, they should still be made to feel part of the club.

A friendly atmosphere and a warm welcome are, therefore, essential to any club. I have known too many clubs where the more established members have only paid lip service to this important aspect of club life. Although seemingly making people welcome, underneath they have resented the intrusion into their world, particularly when a game is in progress and the newcomer is not up to their standard of play. They forget that the game is also being spoilt for him and the obvious result is that the new member never visits the club again. Once this source of new blood into the club dries up, there can be only one inevitable result, the end of the club.

The forward-looking club will not allow itself to be confined to the playing of just one team at a competition level. In trying to ensure a healthy membership it will try to field as many teams as its members will allow. Obviously, it will have what is in effect its first team and it is at this level that the club will endeavour to do as well as it can in the competitive sphere of handball. There is no doubt that the more successful a club is, the more attractive it will seem to new members. It will obviously tend to attract more people to become members than the club that is not quite so successful.

Many of these people will have been persuaded to join the club for the purpose of playing in competitive handball and they must not be disappointed. Provision must be made for people not in the senior team to be members of a team. This will give opportunities for players who are not of first-team standard and for those who are waiting to prove that they are good enough to the coach or the team selectors. Selection to the first team should be the aim of all the handball players of ability.

Handball clubs having a thriving junior section separate from the senior teams are assured of a healthy future. This will provide the nursery for the senior section of the club. Given good coaching and healthy competition junior members will mature and in time graduate to take their place as useful players in the senior teams.

If the demand arises, the club should also provide a ladies' section. It must always be remembered that handball is a sport that can be enjoyed by both sexes. It is not exclusive to men.

The Organization of the Handball Club

If the handball club is to be successful, it must be organized properly from the beginning. There must be people in the club at an administrative level. The administration of the club could well be in the hands of former players or it can just as well be run by people who have very little playing ability but have a great love of the game and are anxious to ensure its development. It is one of the sad things about sport in this country that so many people who derive enjoyment from their playing days are lost to the sport of their choice when those days are over. These are the very people who could do a great deal to help in the development of their sport at an administrative or officiating level. They would be able to pass on to others the benefit of their experiences as players and use this experience to aid the future progress of the game and their club.

The administration of the club should not be left solely in the hands of the playing members. True, they should be allowed to play some part in the running of their own club, particularly in the matters which concern them. By and large, however, the pressures which administration inevitably brings should not have to rest on their shoulders. They will be busy in developing their own talents on the field of play, and be occupied in building and maintaining the reputation of the club at the playing level.

The administration of the club should be in the hands of a democratically elected committee capable of running the affairs of the club in an efficient manner. This committee could be elected on an annual basis at the annual general meeting of the club. Each year at this annual meeting the committee should assemble as a body in front of the whole of the interested membership to tell members what has happened in the preceding twelve months of its office. The meeting would be an opportunity for the ordinary members of the club to evaluate the results of the efforts of their committee and to give their comments and suggestions on those efforts.

The election of the committee could take place at this meeting as it will probably be the only time in the year that the majority of the members will find themselves meeting together in such a way. How many people should serve on the committee will, of course, be for each individual club to decide. However, I would venture to suggest that it will be found to be more workable if the committee is not too big. The committee should not be so large that it becomes too unwieldy; too many fingers in the pie make the business of administration much too difficult. It is important that those people who are elected to the committee accept the responsibility knowing what is expected of them. They must accept this responsibility because they feel that through their efforts they will be able to benefit the club in some way or another. The position offered to them must not be accepted because they look on it as a sort of status symbol. The success of the club will ultimately depend on the actions that are taken by this committee.

The number of people elected to serve on the committee will be decided upon by the members of the club, taking into account the club's needs and the extent of its activities. If it is to be kept small for the reasons I have mentioned then I would suggest the following:

(i) Chairman
(ii) Vice-Chairman
(iii) Hon. General Secretary
(iv) Treasurer
(v) Competitions Secretary
(vi) Membership Secretary

Should the need for more members arise or, for that matter, temporary members, then the committee should be given the powers to co-opt the people they think will be of most help.

In addition to the positions just mentioned, it will probably be found of use to have the more senior people from the playing side of the club as advisory members of the committee. This would enable the elected representatives to seek help when it is needed and would serve to keep them in touch with all sections of the club. Where the members of the committee are all non-playing members of the club, these advisers would be of immense value, ensuring that the voice of the players is heard. Should this idea be acceptable, then I would suggest the following as advisory members of the committee:

(i) The Club Captain
(ii) The Club Ladies' Captain
(iii) The Club Coach.

It might be to the club's advantage, too, to have the elected captain of the youth section, if one exists, as a member of this group. This would be an admirable opportunity of showing to the younger members that they are an important part of the life of the club and that their views are considered important.

A good chairman is essential both to the club and to the committee. It is he who will have to take decisions affecting the club. He must be able to keep the members of his committee together and settle any difficulties which arise whilst he is in office. He must, too, be a person capable of making decisions and standing by his actions, for it is he who, if there is disagreement within his committee, must take the final decision. This obviously means that the position of chairman is an important one and the person taking office must not do so lightly.

The same attributes are required in the vice-chairman, for it is he who must step into the chairman's shoes if he is absent from a meeting at any time.

A sense of responsibility is important for all committee members. The secretary needs to be dedicated to the position he has taken on because his work will involve a great deal of his free time. It is essential that he is capable of handling the club's correspondence in a responsible way because in many cases he will be the only contact that people outside have with the club. He will be dealing with business people over items such as equipment, and with other clubs throughout the country.

No one needs to be told the value of a good treasurer. Unfortunately, they are often hard to find and, where a club is fortunate to have such a person, they should indeed treat him with respect and be appreciative of his efforts, realizing just how much work is involved in running the financial side of the club.

By including a membership secretary and a competitions secretary, the club will have gone a long way to easing the burdens of the treasurer and the general secretary. The membership secretary will provide a personal link between all the members of the club and the committee and be responsible for keeping lists of the members and making sure they keep up to date with the important matter of their subscriptions. He should be responsible, too, for the introduction of new members of the club and ensuring that a welcome is offered to them. The competitions secretary could be resposible for the club fixtures and arranging the internal competitions of the club. He must, too, be knowledgeable about external competitions in which his club teams could take part.

Members of the committee, therefore, must not take their responsibilities lightly. The people concerned must, in their own minds, be sure that their efforts will be of use to the club. They must, too, be prepared to act as ambassadors for the club at regional and national congresses. They must realize that very often they are introducing their club to others for the very first time and it is important that the impression they leave is both lasting and favourable, for it will ultimately have a bearing on the progress of the club.

The Club Coach

For a club to achieve any form of success at the competitive level, there must be a certain amount of coaching from within. Players must accept that if they want to progress as handball players they must put themselves in the hands of the club coach and work with him to their own advantage. Players must realize that the old adage 'play up and play the game' no longer applies in its old sense. True, they must play handball because they want to as sportsmen, but they must develop the more technical side of the game as well if they are to keep pace with the more up-to-date sports club.

The level of coaching within the club is, of course, a matter for each individual club and it will have to take into account the attitude of the players and the ability of the man in charge of the club coaching programme. This does not necessarily mean that a club should restrict itself to having only one person concerned with the coaching, but where a club is fortunate to have the services of more than one person, it is wise to have one of them appointed to the position of senior club coach.

The club coach must take his responsibilities seriously, for on him will ultimately depend the success or failure of the club's teams. He should try to keep abreast of all the latest developments within the game, taking time to attend the coaching clinics organized by the British Handball Association at either a regional or a national level. To function properly as a coach and give of his best to his players, the handball coach must indeed be a dedicated man.

The team coach must be able, through the medium of his own personality, to inspire his players to work for a common cause, the improvement of their personal performance and their development as members of a team. The players must be thoroughly convinced that the efforts of their coach are both sensible and worthwhile. They must be assured, too, that their participation in his methods will improve their performance as team players. The personality of the coach is very important; he must be accepted for what he is, an important member of the team. His contact with his players should be friendly but firm, and they in turn should respond by their efforts to function well as a team. That the personality of the coach is important will be borne out on the field of play in the style of play of the team and of the individual players. This is particularly so when the coach has charge of young players who will quickly emulate the style of their coach in their playing method.

With this in mind, the coach must be wary when demonstrating the individual skills of the game. The cricket coach will always say that it is important to demonstrate the correct method of play only. The wrong way must never be demonstrated. This is particularly so with younger players or those introduced to the game. Demonstrating incorrect methods will only help to confuse them. All this does not mean that there is no place for originality amongst the handball players; far from it. If the player is executing a skill efficiently though in a different way to that taught by the coach, he should be allowed to carry on with this method, providing the coach does not feel that it is harmful to his development.

A sound technical knowledge of the game is absolutely essential, for the coach must know at what stage of the game the various skills and tactics that his team have acquired can be brought into use. This by no means implies that playing methods should become stereotyped, and indeed the coach must be on his guard against this, and be aware of it when it does occur. If he does not detect this when it happens then his team will ultimately suffer. Players will become stale and, as fixtures with other teams are repeated, the opposition will know how to deal with the set patterns of play encountered in previous matches.

The methods used by the coach in his team training must be put over to the players in such a way that they can easily understand the value of what they are doing. That the coach must be able to teach should go without saying. It is not sufficient for him to have acquired a vast wealth of knowledge. He must be able to give this knowledge to his players clearly and they must be able to understand his methods. All progressions must be logical and must keep pace with the progress of the players. He must not fall into the trap of making practices too simple or the players will not take them seriously. On the other hand, they must not be too difficult or the players will become bored and no progress will be made at all. All the practices that the coach evolves which demand team work should be done in such a manner that they simulate a game situation. Individual skills, too, must not be isolated from a game situation for too long or they will prove worthless.

That the coach is considered a member of the team is of vital importance. During a match, the team must have absolute confidence in their coach, relying on him to make the correct decisions at the right time. From his position on the team bench, he must be able to use his powers of observation to the advantage of his team.

Not only in a match situation must the coach be able to draw logical conclusions from his observation of players and methods of play. He must do so during training sessions also, both at group and individual level. He must be able to analyse an individual's movements. It is not enough for him to know that something is wrong either with the action of a player or with the team movements in a practice situation. He must be able to correct these mistakes quickly and efficiently.

It is during the playing of an actual match that the observations of the coach must prove of most value to the team players. He must be able to organize the tactics of his own team and, at the same time, understand where the tactics of the opposition are centred and how they are being utilized against his players. The good team coach should be able to organize his team to counter the movements of the opposing team. His team should be so well drilled that, immediately an order is issued from the bench, they automatically respond to it. Substitution during a game is also the responsibility of the coach and this must be done wisely and at the right moment in the game. In handball, the substitutes who are sitting on the bench are not necessarily the weaker players of the team. The coach should use his substitutes according to the situation within the game being played. If the opposition are employing a six and nought defence formation, the coach must utilize his more powerful players to enable shooting to be executed over the defensive wall. Should the situation change and the defence meet this form of attack by coming out to a four–two formation, then the coach must act accordingly. If he persists in making his attack from a distance, then he will have allowed the opponents to have gained the advantage they had been hoping for. He should call off his strong back line players and substitute for them the players who he knows are more skilful at working closer to the goal.

This applies, too, in the form of defensive cover that the coach utilizes. The whole of his analysis of the game must be adapted to ever changing situations and he must be able to meet all the conditions he is likely to encounter. The players who are on court at any one time should not be there because in the coach's opinion they are his strongest or the best ball players. They must be there because they are the people the coach feels can best meet the situation that has arisen within the game. It is important that the coach does not allow players to remain on the court too long so that they become tired. He must be constantly aware of this point and he should know his players well enough to recognize when they should be taken from the court to stop them becoming over-tired. If players are allowed to remain on court for too long they will be of little further use in the game; even after a period of rest on the sub-stitution bench they will return to the field capable only of playing at a much reduced level.

Organizing ability is essential for a successful coach. He must set a programme of work for his players in their training schedule and, through this work, he must aim for a balanced programme which will benefit his players both individually and as a team. The training programme must be carefully planned and, if necessary, the coach should be prepared to organize schedules for individual players. The presentation of the pro-gramme must take into account the physical and mental make-up of the people who will be involved. The players, for their part, must appreciate the value of the coach's efforts and be prepared to work in order that the programme will prove successful.

What the coaching programme is to include will obviously depend on the coach responsible, but I would like to suggest a framework which might prove of help to club coaches:

1. Personal warm up session.
2. Individual coaching covering the basic techniques.
3. Team practices: (a) defence;
   (b) attack;
   (c) combination of attacking and defensive movements.
4. Tactical talk
5. Developing new tactics
6. Personal training
7. Break
8. Free game.

Obviously, time is an important factor in the training of players. There is never time enough available, but what there is the coach must utilize to the best of his ability for the benefit of his players. Assuming that the club meets for a period of two hours on one evening a week, how should the coach divide the time he has at his disposal? It would be wise for him to set a time for the training session to begin. He should insist that all the players arrive at the club in advance of this time in order that they can have a personal warming up session in preparation for the work ahead. The coach should make sure that the purpose of the warming up period is understood by everyone concerned. If it is tackled correctly, there will be little risk of injury from muscle strain later in the evening. When the coach is sure that his players are ready, he should begin to tackle the first part of his programme, coaching the individual skills of the game. The way that the coach teaches this aspect of the game is most important. It should be within the capabilities of each player. However, where a player is weak in any particular skill, the coach should pay attention to its development and the player must be encouraged to practise it.

The time devoted to this section of the programme should not be particularly long unless the coach has a specific reason

Photos: 'Ormskirk Advertiser'

14. Handball in Britain. Incidents in the Great Britain v. Italy match, 1969

a. John Davies of Britain fists the ball towards the Italian goal in an effort to score

Photo: 'Ormskirk Advertiser'

b. A successful move to draw defenders out of position by an Italian player in order to pass the ball to the Italian player No. 5

Photo: 'Ormskirk Advertiser'

c. John Davies watches as a shot is turned behind by the Italian goalkeeper

Photo: 'Ormskirk Advertiser'

d. Back line player passes the ball to front line player No. 10. Notice how the Italian player in front of the British No. 8, Phil Holden, has succeeded in blocking his forward movement to intercept

for doing otherwise. If too much time is spent here, players will tend to become bored and quickly lose interest in what they are doing and this could affect the whole of the evening's work. Somewhere in the region of ten minutes should be more than enough time spent on the basic skills.

Following this work the coach will move on to team practices, perhaps starting by linking them to the work done in the basic skills training. Team practices should include techniques that are well know to the players. It is wise to begin by using defensive formations and then, when the coach is satisfied with the progress made, he can move on to attacking movements. Again, when he is satisfied, he should move to the next part of this section, the combination of both attacking and defensive movements, using only one half of the court for this work.

Uppermost in the coach's mind at all times must be the need to stimulate interest. Even when his players are practising something they have done many times, the coach must still devise ways of keeping their interest alive. He could devise competitive practices, such as four attackers to three defenders or vice versa. However, both he and the players must remember why the exercise is being undertaken and all the practices must resemble a game situation for them to be of any benefit. Again, time is important and, unless the coach has a definite reason for doing otherwise, the work on this aspect of the game should only take up the amount of time required for it to be undertaken successfully. This should be somewhere in the region of fifteen minutes.

A short time could now be made available to give the players a short rest and enable the coach to have a tactical talk period. The availability of a blackboard would be most useful. This talk could include such things as introducing new tactics or it could be to analyse the play in a recent match. If things went wrong, why did they go wrong, and how can present tactical play be improved? The time spent in this way should not be too long; players should not be allowed to get cold or they will lose the benefit of the earlier part of the evening's training. The coach should move on quickly to put his words into actions, the players trying out the things that have been discussed in a match type of situation. This part of the programme should take up about twenty minutes.

The next part of the programme will be individual fitness training. This must be attempted before the players are too tired. It could be in the form of pressure skills training or circuit training. This we will examine in more detail in a little while.

After the personal fitness training, a short break will prove very welcome. Once the players have overcome their tiredness sufficiently, they should be allowed to immerse themselves in a game as a just reward for all their efforts.

At first, there is no doubt that the coach will encounter difficulties in persuading some players to take a healthy interest in the training sessions. Some will respond almost immediately, realizing the value of coaching and appreciating the efforts of the coach. Others, however, may prove apathetic and resent the intrusion into their playing time. They will not want to be bothered with coaching schedules or team discipline. It is a sad thing that very often the people who have this type of attitude towards organized coaching are the very ones who, if they accepted it, could become the star players of the game. These difficulties must be overcome and the coach must convince his players how useful and rewarding a balanced programme will ultimately be to them.

A sense of team discipline and team loyalty must be introduced, particularly with younger players. When a time is set by the coach for work to begin, he should be reasonably satisfied that his players are doing their best to arrive on time. There may be a tendency for some of the players to arrive late, possibly just in time to take part in the game period of the evening. Once the coach notices that certain players are making a habit of this, he must tell them quite definitely that there can be no place in the team for them unless they are prepared to work with the others for success. Once the coach decides on this course of action, however, there must be no turning back. He must never give an individual player the impression that he is indispensable.

The coach, if he is to be successful, must be prepared to have a great deal of patience. As we said before, he must be friendly as well as firm. Patience will, indeed, prove a great virtue, particularly when the coach is dealing with young players or newcomers to the game, and he will gain a much more favourable response to his efforts. We must not forget that coaches, however good they may be, are still human. They will have their frustrations when things are not going as planned or if players, after hours of practice, find themselves unable to master certain skills properly. The coach must of necessity keep these feelings to himself if there is to be any hope of eventual success.

In his efforts to find a successful formula, the coach must be prepared to experiment with new ideas and he must be imaginative. However, if things do not turn out as he would have hoped, he must accept his failure and experiment further to find out where he went wrong. He must accept also that, to be a successful coach, he will have to be blessed with a certain amount of luck.

Circuit Training

It is not my intention to delve too deeply into the aspects of circuit training. I merely intend to describe it briefly and show how useful it can be in the training of handball players. Coaches who feel that they would like to know more about this form of training are advised to read *Circuit Training* by R. E. Morgan and G. T. Adamson (Bell). They will find it a very useful book.

There are numerous advantages to be gained from including circuit training in the coaching programme. The coach can utilize whatever facilities he has available. It can be done by large numbers in a small amount of space, it calls for vigorous exercise on the part of the performer, and it takes only a relatively short time to complete the exercises. On top of this, it puts the onus to work fairly and squarely on the shoulders of the performer. The amount of effort that he puts into each exercise will be entirely up to him.

Circuit training is an effective way of ensuring development in muscular and circulo-respiratory fitness. There are several ways in which it can be introduced by the coach for inclusion in his training programme. I intend to look at just one of these methods, which we will call individual measurement.

The coach must first decide on which activities he intends to include in the circuit, making sure that he personally is fully conversant with each one before it is introduced. The number of activities to be included is a matter for each individual coach to decide, but it is wise not to include too many. After each activity has been explained in detail, the performers should be given the opportunity of practising.

Circuit training involves repetition of vigorous activities so it is wise to introduce it slowly and deliberately. Players must not be expected to do too much in the early stages, they should take a few weeks to build up to what will eventually be a strenuous full circuit. To begin with, the coach should work on an individual basis, giving each a set of repetitions well within his capabilities. This should be slowly increased. The coach, in using this method of introduction, will also be making sure that the idea of circuit training is fully understood by the performers involved. About three or four weeks should be taken up by this method of introduction. When the coach is satisfied that his players are ready, he should begin to introduce a more positive approach to the work.

When the time has come for the full circuit to be attempted, each performer should be given a circuit card for the purpose of keeping an individual record. This card should be divided into separate columns, with appropriate spaces for the name of the activity, the maximum number of times the activity has been repeated by the performer, the order in which the performer attempts each activity, the number of repetitions to be done in future circuits, and the time each circuit takes to be completed (Fig. 33).

Before attempting the circuit proper, time must be spent to find the number of times the performer can repeat each activity. This is called finding the performer maximum. Whilst this is being done, the individual must record on his card the order in which he does the activity. There need be no specific order laid down by the coach but the individual must understand that, in whatever order he chooses to do the activities when testing his maxima, that must also be the order in which he does his circuit in the future.

It will be found when compiling the circuit that some of the maxima must be ascertained by timing the activity involved. The time should not exceed one minute for each. Other activities will, because of their very nature as strenuous activities, need only a limited number of repetitions for the performer to discover how many he is capable of doing. When all the activities in the circuit have been completed, the performer should divide the maximum obtained for each one by two and enter his findings in the column marked circuit on his record card. Where an odd number is involved, the number entered in the circuit column should be the next higher number above half e.g. Activity: Chins. Maximum 7. Circuit 4. This is the number of repetitions he will be expected to complete on each lap of the circuit.

When the maximum has been found and the entry in the circuit column made, the performer is ready to complete a full circuit on future occasions. When he comes to do his circuit, he must ignore the number in the maximum column and concentrate on his circuit entry. To complete the circuit successfully, he must do each circuit number three times, in the order on the card. By completing three laps of the circuit in this way, he will have done one-third more than the number of repetitions in the maximum column. When this stage has been reached, the coach should introduce the idea of a timed circuit to the performer. It should be found that the time taken will be reduced as the training continues. When the coach considers that the moment has come for a re-testing of the maxima, he should go through the same procedure as before. If the performer has done the circuit exercises correctly, it should be found that he is able to increase the number of repetitions in the maximum column on the record card.

What exercises are included in the circuit is a matter for each individual coach. He can, if he wishes, concentrate on developing certain parts of the body, but he would be wise, at the beginning, to endeavour to build up the level of all-round general fitness in his players.

NAME					
ACTIVITY	MAXIMUM	ORDER	CIRCUIT	DATE	TIME TAKEN TO COMPLETE CIRCUIT
Chins	8	1	4		
1 min. Burpee	20	3	10		
Press up	17	2	9		
1 min. Step up	32	6	16		
Curls	22	5	11		
Rope swing	9	8	5		
1 min. Squats	16	7	8		
Bench press	12	4	6		

FIG. 33. Specimen circuit record card

The specimen card above shows eight activities aimed at developing an all-round general fitness. They are simple to execute and, assuming that the coach has the use of the average type of gymnasium, are well within the scope of the facilities available.

Step-ups require the use of two gymnasium benches, one placed on top of the other. The benches should be positioned near a wall or the wall bars. The performer places one foot on the top of the bench and then lifts the whole of his body on to the bench. He then puts the action into reverse to return to the starting position. This movement should be repeated as many times as possible within the space of one minute and the total number of repetitions is then recorded on the personal record card. It would be advisable for the coach to take charge of this activity himself or at least have someone available to time the performers. This applies in all the activities that require the use of the clock.

Press-ups should be done in a clear space on the floor, with the performer starting the exercise in the front support position. The arms are then bent until the whole of the body is parallel with the floor. The performer then pushes against the floor with his arms and returns to the front support position. The press-up should not be considered satisfactorily done if any part of the body other than the hands and toes comes into contact with the floor. The performer should do as many press-ups as he is able.

Rope swings are a useful gripping and heaving exercise. The performer stands between two ropes grasping them at roughly face height. Running forward, he should aim to swing himself to touch with his feet a beam in front of him at a height of about ten feet. On the way down, he is allowed to take two or three steps backwards when he touches the floor. He should then swing himself forwards to repeat the action. On no account must he touch the floor with his feet during the forward movement or the aim of the exercise will have been defeated.

The burpee is another activity which must be timed. It is aimed at abdominal, leg and general development. The performer begins the activity in the standing position. He then moves into the crouch position placing the hands on the floor and, from there, throws both legs backwards to take up the front support position similar to that at the start of the press-up. The action is then put into reverse until the performer regains the standing position. To be effective, the movement must be rapid.

Chins, or chinning the bar, does not have to be timed as it will be found a very strenuous activity. The beam is used for this activity. The performer should jump on to the beam to obtain an overhand grasp position with the hands. He begins by hanging on the beam and proceeds to pull himself upwards with his arms until his chin is level with the top of the beam. The body is then lowered and the action repeated. The height of the beam should be such that the performer is unable to touch the floor with his feet when in the hanging position.

The trunk curl is aimed at the development of the abdominal muscles. The performer lies on his back with his hands resting on his thighs. The hands are moved slowly down the thigh until they reach the top of the knee-cap, the head and shoulders being lifted from their position on the floor during the execution of this movement. The trunk curl should be repeated as many times as possible.

Squat jumps, aimed at leg and general development, should be timed for one minute. The performer moves from an upright position to a squat position with the hands resting lightly on the floor and one leg in front of the other. He then thrusts himself upwards into the air, stretching his legs and body as he does so, and returns to the squat position, this time with the other leg forward.

The bench press requires the use of a gymnasium bench hooked over one of the higher wall bars at one end and with the other end resting on the floor. The performer assumes a squatting position in front of the bench, grasping the bench with both hands. Lifting the bench, he should aim to rise smoothly into the standing position, lifting the bench over his head as far as he possibly can. When this position has been achieved, the bench is lowered and returned to the floor. The action should be repeated as many times as possible.

Whilst doing the circuit, it is important that the performer is constantly on the move. This does not imply that he should rush everywhere but he must not waste time between each activity. Each time the circuit is completed, the date and time in which it was done should be recorded in the appropriate columns on the card. The player must make sure that the entries on the card are accurate and each time a circuit is completed he should show the card to the coach. The coach, for his part, should watch the time column carefully and, when he feels that the athlete is working well within his capabilities, he should advise him to re-test his maxima. For the new test, the player should be issued with a new card and the old one discarded.

There is, of course, no compelling reason for the coach to use the circuit described in this chapter. There is no reason, either, why he should only use eight activities. He can add more if he wishes or indeed have less in his circuit, but he must see that the balance will achieve an all-round development. The circuit that has been described here is one that has been used with good effect with the players of The Cardinal's Handball Club, Liverpool, who have found it a useful part of their training programme.

On the whole, the coach will find that this form of training is readily acceptable to his players. However, he must impress upon them that, for it to be beneficial, it must be done regularly. There is very little point in a player taking part in the circuit now and again.

8 - COMPETITION

For a club to enjoy a healthy membership, there must be competition for its more enthusiastic members, in the form of competitive matches against other clubs. If players are going to give up their time for methodical coaching and rigorous exercise, then there must indeed be an opportunity for both them and their coach to match their hard-earned skill against players from other clubs. This will be the only practical way for them to discover whether their training has been of good use, and the coach will only be able to improve his methods of coaching if he sees what he has done put to the test.

The task of obtaining fixtures for the club teams should be undertaken by the competitions secretary. If the club is newly formed, he should, when the coach feels his players are ready, write to other clubs in his area to ask if they would be willing to include his club on their fixture lists. He can be sure that he will meet with a favourable reply, but the players must not be disappointed if, in the early stages, the more established clubs do not send their strongest team to play against them. They must realize that these clubs will already have existing fixtures to be honoured. However, once the club players have proved themselves worthy of a visit from a stronger team, they will have no cause to worry. If the players and the club can show that they are capable of upholding a sportsmanlike tradition, they will soon be elevated to the level of first-team fixtures.

If a handball league is in existence, then the work of the competitions secretary will be made very much easier, as he will be able to apply to the league for membership. However, it would be wise, in the case of a new club, to play some matches on a friendly basis before they consider entering into league fixtures. Of course, there are not always leagues available and it may be the club's desire to play matches on a friendly basis anyway.

When this is the case, there is a great need for a highly competent competitions secretary.

The players, however, must realize that the business of obtaining fixtures is not solely the task of the competitions secretary. True, he will be instrumental in making the fixtures materialize, but it is also up to the players to make sure that his hard work is rewarded. They must prove to their visitors that they are worthy opponents, capable of behaving like sportsmen, both on and off the field of play. This does not mean to say that they should not go all out to win, far from it, but they must be able to lose and take defeat, if it comes, in the right spirit. They must accept the decisions of the referee even if they feel that sometimes these are hard. The referee has been appointed to the game because he has a full knowledge of the rules and they must accept his interpretations of them.

Club members, too, must play their part in attracting other teams and show visiting players that they are welcome in the club. Their hospitality will certainly be appreciated and, no doubt, reciprocated when the visit is returned.

If the club is to attract visiting teams, then efficient arrangements must be made and everything must be ready to enable the match to go ahead without interruption. This could be the responsibility of the competitions secretary, but it would be unfair to expect him to do it alone. There is no reason, of course, why a club member should not be co-opted to the club committee to take responsibility for arranging the court before matches are to take place. Again, however, it would be unfair to expect one person to arrange all the tables and benches that will be necessary and it would be better if a small party of volunteers could be persuaded to arrive at the club a little earlier than usual to make all the necessary arrangements.

It is the responsibility of the home club to ensure that the necessary match officials: two referees, a timekeeper and a scorer are available for the match. The British Handball Association's senior area coach will be able to provide a list of people competent to take charge, and the club should provide the timekeeper and scorer. If, however, the club is unable to find a referee from the official source, they should inform their opponents as soon as possible. The two clubs concerned should then try to come to a mutual agreement as to who the officials are to be. As two referees are required in handball, then the wisest thing to do would be to have one member from each club. providing each club has a person who is capable of undertaking the duties of referee.

The appointment of the timekeeper to the game and the scorer could be left entirely to the home club. How they decide to select people for this task is a matter for each individual club. They could call for volunteers before the match begins or they could, if they are more organized, work a rota of the willing people in the club. Before the list of fixtures is drawn up by the competitions secretary, he would be wise to ask the non-playing members of the club if they would be prepared to serve the club in officiating at matches played by the club teams. If there is sufficient interest shown, the competitions secretary can, when publishing his fixture lists, put the names of the willing people by the side of each individual fixture. If there are enough, then this could be worked on a rota basis, thus ensuring that the work will not fall on to the shoulders of the same individuals every time. By publishing the list of officials well in advance, the people concerned will have had ample warning, and if they find that the particular match for which they have been chosen is inconvenient to them, they will be able to inform the secretary in time for him to make alternative arrangements.

The need for encouraging as many people as possible to take up these duties cannot be stressed hard enough. All too often the work of organization falls to a small dedicated few and this can lead to a dangerous situation. If any of them leave the club at any time, they will leave behind an enormous gap in the strength of the club. Every club member should play his part in all aspects of club life and the policy of the club should be to distribute work fairly amongst its members. Playing members who are nearing the end of their playing careers should be encouraged to continue to take an active part in the club, by giving time to pass the referee's examination or taking up duties within the club as match officials.

When the club decides to play inter-club matches it must ensure that it has the facilities and equipment needed for the type of matches it intends to play. The balls that are to be used for the match should be of the correct weight and size. If the ladies' section play matches they should not be expected to play with a handball intended for use by men; it will be found too heavy and too big for them to control properly. A good supply of balls is essential. If a club has sufficient members to warrant it, one of the members could be given the responsibility of equipment secretary to look after the equipment already in the club's possession, to see that it is in good repair, and to deal with suppliers when new equipment has to be ordered.

When a match is to take place it is important that the following items are provided: two match balls, the regulation goals, two team benches, a timekeeper's table and a scoreboard. Care should also be taken to provide enough handballs for both teams to be able to practise with during the warm-up period before the game begins.

The two match balls must be handed to the referee who will then decide which one to use in the game. The other ball will be kept in reserve in case there is a need to change the first ball whilst the game is in progress. Once the game has started the ball may only be changed in exceptional circumstances, so it is wise to make sure that the two balls handed to the referee for approval are in good condition.

The home club are responsible for ensuring that the goals to be used for the match meet the requirements laid down by the rules of the game. For a seven-a-side match the goals must be 2 m. (6 ft. 8 in.) in height and 3 m. (10 ft.) in width. They should be made of wood measuring 8 cm. × 8 cm. (3 in. × 3 in.) and painted in two different colours which contrast effectively with the background. The two colours must alternate with one another and each section of colour must measure 20 cm. (8 in.) in length. If the goals are to be used for five-a-side handball game then they must measure 122 cm. (4 ft.) in height and 182 cm. (6 ft.) in length.

Team benches, placed separately from each other, must be provided for use by the players in each team who are not

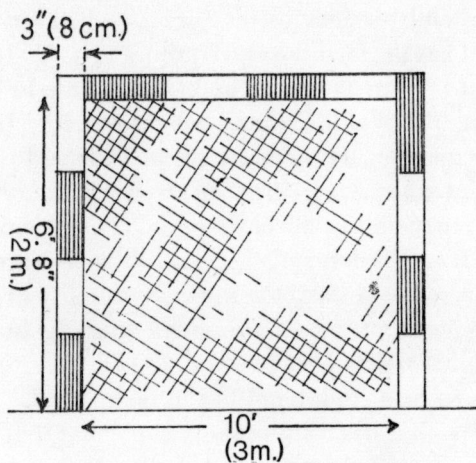

3"(8 cm.)

6' 8" (2 m.)

10' (3m.)

FIG. 34. The handball goal. Front elevation

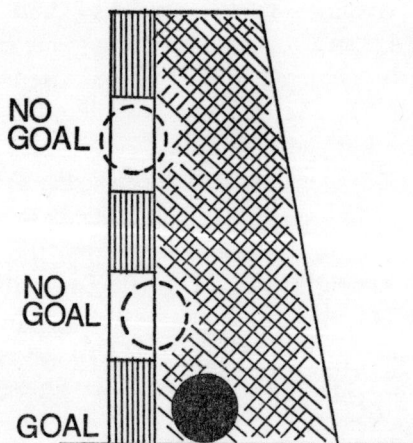

NO GOAL

NO GOAL

GOAL

FIG. 35

This side view of the handball goal shows how the goal net should be positioned and also that the whole of the ball must have crossed over the goal line and into the goal before a goal can be allowed

actively engaged in the game and for the team coach. Both benches should, if possible, be placed near the timekeeper's table. A third bench, known as the suspension bench, must be placed near to the timekeeper's table. This bench will be used during the match by players who have been given a period of suspension by the referee. There are two periods of suspension that can be awarded against an individual player: two minutes or five minutes. If a player is sent from the field for a third time he is not allowed to return. When the suspended player leaves the court he must seat himself near the timekeeper who will tell him when his period of suspension is completed, when he should ask the referee's permission to rejoin the game.

The position of the timekeeper is an important one within the game. As we have seen one of his duties is to control periods of suspension, making sure that the player concerned does not return to the game before his period of suspension has been completed. Before the game begins the timekeeper should make sure that he has in his possession at least two stop-watches and a whistle. One watch is used to time the duration of the game and the other to time suspension periods. The first watch should be started as soon as the whistle is blown by the referee for the throw off at the beginning of the game. When the time set for the end of the game arrives the timekeeper should blow his whistle. The referee will then stop the game when he is ready. However, it should be remembered that the timekeeper is the official responsible for timing the game.

The person who is given charge of keeping the score could quite easily share the table used by the timekeeper. This position also must be regarded as an important one, and the person concerned must take care to see that his entries on the score sheet are accurate and readable. The efficient club will make a point of providing two score record sheets for the scorer to complete. At the end of the game one of the sheets is then presented to the opposing team.

The score sheet used could be the official one issued by the British Handball Association or it could be one peculiar to the club concerned. If a club prefers to print their own sheets then they must be sure that they include the following information and detail. The names of both teams should be marked on the sheet and also each individual player should be named and his number entered alongside his name. There must be space for recording the goals so that it can be seen how many goals each player has scored. Periods of suspension too must be entered. It is useful, for the benefit of the scorer, to have a running total column, similar to that used in cricket score books. This greatly eases the scorer's problems. Each time a goal is scored he simply has to cross out the corresponding number on the sheet. This enables him to have quick reference to the score if it is needed during the game, and to cross-check if there is any doubt at the end of the game. Finally, there must be a space for recording the half time score and the final score of the game, or, in the case of five-a-side matches, the final score and the score at the end of each period in the game (Fig. 36).

Handball can very often be a high scoring game and it would be quite easy for both players and spectators to forget how many goals have been scored. This should not be allowed to happen and a scoreboard should be provided and placed in a prominent position so that it can easily be seen by both players and spectators. The board that is used does not have to be an elaborate one: a blackboard divided into two is sufficient, with the name of each team placed at the top of a column. The person in charge of the blackboard merely has to change the score with a piece of chalk as each goal is scored.

The Invitation Tournament

During the summer months, when handball can more easily be played out of doors, the go-ahead handball club might well think in terms of an invitation tournament, if their facilities will allow it, inviting other clubs in the area to come and take part. However, if such an idea is put into effect the responsibility on the part of the organizing club to make the occasion a successful one will be considerable. The organization required will be far in excess of what has been required for matches against one team on club evenings.

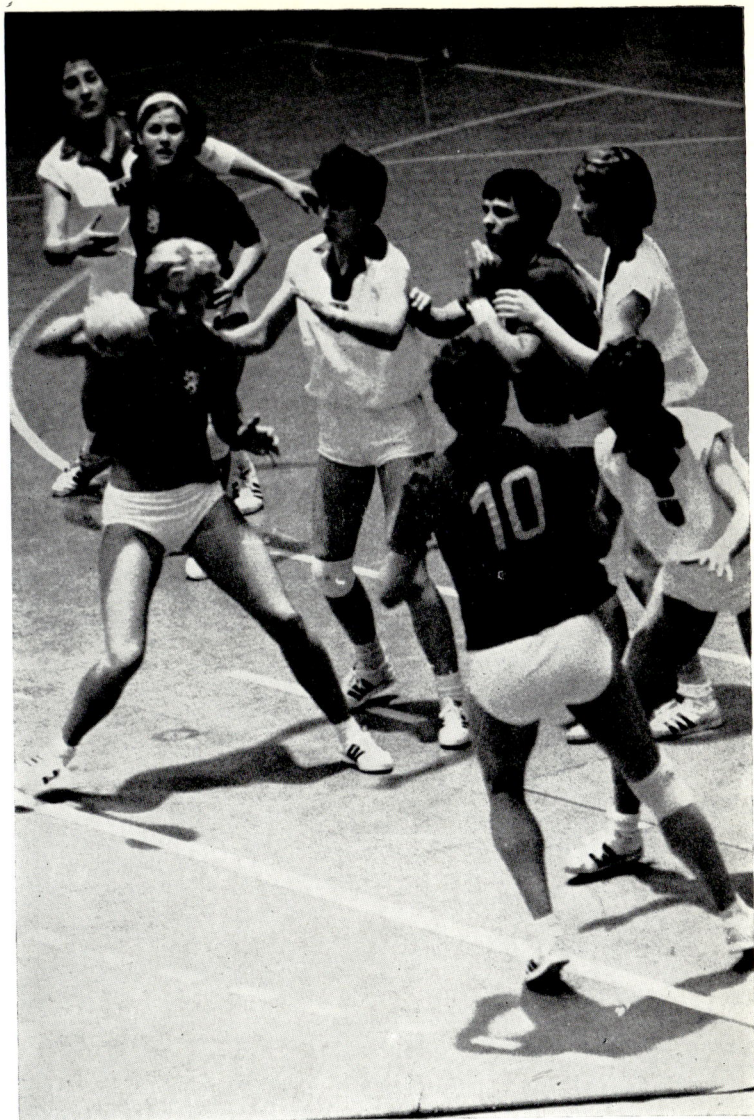

15. Handball for women. Here the Czech ladies' team mounts an attack
in a match against West Germany

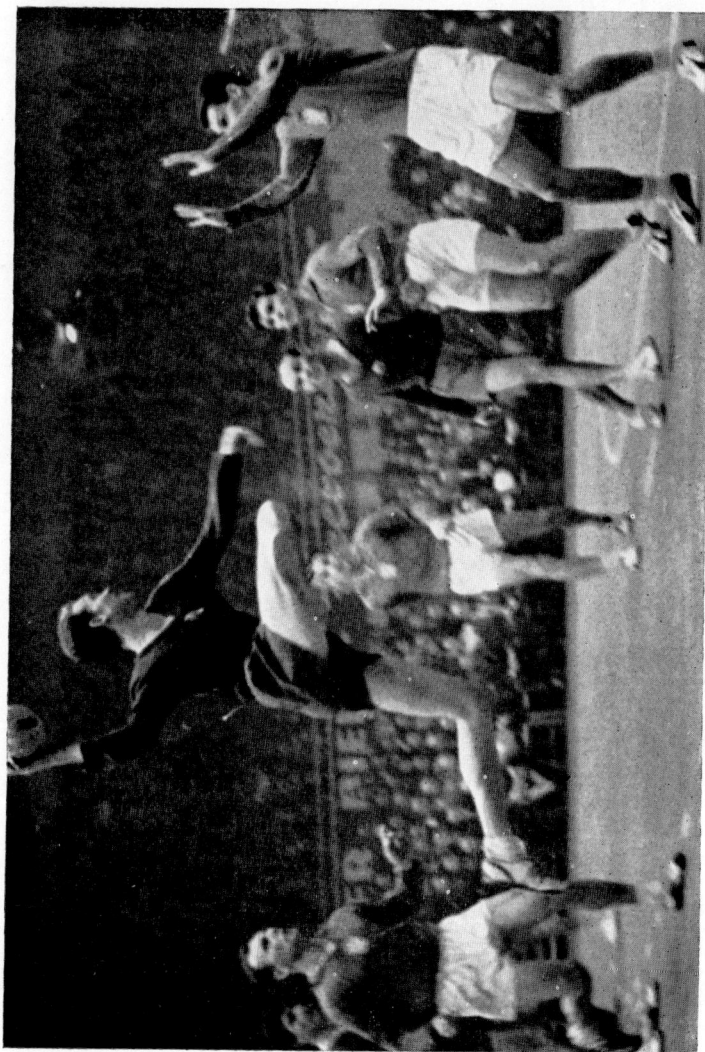

Photo : Hanns Apfel

16. A jump shot before the defence. This photograph shows Hanns Moser, a World Class player, playing for Rumania against Czechoslovakia in the 1960 World Championship, Dortmund

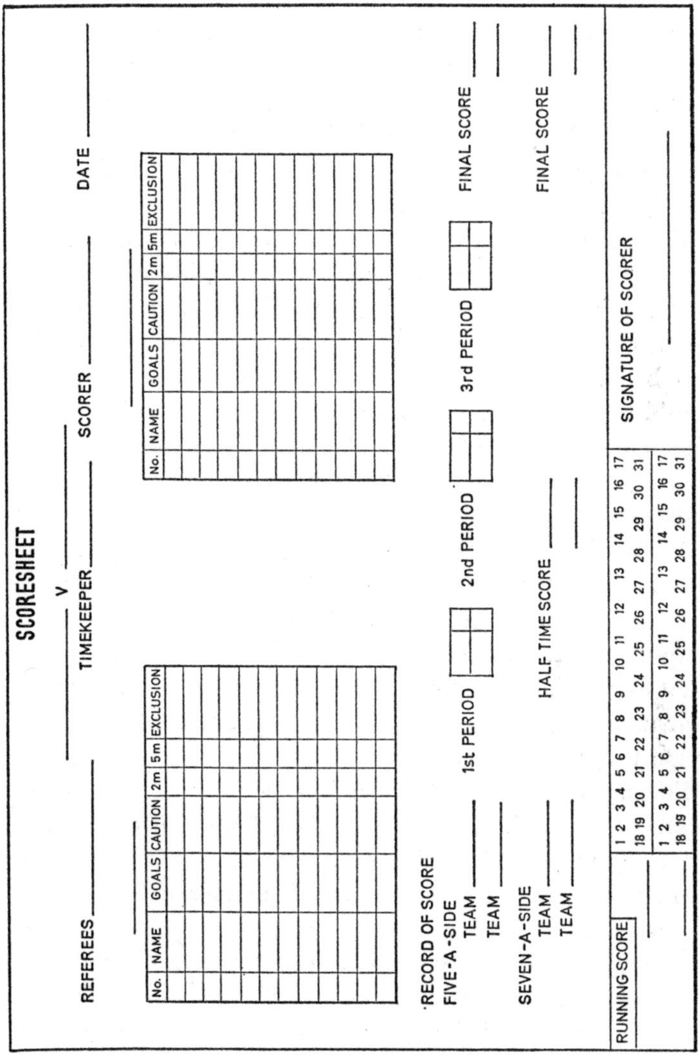

SCORESHEET

REFEREES _____ TIMEKEEPER _____ v SCORER _____ DATE _____

No.	NAME	GOALS	CAUTION	2m	5m	EXCLUSION

No.	NAME	GOALS	CAUTION	2m	5m	EXCLUSION

RECORD OF SCORE

FIVE-A-SIDE
TEAM _____
TEAM _____

SEVEN-A-SIDE
TEAM _____
TEAM _____

1st PERIOD _____   2nd PERIOD _____   3rd PERIOD _____   FINAL SCORE _____

HALF TIME SCORE _____   FINAL SCORE _____

RUNNING SCORE

| 1 2 3 4 5 6 7 8 9 10 11 12 13 14 15 16 17 |
| 18 19 20 21 22 23 24 25 26 27 28 29 30 31 |
| 1 2 3 4 5 6 7 8 9 10 11 12 13 14 15 16 17 |
| 18 19 20 21 22 23 24 25 26 27 28 29 30 31 |

SIGNATURE OF SCORER _____

FIG. 36. Specimen scoresheet

The decision to stage a tournament of this nature must not be taken on the spur of the moment. The implications of the idea must be discussed at length and plans made well in advance. It must not end up as a hit and miss affair. However, where a club does decide to run an invitation tournament and it is successful it can only serve to enhance the reputation of the club. It will also be a wonderful opportunity for handball players to meet together and derive enjoyment from competing against one another.

The decision should in the first instance rest with the executive committee of the club. However, if they think it appropriate they can find out the general opinion of the members before they decide one way or the other. A number of suitable dates should also be discussed at this stage, and the date finally chosen should be convenient for the majority of members concerned. If the committee decides in favour of the tournament being held then time must not be wasted and preparations should be got under way at the earliest opportunity.

A sensible first step would be to form a sub-committee with responsibility for the arrangements, under the chairmanship of the competitions secretary. This committee could if it was desired include members of the executive committee but this is not essential. The sub-committee should report back through their chairman to the executive to keep them informed of the action they are taking.

The sub-committee need not be a large one; three or four people would suffice, but it would be helpful if they can feel free to approach others for guidance when it is needed. The club treasurer would be a very useful member of the committee to give advice on keeping expenditure within the club's budget. The equipment secretary too will have to be available to inform the committee on the extent of the club's equipment and in case there is a need for more equipment to be bought. The equipment secretary will be an important person on the day. He will be needed to see that there are enough balls for the tournament and to make sure that the other equipment needed is made available.

Once the committee is formed they should arrange to start

work straight away. The pace of their work in the early stages must of necessity be slow and deliberate. However, as things begin to fall into place things can begin to be done with gathering speed.

What form the competition should take and how many clubs will be needed to make it flow smoothly should be the first considerations. There are three methods that can be considered. There is the straight knock-out tournament which is simple, but means that the clubs knocked out of the first round will have come to the tournament just to play in one match. Indeed, the committee must realize that their own team might have to sit and watch everyone else for the rest of the day. This form of competition fits into the pattern of club-night handball rather than a whole day competition; it needs to be spread over a period of time to be successful.

Another method is the round robin tournament, where every team taking part plays against every other one some time during the day. This form of tournament is ideal if the number of clubs taking part is small. If there are to be a lot of teams, however, then the round robin tends to go on far too long and people begin to lose interest.

If there are as many as six or eight teams it will probably be found that the best method to adopt will be to pool the clubs taking part into two or more sections. Each team in any one section would then play one another and for each match that it won a team would be awarded two points and for each drawn game the two teams would score one each, the winner of each pool being eventually decided on the total number of points. Semi-final and final matches are then played. If the relative strength of the competing teams is known then care should be taken to ensure that they are evenly distributed so that the strongest teams are not all placed together in the same pool.

The committee must decide how many clubs are to be invited to take part, and who the invitations are to be sent to. But before these are sent out it would be as well to make absolutely sure of the details of all the arrangements such as the time available for the tournament and whether the number of matches envisaged will fit into this period. As the tournament will be taking place during the summer there should be ample time in one full day for a tournament designed to take in eight teams.

The question of the appointment of officials and of help from others in the club must be given careful consideration. There must be enough officials and other helpers available on the day of the tournament if it is to have any chance of success. The committee would be wise to contact the British Handball Association's senior area coach for this purpose and to ask the clubs that are to be invited whether they will be able to help in providing qualified people to act as referees. Two referees must be provided for each match. The referees and other officials for each match should have been arranged well in advance and their names printed on the programme by the side of the matches they are concerned with. Printed copies of the programme should be sent to both the officials and the competing teams before the day of the tournament. It would be advisable also at this stage to consult the ladies of the club to ask whether they would be prepared to help with the preparation of refreshments.

Arrangements for a first-aid post should be made and it will probably be found that an enquiry to the St. John Ambulance Brigade will meet with a sympathetic response. The extent of the changing-room facilities too must be considered as the actual day draws nearer. In effect every detail, no matter how trivial it may appear at first, must be examined. Absolutely nothing must be left to chance.

Only when the committee is entirely satisfied that it can organize the tournament should the letters of invitation be sent to the clubs concerned. Once the letters have been sent the club can only wait to see what the response is going to be. If only a few clubs accept, then the organizing committee must consider whether or not to go ahead. If they decide to do so they would be wise to organize the competition on a round robin basis, taking care to inform the other clubs of their action. However, they must be prepared for all the invited clubs to answer in the affirmative. When all the replies have been received the committee must swing into action.

For a tournament with eight teams competing the following

timetable may prove a useful guide. The teams will be referred to as A, B, C, D, E, F, G and H. It is assumed that the tournament has been arranged so that it will take up the whole of one day, starting in mid-morning and ending in the early evening.

Round I.

Pool 1

A *v*. B 10 a.m.	B *v*. D 11.10 a.m.	D *v*. A 12.20 p.m.
C *v*. D 10.35 a.m.	C *v*. A 11.45 a.m.	C *v*. B 12.55 p.m.

Pool 2

E *v*. F 10 a.m.	F *v*. H 11.10 a.m.	H *v*. E 12.20 p.m.
G *v*. H 10.35 a.m.	G *v*. E 11.45 a.m.	G *v*. F 12.55 p.m.

Round II

Semi-finals: Winners of Pool 1 *v*. Runners-up of Pool 2 3 p.m.
Semi-finals: Winners of Pool 2 *v*. Runners-up of Pool 1 3.30 p.m.

Round III
Final: 5 p.m.

The timetable of matches given assumes that there will be two courts available. If more are available the organization will be easier and can be adjusted accordingly. It would perhaps help the organization if one particular court is allocated to each pool. The timetable above shows that both courts are being used at the same times by teams from different pools. If the same court is kept for the use of each pool, the non-playing teams in that pool will be able to watch their opponents and will know exactly where to go when the time comes for them to take an active part.

The timing of the games must be accurate. In tournaments the usual duration of each game is two halves of fifteen minutes with no break between halves. It will be seen that this is the system of timing that has been used in the timetable above. Each game is scheduled to last half an hour and five minutes has been allowed between the end of one game and the beginning of the next. This should allow for the court to be cleared and for the oncoming teams to have a short period of warming up before the match is due to begin.

The first-round matches take place in the morning session of the competition. When they are completed there should be a break for lunch, and to enable the officials to work out the positions of the clubs in their relative leagues by the method of scoring already described.

If it is found that there is a tie for the final placing in the group then the goal average could be taken to decide the position. The two top teams in each section then go forward to play in the semi-final of the tournament. This will form the afternoon part of the competition.

The break will also, of course, be a signal for the players to rest and eat. Sandwiches could be provided if the organizing club wishes to keep its running costs down. The players will not mind, providing this has been specified in the information sent to their club beforehand. However, if it is to be sandwiches for lunch the host club should at least try to arrange for a cup of tea or coffee to be provided.

In the afternoon the tournament becomes a knock-out competition with the four teams proving themselves the stronger in the morning session fighting for a place in the final. The semi-finals have been timed so that they are played one after the other, and the two leading teams from the morning games have deliberately been kept apart.

After the semi-finals there is another break and the officials of the organizing committee will have time to prepare everything for what should be the climax of the competition. Refreshments should be provided for the two teams that will be playing in the final game in the evening. If there are to be presentations after the game it is now that the trophy table should be set out and any other necessary preparations should be made.

During the tournament the organizing committee must of necessity keep themselves available and the competitions secretary should assume the responsibility of clerk of the meeting. He must have at his fingertips the answers to any queries regarding the tournament and he must be prepared to meet any emergency that might arise. He should, too, ensure that all the voluntary help that is be to given by other members of the club is carried out to his satisfaction. Only when the final match has been played and the speeches made can the organizing committee sit back and relax, knowing that next year things will be made so much easier after their present experiences.

9 - THE HANDBALL REFEREE

In handball as in every other sport there is a shortage of people qualified to take up the responsibility of refereeing. Although handball is admittedly an emerging sport in this country the number of referees available is not keeping pace with the growth in the number of handball clubs. There is and always will be a demand for more people to take the qualifications necessary for entry into the official lists of referees.

How can this demand for referees be met? There can be no clear-cut answer to this problem, but the clubs themselves could do much to help. If each handball club in the country could boast at least one qualified referee amongst its members then this would go a long way towards solving the problem. Clubs must encourage their members to take the referee's examination of the British Handball Association and so become qualified referees.

It is true that the younger players within the club will tend to think of handball purely from the playing side of the game, but what of the older players and the people who do not have sufficient playing ability to warrant inclusion in one of the club teams? The older player who is nearing the end of his playing career could perhaps be persuaded to realize how valuable his contribution to the game could be if he became qualified as a referee. The experience he has gained from playing could be passed on to others and by becoming a referee he would also help to prevent the useless wastage to the sport of those who feel that because they have finished as active players the game has nothing to offer them. This idea must be dispelled from their minds. Their loss to the game can be ill afforded. The experience gained from their participation will prove of immense value to the progress of the game if they use it wisely.

It must not be thought, however, that the only people who

will make good referees are those who have shown that they have ability as players. Where a club has members who do not have particularly strong playing ability, it would be a good idea to introduce to them the idea of refereeing. This could well be the outlet these people have been waiting for. It would give them an opportunity to serve the club in a useful way and they will be helping to secure the game's progress on a much wider basis. It will be a way for them to become valuable members inside the club itself.

Clubs may well find that some of their younger players also show an interest in becoming referees and learning more about the rules of the game. If this happens then these people should be encouraged to take positive steps in this direction. It can only be in the interest of the club concerned for as many of the playing members as possible to become fully conversant with the rules of the game. A start in this direction could probably be made during the activities of the normal club night. After the strenuous session has ended the players quite naturally want to take part in an informal game to round off the evening. However, even these games have to have someone acting as referee to provide some form of organized framework for the game and this could be a good opportunity of introducing the question of serious refereeing. If a situation arises that makes it difficult for the amateur referee to decide how he should interpret the rules, then perhaps the players could have a short discussion on the problem amongst themselves. This itself will be of use, for the more the players study the interpretation of the rules the more they will begin to appreciate the problems that confront the referee when he has to make a decision during a game. This informal approach will be an aid to their playing ability, but later on they might like to take up refereeing on a more serious basis.

By having as many members as possible qualified to referee, the club will have found a way of overcoming the difficulty mentioned in the last chapter of not being able to find a referee to take charge of a game from the official lists in the area. They will always be able to fill the gap with a member from their own club.

There is only one way for a person to become a qualified referee and that is to attend an officially recognized course that leads to the Referee's Certificate of the British Handball Association. If the demand is there the handball club that is a member of the Association should ask the senior area coach of the Association to arrange for a course to be run within the club itself. This he would be very pleased to do. If there are not enough individuals to justify this the club could ask other clubs in the area if they would be interested in providing members for the course, or they could wait until a course is organized by the Association in the area. Interested members could then attend as individuals.

Since the International Handball Federation Congress in Amsterdam in August 1968 the rules of the game concerning referees have been altered, and every handball game should now be controlled by two referees instead of one. Under the old system of one referee per match it was found that because of the speed at which the game is played it was proving too difficult for the referee to control the game as efficiently as was needed. With play moving from one end of the court to the other so quickly the referee was unable to keep a close enough watch on play inside the free-throw line. If he was in front of the defence he could not see everything going on behind because of the continuous movement of the attackers. Similarly, if he placed himself behind the defence there was always the problem of his view being blocked by the defending players. Another problem was that when a team moved from attack into defence it would often move so quickly that the whole of the action was over by the time the referee has managed to take up his new position.

To overcome this difficulty the principle of two referees per game was adopted by the International Federation. This has indeed achieved what was intended. When an attack is being made one of the referees positions himself behind the defence near the goal, whilst the other takes up his position in front of the defence, some way behind the attacking players. In this way the two referees are able to watch the whole of the play and this leaves little chance for the sly fouls that used to occur quite frequently in the free-throw area under the old system. When there was only one referee it was not so much that these fouls went undetected by the referee, but that it was so difficult in a lot of cases to tell whether the offending player was an attacker or a defender, as everything would happen so quickly. The system of two referees has now overcome this problem. The whole of the play is kept under constant review and there is always a referee in front of and behind the players in possession of the ball. We have seen how, when an attack is being made, the referees take up their agreed positions on the court. When the play is switched to the other end of the court the referee in front of the defence keeps this position, moving back with the direction of play until he is behind the defence at the other end of the court. The other referee now takes up the position in front of the defence. By moving backwards and forwards in this manner, the two referees ensure that the game is being controlled from every angle at all times (Fig. 37).

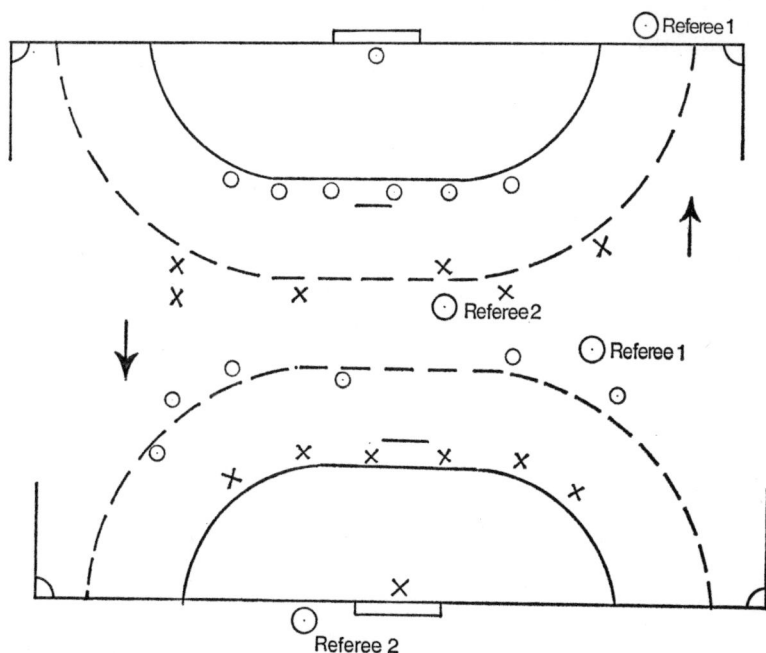

FIG. 37.
The dual refereeing system showing the positions taken up by each referee during the game

It is only by officiating at matches that the young or newly qualified referee can hope to gain experience. Being in possession of the referee's certificate should not be regarded as sufficient by the individual intent on becoming a referee and he should realize that he will mature with match experience. He must be prepared to make mistakes in the early stages of his career but must make sure that he learns from them and be prepared to admit them to himself. He must understand that the standard of his refereeing will improve with every game he takes charge of and he will eventually become in every respect a handball referee.

What are the qualities he should seek to develop in himself? Obviously he must have a thorough knowledge of the rules and their application to the game. However, he must not think that once he knows the rules that will be sufficient. He must also know how to interpret them, and make sure that he is aware of any changes that may be made from time to time. He must be able to control the game that he is refereeing, applying the rules firmly but fairly, taking care to remain strictly neutral. He must never allow his feelings to get the better of him, even in the most trying situations. It is most important that the referee can distinguish between a deliberate attempt to cause an infringement of the rules and an accidental cause. This is particularly important when play is centred around the penalty line and the free-throw area. A mistake on the referee's part could result in an advantage to the wrong team leading to a goal being scored. When a decision is made, however, the referee must stand by it. He must be able to withstand all external pressures brought against him to change his mind and alter his decision. If players do try to undermine the position of the referee then he must not hesitate to give them a period of suspension for their pains.

There is often criticism levelled at referees that are not firm enough with players. It cannot be stressed enough that referees must assert their authority at all times. This is particularly so when an offence warrants a penalty being awarded. If a penalty should be awarded in accordance with the rules of the game then the referee must do so. This is a criticism that has been levelled against continental referees in recent years. They appear to be most reluctant at times to award penalties, awarding instead free throws for the offence that has been committed. The result has been obvious. When a player knows that the referee is in effect going to help him in his plans to break the rules he does it more often. The award of a penalty will show the player that it is the referee who is in control of the game. All this does not mean that the referee makes the players feel that he cannot be approached at all, but it is essential that he is fully capable of dealing with any situation as it arises. The referee must be able to meet the rapidly changing conditions of the game as they occur.

The referee must be an understanding individual as well as a strong one. He must be aware that a player's mood can be finely balanced during a game. The decisions of the referee could upset this balance if he gives too many adverse decisions during the game. He must be constantly aware of this. Of course it is not always due to the referee's decision that a player loses his temper. However, when this situation does arise the referee will be expected to know how to deal with it. He must be fair and make sure he understands the position fully before he commits himself to any action.

The duties of the referee are not confined solely to the time that he is officiating within the game. He is in effect in charge of the players from the moment he enters the dressing-room until the time he leaves the club premises. Club officials and players must make sure that they understand this aspect of the referee's duties. Before the game starts the referee should examine the personal equipment of the players to ensure that it conforms to the rules, and also the goals to make sure that they are satisfactory. He will be handed two handballs by the club officials and he must decide which one is to be used for the match. He should study the scoresheet to make sure that it is accurate and at the same time introduce himself to the officials who will be assisting him during the game.

Before starting the game the referee should make sure that he takes on to the court with him the following equipment: a watch, in order that he can keep an eye on the timing of the game and decide on the length of time to be added, if he so desires, after the timekeeper's whistle has signalled the end of normal time: a whistle, and also a notebook and pencil so that he can keep an accurate check on the number of goals that are scored. This will enable him to check the score sheet at the end of the game. The notebook should also be used if the referee wishes to make a note of any players who he feels should be reported for misconduct. It would be as well, when the match is being played out of doors, for the referee to include a clean handkerchief in his list of possessions in case a player complains of a foreign body in his eye.

To gain respect as a referee and bring credit to the game the referee must present himself in the best way possible. He should take a pride in his appearance, making sure that his referee's uniform is both clean and smart.

10 - HANDBALL IN BRITAIN

Development

The interest in handball in this country has grown tremendously since the formation of the British Handball Association. Handball, which had hitherto been played only occasionally in small pockets of the country, began to be viewed differently by many people concerned with the promotion of sport. People who had said 'Oh yes, we've heard of handball', and were prepared to dismiss the game from their minds suddenly began to be aware of its true values.

Physical education teachers and organizers of physical education who at first were sceptical of the usefulness of the game began to include handball in their programmes, both for its own sake and as an aid in developing other aspects of their school work. Such are the merits of the game that wherever it has been demonstrated or introduced it has been received with tremendous enthusiasm.

The growth of handball has been due largely to the work that has been undertaken by the British Handball Association in the last few years. The Association was formed through the efforts of five people: Chris Powell, Andy Smith, Phil Holden, Ken Watson and myself. With the exception of Ken Watson all are teachers of physical education and it was through work in this sphere that we came to realize how valuable this game can be in the school's physical education programme. The idea of the British Handball Association was born because of the experience of these people in their various schools and colleges, and it is thanks to their untiring efforts that the game has progressed so well. We were all helped and encouraged in the early days of the Association by Wolf Schneggenburger, a handball player from West Germany, who was studying in England for twelve months. His encouragement and technical skill helped us in our determination to succeed, and the fact that handball is becoming an established sport in this country is due to the help he gave at that time. I hope that future generations of handball enthusiasts will never forget the debt that British handball owes to the efforts of this West German player.

Through the technical assistance given by Wolf Schneggenburger, the early work of the Association in introducing handball was made much easier than it otherwise might have been. The members of the newly formed Association quickly became dedicated to the future progress of the game throughout the United Kingdom as a whole. They were so convinced as to the merits of the game that they were prepared to dip into their own pockets to provide the necessary finance in the early stages.

The greatest milestone in the history of the British Handball Association was passed in August 1968 when Phil Holden and I went to Amsterdam to attend the Congress of the International Handball Federation. The Federation is the parent body of the sport throughout the world, and it has its administrative headquarters in Basel, Switzerland. Phil and I went to the Congress to put the British Handball Association's case for membership of the Federation. We were received enthusiastically by all the delegates and when our application was put to the vote its acceptance was unanimous. The friendly way in which our handball colleagues from all over the world received us was, we felt, a wonderful reward for all the work we had done at home. We were also very proud of the high reward our colleagues had for the prestige of sport in Britain. We hear so much nowadays about how our sporting attributes do not compare with other countries that it was refreshing to learn that people overseas still regard British sportsmen with respect.

It was whilst we were in Amsterdam that British handball made another valuable friend in Carl Filip Borgh, who has kindly written the foreword to this book. A member of the International Committee and a pioneer of handball in Sweden, he was most helpful in supporting our successful application for membership of the International Handball Federation.

Through the unselfish efforts of the people I have mentioned, handball has become established as a sport in this country. The original members of the Association are still extremely active, but it is good to see how the number of willing people has expanded to make certain that the development of the game will continue. Handball has at last arrived and is beginning to assume its rightful place in this country. Handball can now be considered as a definite dot on the globe of British sport. With time this dot will undoubtedly grow until the game takes its rightful place amongst the other sports of this country.

Organization

The Headquarters of the British Handball Association, which is the governing body of the sport in this country, are to be found at 32, North John Street, Liverpool 2. This is the nerve centre of British handball where any query about the sport or regarding the acquisition of equipment or other material required by handball enthusiasts will be dealt with as efficiently as possible.

The Association is run at the highest level by the Executive Committee, which in turn is assisted by the National General Committee. From the very beginning it was realized that if a healthy growth and development of the sport was to be maintained then the organization of the game would have to be decentralized as much as possible. With this in mind the United Kingdom was divided into ten separate areas. Each area was eventually, as soon as the right people became available, to be under the control of a senior area coach responsible for the administration of the area. The person so appointed would in turn develop the formation of an area committee to run the Association's affairs in the region. They would also have the responsibility of organizing courses for the training of coaches and referees. This breakdown of the administration of the game has greatly eased the burden that would otherwise have been thrown on to the Executive Committee, and it has helped in overcoming the problem of communication, a problem which in the past has been acute for developing sports.

It is on the Executive Committee of the Association however that the task of administration and organization falls most heavily. This committee is ultimately responsible for all the major decisions that have to be taken. It must co-ordinate all the work that is to be undertaken throughout the various regions and keep all affiliated members of the Association aware of any developments that occur from time to time. It has the responsibility also of developing and maintaining friendships with other associations from overseas. Another important aspect of the work of the Executive Committee is in the development of equipment for the game and making sure that information regarding this important side of the game is constantly brought to the attention of the members of the Association.

The Association is ultimately responsible for the training and examining of both coaches and referees. We have already seen how important these people are for the future success and development of the game. The Association organizes awards for referees and coaches which can be taken by individual members. Courses which lead to the award of either the referee's certificate or the coaching award are run from time to time; successful candidates are awarded the appropriate qualification by the Association, and their names are recorded by the Association.

There is at present only one award open to referees. Senior referees are chosen from experienced people who have proved that they are capable of more responsibility. There is, however, more than one coaching award and the Association organizes coaching clinics for experienced coaches who wish to take the award for senior coaches. It is from the lists of senior coaches that the senior area coaches and staff coaches of the Association are chosen. Not only in this country are courses run for the training of referees and coaches. From time to time international courses take place, suitable for people who already hold one of the Association's qualifications. Details of these are brought to the attention of the Executive Committee through the medium of the International Bulletin. In turn they are passed on to Association members through the medium of the British Handball Association Newsletter.

The British Handball Association is also responsible for the organization of the national championships which are held at adult, youth and school levels. The organization of the area championships is arranged by the committee of each individual area.

National teams at senior, youth and school levels are an important aspect of the work of the Association. It is through this medium that friendship with associations in other countries can be developed further and from the contact received from international matches the Association is able to keep abreast of playing methods in other countries. This is important if the standard of British handball is to improve and keep pace with the latest developments within the game.

Membership of the Association

The success of any association must ultimately depend on the strength of its membership. There are four kinds of membership of the British Handball Association. These are: Individual Membership, School Membership, Club Membership and Block Membership. Block membership is for the convenience of corporate bodies such as education committees who are responsible for the organization of teams on a large scale. This form of membership is offered at a reduced subscription. Membership is open to anyone who wishes to promote the sport and who subscribes to the rules of the Association.

The advantages of membership are numerous. Members are allowed to make use of the facilities that the Association can offer. It allows contact with headquarters when information regarding any aspect of the game is required. Members are kept up to date, through the newsletter, with all the developments in the game and of any events taking place which might be of interest. Another important aspect of membership is the acquisition of the coaching and refereeing awards of the Association. From the club point of view there is the opportunity of participating in organized competitions, such as handball leagues and the national and area championships. It must be remembered too by club secretarties that in order for any of their players to qualify for representative teams the club must be affiliated to the Association. Clubs wishing to have contact with clubs from overseas must be members also. This is laid down by the International Federation. The club wishing to make such a contact will also have the benefit of the help of the Association.

These, then, are some of the benefits of membership of the Association. The Association exists to promote handball and in so doing serve its members. Every member of the Association can take pride in the thought that he too is playing his part in enabling the Association to achieve these aims and that he is making an important individual contribution to the progress of the sport in this country.

GLOSSARY OF HANDBALL TERMS

B.H.A. The British Handball Association. The governing body
for the sport in the United Kingdom.

CAUTION. A warning by the referee to a player guilty of misconduct. The caution is recorded by the officials and any
subsequent warning should be followed by a period of
suspension.

CORNER THROW. When the ball is played over his own goal
line by a defending player (excluding the goalkeeper), on
either side of the goal, the game is restarted by means of a
throw from the corner of the court by one of the attacking
players.

COURT PLAYERS. Members of the handball team excluding the
goalkeeper.

DIVING SHOT. The spectacular way of trying to score a goal by
launching the whole body into the air towards the goal in
order to gain more distance.

DUAL REFEREEING. The new system of two referees for each
game, introduced at the International Congress of the
I.H.F. in Amsterdam in 1968.

FIVE-A-SIDE. The smaller version of the game played in Great
Britain during the winter months. This version is played in
four periods of time instead of two halves.

FREE THROW. Awarded for breach of the rules of the game. It
is executed in similar fashion to the penalty throw but from
where the offence was committed.

FREE-THROW LINE. The broken line drawn parallel to the goal-
area line at an extra distance of 3 metres (10 ft.). It is from
this line that free throws awarded near the goal area are
taken.

GOAL. A goal is considered scored when the ball has passed
wholly over the goal line between the uprights and underneath the crossbar of the goal.

GOAL AREA. The area of playing court inside the goal-area line.

GOAL-AREA LINE. The line which is drawn in the shape of a D at a distance of 6 metres (20 ft.) in front of and on either side of the goal.

GOALKEEPER. The player who is allowed to play freely inside the goal area to defend the goal.

GOAL LINE. The line forming the end of the court which runs between the uprights of the goal and which meets the touch-lines at each corner of the court.

HANDBALL FOR SEVEN. The term used to describe handball for seven players when played out of doors.

INDOOR HANDBALL. Handball for seven played inside the sports hall or gymnasium.

I.H.F. The International Handball Federation. The governing body for the sport throughout the world.

JUMP SHOT. A shot for goal taken when the player shooting wishes to get above the defending players or inside the goal area to shoot.

KEMPA TRICK. Playing the ball over the defence into the goal area for a player to dive forwards and try to propel the ball towards the goal.

OUTDOOR HANDBALL. Handball for eleven.

PENALTY. The penalty taken from the 7-metre line is awarded for particularly bad offences by a defender in his own half of the court and when a clear goal-scoring chance has been prevented by foul means. The player executing the penalty throw is required by the rules of the game to make a direct attempt to score a goal.

PLAYING COURT. The area within the lines marking the perimeter of the playing area.

REFEREE'S THROW. A ball bounced by the referee to restart the game after a stoppage for which no one person is responsible.

SEVEN-METRE LINE. Also known as the penalty line. Drawn as a continuous line, 1 metre in length, 1 metre in front of the goal-area line. It is from here that penalties are taken when they are awarded.

SUBSTITUTION. The changing of one player for another whilst the game is in progress.

SUSPENSION. A period of time in which a player is ordered from the game temporarily by the referee. There are two such periods, two minutes and five minutes. If a player is suspended a third time he is not allowed to enter the court again for the duration of the match.

THREE-SECOND RULE. The time allowed for a player to be in possession of the ball is three seconds. The ball must be either passed or bounced before this period of time has elapsed or a free throw will be awarded against the player concerned. When a free throw is awarded at any time during the game the ball must be played within three seconds of the referee blowing his whistle.

THROW IN. The method of putting the ball back into play after it has crossed one of the touch-lines. The throw is taken by a player from the team which did not cause the ball to go out. In taking the throw the player must have part of both feet on the ground outside the court and must throw the ball with both hands over his head, in a similar fashion to a soccer throw.

THROW OFF. A throw from the centre of the court taken at the beginning of each half of the game and to restart the game after a goal has been scored.

TOUCH-LINES. The two lines marking the sides of the court.

THE RULES OF THE GAME

(Adopted in 1956 and incorporating modifications up to 1969)

Rule 1 The Playing Area

1:1 The playing area, divided into two goal areas and the court, shall be rectangular, no more than 44 m. (147 ft.) and not less than 38 m. (126 ft.) in length, and not more than 22 m. (73 ft.) and not less than 18 m. (60 ft.) in width. The longer boundary lines are called the touch-lines and the shorter the goal lines.

NOTE. The conditions of the playing area must never by any means be altered in favour of one of the teams (e.g. by the strewing of resin in only one of the goal areas).

1:2 The goals shall be placed on the centre of each goal line. A goal consists of two upright posts, equidistant from the corners of the playing area, 3 m. (10 ft.) apart and 2 m. (6 ft. 8 in.) high, firmly fixed to the ground and firmly joined by a horizontal crossbar. The outer edge of the goal line and the back of the goalposts shall be in line. The posts and the crossbar shall be square, 8 cm. × 8 cm. (3 in. × 3 in.), made of wood or similar synthetic material and painted on all sides in two colours which must contrast effectively with the background. Where the goalposts and the crossbar meet they shall be painted in the same colour. Each rectangle of colour shall be 28 cm. (11 in.) in length where the posts and crossbar meet. Elsewhere each colour rectangle shall measure 20 cm. (8 in.) in length. The goal shall be provided with a net attached in such a way that a ball, thrown into it, cannot rebound immediately.

1:3 Each goal area is made by marking a line at a distance of 6 m. (20 ft.) from the goal and parallel to the goal line, and the ends of this line are connected to the goal line by means of quarter circles with a radius of 6 m. (20 ft.) measured from the

136

back inside corner of the goalposts. This line is called the goal-area line.

1:4   At a constant distance of 3 m. (10 ft.) from the goal-area line shall be marked a broken line called the free-throw line. The lines and the gaps between them shall each measure 15 cm. (6 in.).

1:5   At a distance of 7 m. (23 ft.) from the middle of the goal line and parallel to it is marked a line 1 m. (3 ft. 3 in.) long, the penalty line.

1:6   The centre of the two touch-lines are connected by the half-way line.

1:7   All lines shall be clearly visible and must be 5 cm. (2 in.) wide. They all form part of the area they enclose.

1:8   Between the goalposts the goal line must be of the same width as the goalposts.

Rule 2 The Ball

2:1   The ball shall be spherical and consist of a rubber bladder and an outer case of one-coloured leather. It must not be inflated too hard.
NOTE. Balls that have been paint sprayed or painted, or are partly or wholly covered with any other material not originally belonging to it must not be used.

2:2   At the start of play the ball for men and youths shall weigh not more than 475 g. (17 oz.), and not less than 425 g. (15 oz.). Its circumference shall be not more than 60 cm. (24 in.), and not less than 58 cm. (23 in.).
   The ball for women, female and male juniors shall weigh not more than 400 g. (14 oz.), and not less than 325 g. (11½ oz.), and its circumference shall be not more than 56 cm. (22 in.), and not less than 54 cm. (21 in.).

2:3   Two valid balls must be available for every match. They are to be checked by the referees who also chose the one to be used.

2:4 The ball must not be changed during the game but for imperative reasons.

NOTE. If during the game the ball has been changed, it must be taken into use again at the first interruption of the game, provided it is still in accordance with the rules.

Rule 3 The Players

3:1 Each team consists of twelve players (ten court players and two goalkeepers) of whom a maximum of seven players are on the court at the same time (six players and a goalkeeper). (free throw: see rule 13; or penalty throw: rule 14). The other five players are substitutes.

The goalkeepers are never allowed to act as court players. Court players, however, may substitute for a goalkeeper.

NOTE. A court player substituting for the goalkeeper may become a court player again at any time.

3:2 At the beginning of each match at least five players of either team shall be present on the playing area. The number may at any time in the match, including extra time, be increased up to seven. Play continues if, during the course of a match, the number in either of the teams drops below five.

3:3 A player may join the game from the place of substitutes (the bench outside the touch-line where the substitute players are waiting).

The substitution bench shall be close to the timekeeper's table. A player entering the court shall notify the timekeeper and the referee. A free throw shall be taken from where the player actively joined the game (see however 13:2). A player who leaves the court in an ungentlemanly way shall be disqualified for the rest of the game. The disqualification also means that he is banned from the substitution bench. The team shall continue to play with seven players and four substitutes.

NOTE. A player completing his team as sixth or seventh player or when the suspension of a player has expired shall be considered a player entering court.

If a player faultily enters the court and commits an infringement of the rules he shall be penalized as if he had been one of the regular players entitled to participate in the game.

If a player who is not entitled to take part in the game nevertheless enters the court, he shall be disqualified for the rest of the game and a free throw or penalty throw awarded to the opposite team. The disqualified player must leave the court and the place of substitutes. His team may continue to play with seven players and four substitutes unless an excluded player enters the court in which case the team shall continue to play with six players, five on court and the goalkeeper.

3:4   If a player during the game crosses one of the boundary lines, but immediately afterwards re-enters the court, he shall not be regarded as leaving the court.

NOTE. The intentional crossing of the boundary line in order to gain an advantage shall be penalized by the award of a free throw to the opposing team.

3:5   Substitutes may join the game at any time and as often as is wanted without notifying the timekeeper. The players to be substituted must have left the court before the substitute enters (free throw).

NOTE. The goalkeeper can only be substituted from the substitute bench and he must have left the court before the substitute enters.

3:6   Faulty substitution of players shall be penalized by a free throw to the opposing team, to be taken from the place where the substitute actively joined the play (see however 13:2).

The penalty for a second faulty substitution shall be a free throw and the suspension for two minutes of the offending player, and a free throw and five minutes' suspension for all further infringements. If there is a case of more than one substitute entering too early only the first player shall be penalized.

NOTE. For faulty substitution on the part of a team in possession of the ball the referee must at once interrupt play.

For faulty substitution on the part of the team that is not in possession of the ball the referee shall not interrupt the play unless it is directly influenced by the faulty substitution.

If by faulty substitution a clear chance of scoring a goal is taken away from the opposing team the offending player shall be disqualified from the rest of the game and a penalty throw awarded. The disqualified player must leave the court and the place of substitutes. His team may continue to play with seven players and four substitutes.

3:7 All the court players must be dressed alike. The goalkeeper shall wear colours that distinguish him from the other members of the team and the opposing team.

The players should be numbered from 1–12 on the backs of their shirts. The first goalkeeper being number 1 and the substitute goalkeeper No. 12. The figures shall be at least 20 cm. (8 in.) high and the colour must contrast with that of the shirt.

Players shall wear shoes or boots. When playing on hard ground light shoes or boots are allowed. When playing on soft ground bars or studs of leather are allowed. Rubber or other synthetic material is also permitted. Bars must be flat and at least 12 mm. ($\frac{1}{2}$ in.) in width and studs must be cylindrical and not less than 12 mm. ($\frac{1}{2}$ in.) in diameter. Spikes and pointed studs are prohibited. The wearing of wristlets, wrist watches, rings, frameless or rimless glasses as well as anything else that might be considered dangerous to other players shall be prohibited.

Before the game is started the referee shall examine the equipment of players and if he finds anything liable to cause injury to other players these things must be removed before the player is allowed to take part in the game.

Rule 4 The Duration of the Games

4:1 The playing time is as follows:

For men two equal halves of thirty minutes duration with an interval of ten minutes (in tournaments, as a rule, two equal periods of fifteen minutes without any interval); for male juniors two equal periods of twenty-five minutes with an interval of ten minutes (tournaments, two equal periods of twenty minutes without interval); for all other teams two equal periods of twenty minutes with an interval of ten minutes (tournaments, two periods of ten minutes without interval).

The time taken at the interval may be shortened by the referees after requests from both teams concerned.

4:2 Before the game is started and in the presence of both captains the referee will toss a coin, and the team winning the toss shall have the option of choosing which goal they will defend or starting the game with the throw off.

4:3 When the referee has started the game by blowing his whistle the throw off shall be taken within three seconds from the centre of the court (free throw). (See also 16:1, 2, 4, 5, 7, 8.)

4:4 Every player shall be in his own half of the court and all players of the team opposing that of the thrower shall remain not less than 3 m. (10 ft.) from the thrower until the ball has left his hand (free throw).

4:5 A goal cannot be scored direct from a throw on (goal throw).
NOTE. Direct means without first having touched another player.

4:6 After the interval, ends shall be changed and the throw off shall be taken by a player of the opposite team to that which started the game.

4:7 Allowance shall be made in either period for time lost and the amount of time to be added shall be a matter for the referee alone (17:6).
The referee shall notify the timekeeper, his colleague and the captains of the teams of the extra time that will be played.

4:8 Time shall be extended to permit the execution of a free throw or penalty throw being taken on or after the full time of the period has expired. As soon as the result of the throw is ascertained, the timekeeper shall signal the end of the period.

4:9 If the referee is aware that the timekeeper has signalled half-time or the end of play too early, he shall at once restart play if none of the players has left the court. If the ball was in play on the court when the wrong signal was given the game shall be restarted by a referee's throw from the centre of the court or with a goal throw from the area where the ball was when the wrong decision was given. In either case the referee shall blow his whistle before the throw is taken.

In all other cases, i.e. if the game was interrupted without a wrong signal being given, the game shall be restarted by the throw which had been awarded before the interruption took place.

If half-time is signalled too early and some of the players have left the playing area before the referee is aware of the mistake, the ordinary interval shall be taken. When the players return they will restart the game to complete the first period of the game. The game shall be restarted from the centre by a referee's throw. When the ordinary time of the first period has been completed, i.e. when the outstanding amount of time has been played the referee shall stop the game and the teams will then change ends to begin the second period. There is no break between the end of this period of the first half and the beginning of the second half. The second half shall be started in accordance with the rules.

NOTE. If the timekeeper has signalled half-time too late the second half is shortened accordingly.

4:10   If it is previously decided that a match shall have a winner, and if at the end of the second half it is a draw, two extra halves must be played, after an interval of five minutes. The referee shall again toss a coin and the team winning the toss shall have the option of ends or a throw off.

For men the two halves shall be of five minutes each. Ends shall be changed without an interval. For all other teams the duration shall be three and a half minutes. If after the completion of these two halves there is still no decision another two halves of the same duration shall be played after an interval of five minutes and after a new toss has been made. There shall be no interval between the halves. If after this further extension of play there is still no result the game must be considered a draw and rearranged for another time.

4:11   During extra time no other players other than those originally forming the teams may be used.

Rule 5 Playing the Ball

5:1   It shall be permitted:

To stop, to catch, to throw, to bounce or to strike the ball in any manner and in any direction by using hands (fists or open hands), arms, head, body, thighs and knees.

5:2   To hold the ball for a maximum time of three seconds, also when it is lying on the ground.

5:3   To take a maximum of three steps while holding the ball. One step has been taken, (a) when one foot is lifted from the ground and put down again, (b) when one foot is moved on the ground from one place to another. In both cases it is permissible to move one foot in the air or on the ground until it is level with the first.

NOTE. If a running or jumping player catches the ball, the counting of steps shall not begin until both of his feet have touched the ground. A hop on one foot shall be considered a step even if the other foot has not touched the ground. If after such a hop on one foot the other foot touches the ground it shall not be considered a step.

5:4   It is permitted to bounce the ball once and to catch it again with one or both hands either whilst running or standing; to catch, to bounce, and to catch the ball again when it has touched another player or the goal; repeatedly to bounce the ball with one hand either whilst running or standing.

When a player, after having bounced the ball, catches it again with one or both hands he is permitted to take a maximum of three steps and to hold it for three seconds, then he must pass it (free throw).

A player may take as many steps as he wishes between the bouncing and re-catching of the ball.

NOTE. It shall be permitted to roll the ball repeatedly on the ground with one hand.

Bouncing of the ball can only take place when the player is in control of it. It is bouncing if the player in control of the ball drops it on the ground and takes it again.

143

If a player tries to catch the ball and fumbles he shall be considered to have not touched the ball.

5:5 It is permitted to pass the ball from one hand to the other:

5:6 To stop the ball with one or both hands and immediately afterwards catch it if the player does not move when doing it:

5:7 To pass the ball when kneeling, sitting, or lying on the ground.

It shall be prohited:
5:8 To touch the ball more than once, unless in the meantime it has touched the ground, another player or the goal (free throw), (exceptions: 5:4, fumbling, and 5:6):

5:9 To touch the ball with any part of the leg below the knee or with the foot (free throw). It shall not be punished, however, if it does not give the offender or his team an advantage, and it shall be no infringement of the rules if the ball is thrown on the player's leg or foot by an opponent:

5:10 To dive for the ball lying or rolling on the ground (free throw), except for the goalkeeper in his area.
NOTE. It shall not be permitted, however, to dive for the ball that is going to roll across the touch-line or the goal line no matter whether it is dangerous or not to a player on the opposing team:

5:11 Intentionally to play the ball across the touch-line or the goal line outside the goal (free throw 13:1d).

5:12 The game shall not be interrupted if the ball happens to touch the referee.

Rule 6 Approach to Opponent

It shall be permitted:
6:1 To make use of the hands and arms to get hold of the ball:

6:2 In any direction to play the ball from an opponent using the flat of the hand:

6:3   To obstruct an opponent with one's body.
NOTE. It shall be permitted to obstruct an opponent also when he is not in possession of the ball.

It shall be prohibited:
6:4   With one or both hands to snatch or violently to strike the ball from the hands of an opponent (free throw, see however 6:9).

6:5   To obstruct an opponent with arms, hands or legs (free throw; see however 6:9).

6:6   To catch hold of an opponent with one or both hands, in any way to handle him roughly by hitting, pushing, running into, jumping into or tripping him or by throwing oneself before him (free throw; see however 6:9):

6:7   To force an opponent into the goal area (free throw; see however 6:9):

6:8   Intentionally to throw the ball on an opponent or move the ball towards him as a dangerous feint (free throw; see however 6:9).

6:9   In the case of serious infringements of the rules 6:4–8, committed in the offender's own half of the court, and in the case of infringements of the rules 6:4–7, committed in any part of the court, by which a clear chance of scoring a goal is destroyed, a penalty throw shall be awarded.

6:10   If a player falls with the ball underneath him in such a way that the play is unduly delayed, the referee shall interrupt the game and restart it with a referee's throw unless one of the teams is to be punished.

Rule 7 The Goal Area

7:1   Only the goalkeeper is allowed to enter or to be in the goal area. The area is considered entered if in any way it is touched by a court player. The goal area includes the goal area line (1:8).

7:2 The penalties for entering the goal area are as follows: (a) free throw if the court player is in possession of the ball; (b) free throw when the court player is not in possession of the ball but gains a clear advantage by entering the goal area (see however 7:2c); (c) penalty throw if a court player of the defending team intentionally and clearly for the purpose of defence enters the goal area.

7:3 A court player entering the area after playing the ball shall not be punished providing the entering does not give a disadvantage to the opponents.

7:4 The ball in the goal area belongs to the goalkeeper. No court player shall be allowed to touch the ball lying or rolling in the goal area or held by the goalkeeper being in the goal area (free throw).
NOTE. The ball shall be considered in the goal area and belonging to the goalkeeper when it touches the goal area line.

7:5 A ball entering the goal area and getting out on to the court again, without touching the goalkeeper, remains in play (see however 7:6).

7:6 If a player intentionally plays the ball into his own goal area, and it does not by itself get out on court again the following awards shall be given: (a) goal, if the ball enters the goal; (b) penalty throw if the goalkeeper touches the ball and no goal is made; (c) free throw in all other cases (13:1g).

7:7 Play shall continue if in the act of defence a player of the defending team touches the ball and it immediately afterwards is taken by the goalkeeper or comes to rest in the goal area.

Rule 8 The Goalkeeper

8:1 The goalkeeper may defend his goal in every way. He is, however, only allowed to use his feet or his legs below the knees if the ball is moving towards the goal or the goal line (free throw).

8:2 In his goal area the goalkeeper may move about with the

ball without any restrictions about steps and time (see however 16:9).

8:3   The goalkeeper may leave his goal without the ball. On the court he shall follow the rules of the court players, with the exception that he cannot be punished for entering his goal area.

The goalkeeper is considered to have left his area as soon as he touches the ground outside the goal area line.

Note. With or without the ball in his hand the goalkeeper is considered to be out of his own goal area as long as he touches the ground outside the goal area line. If he enters the goal area with the ball a penalty throw is awarded (8:7).

8:4   The goalkeeper shall not leave the area with the ball under his control (free throw).

Note. If, in the act of defence, the goalkeeper tries to get the ball under control and at the same time happens to get outside his goal area he shall not be considered to have left the area and shall be allowed to pass the ball.

8:5   Whenever the goalkeeper throws the ball from his area out on to the court he shall not be allowed to touch it again until it has first been touched by another player (free throw).

Note. If the ball gets into the area and is still in play the goalkeeper shall throw it out again by means of a throw out. The opponents shall be allowed to place themselves immediately at the goal area line when the throw is taken. A goal may be scored direct from a throw out.

8:6   The goalkeeper shall not touch the ball lying or rolling on the ground outside his goal area line as long as he himself is in the goal area (free throw).

8:7   During the play the goalkeeper shall not take or play the ball into his own area (penalty throw).

8:8   If during the play a court player is going to substitute for the goalkeeper, the referee shall be notified before the court player enters the goal area (penalty throw, 3:1).

The court player shall not enter the goal area before it is left by the goalkeeper (penalty throw, 7:2c). He must also change his colours.

Rule 9 Scoring

9:1   A goal is scored when the whole of the ball has passed over the opponents' goal line between the goal-posts and underneath the crossbar, provided that in connection with the scoring no infringements of the rules were committed by the scoring player or his team mates.

A goal made in one's own goal is to the advantage of the opposing team (own goal).

NOTE. If a player of the defending team commits an infringement of the rules with the result that the ball goes into goal, a goal is made to the advantage of the opposing team (own goal).

The play is interrupted at the moment the referee or the timekeeper gives his signal, and if the whole of the ball has not passed over the goal line between the goalposts and underneath the crossbar before the signal is started a goal must not be allowed.

If the ball is prevented from going into the goal by anybody or anything not authorized to be on the court, the referee shall award a goal if he is absolutely convinced that the ball would normally have passed over the goal line into the goal.

If the ball being in play and being held by the goalkeeper in his goal area should, in the air, be dropped into or, on the ground, be carried into the goal behind the goal line, a goal shall be awarded to the opposing team (own goal).

9:2   After a goal has been scored, the game shall be restarted with a throw off from the centre of the court by a player from the team conceding the goal.

NOTE. If a goal has been scored and the play has been restarted by a throw off from the centre of the court, the goal shall not be disallowed.

Rule 10 Throw in

10:1   If the whole of the ball crosses the touch-line on the ground or in the air, play shall be restarted by a throw in (except 5:11).

10:2　The throw in shall be taken from the point where the ball crossed the touch-line by a player of the team opposite to that of the player who caused the ball to leave the court (see also 16:1, 5, 8, 9).

Note. If a throw in is taken from a wrong point the referee shall blow his whistle to have the throw repeated from the right place.

10:3　The thrower shall face the court and stand with both feet outside the touch-line. He shall use both hands and deliver the ball from over his head (free throw).

10:4　While throwing in the player must touch the ground with some part of each foot (free throw).

10:5　No goal can be scored (i.e. against the opponents) direct (4:5) from a throw in (goal throw).

Rule 11 Corner Throw

11:1　If the whole of the ball passes over the goal line outside the goal, either in the air or on the ground, having last touched a player of the defending team, a corner shall be awarded to the attacking team (except 5:11).

This rule does not apply to the goalkeeper in his area (goal throw).

11:2　The corner throw shall be taken within three seconds of the referee blowing his whistle, from the point where the side line and the goal line meet, on the side of the goal where the ball went out (see also 16:1, 2, 4–8).

Note. While taking a corner throw the player shall touch the ground with one and the same foot until the ball has left his hand. It is permitted to repeatedly lift and put down the other foot inside or outside the court (see also 16:1, 2, 4–8).

11:3　A goal may be scored direct from a corner throw (see commentary on 4:5).

Rule 12 Goal Throw

12:1　A goal throw shall be awarded:

(a) if the whole of the ball passes over the goal line outside the goal either in the air or on the ground, having last touched an attacking team player or the goalkeeper of the defending team in his goal area;

(b) if the ball goes direct into the goal of the opposite team from a throw off (4:5), a throw in (10:5), or a goal throw (12:4).

12:2   The goal throw shall be taken by the goalkeeper from his goal area into the court (free throw) (see also 16:5–9).
NOTE. If the goalkeeper tries to take a goal throw from outside his area, the referee shall order him into the area before the goal throw can be taken.

12:3   The goal throw can be taken in any way preferred by the goalkeeper.
   A goal throw shall be considered taken when the ball after leaving the hands of the goalkeeper has crossed the goal-area line.

12:4   A goal cannot be scored direct from a goal throw (i.e. against the opposing team) (see commentary 4:5) (goal throw, 12:1).

12:5   The players of the opposing team must neither enter the area between the free-throw line and the goal-area line nor even touch the free-throw line before the goal throw has been taken by the goalkeeper (free throw).

Rule 13 Free Throw

13:1   A free throw shall be awarded:
   (a) for faulty entering or leaving the court (3:1, 3, 5, 6);
   (b) for faulty throw off (4:3, 4)
   (c) for infringements of the rule 5:8–10 (playing the ball);
   (d) for intentional playing of the ball across the touch-line or the goal line outside the goal (5:11);
   (e) for infringements of the rules 6:4 (approach to opponents);

(f) for infringements by court players of the rules 7:2a, 2b, 4 (the goal area);

(g) for the goalkeeper's infringements of the rules 8:1, 4–6; 12:2; 16:9;

(h) for the intentional playing of the ball into one's own goal area (7:6c);

(i) for infringements of the rules 10:3–5; 16:7, 9 (throw in);

(j) for infringements of the rules 16:2, 4, 5, 7 (corner throw);

(k) for infringement by the attacking team of rule 12:5 (throw off);

(l) for infringements of the rules 13:3; 16:4–7, 9 (free throw);

(m) for infringement of the rules 14:2, 3, 5c; 16:2, 4, 5, 7, (free throw);

(n) for infringements of the rule 15:3 (referee's throw);

(o) for ungentlemanly conduct (17:6, 7, 11).

13:2 The free throw may be taken immediately without the referee blowing his whistle, from the place where the infringement occurred (see also 16:1, 3–8).

If the infringement was committed by a player of the defending team between the goal-area line and the free-throw line, the free throw shall be taken from the nearest point outside the free-throw line.

If for some reason the free throw is delayed, the referee shall blow his whistle and the free throw be taken within three seconds (16:9).

13:3 The players of the attacking team shall neither touch nor cross the free-throw line of the defending team before the free throw is taken (free throw).

Note. If some of the thrower's team-mates are placed between the free-throw line and the goal-area line when the throw is taken and if their placing may have any influence on play, the referee shall interrupt the game and order the wrongly placed players to move to the other side of the free-throw line. The game shall then be continued by the referee blowing his whistle.

13:4 When a free throw is to be taken from the free-throw line, the players of the defending team may place themselves immediately at their goal-area line. ‑

13:5 If a free throw is going to be taken and some of the opponents of the thrower are wrongly placed, the referee shall not blow his whistle but let play continue if he is of the opinion that it will be to the advantage of the thrower's team not to have the game interrupted.

NOTE. If the referee blows his whistle for a free throw to be taken although some players of the opposing team are wrongly placed, these players shall be entitled to actively take part in the play as soon as the throw has been taken. Their wrong position shall not be penalized after being accepted by the referee.

If a free throw is going to be taken, and some of the opponents try to delay the restarting of play by getting too near to the thrower or by committing other infringements of the rules, they shall be cautioned. In the case of the infringements being repeated the players concerned shall be suspended or excluded from the game (17:6, 8).

13:6 A goal may be scored direct from a free throw (see commentary on 4:5).

13:7 The referee shall not award a free throw if an interruption of the game might be an advantage for the team that committed the infringement.

Rule 14 The Penalty Throw

14:1 A penalty throw shall be awarded:
    (a) for serious infringements of the rules 6:4–9, committed on one's own half of the court;
    (b) for serious infringements of the rules 6:4–7 and 9 committed in any part of the court and destroying a clear chance of scoring a goal;
    (c) if a player intentionally enters his own goal area for defensive purposes (7:2c);
    (d) if a player intentionally plays the ball into his own goal area and the ball touches the goalkeeper(7:6b);

(e) if the goalkeeper carries or throws the ball into his own area (8:7);

(f) for faulty substitution of the goalkeeper (3:1; 8:8).

14:2   The player taking the penalty throw shall neither touch nor cross the penalty throw line before the ball has left his hand (free throw; see also 16:1, 2, 4, 5, 7, 8).

NOTE. If a suspended or excluded player enters the court and takes the penalty throw, he shall be excluded for the rest of the game (see commentary on 3:3) and the penalty throw repeated.

While a penalty throw is being taken opponents shall not try in any way to make the thrower nervous or to disturb him. Offenders shall be cautioned, possibly suspended or even excluded from the game, and if no goal is scored the penalty shall be repeated.

14:3   When taking the penalty throw the thrower shall throw the ball in the direction of the goal of the opposing team (free throw).

14:4   While a penalty throw is being taken, all players with the exception of the thrower shall be outside the area between the goal-area line and the free-throw line, and the players of the opposing team shall be at least 3 m. (10 ft.) from the thrower until the ball has left his hand.

14:5   If a player of the attacking team touches or crosses the free-throw line before the ball has left the thrower's hand, the referee shall award as follows:

(a) the penalty throw to be repeated if a goal is scored;

(b) goal throw if the ball has passed the goal line outside the goal;

(c) free throw in favour of the defending team if the ball bounces back on to the court from the goalkeeper or any part of the goal. If the goalkeeper stops or keeps the ball it remains in play, and the game shall be continued by his throwing the ball out on to the court.

14:6   If a player of the defending team crosses the free-throw line or even touches it before the ball has left the thrower's hand, the referee shall award as follows:

(a) goal if that was the result of the throw;

(b) the penalty throw to be repeated in all other cases.

14:7 While the penalty throw is being taken, the goalkeeper may move about as much as he likes in his goal area. He shall, however, be at least 3 m. (10 ft) from the thrower until the throw has been made, and if he infringes this rule the penalty throw shall be re-taken if a goal is not scored.

14:8 The referee shall not award a penalty throw if an interruption of the game might be an advantage to the team committing the infringement.

Rule 15 The Referee's Throw

15:1 The game is re-started with a referee's throw:

(a) if the game has been interrupted by the referee, when the ball was in play, after infringement of the rules by both teams simultaneously;

(b) if the game has been interrupted without any infringements of the rules being committed.

15:2 The referee's throw shall be taken by the referee bouncing the ball vertically on the ground at the point where play has been interrupted (see however 4:9). If this point should be between the goal-area line and the free-throw line the referee's throw shall be taken from the nearest point outside the free-throw line.

The position of the players is the same as given in 13:3, 4. The referee need not blow his whistle (see however 4:9).

15:3 While the referee's throw is taken, no players shall be nearer to the referee than 3 m. (10 ft.) before the ball has touched the ground (free throw).

Rule 16 How to Take the Throws

16:1 Before a throw is taken the ball must rest in the thrower's hand, and the positions of the players shall be in accordance with rules of the game (see however 13:5).

Note. Only the thrower shall be permitted to touch the ball before the throw is taken.

16:2 Throw off (4:3), corner throw (11:2) and penalty throw (14:2) shall be taken not later than three seconds after the referee has blown his whistle (free throw). The ball may be thrown in any direction (except penalty throw, 14:3).

16:3 The free throw may be taken immediately without the referee blowing his whistle. The ball may be thrown in any direction. If the free throw is taken before the positions of the players are in accordance with the rules and if the wrong positions may influence play, the referee shall interrupt the game, correct the wrong positions and then blow his whistle for play to continue (13:2, 3, 5).

If the game is interrupted owing to intentional delay of the play, owing to warning, suspension, exclusion (17:8) or disqualification of a player, the referee shall restart the game by blowing his whistle.

16:4 When taking the throws mentioned in 16:2 and 3 the thrower shall keep one of his feet continuously on the ground until the ball has left his hand (free throw).

He is permitted however, to repeatedly lift and put down again the other foot or to move it on the ground in any direction (4:3; 11:2; 13:2; 14:2).

16:5 Having taken a throw off (4:3), a throw in (10:2–4), a corner throw (11:2), a goal throw (12:2, 3) or a free throw (13) the thrower shall not touch the ball again until it has touched another player or part of the goal (free throw). When a penalty throw has been taken, the ball shall not be touched by any player till it has touched the goalkeeper or the goal (free throw).

16:6 When taking a corner throw (11:2), a goal throw (12:2, 3) or a free throw (13) the thrower may hold his hand with the ball outside the boundary lines provided his position on the playing area is in accordance with the rules.

16:7 When the above-mentioned throws are taken the opponents shall be at least 3 m. (10 ft.) from the thrower until the ball has left his hand (free throw).

NOTE. Faulty positions of the players of the opposing team shall not be corrected by the referee if the immediate taking of the throw gives an advantage to the throwing team.

16:8   A throw is considered taken when the ball has left the hands of the thrower.
NOTE. While taking the throw, the player shall throw the ball, not hand it to a team-mate.

16:9   If a player intentionally delays the taking of a throw in, a goal throw, a throw out or a free throw the referee shall blow his whistle for the throw to be taken within three seconds (free throw) (8:2; 10:2–4; 12:2–3; 13:2).

Rule 17 The Referee

17:1   Every game shall be conducted by two referees, assisted by a timekeeper and a scorer.

17:2   The referees shall be in charge of the game from the moment they enter the playing court until the moment they leave it.
NOTE. The referees shall be entitled to caution or to disqualify (3:3) a player before the start of the game and they may also caution a player after the game.

17:3   The referees shall examine the condition of the playing ground before the start of the game. One of them shall start the game and both have the right to interrupt or stop the game.
    They shall endeavour to keep as close to the ball as possible and to enforce the rules of the game. One referee shall take up a position in front of the attack and behind the defence and shall be known as the goal-line referee. The other referee shall be behind the attack and in front of the defence. He shall be known as the court referee. When play switches to the other end of the court the positions of the referees change also. The court referee moves backwards to become the goal-line referee and the goal-line referee moves forwards to become the court referee. At half time the referees stay at their respective ends of the court in order that they might change teams.

The referees shall enforce the rules of the game and their decision shall be final. It is permissible for team captains to appeal against decisions which are against the rules of the game.

17:4 In principle a game shall be conducted throughout by the same two referees.

17:5 The referees shall count the goals.

17:6 In case of ungentlemanly conduct the player(s) shall be cautioned by the referees. If the ungentlemanly conduct is repeated the player(s) shall be suspended for two or five minutes or be excluded from the game (17:8).

In the case of serious infringements the player(s) may be suspended or excluded without being previously cautioned.

If the game is interrupted owing to ungentlemanly conduct it shall be resumed by a free throw.

Allowance shall be made for time lost in each half (4:7).

Note. If the referee wants to caution a player, he must use the word caution and he must also lift one of his arms, with the fist clenched, in the air in such a way that it is distinctly seen by the players and by spectators that a caution has been given.

17:7 Ungentlemanly conduct against the referee shall always be penalized by a free throw being awarded against the player(s) concerned. The player(s) shall be cautioned, suspended, or excluded (17:8).

17:8 Players may be suspended, i.e. be sent off the court for two or five minutes, or they may be excluded, i.e. sent off the court for the rest of the game. If a player should be sent off the court for a third time he shall be excluded for the rest of the game (see however 3:6 and 17:11).

If the time of a suspension has not expired by the end of the first half, the rest of the suspension must be taken from the beginning of the second half.

If the suspension has not expired by the end of normal time and extra time is to be played (4:10), the rest of the suspension must be taken from the beginning of the extra period.

Note. Suspended and excluded players shall remain in the place of substitutes. The time of suspension begins: (a) when the referee blows his whistle for the play to continue, if it was interrupted, (b) when the suspended player crosses the touchline, if the game was not interrupted.

17:9 Suspended or excluded players shall not be substituted. NOTE. If the goalkeeper is suspended or excluded, the substitute goalkeeper may take his place. In that case one of the court players shall leave the court.

17:10 When the time of suspension has expired, the entering player shall notify the timekeeper (free throw, 3:3).

17:11 If a team intentionally delay the progress of play and among other things refrain from attempting to score a goal the referee shall award as follows:

(a) first offence: free throw and cautioning;
(b) second offence: free throw and suspension for two minutes of the chief offender.
(c) further offences: free throw and suspension for five minutes of the chief offender.

Any other kind of delaying tactics shall be considered ungentlemanly conduct and be penalized accordingly (17:6).

17:12 Only the referees and their assistants shall be permitted to wear black dress.

17:13 The referee shall blow his whistle:

(a) to start play;
(b) when a goal is scored;
(c) when an infringement of the rules is committed (except 13:7 and 14:8);
(d) when the ball has crossed the boundary lines;
(e) for a throw on, a corner throw or a penalty throw to be taken;
(f) for a free throw to be taken in accordance with 16:3;
(g) to interrupt the intentional delay of the progress of play (16:9):
(h) before a referee's throw in accordance with 4:9.

17:14 The scorer shall keep the record of the game and together with the timekeeper he shall also control the entering of the players.

17:15   The timekeeper shall control:
  (a) the time;
  (b) the substitutes entering and leaving the playing area;
  (c) the time of suspensions;
  (d) together with the scorer, the entering of players.

The timekeeper shall also give a loud and distinct signal for the end of half-time and the end of the game (4:8).

The duties of the timekeeper and the scorer can be entrusted to one person.

Referees, their assistants and players are required to acquire a thorough knowledge of the rules of the game and to apply them with sporting spirit.

INDEX

Page references to the Rules of the Game are in **bold type.**
References to Illustrations are in *italic type.*

INDEX

HOFMANNSTHAL
STUDIES IN COMMEMORATION

Hofmannsthal:
Studies in
Commemoration

University of London
Institute of Germanic Studies

HOFMANNSTHAL

Studies in Commemoration

Edited by
F. Norman
Director

London
1963

University of London
Institute of Germanic Studies

VOLUME 5. HOFMANNSTHAL STUDIES IN COMMEMORATION

Previous Publications

1   UNION LIST OF PERIODICALS dealing with Germanic Languages and Literatures, in the University Library and in Libraries of the Colleges and Institutes of the University, 58 pp. 1956. 5/-

2   SCHILLER BICENTENARY LECTURES (Ed. by F. Norman), 168 pp. 1960. 21/-

3   SCHILLER IN ENGLAND 1787—1960. A bibliography compiled under the direction of R. Pick, 123 pp. 1961. 25/-

4   THESES IN GERMANIC STUDIES. A catalogue of theses and dissertations in the field of Germanic studies (excluding English) approved for higher degrees in the universities of Great Britain and Ireland between 1903 and 1961, 46 pp. 1962. 10/6

All publications are obtainable direct from the Institute of Germanic Studies, 29 Russell Square, London, W. C. 1.

CONTENTS

PREFACE

In the autumn of 1960 Dr. H. Ritschl, at that time Director of the Austrian Institute in London, which has made such a notable contribution to our musical and general cultural life, approached the Institute of Germanic Languages and Literatures with the idea that there might be a Hofmannsthal exhibition; this would be organized as a joint venture of the two institutes. We readily agreed.

During the summer there had been a most successful commemorative exhibition at Salzburg though on a scale that would not have proved possible in London. Clearly, not everything that had been assembled at Salzburg could be shown, and here we had the good fortune to be advised by Dr. F. Hadamowsky, of the Österreichische Nationalbibliothek in Vienna. Dr. Hadamowsky made an admirable selection, came over to England himself and took immense care and trouble in displaying a remarkably representative amount of material most skilfully within very limited space and in a room which was by no means ideal for such a purpose. He has contributed to this book an informative introductory essay in which he discusses succinctly and authoritatively the complicated technical aspects which must guide any attempt to arrange this type of literary exhibition. We are most grateful to him for his interest and help, given cheerfully, modestly and expertly.

At the opening ceremony on 6 February 1961 we were happy to welcome His Excellency the Austrian Ambassador, many prominent members of the Austrian community, the Principal of the University of London and many academic friends and well-wishers.

In connexion with the exhibition there was delivered a series of lectures which are here presented to a wider public. We have contributors from the Universities of London, Oxford, Reading and Wales which shows how widely scholarly interest in Hofmannsthal is spread in academic circles. We should like to express our thanks to the lecturers for consenting, at rather short notice, to contribute to our scheme, and for all the subsequent trouble they took in preparing their manuscripts for publication.

Whilst our exhibition was not as rich as the one at Salzburg we were able to include quite a number of items which had not been exhibited before. This was almost entirely due to the generosity shown by Mr. Raimund von Hofmannsthal who allowed free access to his house, and permitted us to borrow any manuscript, book or picture which we thought would be of interest. Indeed, without the ever-ready co-operation of Mr. von Hofmannsthal there would have been no exhibition. The poet's daughter, Mrs. Christiane Zimmer, was unfortunately in the United States though she watched our efforts from afar with benevolent eye.

In a more modest way the Institute itself was in a position to supply some items, notably such as fell under the general designation "Hofmannsthal and England".

The only pleasant duty that remains is to thank contributors, helpers and well-wishers. Dr. R. Pick, our former Secretary-Librarian, compiled, together with Mrs. Ann C. Weaver, B.A., the bibliography of Hofmannsthal in England. One almost takes it for granted that the work was done with their usual meticulous accuracy and attention to detail. Dr. Ritschl's most able and courteous aide, Dr. R. Sickinger, under his direction devoted a great deal of time and energy to the negotiations which preceded the exhibition. Dr. Knight, our present Secretary-Librarian, was responsible for the more immediate arrangements and it would be tedious to enumerate the odd variety of tasks that had to be accomplished, from producing show-cases, arranging safe transport, to giving the exhibition adequate publicity. The burden of supervising the preparation of the manuscripts for the press, and of ensuring uniformity of references—no easy task when a number of contributors present well-documented articles—has also fallen largely to his lot. Our staff has helped him in this, as always, willingly and ably.

First and last we are indebted to the Austrian Government, in particular to Dr. Heinrich Drimmel, the Bundesminister für Unterricht, for unfailing kindness and support. The moment Dr. Ritschl suggested the exhibition the idea was taken up with his accustomed enthusiasm and energy by Ministerialrat Dr. Alfred Weikert, and the Bundes-

minister für Unterricht authorised the necessary financial support. There could not have been any exhibition at all without this aid, nor would it have been easy to finance the present publication without a generous subvention from the Bundesministerium.

Hofmannsthal was a great Austrian and that means, almost inevitably, a great European. There are many different ways in which the traditional friendship of Great Britain and Austria expresses itself, yet there could surely be no happier way of emphasising this friendship than by commemorating the genius of Hugo von Hofmannsthal.

F. Norman

ABBREVIATIONS

Wherever possible quotations from Hofmannsthal's works are taken from his *Gesammelte Werke in Einzelausgaben*, edited by Herbert Steiner, S. Fischer Verlag, Frankfurt am Main, 1947—1958. In the footnotes the following abbreviations are used:

A: Aufzeichnungen
D: Dramen
E: Erzählungen
G: Gedichte und lyrische Dramen (1952)
L: Lustspiele
P: Prosa

DIE HOFMANNSTHAL-AUSSTELLUNG

ALLGEMEINES UND BESONDERES ZU EINER GEISTESGESCHICHT-
LICHEN EXPOSITION

„Zum Sehen geboren, zum Schauen bestellt": dieses Wort aus Goethes
„Faust II." scheint die Menschheit — wenigstens in einem Teil —
immer stärker verwirklichen zu wollen; der Film bringt die Welt
nah, das Fernsehen sie ins Haus, selbst bei den Erholungsreisen fällt
für die Bildung des Menschen (des Wortes Bedeutung in Goethes Sinn)
etwas ab. Noch ist die Schaufreude mehr auf die Quantität als Quali-
tät des Geschauten gerichtet, doch ist zu hoffen, daß der Weg von der
materiellen Breite in die geistige Tiefe geht. Die Bauwerke der Antike
waren bis vor einem halben Jahrtausend ja auch nur willkommenes
und gern genütztes Material zur Kalkgewinnung für die Bauten der
Zeit und haben dann doch die Anregung zur Beschäftigung mit den
Menschen, die sie 1½ Jahrtausende vorher geschaffen hatten, ihrem
Leben und ihren Werken gegeben, und diese wurde wieder der Aus-
gangspunkt einer geistigen Bewegung, welche die weitere Entwicklung
der Menschheit bestimmte und heute noch fruchtbar weiterwirkt.

Die Freude am Schauen steckt zutiefst im Menschen; sie wird heute in
einem Ausmaß kultiviert, das fast einer Erziehung zur Oberflächlich-
keit gleichkommt; die von allen Seiten gebotenen Reize stumpfen ab
und erschweren Wahl und Wirkung des Wertvollen. Der Kirche, die
im Mittelalter begann, Glaubenslehren und heilige Geschichte durch
Schau-Spiele dem Volke näherzubringen und so das bis dahin ver-
dammte Theater in den Dienst ihrer Sache stellte, folgten die Fürsten,
die ihre Macht in prunkvollen Aufzügen und Festen *schau*bar demon-
strierten; die Gewerbsleute brachten auf Messen und Jahrmärkten die
Ergebnisse ihrer Arbeit unters Volk. Es war allen, die Materielles zu
bieten hatten, ein Leichtes, es vorzuweisen und auf die Menge zu wirken; wie aber soll sich Immaterielles, wie Geist und geistige Betätigung
ins Schaubare übersetzen? Diese bedürfen eines materiellen Mediums,
das vermittelt und durch die Sinne von Auge und Ohr auf uns wirkt;

es waren bislang in erster Linie Schrift und Buch, Lektüre und Vorlesung; nunmehr aber schiebt sich gleichbedeutend als Drittes das Bild in den Vordergrund.

Aus dem Zug der Zeit nach dem Schaubaren ergab sich für die visuellen Künste keine Änderung ihrer Arbeitsweise; nur neue Anregung und Steigerung; wie seit dem Altertum stellen Architekten und Plastiker ihre Kunst ja auf der Straße zur Schau; schwieriger schon haben es Maler und Kunsthandwerker, deren Werke man, in Museen gesammelt, aufsuchen muß. Was aber sollen die Geisteswissenschafter tun, um dem Zug der Zeit, der zum Teil auch ihres ferneren Schicksals Stimme ist, zu folgen? Sie müssen das Geistige schaubar machen und über das Schaubare zum Geistigen führen, sie müssen den Menschen, den die Technik bequem gemacht hat, der den faustischen Drang weithin verloren hat, um seiner selbst willen vor Leere und Vermassung retten, indem sie ihm immer wieder — mit materiellen Unterlagen — seine geistigen Besitztümer vor Augen — und Ohren — führen.

Forschung und Lehre haben die Aufgabe, den geistigen Besitz zu erschließen; Archive, Bibliotheken und Museen aber die gleich wichtige Aufgabe, die materiellen Grundlagen des Geistigen zu sammeln. An sie wird aber heute mehr denn je auch die Forderung gestellt, das Gesammelte einem größeren Kreis zu zeigen; Sammlungen jeder Art, vor allem Archive und Bibliotheken, dürfen ihre Aufgabe nicht nur darin sehen, ihren Besitz zur Benützung bereitzuhalten; eine Fafnerrolle: „Ich lieg' und besitz, laßt mich schlafen" zu spielen widerspräche den Forderungen der Zeit. Die Sammlungen aller Art müssen soweit sie ihre Schätze nicht ohnedies in Museen zeigen, aus einer passiven Rolle heraustreten, ihren Besitz mit einem auf ihrer Wissenschaft basierenden Konzept anbieten. Am besten geschieht dies in temporären Ausstellungen.

Ausstellungen sind fast so alt wie die Menschheit; sie ergaben sich natürlich, als diese begann Handel zu treiben, der die Erzeugnisse des Gewerbes zeigen mußte, um Käufer zu gewinnen. Mit der Entwicklung der Künste waren diese bestrebt, möglichst viele Mitmenschen an ihren Werken Anteil nehmen zu lassen. Es entwickelten sich zwei Gruppen von Ausstellungen: dauernde, die mit dem Besitz und der musealen Verwahrung der Gegenstände verbunden waren, und fallweise, die von einem sachlichen Gesichtspunkt her Gegenstände aus verschiedenstem Besitz für kurze Zeit vereinigten, um sie an einem Ausstellungsort der Allgemeinheit zugänglich zu machen. Das Ausstellungswesen im großen Maßstab entwickelte sich in der zweiten Hälfte des 19. Jahrhunderts, in der die Fortschritte der Technik die Menschen einander näher brachten. Bald wurde alles in Ausstellungen gezeigt; Gegenstände des täglichen Lebens ebenso wie solche der höchsten Kunst.

Wie bei den großen Schaufesten der Barockzeit nimmt unsere Zeit meist einen Anlaß, um für ein bestimmtes Thema oder für einen Einzelnen eine Ausstellung zu veranstalten; früher war es der 50. oder 100. Jahrestag der Wiederkehr eines besonderen Ereignisses; jetzt nimmt man schon Dekaden, ja Lustren zu Anlässen, Ausstellungen zu veranstalten.

Ausstellungen für einen einzelnen Menschen werden selten bei seinen Lebzeiten veranstaltet, es wäre denn, eine einmalige, alles überragende Tat gäbe den Anlaß zu einer solchen; meist aber wird, wenn über Bedeutung und Umfang eines Lebenswerkes einigermaßen Klarheit gewonnen ist, eine Dekade des Todestages zum Anlaß genommen, Leben und Werk in seiner ganzen Breite aufzuzeigen.

Bei einer Ausstellung für einen Einzelnen, und sei er noch so bedeutend, darf man nie vergessen, daß jeder Mensch, und sei er der genialste, auch ein Produkt seiner Zeit ist; die Ereignisse in der großen wie kleinen Gemeinschaft, in der er aufwächst, im Staate wie in der Familie, wirken auf seine naturgegebenen Anlagen ein, hemmen die einen, fördern und steigern die andern. Darum wird, wenn es der Raum nur irgendwie zuläßt, in Ausstellungen, die einzelnen Persönlichkeiten gewidmet sind, ihre Umwelt und ihre Zeit gezeigt werden; durch dieses notwendige Beiwerk darf aber natürlich die Hauptgestalt nicht überwuchert werden.

Jede Ausstellung fordert eine nicht unbeträchtliche Vorbereitungsarbeit. Sie beginnt mit der Überlegung, wie das vielschichtige Leben und Werk eines Menschen oder einer Epoche schaubar gemacht werden kann und der Aufstellung eines Plans, mit welchen Objekten dieser in die Wirklichkeit umgesetzt werden könnte, sowie der Wahl des Ortes, an dem die Ausstellung stattfinden soll.

Das Schwierigste bei einer temporären Ausstellung ist immer, für sie geeignete Räume zu finden. Es gibt zwar zahlreiche Ausstellungsgebäude, die Museen, aber sie haben ihre ständigen Ausstellungen und nehmen vorübergehende Fremdlinge nur sehr selten auf. Sie bleiben durch Jahrzehnte unverändert und sind bestrebt, nur das Beste und Wesentlichste aus ihren Beständen zu zeigen. Ein eigenes Haus für temporäre Ausstellungen zu schaffen, ist noch niemandem in den Sinn gekommen; es wäre dies eine Aufgabe für die Kulturverwaltung eines öffentlichen Gemeinwesens, des Staates, Landes, einer Stadt. Für materielle Zwecke gibt es solche Einrichtungen: oft riesige Gebäude für Messen, die dann 11 Monate des Jahres leer stehen. Ausstellungen des Geistigen aber müssen meist Notunterkünfte beziehen, in Sälen einer öffentlichen Institution, einer Universität, in einem Palais. Es müßte den kapitalskräftigen Brüdern der Wirtschaft bei einigem guten Willen schon möglich sein, ihren kapitalsschwachen Brüdern im Geiste zu helfen; aber im Denken der Wirtschaft scheint für Immaterielles kein Platz zu sein.

Die Zahl der Exponate kann bei kleinen Ausstellungen mit 200 bis 300 angenommen werden, bei größeren gegen 600, bei großen 1000 und darüber. Aus der Überlegung heraus, daß eine Vielfalt den Beschauer ermüdet und damit das Gegenteil tiefergehender Wirkung erreicht wird, daß eine erheblich größere Zahl von Objekten die Wirkung nicht erhöht, die Eindrücke nicht verstärkt und vervielfältigt, sondern vermindert und verflacht, soll die Zahl der Ausstellungsgegenstände möglichst beschränkt werden. Es wird zwar der, der Vieles bringt, auch manchem etwas bringen, aber in der Gesamtheit ist Überfülle nur schädlich. Je weiter ein Ausstellungsthema gespannt ist, desto größer wird freilich, auch bei Beschränkung auf das Wesentliche, die Zahl der Objekte sein.

Wie man früher in Gemäldegalerien Bilder reihenweise übereinander und dicht nebeneinander hängte, so stopfte man auch Schaukästen mit Gegenständen zum Bersten voll: davon ist man heute abgekommen. Wie man stark aufgelockert hängt, legt man nur wenige Objekte in eine Vitrine, versucht aber, mit ihnen die stärkste Aussage zu erreichen. Diese Änderung in der Aufstellung ist ein Zeichen der Zeit: man hatte früher wohl die Ruhe, eine Überfülle im einzelnen zu betrachten, sie fehlt uns aber heute in weitem Ausmaß.

Wie die einzelnen Schaukästen mit Objekten, darf auch der Raum mit Schaukästen nicht überladen werden; es gehört zu den schwierigsten

Fragen einer Ausstellung, auf Grund der Gegebenheit des Raumes die Zahl der benötigten Vitrinen und Objekte festzulegen. Bei großen Ausstellungen zieht man meist einen Innenarchitekten bei, dem die Gestaltung, also die räumliche Aufstellung der Ausstellung und ihrer Objekte übertragen wird; damit tritt neben den oder die (bei größeren Ausstellungen, deren Gegenstände aus mehreren Fachgebieten stammen, sind naturgemäß auch mehrere Wissenschafter am Ausstellungswerk) für die sachlich-fachlichen Belange Verantwortlichen eine zweite Person oder ein zweites Team, das die gesamte äußere Gestaltung der Ausstellung durchführt. Dies kann, da nicht alle Wissenschafter fähig sind, den heute sehr hoch gestellten Anforderungen in Bezug auf räumliche Gestaltung zu entsprechen, für die Ausstellung von größtem Vorteil sein, und zwar dann, wenn der Architekt seine Absichten mit den Forderungen des Wissenschafters in Einklang bringt und sich nicht in den Vordergrund spielt; die Ausstellungsgegenstände müssen immer Selbstzweck sein und dürfen nie Mittel zum Zweck werden.

Liegt nun der Plan der Ausstellung, das geistige und räumliche Grundkonzept, fest, dann gilt es, die Objekte auszuwählen. Staatliche und private Eigentümer werden gebeten, sie zur Verfügung zu stellen. Nun kann man von freundlichster Zusage, ja von Stolz, etwas besonders Schönes der Allgemeinheit zu zeigen, bis zur schroffsten Ablehnung ohne Begründung und ohne Grund alle Spielarten von Zustimmung und Ablehnung erleben. Grundsätzlich ist zu sagen: je weniger Leihgeber, desto weniger die Arbeit; hier gilt in Abwandlung eines alten Wortes: quot possessores, tot sensus. Die Leihgeber bestehen meist auf einer Versicherung ihrer Objekte; manche verlangen den Wert vielfach übersteigende, manche lächerlich geringe Versicherungssummen; man sollte eine dem tatsächlichen Wert — der selten ein materieller, sondern meist ein Liebhaberwert sein wird — entsprechende Summe annehmen, denn Überwertung könnte den Verdacht unmoralischer Bereicherung erwecken, Unterbewertung Schaden und nachträglichen Streit zur Folge haben. Man versichert „von Nagel zu Nagel" gegen alle möglichen Risken, zu denen nicht nur Transportschäden, Feuer, Einbruch, Diebstahl usw., sondern auch Schäden durch Wasser oder Heizung (geborstene Leitungen, undichte Dächer), ja sogar Klimaschäden (in außergewöhnlich feuchten oder trockenen

Gegenden) gehören können. Im allgemeinen ist zu sagen, daß selbst die höchste Versicherungssumme ein originales Werk auch von geringstem Wert nicht ersetzen kann.

Es empfiehlt sich, *eine Stelle* auch dann, wenn mehrere große Leihgeber die Ausstellung beschicken, zu bestimmen, die alle Ausstellungsgegenstände sammelt; sie soll das gesamte Ausstellungsgut auch in Listen verzeichnen. Umständlich ist der Transport von Ausstellungsgut ins Ausland. Denkmalschützer müssen ihre Genehmigung geben, Zollbehörden des Absendungs- wie des Ankunftslandes prüfen die einzelnen Stücke, bevor sie siegeln respektive die Objekte freigeben. Man beauftragt mit diesen Manipulationen am besten eine bewährte, wenn möglich auf Kunsttransport spezialisierte Speditionsfirma.

Die äußere Gestaltung einer Ausstellung bedarf verschiedener Schaustellungsmöglichkeiten; sie müssen gute Sicht gewähren, gegen Verschmutzung und Diebstahl sichern und eine geschmackvolle Repräsentierung der Objekte ermöglichen. Es sind dies Schauflächen oder Schaukästen (Vitrinen) und Rahmen. Schauflächen können behelfsmäßig auch aus Tischen angefertigt werden; auf die Tischfläche wird passendes Unterlagspapier gelegt, darauf die Objekte und schließlich eine 3 mm starke Glasplatte, die mit glasklaren Klebestreifen am Rand des Tisches befestigt wird. In solchen Schauflächen können zweidimensionale Objekte, wie Schrift (einzelne Blätter von Gedichten und Briefen), Drucke (Einblattdrucke, Theaterzettel, Zeitungsausschnitte) weiters Photographien gezeigt werden. Pultvitrinen müßten eigentlich immer angefertigt werden; erfahrungsgemäß sind die Vitrinen, die Museen und Sammlungen zur Verfügung haben, meist mindestens ein Menschenalter alt; man muß sich mit ihnen behelfen, wenn die Mittel zur Anschaffung neuer Vitrinen nicht vorhanden sind. Schaukästen haben die Form von Kuben oder Trapezoiden und sollen gleicherweise in liegender wie in stehender Form aufgestellt werden können; sie sollen dreidimensionale Gegenstände und kleinere museale Objekte aufnehmen. Für größere museale Objekte, wie Waffen, Kostüme, Instrumente müssen eigene Stehvitrinen angefertigt werden. Bilder kommen in Passepartouts und in Rahmen; am besten bewähren sich Wechselrahmen.

Bei dem Aufbau einer Ausstellung wird man ohne Hilfskräfte nicht auskommen; sie sollen geschult sein, damit die Objekte nicht beschädigt

werden; es ist erstaunlich, in welchem Ausmaß sogar manchen Fach-
leuten der Sinn für pflegliche Behandlung musealer Gegenstände
fehlt; die geübte und sorgsame Hand des Verwahrers erspart den
Restaurator.
Für jede Ausstellung sollte ein Katalog hergestellt werden. Er soll
nicht nur eine trockene Aufzählung der Ausstellungsobjekte sein,
sondern eine Einführung in Leben und Welt des Menschen oder der
Epoche, denen die Ausstellung gilt. Der Katalog wird über seinen pri-
mären Zweck, dem Ausstellungsbesucher zur Orientierung zu dienen,
für die Wissenschaft und die Nachwelt einen dauernden Behelf und
Besitz darstellen.
Schließlich ist es auch notwendig, für die Bekanntmachung der Ausstellung durch Presse, Rundfunk und Fernsehen zu sorgen, einführende
Vorträge zu veranstalten, Führungen zu organisieren, kurz der Ausstellung zu breiter Wirkung zu verhelfen.
In unserem besonderen Fall war die Wiederkehr des 30. Todestages
von Hugo von Hofmannsthal im Jahr 1959 der Anlaß zu einer Ge-
denkausstellung; die Erinnerung an jenen heißen Sommertag, an dem
der Dichter unter der Last des Schmerzes und der Aufregungen über
den Tod seines älteren Sohnes auf der Stiege seines theresianischen
Schlößls vom Schlag getroffen zusammenstürzte und kurz danach in
seinem Arbeitszimmer verschied. Die Bedeutung seiner dichterischen
Erscheinung steht heute im großen und ganzen fest. Für seine Zeit-
genossen war er der Schöpfer von lyrischen und lyrisch-dramatischen
Dichtungen, die mehr um ihrer dunklen Schönheit, eigenartigen Ge-
fühlswelt und sprachlichen Gewalt willen als der Tiefe und Weite
ihrer Gedanken faszinierten und besonders die Jugend in ihren Bann
zogen; zum zweiten war Hofmannsthal seiner Generation der Librettist von Richard Strauss, der Textdichter des „Rosenkavaliers", der
„Elektra", der „Frau ohne Schatten". Bald nach seinem Tod begann
— wie bei jedem Dichter — eine Zeit der Unterschätzung, die bei ihm
wegen seiner geistigen und persönlichen Herkunft in der Folge zu
fast völliger systematischer Unterdrückung wurde; er wäre vollkom-
men verschwunden, hätte er nicht zu den Opern von Richard Strauss
die Texte geschrieben.
Nach dem Jahr 1945 begann man sich der Bedeutung Hofmannsthals
bewußt zu werden; in Werk und Betrachtung erfuhr der Dichter eine

Auferstehung, die ihn nach dem Dunkel der Verkennung mitunter in fast zu grellen Lichtschein absoluter Bewunderung setzte. Man erkannte nun, wie er, vom Vielvölkerstaat der österreichisch-ungarischen Monarchie, seiner österreichischen Heimat ausgehend, zu einer größeren, europäischen Gemeinschaft strebte, in der die europäischen Völker in geistigem Wettstreit ihre Anlagen im Geiste des Humanismus weiterbilden sollten. Auch das dichterische Werk rückte nun in eine neue Wesenheit, Deutung und Bedeutung. All dies zusammenfassend zum Bewußtsein zu bringen, war die Absicht der Hofmannsthal-Ausstellung.

Die Anregung zur Ausstellung ging vom Kulturreferat der Salzburger Landesregierung aus, das mit Erfolg bestrebt ist, den zur Zeit der Salzburger Festspiele im Juli und August besonders zahlreichen Besuchern der Stadt zu den überall sichtbaren Zeichen ihrer barocken Vergangenheit auch ihre Beziehungen zu Kunst und zum Geistesleben der letzten Jahrhunderte vor Augen zu führen. Bei Hofmannsthal kam ja noch eine besonders starke Verbindung zu den Salzburger Festspielen dazu; er war einer ihrer Begründer, mit seinem „Jedermann" wurden sie im Jahr 1920 eröffnet.

Die Hofmannsthal-Ausstellung fand in Salzburg in Schauräumen in der erzbischöflichen Residenz, zwei großen Sälen, statt; der eine, neutraler, war für Ausstellungszwecke sehr gut geeignet, der andere mit seinen schweren, prachtvollen Tapeten und einem herrlichen Deckengemälde nur eine Notlösung. Die Hofmannsthal-Ausstellung war von vornherein nicht als Wanderausstellung gedacht; sie fand aber so viel Interesse, daß sie dann auch in Straßburg, Luxemburg und London gezeigt wurde; auch dort standen ihr nur Behelfsräume zur Verfügung; in Straßburg ein Sitzungs- und ein Festsaal der Universität, in Luxemburg die Halle eines Ministeriums und in London ein Bibliotheksraum des germanistischen Instituts der Universität.

In jeder der vier Städte wurde, den örtlichen Gegebenheiten entsprechend, das Thema der Ausstellung variiert; es war in allen Fällen der Mensch Hofmannsthal und sein dichterisches Werk. Da wurden zunächst die Zeugen seines äußeren Lebens gezeigt: der wegen seiner Wohltätigkeit und erfolgreichen Förderung der Wirtschaft Österreichs geadelte Urgroßvater, die Großeltern und die Eltern, der kultivierte altösterreichische Bankmann und die sensible Mutter, deren bäuerliche

Hugo von Hofmannsthal. 1891

Hugo von Hofmannsthal and Max Reinhardt at the rehearsal of "Das Salzburger Große Welttheater". 1925

Hugo von Hofmannsthal. 1929

Hugo von Hofmannsthal's Study

Vorfahren im niederösterreichischen Waldviertel gelebt hatten; es war in drei Generationen gleichzeitig ein Stück österreichischer Geschichte bis zur Auflösung des alten Habsburgischen Reiches und österreichisch-ungarischen Vielvölkerstaates. Und dann, breit angelegt, die Entwicklung des Sohnes, unseres Dichters; die Eintragung der Taufe in der ehrwürdigen Karlskirche, das Geburtshaus und die Räume der elterlichen Wohnung; Kinderbriefe mit rührenden kleinen Bemerkungen des Tages und Festtagswünschen für Großeltern und Eltern, Zeugnisse aus dem Akademischen Gymnasium; Gleichstrebende, wie Schnitzler, Beer-Hofmann, Karl Kraus, aus dem Kreis einer österreichischen „Moderne" um Hermann Bahr; erste Gedichthandschriften und Bilder des Gymnasiasten und Maturanten. Dann die frühesten Drucke seiner Gedichte, der lyrischen Dramen, der ersten Prosa. Universität und Militärdienstzeit. Doktorat und Versuche, das reale Leben zu bewältigen; die Verbindung mit der geliebten Frau. Dann die Verbindung mit der Realität Theater (in der sich Wien versagte und Berlin als geistige Heimat anbot) und die entscheidenden Begegnungen seines Lebens: Max Reinhardt und Richard Strauss. Die Werke des Jahrzehnts bis zum Ausbruch des Weltkrieges, das im Erfolg des „Rosenkavalier" gipfelt; Ausbruch des Weltkriegs: Besinnung auf die Heimat Österreich und ihrer politischen wie geistigen Bedeutung in und für Europa: vergebliches Bemühen, die anderen davon zu überzeugen; dann der unvermeidliche Zusammenbruch und Resignation. Neuer schöpferischer Auftrieb aus dem Untergang, neue Zukunftshoffnung auf das größere geistige Vaterland an Stelle des verlorenen; die altösterreichischen Lustspiele, Festspiele in Salzburg und Paneuropa. Ständiges Reifen und Wachsen, Zusammenbruch und erschütterndes Ende. Während die Dokumentation zu Leben und Werk in Handschrift, Druck und Bild in allen vier Ausstellungen gleich blieben, war in Salzburg entsprechend dem Ort das Theater, vor allem die Salzburger Festspiele, in Entwürfen von Bühnenbildern und Kostümen, in Szenenbildern während des Spiels und Rollenphotos stärker betont; museale Objekte, wie die biedermeierisch bürgerlich-behäbige Reisetasche der Großeltern, die Rose, die Oktavian der geliebten Sophie bei der Wiener Erstaufführung des „Rosenkavalier" überreichte, ein Bühnenmodell des Schwierigen, das berühmte Rollenbild von Richard Mayr als Ochs auf Lerchenau von Anton Faistauer waren als kleine Glanzlichter darübergesetzt. In Straßburg waren die Bilder des österreichischen Theaters stark vermindert worden, sie wurden in Luxemburg weiter reduziert; an beiden Orten konnten die musealen Objekte nicht gezeigt werden. In London trat das Theater in seine großen internationalen Bezüge zurück, dafür aber wurde das literarische Werk stärker betont; es fehlte keine wesentliche Erstausgabe. Hofmannsthals Beziehungen zu England und die stetige Verbreitung seines Werkes im Buch und im Theater wurden in hohem Maße berücksichtigt. Da der Sohn Hugo von Hofmannsthals, Raimund, in London lebte und die Ausstellung tatkräftig förderte, konnte dort auch ein gutes Bild des Dichters im Alter von etwa 30 Jahren von seinem Schwager Hans Schlesinger gezeigt werden.

Der Erfolg der Ausstellung war an allen Orten sehr erfreulich; nicht nur die fachlichen und sachlichen Interessenten fanden sich bei ihr ein, sondern auch der weite Kreis geistiger Menschen fand Bestätigung und Anregung. Und wenn wie hier ein österreichischer Dichter im europäischen Westen gezeigt wird, dann ist dies ein kleiner Faden einer geistigen Verbindung, die in Europa immer bestanden hat, und die zu verstärken eine unserer wesentlichsten Aufgaben sein soll.

Fr. Hadamowsky

HOFMANNSTHAL AND ENGLAND

BY MICHAEL HAMBURGER

This title and subject demand a few words of explanation; the title, because it could be ambiguous; the subject, because it may seem far-fetched, tenuous and marginal. The ambiguity can be eliminated at once; I shall be dealing with Hofmannsthal's debt to England, not with England's debt to Hofmannsthal. As for the marginal character of the subject, I think that a student of Hofmannsthal does well to ponder the words which Goethe addressed to the Physicist. Like Nature in Goethe's poem, Hofmannsthal had "neither core nor outer rind, being all things at once". And the corollary, too, applies to the Hofmannsthal scholar:

> It's yourself you should scrutinize to see
> Whether you're centre or periphery.

With Hofmannsthal, as with Goethe's Nature, "at every place we're at the centre", if only we beware of the temptation to lose sight of the centre in pursuing the astonishing wealth and variety of minute particulars on the periphery. Both in his work and his life Hofmannsthal believed in "concealing the depth in the surface"; once this peculiarity has been recognized, there is no part of the extensive surface of his mind that does not yield some intimation of the depth.

Writing on Hofmannsthal and England some twenty-five years ago, Dr. Mary Gilbert found it "perplexing" that this writer, whose "Europe was the Catholic Europe of the baroque period" [1] should himself have laid such great emphasis on his debt to "northern and Protestant England". If we turn to a more recent view of Hofmannsthal, in Professor Fritz Martini's history of German Literature, we also read that Hofmannsthal "lived deeply within the Catholic-Baroque heritage of Vienna"; but Professor Martini goes on to say that "the Middle

---

[1] Mary E. Gilbert: 'Hofmannsthal and England', *German Life and Letters*, I (1937), 182—193.

Ages and the Baroque, Venice and Florence, Spain, classical antiquity and the East" were Hofmannsthal's "spiritual home". If to this "spiritual home", or to these spiritual homes, we add Germany, France, the Low Countries, Britain, America, Scandinavia and Eastern Europe, all of which made significant contributions to Hofmannsthal's work and development, we are coming closer to the complex truth of the matter.

Although she appeared to accept the more exclusive view of Hofmannsthal, Dr. Gilbert very clearly demonstrated that Hofmannsthal's affinity with "the Catholic Europe of the baroque period" was far from being his only one; in quoting the following passage from Hofmannsthal's letter to Felix Baron Oppenheimer of 4th April 1899, she was the first to draw attention to a very different source:

> London nimmt in meinem Vorstellungsleben einen ungeheuren Raum ein: mehr Fäden, als mir aufzuzählen möglich wäre, laufen von dort aus, und die wichtigsten Einflüsse für mein inneres Leben lassen sich mehr oder weniger auf englische Kunst, englische Weltanschauung und das intensive und weltumspannende Gegenwartsleben, das sich dort konzentriert, zurückführen [2].

Before going on to particularize and substantiate this indication of Hofmannsthal's—and there is more evidence for it than can be adduced here—I must return very briefly to the larger question of perspective. It is certainly true that in later life, after 1916 to be precise, Hofmannsthal tended to stress his links with "the Catholic Europe of the baroque period" and, guided in part by the theories of Professor Josef Nadler, to see himself primarily as a late representative of the Bavarian-Austrian or South German theatrical tradition [3]. Yet to pin Hofmannsthal down to this single tradition—if indeed it is a single tradition—would be as wrong as to assume a radical change of heart or outlook on his part between the early statement just quoted and the later ones. For all his complexity and diversity, few writers were more consistent than Hofmannsthal. Only by balancing one statement against another, with constant reference to the whole of his work and its centre, can we avoid violating either the complexity or the con-

---

[2] *Briefe 1890—1901,* Leipzig, S. Fischer Verlag, 1935, p. 285.
[3] See P IV 105, 324—325 and *passim.*

sistency; and it is the two together that constitute Hofmannsthal's chief distinction among the imaginative writers of his time. Hofmannsthal's consistency in this matter of his relationship to England can be shown by citing three other passages written at various times in his life; the first as early as June 1894, at the age of twenty, the last in February 1929, only a few months before his death at the age of fifty-five. The first two are from his notebooks:

> Englischer Ästhetismus als Element unserer Kultur. I. Erstes Entgegentreten: als Sonderbarkeit, wohl etwas Affektionen, Kostümtragen etc. II. Oscar Wilde, "Intentions": starker narkotischer Zauber, sophistisch verführerisch, unelegant paradoxal, Reaktion gegen englischen Utilitarismus. III. Ruskin, Pater, Madox Brown, Rossetti, Burne-Jones — die tiefen Zusammenhänge mit Seelenleben, das Ganze als Versuch einer inneren Kultur [4].

Here, in a nutshell, we have Hofmannsthal's own account of his early debt to English art and literature, that is, to the English aesthetic movement and its various representatives; that this account is not uncritical of the influence points to an inner conflict also present in Hofmannsthal's playlets of the same period, as well as in his critical essays on Pater [5], Wilde, Swinburne and many other contemporary writers. It is worth noting, too, that Hofmannsthal ascribes the excesses of the aesthetic movement to a reaction against utilitarianism; even at the age of twenty he had a sharp eye for political and cultural realities. Hofmannsthal's notebook for the same year contains quotations from poems by Browning—another important influence on his work—and there is another entry on Browning in the following year. In July of that year, 1895, he returned to the subject of aestheticism in a longer entry, from which I shall quote only a few relevant extracts:

> Große Anfänge, jetzige Depravation. — Ein Kreislauf, sich wechselseitig steigernd, befruchtend-verderblich, zwischen England—Belgien—Frankreich. Künste neigen sich einander zu, entfernen sich vom Publikum ... — Die erste Wirkung von England (Rossetti) ... Swinburne ein Höhepunkt; jetzt das Raffinement der jungen halben Talente. — Pater schon *morbide* Ausschreitung der Kritik ...[6].

---

[4] A 108.

[5] It is significant, too, that for his essay on Pater of 1894 Hofmannsthal chose the pseudonym "Archibald O'Hagan, B. A.—Old Rookery, Herfordshire" [sic].

[6] A 123.

14

The still more censorious tone of this passage does not mean that Hofmannsthal had broken once and for all with English aestheticism, or aestheticism in general; the hyphenated words "befruchtend-verderblich" render the conflict in his own mind between its attractive and repellent qualities. How crucial this conflict remained for at least another decade, how many of Hofmannsthal's works sprang from the tension between a sensuous and an ethical impulse, cannot be elaborated here; but his debt to English aestheticism is inseparable from this central preoccupation.

The last passage is from Hofmannsthal's letter of 20th February 1929 to his friend Professor Walther Brecht, most of which is devoted to an account of his relationship with Stefan George. Hofmannsthal wrote here of his early encounter with George:

> Im Ganzen kann man sagen, daß die Begegnung von entscheidender Bedeutung war — die Bestätigung dessen, was in mir lag, die Bekräftigung, daß ich kein vereinzelter Sonderling war, wenn ich es für möglich hielt, in der deutschen Sprache etwas zu geben, was mit den großen Engländern von Keats an sich auf einer poetischen Ebene bewegte und andererseits mit den festen romanischen Formen zusammenhing . . . [7].

Even at the end of his life, then, Hofmannsthal regarded his early poetry as an attempt to emulate the "great Englishmen after Keats"; and he did not regard this influence as opposed to that of Romance literature and culture on his development, because these in turn had so greatly influenced the English poets of the nineteenth century.

The eminence of these poets alone explains why Hofmannsthal attached such great importance to them. However, since Hofmannsthal chose to study Romance languages and literatures at Vienna University, and came close to an academic appointment in this discipline, his emphasis on English literature may still seem astonishing. The most important circumstance to be borne in mind is that Hofmannsthal's scholarly and antiquarian interests were always subordinated to his needs as a poet and writer; another is that whatever his spiritual homes may have been, Hofmannsthal's immediate starting-point was the world in which he grew up and the literary culture of his own

---

[7] *Der Briefwechsel zwischen George und Hofmannsthal*, Düsseldorf, 1953, pp. 235—236.

time. This culture was cosmopolitan and liberal; and the British component in it was very pervasive. Moreover, Hofmannsthal's attitude to the aestheticism of the eighteen-nineties was characterized by those reservations which were to determine his later development. English aestheticism differed from the French in one important respect; from Gautier onwards, the French advocates of "Art for Art's sake" had deliberately and progressively widened the gulf between "art" and "life", art and society—the very gulf of which Hofmannsthal complains in his notebook entry of 1895. Hofmannsthal's difference with Stefan George hinged on the same issue. In his essays of the same period on English art and literature Hofmannsthal repeatedly commented on the ethical and social aspects of English aestheticism—"die englische ästhetisch-moralische Form", as he called it—in contrast with the greater sensuousness of the French school. Thus, in the essay *Über Englische Malerei* of 1894, in connection with Ruskin and the Pre-Raphaelites, Hofmannsthal observed: "Zumal diese englische Kunst der psychisch-leiblichen Schönheit ist durch und durch ethisch" [8]. Where the English aesthetes, too, tended towards the doctrine of an autonomous aestheticism, like Walter Pater in the Third Book of *Marius the Epicurean,* or cultivated a hypertrophy of the senses, like Swinburne in much of his poetry, Hofmannsthal did not exempt them from his general critique of modern decadence.

Dr. Gilbert has already given a fully documented account of what the English way of life meant to Hofmannsthal ever since his adolescence:

> He behaved like an Englishman, in francophile Vienna ... He laid stress on the fact that he was acquainted with members of the British Embassy in Vienna; he played tennis rather ostentatiously, when the game had not yet become fashionable on the Continent. He was so well acquainted with English customs as to promise his friend Bahr English recipes. He alluded to the habit of sending Christmas cards; he imitated English headings of letters and interspersed his own letters with English words ... He was attracted to the idea of the 'gentleman', in which he saw his own ideal of a cultured life personified [9].

[8] P I 233.
[9] Gilbert: *op. cit.*

Dr. Gilbert cited the *Letter of Lord Chandos* and the *Briefe des Zurückgekehrten* as examples of how this conception of the gentleman entered into Hofmannsthal's imaginative works; and she quoted the following definition of the gentleman from Hofmannsthal's letter to Edgar Freiherr Karg von Bebenburg of 21st August 1894: ". . . ich glaube, der tiefste Sinn von dem, was man mit gentleman bezeichnet, ist das, daß man besser und vornehmer ist als das Leben" [10]. On the other hand, it is only fair to add, Hofmannsthal's very early essay *Englisches Leben*, published when he was seventeen, contains this comment on the biography of the English adventurer and occultist Laurence Oliphant; "Und Englands Geist ist ganz in diesem Buch mit seinem Reichtum und seiner Beschränktheit, entbehrend der höchsten Höhen und der tiefsten Tiefen" [11].

English life continued to fascinate Hofmannsthal during the next decade of his life. His library contains a copy of the second edition of *An Onlooker's Notebook* (London, 1902), a collection of sociological articles from the *Manchester Guardian*, which he read and annotated in December 1904. He was especially interested in the sections dealing with economics; thus he referred in a note to a passage on 'Manchesterism', which the writer defined as "unrestricted competition, every man for himself, 'the devil take the hindmost' and the survival of the fittest". A second note of Hofmannsthal's in this book refers to the historical origins of this trend in the eighteenth century: "Pitt erklärt, jeder der 1000 Pfund jährlich hat, hat ein Recht auf das peerage S. 50." Another English book that Hofmannsthal read with care at this time, in June 1906, was *A Modern Symposium* by G. Lowes Dickinson. The many passages marked by Hofmannsthal in his copy of this work show that he was no less interested in the Socialist point of view than in the Conservative. Hofmannsthal also marked a passage about a possible synthesis of the two points of view and the creation of a "Tory-Socialist party". A passage on the artist's plight in democracies is especially heavily marked; but against an attack on the philistinism of America Hofmannsthal has entered the words "Poe! Whitman!" in protest. At the back of the book he has noted "culture!"—meaning

[10] *Briefe 1890—1901*, p. 113.
[11] P I 72.

17

the high cultural level of Lowes Dickinson's book, and of England
generally—but also: "Ungleichheit — das ganze Land voll davon".
Hofmannsthal's interest in economic questions and the evils of
capitalism is confirmed by several other books in his library.
Little has become known as yet about Hofmannsthal's visits to England [12] or his relations with British friends and acquaintances such as
Robert Vansittart, Edward Gordon Craig, Cyril Scott, Ethel Smyth,
John Drinkwater and Gilbert Murray. Scattered references in his
works and published letters suggest that personal contacts with English
men and women were as important to him as his wide acquaintance
with English literature and English institutions. There is the Englishwoman of *Erinnerung Schöner Tage* (1907), "eine von den Englände-
rinnen, die antiken Statuen gleichen. Wunderbar war der junge Glanz
ihres fast strengen Gesichtes und der Schwung ihrer Augenbrauen, die
geformt waren wie Flügel" [13]. Hofmannsthal's notebook of 1908
records one of his meetings with the young Englishwoman Gladys D.,
of whom he writes that she was "in gewissem Sinne die glänzendste
Person, die ich je gesehen habe . . . Sie hat immer unter fünfundzwan-
zig Personen die alleinige Führung des Gesprächs; schmeichelt, insul-
tiert, durchdringt. Die Raschheit und Elastizität ihres Geistes ist erstaunlich" [14]. In a plan for his periodical *Neue Deutsche Beiträge*,
drafted about 1920, Hofmannsthal names Gilbert Murray, Lowes
Dickinson and Granville Barker among the prospective contributors
and describes them as "die bedeutenden reingesinnten Engländer" [15].
To such references we can add the evidence of the Rodaun Visitors'
Book, which records visits by Cyril Scott, Ethel Smyth and Robert
Vansittart, as well as the American dancer Ruth St. Denis. Hofmannsthal's association with Edward Gordon Craig was mainly professional, and 'theatre business' thwarted most of their projects for collaboration. In 1906 Craig presented Hofmannsthal with a copy of his
book *The Art of the Theatre* with the inscription "To the Poet in all
admiration." This admiration is borne out by Craig's unpublished

[12] Hofmannsthal visited Brighton and London in 1900, London again in 1925. Both
visits were brief.
[13] P II 403—406.
[14] A 160—161.
[15] *Ibid.*, 367

2

letters to Hofmannsthal—whom he called "the most intelligent man in Germany"—and it also transpires from these that Craig wanted Hofmannsthal to write a preface to the German edition of his book.

The letters of Arthur Symons to Hofmannsthal reveal that it was Mrs. Patrick Campbell who asked him to translate Hofmannsthal's *Elektra;* unfortunately their correspondence was confined to practical matters arising over the translation, and there is no reason to suppose that Hofmannsthal knew of Symon's importance as a link between the French Symbolists, the English poets of the 'nineties and such twentieth century writers as W. B. Yeats, James Joyce and Ezra Pound. Hofmannsthal's unpublished papers also include letters from Granville Barker, Ethel Smyth, Cyril Scott, John Galsworthy, Gilbert Murray and other English acquaintances; his library, inscribed copies of books by Robert Vansittart and John Drinkwater. Hofmannsthal had some correspondence with T. S. Eliot over a contribution to *The Criterion;* and Eliot's *The Sacred Wood* is still extant among the books in Hofmannsthal's library. Incomplete though they are, these names may suffice to indicate the range of Hofmannsthal's personal associations with England; it is characteristic of him that they should have included representatives not only of all the arts, but of diplomacy and the world of learning.

The extent of Hofmannsthal's reading in English was such that only a rough general outline can be given here, followed by a few instances of borrowings, influences and parallels. As one would expect from indications in his notebooks and letters, the nineteenth century writers are prominent in his library. Besides the poetry of Coleridge, Wordsworth, Byron, Keats and Shelley, Poe, Whitman, Browning and Swinburne, he read Coleridge's letters, Lamb's and De Quincey's essays, the *Imaginary Conversations* of Walter Savage Landor, novels by Jane Austen, Dickens and Conrad, various prose works by Ruskin, Pater, Wilde and Yeats. The poets after Milton and before Blake do not appear to have interested him; but the eighteenth century is represented by Sheridan's comedies, Addison's essays, Gibbon's *Decline and Fall,* the letters of Horace Walpole and Lord Chesterfield, Boswell's *Life of Johnson,* novels by Defoe, Smollett, Sterne and Fielding, and William Beckford's *Vathek.* Hofmannsthal's knowledge of Shake-

speare and Francis Bacon needs no emphasis; his interest in the sixteenth and seventeenth centuries led him to study many minor Elizabethan, Jacobean and Restoration dramatists, including Dekker, Beau-
mont and Fletcher, Ford, Webster, Thomas Middleton, Philip Massinger, Thomas Shadwell, Vanbrugh, Otway and Congreve. Of seventeenth century prose works, Burton's *Anatomy of Melancholy* is extant in Hofmannsthal's library.

Adaptations of Coleridge's *Fact and Phantom* and of Browning's
A Serenade at the Villa are to be found among Hofmannsthal's
poems [16], the former among the few which Hofmannsthal published
in his lifetime. As late as 1901 Hofmannsthal also worked on a play,
Pompilia oder das Leben, on a subject derived from Browning's *The
Ring and the Book*. What is much more significant, it was mainly to
Browning's example that Hofmannsthal owed the very idea of both
lyrical drama and those dramatic monologues and studies which he
called *Gestalten*. If we consider that these two intermediate genres
enabled Hofmannsthal to make the difficult transition from an essentially lyrical to an essentially dramatic output, it is to Browning,
above all, that we should apply Hofmannsthal's acknowledgement
to the English poets after Keats. Hofmannsthal read Browning's work
repeatedly after 1892; his copy of *Poems by Robert Browning* (London, 1898) records the dates 1903, 1905, 1913 and 1925.

In other respects, it is true, Hofmannsthal's affinity with Keats himself is more apparent than his affinity with Browning. The following
lines from Keats's poem 'On Death', for instance, are strikingly close
in mood and tone to the concluding lines of *Der Tor und der Tod:*

> How strange it is that man on earth should roam,
> And lead a life of woe, but not forsake
> His rugged path . . .

> Wie wundervoll sind diese Wesen,
> Die, was nicht deutbar, dennoch deuten,
> Was nie geschrieben wurde, lesen,
> Verworrenes beherrschend binden
> Und Wege noch im Ewig-Dunklen finden.

[16] G 93 and 23 respectively.

2*

as well as to the following lines from 'Ballade des Äußeren Lebens':

> Was frommt das alles uns und diese Spiele
> Die wir doch groß und ewig einsam sind
> Und wandernd nimmer suchen irgend Ziele?

The edition of *The Poetical Works of John Keats* in Hofmannsthal's library was published in 1892. Hofmannsthal's notes in the book suggest that he read the shorter poems at about this time, though he read 'The Eve of St. Agnes', 'Isabella' and 'Lamia' as late as 1912, when he also marked the poem 'Welcome joy and welcome sorrow' with a note for *Die Frau ohne Schatten:* "für den Kaiser/was er der Kaiserin vorenthalten hat".

Another English influence on the poems goes back to Hofmannsthal's childhood, when he owned picture books by Kate Greenaway, as we learn from the early autobiographical piece to which he gave the English title *Age of Innocence* [17]. In the slightly later essay *Englischer Stil* of 1896 [18] he writes in connection with a performance by the Barrison sisters:

> Wenn die Barrisons auftreten, erwartet man, daß auf der staubigen Tingeltangel-Bühne hinter ihren gelben Haaren und kindischen Schultern auch einmal der Mond aufgehen wird, der übergroße japanische Vollmond, so wie in den Bilderbüchern von Kate Greenaway hinter den fünf Schulmädeln mit gelben Haaren, Baby-Hüten und rosa Kleidern.

It is not difficult to recognize the same association once more in the second and third parts of Hofmannsthal's 'Terzinen über Vergänglichkeit', written some two years before the essay, but quite especially in these lines:

> Und Träume schlagen so die Augen auf
> Wie kleine Kinder unter Kirschenbäumen,
>
> Aus deren Krone den blaßgoldnen Lauf
> Der Vollmond anhebt durch die große Nacht.

The same childhood association may account for Hofmannsthal's emphasis on the virginal, youthful or androgynous character of Eng-

---

[17] P I 147.
[18] *Ibid.*, 292.

lish art and style generally, what he calls their "merkwürdige Kind-
lichkeit" in the essay—a quality which he also sensed in the work
of the Pre-Raphaelite painters. In the same essay Hofmannsthal speaks
of the design of tennis clothes, furniture and picture books as examples of English style. Since it was one of the foremost aims of the
aesthetic movement to effect a synthesis of all the arts, it is not surprising that a visual association should have had such power over him.
A thorough examination of Hofmannsthal's imagery in this light
would almost certainly reveal other debts to English graphic and de-
corative art. Walter Crane and Aubrey Beardsley were among the
English illustrators whom he admired. The sketches for his unfinished
tragedy on the *Pentheus* theme (1904) begin with an epigraph from
Walter Pater and the note: "Costumes in the spirit of Aubrey
Beardsley" [19].

Richard Alewyn [20] has remarked on the implications for Hofmannsthal not so much of the work as of the fate of Oscar Wilde, whom in
the essay *Sebastian Melmoth* of 1905 Hofmannsthal celebrated as a
tragic hero of the age:

> Oscar Wildes Wesen und Oscar Wildes Schicksal sind ganz und gar
> dasselbe. Er ging auf seine Katastrophe zu, mit solchen Schritten
> wie Ödipus, der Sehend-Blinde. Der Ästhet war tragisch. Der Geck
> war tragisch . . . Er insultierte die Wirklichkeit. Und er fühlte, wie
> das Leben sich duckte, ihn aus dem Dunkel anzuspringen [21].

No contemporary writer was more aware of both the temptations
and the perils of extreme aestheticism than Hofmannsthal; his early
playlets and stories are variations on this theme. It was Oscar Wilde
who asserted that life imitates art; and, as Professor Alewyn has shown,
Oscar Wilde's fate is prefigured in Hofmannsthal's magnificent story
of the merchant's son, *Das Märchen der 672. Nacht,* published in 1895,
before Oscar Wilde's trial and fall. This strange concordance, then,
is not one of literary influence; rather it is to be ascribed to the *Zeitgeist* itself, and to the intuitive and imaginative power that enabled
Hofmannsthal to grasp and interpret it.

[19] D II 523.
[20] Richard Alewyn: *Über Hugo von Hofmannsthal,* Göttingen, 1958, pp. 143—144.
[21] P II 135.

The same is almost certainly true of the remarkable parallels between certain works of Hofmannsthal and certain works by his Irish contemporary W. B. Yeats. Since I have dealt with some of the more striking of these parallels elsewhere [22], I shall only confirm here that Hofmannsthal does not appear to have known these works by Yeats at the time. Much later, in 1916, Yeats's German translator Friedrich Eckstein presented Hofmannsthal with an inscribed copy of his selection of prose works by Yeats, *Erzählungen und Essays* (Leipzig, 1916), now the property of Dr. J. C. Middleton. Hofmannsthal read this book with care and marked many passages that shed light on his affinity with Yeats, as well as on their common debt to the English Romantics, Neo-Platonist thought, theosophy and Symbolist aesthetics. It is from this book also that Hofmannsthal took the two quotations from William Blake which he included in his *Buch der Freunde* [23]. Hofmannsthal's only published reference to Yeats occurs in his 'Vienna Letter' of 1922, written for the American periodical *The Dial;* there he spoke with sympathy of Yeats's endeavours to found an Irish National Theatre that would provide both for an educated and an uneducated public, compared this undertaking with the more favourable conditions in Vienna, with its long tradition of popular drama, and quotes from one of Yeats's early reports on his and Lady Gregory's work for the Irish Literary Theatre [24]. It is possible that Edward Gordon Craig, who was associated with both poets, gave Hofmannsthal an idea of Yeats's theatrical aspirations, although neither poet refers to the other in his published correspondence, and no book of poems or plays by Yeats is extant in Hofmannsthal's library. Both poets adapted parts of Sophocles's Oedipus trilogy for the modern stage. Hofmannsthal's dramatic fragment *Leda und der Schwan* constitutes one of an extraordinary number of thematic parallels with poems and plays by Yeats. The influence of Walter Pater on both poets—and quite especially of his passage on the Mona

---

[22] In the Introduction to Hofmannsthal: *Poems and Verse Plays*, New York and London, 1961, pp. xliii—xlv, lvi—lviii.

[23] A 45 and 48 and D III 458.

[24] Hofmannsthal's quotation is from Yeats's essay *The Theatre* of 1899, recently reprinted in W. B. Yeats: *Essays and Introductions*, London, 1961. The passage in question is to be found on p. 167.

Lisa which Yeats thought important enough to place at the head of his *Oxford Book of Modern Verse*—was another link between them. Because of his habit of appropriating and adapting not only whole works, but isolated lines, thoughts, metaphors and images taken from the works of his predecessors, Hofmannsthal's poems and plays abound in evidence of his wide reading. Those who assert that Hofmannsthal's originality and creative energy declined after his youth are also apt to assume that this practice is more marked in his later work than in the earlier; but the poems and playlets which he wrote in the 'nineties are as rich in direct and indirect borrowings as the comedies and libretti of his maturity. This applies to his reading in English also; as early as June 1892, even before the first mention of Browning in his letters, Hofmannsthal writes of using "ein technisches Requisit von Shakespeare" for his unfinished Renaissance tragedy *Ascanio und Gioconda* [25]. The ten-volume edition of Shakespeare in Hofmannsthal's library (ed. Singer, 3rd Edition, London, 1883) corroborates his concern with Shakespeare's stagecraft. To cite only one instance: in Act III, Scene III of *Othello*, against Iago's "My lord, I take my leave", followed by the direction "Going" and Othello's next words: "Why did I marry?", Hofmannsthal has entered the words: "fausse sortie". At the back of the same volume Hofmannsthal has entered sketches for his comedy *Cristinas Heimreise*. In 1892 also, at the age of eighteen, Hofmannsthal had begun to study the dramatic works of Ford, Webster and Massinger.

Hofmannsthal's borrowings or plagiarisms, as some would call them, are a controversial matter [26]; all that need be said here is that his practice rested on the deep and constant conviction that there can and should be no such thing as private property in literature. In many cases his unacknowledged quotations or translations must be construed as tributes to the authors and works he admires; in others, as something that belonged to Hofmannsthal as much, and in the same way, as the air he breathed or the streets in which he walked. To give an example of the former kind, in his lecture *Shakespeares Könige und*

---

[25] *Briefe 1890—1901*, p. 44.
[26] Discussed in the present writer's article 'Hofmannsthals Bibliothek', *Euphorion*, LV (1961), 15—76.

Große Herren of 1905, Hofmannsthal praises the lines in which Brutus apologizes to Lucius for shortening his sleep: "Wie er sich entschuldigt, daß er ihm den Schlaf verkürzt, auf den seine Jugend so viel Anrecht hat" [27]. Hofmannsthal must be referring to these lines from Act IV, Scene III of *Julius Caesar:*

> I should not urge thy duty past thy might;
> I know young bloods look for a time of rest.

In Hofmannsthal's own tragedy *Oedipus und die Sphinx,* published in the following year, Creon says to the Boy [28]:

> Schlaf fort, das junge Blut
> braucht seinen Schlaf.

Clearly, Hofmannsthal felt no guilt over such stolen goods, since he himself drew attention to the appropriation in this case.

In the same lecture Hofmannsthal remarked about Claudio in *Measure for Measure:* "Wie preßt der Tod den besten Saft aus ihm heraus" [29]. The remark applies equally well to Hofmannsthal's Claudio in *Der Tor und der Tod;* and it was no accident that Hofmannsthal chose this name for the man enclosed, immured and isolated within his own egotism. It seems likely, too, that the name Faninal in *Der Rosenkavalier* is an anagram of the name Fainall in Congreve's *The Way of the World,* though here the connection is more tenuous.

Another Shakespeare echo, also connected with sleep, occurs in *Der Abenteurer und die Sängerin* [30], when Lorenzo says:

> Nun schon ich ihren Schlaf — und bald vielleicht
> Ermord ich ihr den Schlaf von vielen Nächten —

an obvious reminiscence of "Macbeth has murdered sleep". It would seem, in fact, that English poetry is quite especially prodigal of allusions to sleep, or that Hofmannsthal found it so. In his playlet *Der Weiße Fächer* [31] the Mulatto Woman says:

[27] P II 168.
[28] D II 329.
[29] P II 156.
[30] D I 225.
[31] G 250.

> Denn was hat Schlaf mit Nacht zu tun, was Jugend
> Mit Treue?

linking a new train of thought to a literal translation of Milton's line from *Comus:*

> What hath night to do with sleep?

Hofmannsthal's knowledge of Milton's poetry is attested by an entry in his notebook of 1911 and by a short note which he entered in his copy of Boswell's *Johnson,* one of Hofmannsthal's favourite English books. Since there is no evidence that Hofmannsthal knew William Blake's poetry at this early period, one cannot be quite sure about the following lines from *Das Bergwerk zu Falun* [32]:

> Du kannst das Glück nicht in verschlossnen Höhlen
> Dir halten, denn es atmet nur im Flug!

but these lines certainly suggest that Hofmannsthal had read Blake's *Eternity,* perhaps in an anthology:

> He who binds to himself a joy
> Does the winged life destroy;
> But he who kisses the joy as it flies
> Lives in eternity's sun rise.

If we add Hofmannsthal's adaptations of *Everyman* and *Venice Perserv'd,* or his film scenario based on the life and works of Daniel Defoe, to a great variety of concealed allusions and borrowings, the English background of his most revealing confession, the *Chandos Letter,* and of his projected imaginary conversation *Essex und sein Richter,* to the many references to English works in his essays, Hofmannsthal's debt to England becomes very substantial indeed. The influence of Landor on the dialogue form of some of Hofmannsthal's finest essays, and of English criticism generally on all of them, are other matters that would repay study. Hofmannsthal himself acknowledged the superiority of English journalism [33], using this word in a sense neither derogatory nor patronizing, since he included H. G. Wells, the "philosophical journalist", Lowes Dickinson and the "poetic jour-

---

[32] G 377.
[33] P II 299.

nalist" Lafcadio Hearn in this category, just as he would have included his own essays.

Lafcadio Hearn is one of several authors to whom Hofmannsthal was indebted for his knowledge of the East; his library contains other works by English orientalists, travellers and translators from oriental languages, such as Arthur Waley's translations of Chinese poems. The importance to him of Kakasu Okakura's *The Ideals of the East, with special reference to the Art of Japan* (London, 1903), a marked copy of which is extant in his library, becomes apparent in Hofmannsthal's notes for his lecture *Die Idee Europa* of 1916 [34].

The works of two British classical scholars, Gilbert Murray and J. W. Mackail, were no less important to him, as his notes in copies of their books testify. Hofmannsthal read Gilbert Murray's *The Rise of the Greek Epic* in 1912; besides marking many passages on Homer and Hesiod, he used the blank pages at the back for sketches later incorporated in the most outstanding of his own works bearing on classical antiquity, *Augenblicke in Griechenland*. Of the passages marked, two are especially interesting as indirect comments on Hofmannsthal's own peculiarities; and one of these peculiarities was to mark passages especially relevant to himself. "First of all", Murray writes, "I think we are apt to confuse originality with a much less important thing, novelty"—a distinction also made by Hofmannsthal. The relevance of the other passage to Hofmannsthal is equally clear: "And it is very noteworthy how many great poets seem to have drawn most of their inspiration not directly from experience, but derivatively from experience already interpreted by other men's poetry." Gilbert Murray's *A History of Ancient Greek Literature,* also in Hofmannsthal's library, was published in 1911; and so was the edition of Mackail's *Lectures on Greek Poetry* which Hofmannsthal read in 1912, and again in 1916. This work, too, occupied Hofmannsthal's attention at the time of his work on *Augenblicke in Griechenland*.

What Hofmannsthal wrote in 1899 about the many threads running out from London, and the important influences on his mental life,

[34] P III 380.

[35] William James. The source is described in detail in 'Hofmannsthals Bibliothek', *op. cit.*, p. 29.

applies to every period of his life, from childhood to maturity. It may well be that the most vital of these influences have evaded me here, because they are not attached to specific authors, works and references, but to moments of vision—epiphanies, as Joyce called them—to auras and associations. Thus, in the essay *Der Dichter und diese Zeit*, one is struck by an unexpected evocation of London itself, not unlike certain passages in T. S. Eliot's *The Waste Land* in its power to illuminate by sudden juxtapostion: "Er ist der leidenschaftliche Bewunderer", Hofmannsthal writes of the poet, "der Dinge, die von ewig sind, und der Dinge, die von heute sind. London im Nebel mit gespenstigen Prozessionen von Arbeitslosen, die Tempeltrümmer von Luxor, das Plätschern einer einsamen Waldquelle, das Gebrüll ungeheurer Maschinen: die Übergänge sind niemals schwer für ihn ..."
Here London becomes the very paradigm of the modern city and the modern age, its unemployed like those spirits of whom T. S. Eliot, quoting Dante, was to write:

> Unreal city,
> Under the brown fog of a winter dawn,
> A crowd flowed over London Bridge, so many,
> I had not thought death had undone so many.

Whether or not Hofmannsthal's vision of London in the fog was a reminiscence of immediate experience—as "the ruined temples of Luxor" were not, since Hofmannsthal did not visit North Africa until 1925—may be of biographical interest, but it is quite irrelevant to an apprecation of his art. What matters in the case of either passage, Hofmannsthal's and Eliot's, is not the extent of the poet's reading and borrowings, but his capacity to absorb and organize disparate material, fuse immediate with vicarious experience, and make those transitions which give them new life and meaning.
It is in this light that Hofmannsthal's debt to English literature and English institutions should be considered. Exciting though it is to discover that the Captain in Hofmannsthal's comedy *Cristinas Heimreise* owes much of his past life to the real experiences of an English sailor in the year 1689, of which Hofmannsthal read in a twentieth century work by an American [35], what is much more important is that no one would have guessed as much without stumbling on the evidence. The transitions have been made with the utmost delicacy of

thought and imagination, and the alien material naturalized to the wholly different atmosphere of Hofmannsthal's play.

Nevertheless, and granted that Hofmannsthal's debt to England was one of many debts to other nations and cultures, the extent of his interests and sympathies should never be left out of account in determining his status, allegiances and "spiritual home". These have been, and still are, persistently misrepresented by those who cannot or will not allow for his liberality and comprehensiveness of mind. Hofmannsthal was more than a "good European"; he attempted nothing less than to attain and uphold a Goethean universality in an age of which Yeats wrote:

> Things fall apart; the centre cannot hold;
> Mere anarchy is loosed upon the world.
> The blood-dimmed tide is loosed, and everywhere
> The ceremony of innocence is drowned;
> The best lack all conviction, while the worst
> Are full of passionate intensity.

To this state of anarchy Hofmannsthal struggled to oppose a "passionate intensity" quite unlike the fanaticism of "the worst", a passionate intensity tempered with understanding, committed to the centre and yet as all-embracing as the other is exclusive and destructive. Hofmannsthal's concern with England was part of that larger concern.

HOFMANNSTHAL'S ESSAYS, 1900—1908

A POET IN TRANSITION

BY MARY E. GILBERT

Shortly after the publication of the Lord Chandos letter (*Ein Brief* 1901) Hofmannsthal wrote to his friend, the poet Andrian [1]:

ich dachte und denke an eine Kette ähnlicher Kleinigkeiten. Das Buch würde heißen "Erfundene Gespräche und Gedichte". Ich denke, darin kein einziges formales Totengespräch zu geben — der Gehalt soll überall für mich und mir nahestehende aktuell sein — aber wenn Du mich wieder heißen wolltest diesen Gehalt direkt zu geben, so ginge für mich aller Anreiz zu dieser Arbeit verloren, der starke Reiz für mich ist, vergangene Zeiten nicht ganz tot sein zu lassen, oder Fernes, Fremdes als nah verwandt spüren zu machen. Ich würde folgendes hineinbringen: ein Gespräch zwischen einem Menschen wie Bui [2] und einem alten, klugen mit Europa wohl vertrauten Japaner; den Brief des letzten Contarini, der, bettelarm, eine Rente ablehnt, welche Freunde ihm anbieten, damit er standesgemäß leben könne; den Abschiedsbrief A. de Vignys an den Kronprinzen Max von Bayern, mit welchem er eine erziehliche Korrespondenz geführt hat. Einige antike Briefe. Ein Gespräch zwischen einem einfachen Menschen und einem Schauspieler usw. In der Weihnachtsbeilage der Neuen Freien Presse findest Du eines zwischen Balzac und Hammer-Purgstall, das einzige, welches nicht über literarische und Artistenprobleme hinausgeht.

Hofmannsthal here talks of a book he plans containing imaginary letters and conversations, stressing the unity and coherence of these "Kleinigkeiten". This is not the only trace of such a plan, for in several letters of these years he mentions such dialogues. On September 20,

---

I should like to acknowledge my gratitude to Herr Raimund von Hofmannsthal for allowing me to work in his father's library.

[1] Letter dated 16 January, [1903]. *Briefe 1900—1909*. Vienna, 1937, p. 100.

[2] Short name for their mutual friend Georg von Franckenstein who had spent several years in the Diplomatic Service abroad.

1902 [3], he writes to his publisher Bie: "Vielleicht kündigen Sie besser einen Dialog an, wie ich deren mehrere ganz skizziert habe ... Sie beziehen sich auf sittlich-politische Gegenstände des gegenwärtigen Lebens, auf Reichtum, auf Vergleich unserer Kultur mit orientalischen Kulturen".

Such is the programme; however, as with so many plans of these years, this remains fragmentary. Of the imaginary letters and dialogues all we have in print are *Ein Brief* (Lord Chandos letter 1901), *Über Charaktere im Roman und im Drama (ein imaginäres Gespräch)* (1902) and fragments and different versions of *Der Brief des letzten Contarini* (undated). But in the following years the form of "Erfundene Briefe und Gespräche" is taken up again and again. There are: *Gespräch über Gedichte* (1903); *Unterhaltungen über ein neues Buch* (1906); *Unterhaltung über den "Tasso" von Goethe* (1906); *Unterhaltung über die Schriften von Gottfried Keller* (1906); *Das Gespräch der Tänzerinnen* (1906); *Die Briefe des Zurückgekehrten* (1907) [4].

Why does Hofmannsthal choose the form of conversations and dialogues? There is, of course, a literary tradition of such dialogues (Gespräche) on philosophical and literary subjects of which he is well aware [5]. But the conversations, "Unterhaltungen" as he calls them, are of a very different type. They are discussions between young people of Hofmannsthal's own age group—anyone interested in such biographical facts can easily identify his friends in the speakers [6]. They

---

[3] *Briefe 1900—1909*, p. 84. In a folder among Hofmannsthal's manuscripts there is a plan for the prose essay on "Reichtum" or so it seems. See Norton: 'Hofmannsthals Magische Werkstätte'. *Germanic Review*, XXXVI (1961). Here we read: "Reichtum und Armut zu behandeln nicht vom Standpunkt der Reichen oder der Armen sondern als die beiden großen mythischen Potenzen, welche unsere Zeit beherrschen, Vorratsbecken ungeheurer Metaphern. An die ganz Reichen und die ganz Armen denken wir unaufhörlich. Jeden umkleiden wir abwechselnd mit Glorie in unserm Traum."

[4] These essays appeared in different newspapers and periodicals: *Neue Freie Presse, Der Tag, Die Zeit, die Neue Rundschau, Morgen, Kunst und Künstler*.

[5] Hofmannsthal was well acquainted with Novalis and knew Landor as well as Wilde. Of his personal friends, Kassner, Wassermann and Bahr used the form of dialogue on literary subjects at about the same time, and Borchardt translated Landor's 'Imaginary Conversations' in 1908—note the closeness of the two titles.

[6] cf. my introduction to *Hofmannsthal: Selected Essays*. Blackwell, 1955. p. xviii. "Der Zurückgekehrte" is a composite figure embodying moods, experiences and reactions of Hofmannsthal as well as his friends—as can be shown from the

are a give and take in which the speakers aim at gaining clarity about their own positions, and indeed they often modify their views. The predilection for this form seems to reflect one side of Hofmannsthal's nature who, as all his friends testify [7], was the most wonderful of conversationalists. "Gespräche" to him were a spiritual need and a great part of his thinking seems to have been done in this form. Nevertheless the preponderance of "Gespräche" and "Unterhaltungen" at this particular time of his life seems strange. For we think of this period, the period inaugurated by the Lord Chandos letter, as one of deep withdrawal: of the most tormenting doubts on the part of Hofmannsthal about his capability as a poet—perhaps even about the possibility of poetry itself? About his ability to communicate through words, perhaps even about the capacity of words *per se* to communicate. And yet, it is just at this juncture that he resorts so frequently to this form. Why? He could have presented his insight into matters political, cultural and literary in the form of so many straightforward arguments—yet he consistently chose "Gespräche" and "Unterhaltungen", a form which entirely depends upon the demonstrable capability of the figures to communicate through words. For in these essays insight is not there *a priori;* it grows and deepens perceptibly in the give and take of sympathetic minds [8].

And then Hofmannsthal's withdrawal into himself, the cessation of that inexhaustible responsiveness to the world around him which marks his early lyricism? The doubts that assailed him as this inner source dried up? Again the essays written at this period provide a startling answer. For in these essays it is not the poet, the specialist, the expert who has the creative insight into works of art—with the exception of Balzac in the earliest essay *Gespräch über Charaktere im Roman und im Drama*—it is rather the ordinary reader, the fictitious representa-

correspondence—of Leopold Freiherr von Andrian, Legationssekretär in Brazil from 1903 onwards, of Egdar Karg Freiherr von Bebenburg, naval officer in the Far East 1894, and of Eberhard von Bodenhausen, who had entered the big industrial concern of Krupp in 1906.

[7] cf. the articles in Fiechtner: *Hofmannsthal, die Gestalt des Dichters im Spiegel der Freunde.* Vienna, 1949. i. e. Wassermann, p. 105; W. Müller-Hofmann, p. 142; E. Lang, p. 199; E. Buschbeck, p. 222 and R. A. Schröder, p. 343.

[8] Several of these essays are divided into two parts, time elapsing in between. Hofmannsthal can thus show how what has been said has its effect on the speakers.

32

tive of his generation to whom Hofmannsthal has assigned the task of creative critic. Hofmannsthal, whilst ostensibly despairing of poetry, peopled his literary universe with ordinary human beings endowed with a natural sensibility of the highest order and capable of the most differentiated poetic response, for it must be remembered that these are creations of his imagination. The following are the words in which the characters themselves describe their experience of poetry. The appreciation of a work of art leaves the reader in "einer schwebenden erhöhten Stimmung" [9], gives him a rare intensity of living, a heightening of sensibility: "das Leben schien mir schöner und gefährlicher als je zuvor" [10]. To one of them poetry is „ein höchstes Genießen, und das ist flüchtig wie der Blitz, ist ein zuckendes Ahnen, flüchtigste Intuition, ist ein raumloses, zeitloses: 'Ich hab's gefühlt'" [11]. To another, "mir war, als jagte ein dunkles Wasser mit mir zwischen steilen Ufern hin, und doch stieß ich nirgends an ... dreimal kam ich durch ein ganzes Menschenleben hindurch, dunkel ahnte mir, als beginge ich einen Frevel, finstere Geschicke so hinunterzutrinken wie einen aufschäumenden Becher ... aber die Lust überwog" [12]. In these moments the reader transmutes reality "und noch jetzt ... sehe ich mein Haus ... eure Gesichter mit Befremden, als käme ich von weither" [13]. The reader reacts by seeing the world differently as if by magic and by being related to a world that had been alien to him. Such is the figure of the creative reader—"der erlebende Leser".

What is more interesting still is that such an account on the part of the reader-critic—and I have selected only a few of many—is virtually identical with accounts of the poet's own moments of creative inspiration. Not only is the ordinary reader the reliable interpreter of these works of art, he also speaks with the authentic voice and knowledge of the poet. And these reader-poets are Hofmannsthal's creations.

Lastly there were his doubts about the power of the word, the medium of communication, of which Hofmannsthal despaired in what is called

[9] *Unterhaltungen über ein neues Buch*, P II 246.
[10] *Ibid.*, p. 245.
[11] *Unterhaltung über den "Tasso" von Goethe*, P II 220.
[12] *Unterhaltungen über ein neues Buch*, P II 245.
[13] *Ibid.*, p. 246.

his "Sprachverzweiflung". In the essays of this period we read the following lines about poems and words put into the mouth of one of his imaginary speakers: "Aber daß ihrer überhaupt welche entstehen [i. e. "Gedichte"], ist es nicht wie ein Wunder? Daß es Zusammenstellungen von Worten gibt, aus welchen, wie der Funke aus dem geschlagenen dunklen Stein, die Landschaften der Seele hervorbrechen, die unermeßlich sind wie der gestirnte Himmel, Landschaften, die sich ausdehnen im Raum und in der Zeit, und deren Anblick abzuweiden in uns ein Sinn lebendig wird, der über alle Sinne ist" [14]. It is true that at this juncture Hofmannsthal could not bring himself to employ the 'Ich-Form' for experiences which he makes his figures discuss. He could no longer bring himself to make the simple statement which had become an extremely difficult statement: 'I communicate, I respond to the world around me, I am a poet.' But did he not affirm his belief in the validity of these statements indirectly through the communicating and responding creative figures which he invented?

Did he not indeed confirm that to him poetry was still a reality, not by what he says but by the way he says it? These essays are more than critical arguments, they are themselves a form of poetry.

We know that Hofmannsthal himself felt like this, for when *Das Gespräch über Gedichte* was to appear in *Die Neue Rundschau,* he asked Bie: "ihm eine auch äußerlich ausgezeichnete Stellung zu geben, damit er nicht in die Kategorie der Aufsätze, sondern die der Dichtungen fällt" [15], and Bodenhausen calls it in a letter to the poet "Gedicht über Gedichte" [16]. And again in a letter to his father the poet describes *Die Briefe des Zurückgekehrten* as "eine Art Novelle in Briefen" [17]. The letters were to be continued and were to end with the marriage of the correspondent [18], thus being modelled on the structure of a "Bildungsroman", the form of novel which Hofmannsthal was to choose for his *Andreas.*

[14] *Das Gespräch über Gedichte,* P II 112.
[15] Letter dated 9 October, [1903]. *Briefe 1900—1909,* p. 130.
[16] Letter dated 20 February, 1904. *Briefe der Freundschaft: Hugo von Hofmannsthal — Eberhard von Bodenhausen.* Berlin, 1953. p. 42.
[17] Letter dated 17 July, 1907. *Briefe 1900—1909,* p. 283.
[18] This remark is based on information of H. Steiner which I have, so far, been unable to follow up in detail.

A closer look at these essays will show how theme, setting and speaker are one indivisible whole and how each is pervaded by its unmistakable and individual atmosphere. The two urbane young couples driving home from a performance in Vienna of Goethe's *Tasso* to their "Villenvorstadt" on a mild summer's night with the roses in full bloom—is this not the right framework for a talk on *Tasso?* How deliciously appropriate that the painter, one of the participants in the conversation on Keller's realistic and visual art should be sitting "in einer hölzernen, luftigen Laube" doodling a "Weinbergschnecke" [19]. Hofmannsthal could not have found a more suitable speaker to discourse on the theme of life fulfilled in the present moment than the Greek dancers in *Das Gespräch der Tänzerinnen,* for there is no race that stands as the Greeks do for oneness of body and mind and no art which achieves so perfectly as the art of dancing the articulation of the heightened sense of reality that springs from such oneness. In *Unterhaltungen über ein neues Buch (Die Schwestern* by Wassermann), where the modern form of fiction is contrasted with the traditional one, the speakers represent fittingly the younger and the older generations, each defending his case. Yet the uncle is not the serene man of wisdom; he is quarrelsome, temperamental, restless, whereas the nephew although travelled and sensitive is of peasant stock and firmly rooted. This complexity cuts across the simple and schematic distribution of the theme of discourse amongst its participants. The old man feels threatened by what is new not because he is old and rooted in the past but because he is as unstable as that which confronts him; the young man, on the other hand, can go out towards the new, not because he swims with the stream, but because his roots are deep in the past. What better symbol for this manifold blending of the stable and the differentiated than the house of which we read: "auf diesem [dem kleinen runden Hügel] standen zwei Ahorn, uralt, riesig; wie zwei Wächter blickten sie das Haus an ... das Haus war sonderbar genug; es mochte aus den mittleren Zeiten des 18. Jahrhunderts stammen, Edelsitz, Stallung und Scheune vereinigte es unter einem riesigen, verwitterten Schindeldach. Der vordere Teil war von Stein; hier trugen schöne Säulen, vor dem Haustor eine Loggia bildend, den Balkon; die

---

[19] *Unterhaltung über die Schriften von Gottfried Keller,* P II 192.

mächtige, rückwärtige Hälfte des Hauses aber war hölzern, mit dem gewaltigen Scheunentor in der Flanke" [20].

Such reflections suggest that these essays are products of the creative imagination rather than the critical intelligence and indeed there is further evidence to support such a view; each essay differs in language and style. Not only is the Chandos letter written in the rhetorical style of the seventeenth century. An equal regard for the "Sprechton" can be found in the other essays, down to the uncle's language in the Wassermann discussion which is distinctly different from that of the younger generation [21].

Most important of all, what gives the essays their coherence and density is their poetic structure round a key word, a complexity of organisation that cannot be shown in detail here; this structure is the final proof of their poetic character.

Hofmannsthal's historical letters and dialogues impress the reader as a highly successful evocation of the atmosphere of a bygone period; this impression is supported by his own admission, "der starke Reiz für mich ist, vergangene Zeiten nicht ganz tot sein zu lassen". In fact, if one follows up the allusions in his text, as I have lately had the chance of doing with the help of the books in Hofmannsthal's own library, one is rather overwhelmed by the abundance of stray facts, connexions, allusions and borrowings that seem to have found their way into these pages and one wonders whether such checkered material serves any poetic purpose or whether it is merely an expression of a delight in historic oddity for its own sake. Here are just a few instances of such connexions. Why does Hofmannsthal attribute to his Lord Chandos a literary purpose which had, in fact, been executed by the recipient of this letter, Lord Bacon, i. e. the interpretation of the ancient fables and myths [22]? Why does he choose to borrow from

---

[20] *Unterhaltungen über ein neues Buch,* P II 240, 241.

[21] Hofmannsthal re-creates the atmosphere of the seventeenth century through choice of words, sentence structure of Latin periods and rhetorical devices. The uncle with his great number of foreign words: 'Delikatesse', 'supplieren', 'eskamotieren' anticipates the language of the aristocratic Viennese society of *Der Schwierige.*

[22] In the letter of January 1903, quoted at the beginning of this article, Hofmannsthal mentions as one of the reasons for the historical costume of the Chandos letter: "ich blätterte im August öfter in den Essays von Bacon, fand die Intimität dieser Epoche reizvoll ... bekam Lust, etwas in *diesem Sprechton* zu machen ..."

Bacon's *Apophthegms* the extraordinary anecdote of Crassus the orator who forms a passionate attachment to a lamprey in his fish pond and sheds bitter tears at its death? Such freakish borrowings can hardly be caused by the poet's wish for historical authenticity!

A little research into the background of the essay *Über Charaktere im Roman und im Drama*, originally entitled *Gespräch in einem Döblinger Garten*, reveals a wealth of unsuspected biographical detail. Why Döbling of all places as a setting for this conversation in which Balzac is the dominant figure? And why is his partner the orientalist Hammer-Purgstall? Now Balzac did in fact stay in Döbling, to be precise in the Hotel zur Birne situated near the villa of his beloved, Frau von Hanska [23]. Furthermore, Hammer-Purgstall was not only related to this lady, but had in fact a villa in Döbling and was on friendly terms with Balzac, who actually did meet him there and to whom he eventually dedicated his *Cabinet des Antiques*. Again, Balzac, of whom we think as a writer of novels, did try his hand at drama, though unsuccessfully, and was therefore well equipped to talk on the difference between the type of characters required by the two genres. And yet if Hofmannsthal wanted to be a chronicler he certainly had his lapses! It could not have escaped him that Balzac visited Vienna in 1835 and not in 1842 as he has us believe; nor that Lord Chandos, himself so respectably equipped with a fully historically credited line of ancestors, should refer to Queen Elizabeth as amongst the living, though she had been dead for six months at the date of writing!

It would take me far beyond the scope of this essay to show how such borrowings, allusions and falsifications serve a different, non-historical, poetic purpose. One example must suffice, the anecdote mentioned above, borrowed from Bacon and related by Lord Chandos, of the orator who became enamoured of a fish. Has this absurd eccentricity

In the Hofmannsthal library there is an edition of Bacon's work, London, G. Newnes Ltd., 1902. One may perhaps surmise that his interest was roused through the acquisition of this, then, new edition, and it is noteworthy that this one volume contains the 'Wisdom of the Ancients' and the 'Apophthegms' both of which play a part in Hofmannsthal's essay.

[23] Hofmannsthal's introduction of Frau von Hanska at the end of the *Gespräch in einem Döblinger Garten* seems less arbitrary when we realise that the first book on Balzac's relation to her had appeared in 1899 as well as the first volume of *Lettres à l'Etrangère*. The latter is in Hofmannsthal's library.

any connexion with the sufferings of the man who is the intellectual peer of the greatest intelligence of his day, whose rhetorical fireworks astonished the world when he was nineteen, whose passionately curious spirit ranged far and wide in the domain of the human spirit, fascinated by its every manifestation and who moved amongst the great figures of antiquity—Caesar and Sallust, Seneca and Cicero—as if he were their equal? It seems incongruous indeed that this man should be feverishly interested in another's attachment to a fish, and should relate it with great detail as the culmination of the letter. And yet, Crassus is a rhetorician too, like Chandos, before the crisis of which he writes to Bacon, in which language lost its meaning. Could it not be that the orator's attachment to a dumb creature was after all significant for the rhetorician who has despaired of language? For the fish is the dumbest of creatures, it has no language and cannot be reached by words. It was a "dumpfer, rotäugiger, stummer Fisch" with whom the Roman Senator had the deepest contact, and it is to the "stummen und manchmal unbelebten Kreaturen", to the rats, the beetles, the cricket, to the ugly young dogs, and to the strolling cat— that Lord Chandos turns from the human world, the reality of which has disintegrated, in order to be healed by contact with their un-questioned reality: their "stumme Wesenheit". And it is, as the last sentence of this letter tells us, no human tongue but "eine Sprache, in welcher die stummen Dinge zu mir sprechen", in which he can conceive of ever thinking or writing again in any imaginable future. It is thus that seemingly most wayward allusions or borrowings are assimilated by the poet's "integrierende Phantasie" [24].

In 1906, Hofmannsthal wrote to his friend Bodenhausen about one of these dialogues: "denn es steckt auch in den Sachen so viel Persön-liches, es ist meist das darin, was ich grade in dem Augenblick zu geben

[24] A similar process could be shown in the case of the anecdote of the white cranes in letter five of *Die Briefe des Zurückgekehrten* — one of the letters originally published under the title: 'Das Erlebnis des Sehens' in *Kunst und Künstler*, Feb-ruary 1908. This story is to be found in W. Müller: *The Life and Sayings of Ramakrishna* (p. 34, ed. 1901), the only biography that existed at the time. This book is in Hofmannsthal's library and is heavily marked; it also says in Hof-mannsthal's handwriting "zum zweiten Mal gelesen Grundlsee 1905" and a marginal comment reads "an die Spitze eines Aufsatzes über das Eindringen der Farbe in die Phantasie der Deutschen". I hope to discuss the genesis of the *Briefe des Zurückgekehrten* at a later date.

habe, und viele Menschen fassens auch so auf" [25]. And this is perfectly true: it could be shown down to the last detail that what fascinated and puzzled Hofmannsthal in books, newly published or re-read, in intellectual events, even in fads and fashions found its way straight into these conversations [26]. What may seem a casual choice of subject matter is indeed invariably a most personal one [27]. These essays reveal

[25] Letter of 5 December, 1906. *Briefe der Freundschaft*, p. 87.

[26] To give two examples only. The passage in the Keller essay (P II 199) on Maurice Denis, "die Schule von Beuron" and Pater Desiderius Lenz becomes very much more significant and alive when one realises that the speakers side here with the new religious symbolic art as represented by Maurice Denis in his own paintings and his theories on art, and that Maurice Denis, himself contributor to *Kunst und Künstler*, was very much in vogue with the circle of art connoisseurs and art historians among whom Hofmannsthal moved at that time: Eberhard von Boden-hausen, Harry Graf Kessler, Van de Velde, Meier-Gräfe. Hofmannsthal him-self had acquired a picture by Maurice Denis just at that time. See his correspon-dence with Bodenhausen, letters of 23 April, 1904 and 26 June, 1904. — In *Die Briefe des Zurückgekehrten* (P II 336), the writer mentions "und stören in den Kaisergrüften herum ... und zerren Karl den Großen aus seinem Sarg ... und restaurieren ihre ehrwürdigen Dome zu Bierhäusern ..." without doubt referring to the events of 13 July, 1906, to the dedication of the new crypts and the imperial tombs in Speyer, an event which is also reflected in George's poem in *Der Siebente Ring*: 'Die Gräber in Speyer'; whereas the wilful restoration of the old cathedrals is also commented upon by Borchardt in his essay on Worms. Hofmannsthal refers to it in his letter of 18 February, 1907, and Borchardt's formulation "zwischen diesem Dom und den Fratzen stilgerechter Bierhäuser im schlimmsten Berlin ... bald kein Unterschied mehr" — seems to be re-echoed in Hofmannsthal's essay. There is no question that for the contemporary reader the essays were far more 'topical' than they seem at first glance.

[27] Hofmannsthal had re-read George's *Jahr der Seele* (published 1898) in 1903 and was deeply impressed as we can gather from his letters of 5 June and 10 June: *Briefwechsel zwischen George und Hofmannsthal*. Berlin, [1938]. pp. 189, 191. Hofmannsthal read Keller's *Leute von Seldwyla* for the first time in Rome in the spring of 1906, or so he alleged. (He seems to have forgotton his earlier acquain-tance with the *Leute von Seldwyla: Briefe 1890—1901*. Berlin, 1935. p. 40.) "Es hat eine unglaubliche Weltklugheit und soviel Glanz und Licht und Farbe" we read in a letter of 26 April, 1906. *Briefe 1900—1909*, p. 227, and in the essay of 1906 we hear "und später dann in Rom las ich öfter darin ... ein Glanz ist auf all dem, ein Glanz der Jugend, ein Glanz des Lebens." The same, namely that personal impressions and value judgements determine choice and argument of these critical essays on literary subjects, can be proved also in the case of the Wassermann essay. Here we may note an amusing detail: Ferdinand in *Unterhal-tungen über ein neues Buch* states: "ein kleines, broschiertes Buch, das einem Band aus den vierziger Jahren glich", an unusual cover it seems. Eloesser in his review of Wassermann's *Die Schwestern* in *Die Zeit*, 18 October, 1906, mentions that the book appeared "im geschmackvollen Empireband wie vor ungefähr 100 Jah-

his interest in and his critical attitude to literary and general problems
of his time.
Hofmannsthal is fully aware of the crucial importance of *Das Gespräch über Gedichte*. "Ich hoffe nicht vieles zu übersehen, was sich
zu diesem Thema, mehr in Metaphern als in dürren Terminologien,
sagen läßt" [28], he wrote to Stefan George. Apart from very casual
tributes to the poetry of personal friends and one short note on C. F.
Meyer it is his final word on lyric poetry. The ideas of the French
symbolists on poetry made known through the *Blätter für die Kunst*
and aesthetic ideas found in Jean Paul or Novalis are delicately woven
into a poetic whole.
Yet there are a few remarks that seem to show a certain reserve on
the speaker's part towards these views. The symbol is indeed the centre
of all poetry; yet, does Clemens' explanation of the symbol in terms
of the magical relation between sacrificer and the beast he sacrifices
not sound a warning against the glib use of terms such as symbol, or
the use of symbols in a facile fashion? Implicitly the speaker seems to
reject poetry that aims exclusively at the rendering of sense impressions—after all a frequent poetic form in his days—when he emphasises
that poetry articulates not the ephemeral but the intrinsic nature of the
object: "die Poesie schlürft aus jedem Gebild der Welt und des
Traums . . . sein eigenstes, sein Wesenhaftestes heraus". This search for
the essential in a world of phenomena is echoed in *Die Briefe des Zurückgekehrten*, a view that looks forward to the world of expressionism after 1912. Lastly, the speaker admits that no single type of
poetry is the right one; great poetry need not be exclusively magic or
evocative, it can equally well be plastic or objective [29]. The view that
each age needs its own poetic form springs from an undogmatic and
unprejudiced approach which sees a literary movement or dogma in
its historical perspective instead of hailing it as the absolute truth.

ren" —. As for the topicality of the essays on Tasso and Van Gogh, see my introduction to *Hofmannsthal: Selected Essays*, pp. 147 and 154, footnote 8.
[28] Letter to Stefan George, 27 July, 1903. *Briefwechsel zwischen George und Hofmannsthal*, p. 193.
[29] It is interesting to note that when the essay appeared in Brandes' *Literatur*, Vol. I.,
the editor emphasised this aspect of the dialogue when he described the theme of the
essay as "die die Unterhaltung beherrschende Antithese zwischen dem antiken
und modernen Stil der Lyrik".

Between 1902 and 1908 Hofmannsthal, alternating between moods of confidence and dejection, struggled with a great number of tragic projects: *Das gerettete Venedig, Elektra, Oedipus, Pamphilia, Volpone, Tochter der Luft, Bacchae, Jedermann* etc. This preoccupation found its precipitate in the two essays *Über Charaktere im Roman und im Drama* and *Unterhaltung über den "Tasso" von Goethe*. Whilst in practice Hofmannsthal turned to Calderon, to classic antiquity and to Elizabethan drama, in theory he discusses the dramatic art of Shakespeare and Goethe. What both essays have in common is that they discuss "haute tragédie". It is remarkable that Hofmannsthal, who himself is in the vanguard of modern poetry and who in the other "Erfundene Gespräche" discusses modern psychological novels with considerable insight, takes so little notice of modern drama [30]. Indeed, in the essay on *Tasso* he explicitly rejects the drama of realism and he does the same implicitly in the Balzac essay when he dismisses the 'true to life' theory of characterisation. To the speakers in these essays the dramatic characters are "kontrapunktliche Notwendigkeiten" or, in a different formulation, "der dramatische Charakter ist eine Verengerung des wirklichen". Drama is taken in its widest sense, the speaker defines it as "die Katastrophe als symphonischer Aufbau", and again "Wir sehen etwas sich vollziehen, was nicht aufzuhalten ist. Das Ereignis selbst, durch das scheinbar alles ins Rollen kommt, ist belanglos ..."

On the other hand, the two essays reveal an important difference in the interpretation of drama. In both essays Goethe and Shakespeare are juxtaposed as the two poles of dramatic art, but while the first essay is an enthusiastic glorification of Shakespeare through the mouth of Balzac, the *Unterhaltung über den "Tasso"* attempts to justify Goethe's dramatic art. This shift of emphasis is more than accidental, it corresponds to Hofmannsthal's own development. The admiration that Balzac feels for Shakespeare's dramatic art is a reflection of Hofmannsthal's own attitude. Already in 1901, in a plan for a lecture to the *Wiener Goethe Verein* on "Der dramatische Stil in der Natürlichen Tochter", he had praised Shakespeare at the expense of

---

[30] Apart from his appreciation of Maeterlink, his analyses of some of Ibsen's dramas, his casual mention of Hauptmann's dramas, he refers several times and admiringly to Wedekind's dramas.

Goethe. His admiration is expressed once more in his "Shakespeare Rede" of 1905—his own dramatic experiments of these years he had called "shakespearisierende Gebilde". It is therefore indicative of a major change that in 1907 he should rise to a defence of Goethe and that by 1908 he should refuse outright to lecture on Shakespeare: "für mich ist nicht der Augenblick, über Shakespeare zu schreiben". In the *Unterhaltung über den "Tasso" von Goethe* he is at pains to prove that if Shakespeare's plays are dramatic, so is Goethe's "Schauspiel", if in another manner. "Ich weiß nicht was die Leute wollen, die das nicht dramatisch nennen", so Hofmannsthal has the Major say—is he not here ironically alluding to his own earlier attitude? That this attitude became confirmed and deepened in the course of the years is proved by the following statement as late as 1920, juxtaposing once more Shakespeare and Goethe: "Goethe hat man mit Unrecht undramatisch genannt, gerade weil er unablässig nach den heilenden Kräften sucht, selbst im Furchtbarsten ist das Verhängnis bei ihm so bedeutungsvoll, nie losgerissen immer als Funktion eines höheren Plans vorhanden; findet es im Menschlichen keine Lösung mehr, so liegt das Erlösende jenseits des Menschenlebens, immer im Bereich der die Welt über dem Abgrund des Nichts haltenden lebendigen Kräfte" [31].

In the essay on Tasso the speakers conclude that Goethe creates a form of drama in which the characters are "formgewordenes Tun", static, "jeder, ein grenzenloser Zustand" in which the action becomes symbolic, the plot is not temporal but eternal and the dramatic element is to be found in the "Entschleiern eines unabänderlichen Verhältnisses." It is lyric drama that the speakers try to describe and to establish in its own right. Having avoided it for some time in his attempts to break away from his own lyric past—this is the phase when he tried to come close to Shakespeare's tragedies—Hofmannsthal once more seems now free to accept this past. One can hardly help thinking of the figure of "Der Schwierige" when the speakers discuss Goethe's difficulties in making the character of the Prinzessin come alive; how can a dramatist —so they say—present characters that make their impact not through what they say but by what they are, since "im Drama die Figuren sich

---

[31] Carl J. Burckhardt: *Erinnerungen an Hofmannsthal*, Sammlung Klosterberg, p. 40.

nur durch Reden zeigen können, nicht durch stilles Dasein und lautloses Reflektieren der Welt in ihrem durchscheinenden Innern" [32]. Hofmannsthal was to give his final answer to this problem twenty-two years later, one year before his death, in his comment on his *Aegyptische Helena*. "Er [der Dichter] ist zu allem fähig, wenn er darauf verzichtet, daß seine Figuren durch direkte Mitteilung ihre Existenz beglaubigen sollen" [33].

When one compares the three "Gespräche" on epic art with the Loris essays on the same subject, it becomes clear that Hofmannsthal has moved away from his interest in modern novelists and their craft. In the "Gespräche" there is a tendency to contrast the contemporary with the traditional: Keller versus Dostojewsky; Goethe, Stifter, Balzac versus Wassermann; Goethe and Greek poetry versus George. Loris was out and out modern, not uncritical but contemporary in the choice of his reading material ; in the "Erfundene Gespräche", however, we find a thoughtful weighing of relative merit and a strong underlying sense of tradition.

Needless to say, the genre of the novel had not yet become questioned. On the contrary Hofmannsthal makes the highest aesthetic claims for this art form and on one occasion he calls it "die erzählende Poesie". The underlying assumption is that the writer is never seen as the imitator of nature; he must create the poetic world out of his vision. In these three essays Hofmannsthal is fundamentally concerned with the problem that is inherent in all epic art, the interplay between the individual and his surrounding world. Yet Hofmannsthal's predilections change. The very quality in Balzac's characters which the latter had called "pathologisch" (in Goethe's sense of the word) and which Hofmannsthal at first found so attractive—"Alle sind sie so wahnsinnig, meine Geschöpfe, so verrannt in ihre fixen Ideen, so unfähig, das in der Welt zu sehen, was sie nicht mit dem Flackern ihres Blickes in die Welt hineinwerfen" [34], — four years later seems to become doubtful to him. Of Wassermann we hear "da ruft er, um uns mit dem Gefühl des Lebens zu blenden ... das Pathologische herbei ... Das

---

[32] *Unterhaltung über den "Tasso" von Goethe*, P II 217.
[33] *Die ägyptische Helena*, P IV 458.
[34] *Gespräch über Charaktere im Roman und im Drama*, P II 52.

Pathologische ist ein Schatten, der innere unsichere Verkürzungen verdecken soll. Es wird dort hingesetzt, wo das Eigentliche, die schöpferische Kraft nicht hingekommen ist" [35]. Granted that there is difference between the order of the imagination of a Balzac and a Wassermann, and granted again, that there is a difference between the stature of Wassermann's and Balzac's characters and that the fanatics of the novels of the mid-century have become the neurotics of the *fin de siècle*, it still remains true that Hofmannsthal's essays move away from the maniacal type of character—characters akin to his Elektra— to the mixed characters of Keller's novels, in whose world one meets "die sonderbarsten Kombinationen von Anmaßung und Unsicherheit, von Hochmut und Bassesse . . . von Prahlerei, die in Hilflosigkeit umschlägt, oder von Eitelkeit, die zur Böswilligkeit abbiegt" [36]. It is a world that remains closer to the reality we know, except that the poet reveals with poetic insight what in real life remains hidden.

The same groping for a re-orientation is perceptible in the poet's recurrent reflections on what he calls the "Welthaftigkeit" of a novel. In the essay on Balzac the world of that poet is praised for its chaotic turbulence. As against this the later essays are at one in demanding that the novel should evoke in the reader the perception of a harmony which may not be discernible in empirical reality, which none the less is there in truth. This is just what Keller presents: "es ist eine Welt, in der eine gute und starke Harmonie herrscht"[37]. This ultimate feature of sanity is sadly lacking in the modern novels, not only in those of a Wassermann but more significantly in works of European stature as are those of Dostojewsky.

The same qualities that are demanded on the metaphysical level are urged on the formal level: order, harmony and symmetry are the most distinguished structural principles—a homogeneity of view that the poet explicitly formulates in the reiterated statement "darüber sind wir doch endlich hinaus in der Kunst oder im Leben ein Äußeres von einem Inneren scheiden zu wollen" [38]—the credo of the *Blätter für die*

---

[35] *Unterhaltungen über ein neues Buch*, P II 249.
[36] *Unterhaltung über die Schriften von Gottfried Keller*, P II 193.
[37] *Ibid.* p. 199.
[38] *Unterhaltungen über ein neues Buch*, P II 243, and *Unterhaltung über die Schriften von Gottfried Keller*, P II 196.

Kunst. And in the measure in which Hofmannsthal now demands a balanced poetic world he also becomes insistent upon corresponding maturity in the writer himself. About the connexion between these two, character and poetic quality, he has no doubt whatever.

In all the facets of his thoughts on poetics the same underlying trend can be observed, a trend towards a fuller engagement with reality, noticeable in the demand for "Welthaftigkeit", harmony, order and plasticity; indeed, an approximation to the classic Goethean world [39]. However, these imaginary conversations and letters do more than elucidate some basic problems of aesthetics or, to be precise, of poetics; in their essence they constitute an act of self-clarification. It is nothing less than the quintessence of Hofmannsthal's experience, as we know it from his early lyric period, now reviewed and revised. It is the old problem of personality, its identity and continuity that occupies him throughout these essays.

The receptivity of the young poet who surrendered to the impressions and experiences of the moment was such that at times he was threatened with a loss of any sense that he himself was a continuous entity in time, capable of enduring and assimilating these experiences. This is the poet of *Der weiße Fächer* who says:

> Wir selber nur der Raum,
> Drin tausende von Träumen buntes Spiel
> So treiben wie im Springbrunn Myriaden
> Von immer neuen, immer fremden Tropfen,
> All unsre Einheit nur ein bunter Schein,
> Ich selbst mit meinem eignen Selbst von früher,
> Von einer Stunde früher grad so nah,
> Vielmehr so fern verwandt, als mit dem Vogel,
> Der dort hinflattert.

[39] There is evidence that between 1904 and 1907 Hofmannsthal studied Goethe's and Schiller's views on aesthetics. "Ich möchte alles, was mir in die Hand fällt, dramatisieren, selbst den Goethe-Schillerschen Briefwechsel", he writes on 22 July, 1904, *Briefe 1900—1909*, p. 152. As the necessary preparation for an examination of basic formal problems which he had planned to discuss with R. A. Schröder in the form of dialogues, he suggests "die sämtlichen kunstphilosophischen Aufsätze und Briefe von Schiller, die Sprüche und nichts Sonstiges von Goethe", *Briefe 1900—1909*, p. 239. While he works on his lecture 'Der Dichter und diese Zeit', he read Schiller's *Briefe über die aesthetische Erziehung*. He recommends Goethe's *Farbenlehre* and his "kleinere Aufsätze" to Bodenhausen. (10 February, 1905).

This is the poet of *Gestern* who expresses by the very title of his playlet that that residue of personality beyond the immediate here and now of experience is felt as an obsolete remnant, an appendage that cannot be removed from consciousness but which does not truly belong there. In this almost *pointilliste* experience of personality, which could be testified by many more examples, Hofmannsthal was not alone. There was the philosophy of Mach, whose lectures incidentally he had attended [40],—Mach who saw the individual as a bundle of reactions and sense perceptions without any organising centre— furthermore the *fin de siècle* cult of experience for experience's sake with its attendant danger of the disintegration of the personality and the relativisation of all values.

These were unquestionably formative influences confirming his personal bias so that the writer of the Chandos letter, although relating a personal predicament, was truly a child of his time. But there is also little doubt that he did not swim with the stream without being aware from the earliest time onwards that a price had to be paid for the cult of experience in terms of the development of the personality as a whole. What is new is the awareness that this disintegration of personality, this threat to a stable consciousness, is a problem of European dimensions. Hofmannsthal sees his personal crisis in this larger context. "So verwischt sind die meisten Gesichter, so ohne Freiheit, so vielerlei steht darauf geschrieben, und alles ohne Bestimmtheit" [41]. This is the observation of "der Zurückgekehrte".

Corresponding to this new insight is the dawning awareness of a remedy and his turn to other races and civilisations in search of an answer. In these essays Hofmannsthal contrasts Europeans with representatives of primitive or Asian races who have not yet lost their wholeness through excessive consciousness. "Muß ich zurück nach Uruguay oder hinunter nach den Inseln der Südsee, um wieder von menschlichen Lippen diesen menschlichen Laut zu hören, der in ein schlichtes Abschiedswort ... manchmal das Ganze der menschlichen Natur zu legen vermag" [42], says "der Zurückgekehrte". Or, there is

---

[40] He attended Mach's lectures during the 'Sommersemester' 1896/97.
[41] *Die Briefe des Zurückgekehrten*, P II 331.
[42] *Ibid.*, p. 334.

his Greek dancer, Laidion, longing for the barbaric islanders in an original state of grace before consciousness sets in, divides the personality,—and with self-consciousness brings shame.

In his inclination towards primitive civilisations Hofmannsthal is not alone. Picasso's so-called Negro period is dated 1906, Gauguin's diary *Noa-Noa* appeared in 1908. With seismographic precision Hofmannsthal registers here, as always, the intellectual climate; he is the wave that yields and reflects. Surely it is this boundless susceptibility to the pressures of his civilisation, threatening his very being and threatening him doubly as an artist, that drove him to see as the one solution that could save the man and the poet, a new singleness of being; or to put it in Addison's formulation, which Hofmannsthal loved and which is the central statement of the first two letters in *Die Briefe des Zurückgekehrten:* "The whole man must move at once."

The second problem under review in these essays is the relationship between reality and the individual. In the state of "Praeexistenz", as expressed in his early magic poetry, there was no barrier between the finite and the infinite, the ego and the universe. As Claudius in *Der Tor und der Tod* puts it,

> Wenn Überschwellen der Gefühle
> Mit warmer Glut die Seele zitternd füllte
> Wenn sich im plötzlichen Durchzucken
> Das Ungeheure als verwandt enthüllte
> Und du hingebend dich im großen Reigen
> Die Welt empfingest als dein eigen.

It is this stage that Lord Chandos describes retrospectively and nostalgically: "Mir erschien damals in einer Art von andauernder Trunkenheit das ganze Dasein als eine große Einheit ... in allem fühlte ich Natur ... in aller Natur fühlte ich mich selber ... überall war ich mitten drinnen, wurde nie ein Scheinhaftes gewahr" [43]. But at the time of writing he has lost this feeling of oneness with life around him. The 'Ich' has become isolated. Not only, as we have seen, has the identity of the 'Ich' become problematic—Chandos is led to question the meaning of the words 'Leib', 'Seele', 'Körper'—but the intellectual and moral premises of his thinking have become meaningless.

[43] *Ein Brief,* P II 10, 11.

In *Die Briefe des Zurückgekehrten* the process of dissociation has gone a step further. The familiar world of objects has become ghost-like and unreal: "Zuweilen kam es des Morgens . . . daß mir der Krug und das Waschbecken . . . oder eine Ecke des Zimmers . . . so nicht-wirklich vorkamen . . . so ganz und gar nicht wirklich, gewissermaßen gespenstisch" [44]. And with the world of objects staring at him meaninglessly the writer doubts existence, life as such, and he is gripped by panic of nothingness, by "ein Anwehen des ewigen Nichts". But despair is not the last word in these essays. At rare moments both Lord Chandos and "der Zurückgekehrte" find release from what is described by the latter as "der Starrkrampf fürchterlichster Zweifel" and by the former as "Starre seines Innern"; one finds it through contact with ordinary things, the other through contact with works of art. Lord Chandos finds release from his terror of isolation through a new contact with dumb things: not through language nor yet through the mind, but through a kind of immediate bodily awareness. "Es ist mir dann, als bestände mein Körper aus lauter Chiffern, die mir alles aufschließen." In such moments he feels his way towards a new mode of experiencing and has an intimation that such an experience might open up to him "ein neues ahnungsvolles Verhältnis zum ganzen Da-sein".

"Der Zurückgekehrte" finds a comparable release through the world of objects mediated through the vision of paintings. Van Gogh's colours in their blazing intensity and their composition restore to the object that unquestioned reality they had lost and their relatedness to each other. A new world, a "Welt der Bezüge" is created; a coloured cosmos out of the chaotic jumble of isolated, meaningless things. "[Die Farben sind eine Sprache,] in der das Wortlose, das Ewige, das Ungeheure sich hergibt" [45]. Clearly discernible in the language of colour, he can see "Das wütende, von Unglaublichkeit umstarrte Wunder ihres Daseins", and can say that ". . . jedes Wesen — *ein Wesen* jeder Baum jeder Streif gelben oder grünlichen Feldes, jeder Zaun, jeder in den Stein-hügel gerissene Hohlweg, ein Wesen der zinnerne Krug, die irdene Schüs-sel, der Tisch, der plumpe Sessel — sich mir wie neugeboren aus dem

[44] *Die Briefe des Zurückgekehrten*, P II 344.
[45] *Ibid.*, p. 355.

furchtbaren Chaos des Nichtlebens, aus dem Abgrund der Wesenlosigkeit entgegenhob, daß ich fühlte, nein, daß ich wußte, wie jedes dieser Dinge, dieser Geschöpfe aus einem fürchterlichen Zweifel an der Welt herausgeboren war und nun mit seinem Dasein einen gräßlichen Schlund, gähnendes Nichts, für immer verdeckte"! [46]

Young Loris, receptive in the extreme and as yet protean, had felt time to be an incessant flight of moments. He knew of no means to counter such uneasy awareness of transience than to surrender to each moment, experiencing it to the full. During the period we are discussing this solution is once more scrutinised—in the *Gespräch der Tänzerinnen,* originally called *Furcht* [47]. Constant fear haunts Laidion the dancer, the causes of which she cannot specify and of which nowadays we would probably use the term "Angst" [48]. Laidion realises that hope is the reverse of this fear and closely related to it. As she says: "Ich glaube manchmal, es ist noch gräßlicher zu hoffen als zu fürchten. Ganz ausgehöhlt liegt man da, nach einer Nacht der Hoffnung. Nichts saugt einem so tief die Seele aus dem Leib" [49]. However different fear and hope may seem, they have this in common that in both states consciousness gravitates towards the future, preventing a person from living in the present, in happy freedom from wishes and expectations, remorse and regret, pulling him now backwards now forward. And yet, even the Greek dancer—most fitted by her civilisation and her talent alike to fuse bodily and spiritual experience in a pure awareness of the present—fails to do so. Only the barbaric dancers of her vision who have not yet emerged into an individual existence and consciousness can truly lose themselves in the ecstatic moment. It is the description of their dances by one who has witnessed them that brings

[46] *Ibid.,* p. 350.

[47] The version 'Furcht, ein Dialog' as printed in *Neue Rundschau,* October 1907, was more poignant in its descriptions of the exotic islands as well as of the dancer's harassed state of mind.

[48] We may, I think, do so as the terms "Furcht" and "Angst" were in those days not yet as subtly defined and distinguished as in the post-Kierkegaard days. Hofmannsthal had read Kierkegaard soon after the German translations had appeared as we can conclude from the editions in his library that show traces of having been carefully studied by him, especially also the chapter on 'Der Begriff der Angst' in *Zur Psychologie der Sünde* (ed. 1890).

[49] *Furcht, ein Dialog,* P II 365.

home to Laidion the unbridgeable gulf that separates her from such timeless bliss. And it is clear that Hofmannsthal's verdict is that what this most favoured representative of western civilisation fails to achieve is out of reach for the rest of us [50].

This negative answer is not the poet's last word. Even during this period we can discern the contours of the two solutions between which he was to alternate for the remainder of his life. The one, the conquest of time and transience *sub specie aeternitatis,* an essentially religious and dualistic solution which the poet often approached and never abandoned, is formulated in *Jedermann,* on which he had begun working in these years, *Das Salzburger Große Welttheater* and *Der Turm.* The other—and this seems to be the indispensable solution for a creative artist so delicately organised—is the conquest of the fugitive moment and of the fear it breeds in the timelessness of the aesthetic act. In the aesthetic experience, his innermost domain, the poet finds all that he had vaguely sought in the primitive rites of far-away dancers. It is an experience of religious quality, annihilating past and future, annihilating time itself, restoring wholeness and inducing a state of serenity freed from the "Stachel der Hoffnung", as the Greek dancer was not. "Für einen bezaubertenAugenblick ist ihm alles gleich nah, alles gleich fern: denn er fühlt zu allem einen Bezug. Er hat nichts an die Vergangenheit verloren, nichts hat ihm die Zukunft zu bringen. Er ist für einen bezauberten Augenblick der Überwinder der Zeit ... er ist glücklich ohne den Stachel der Hoffnung. Er vergißt sich nicht, er hat sich ganz." So we read in *Der Dichter und diese Zeit* [51].

It is customary in Hofmannsthal scholarship to read the Chandos letter as a personal confession and to find in it the motives which prompted the young poet to abstain from all lyric poetry after the turn of the century.

I would suggest that the Contarini letter is yet another piece of self-revelation, showing another facet of the crisis in which Hofmannsthal found himself. This can only be done tentatively as the letter is frag-

---

[50] Of late this essay of Hofmannsthal's has aroused great interest; it has been interpreted by Bollnow in *Neue Geborgenheit,* p. 88 ff., and alluded to by Höllerer in *Zwischen Klassik und Moderne,* p. 455.

[51] *Der Dichter und diese Zeit,* P II 296.

4

mentary and the different versions are not dated [52]. The situation described is that of a man who is the last descendant of a great family and heir to a great tradition. He realises that in accepting his privileges unquestioningly he has, in fact, been living on false pretences and he is seized by a feeling of inner bankruptcy. This "Scheinexistenz" where inner and outer situation no longer tally, where he doubts his inner claims to outer fame, where the feeling of self-esteem and self-respect is undermined, causes him to live under continuous strain and pressure. After his confidence has been shaken, Contarini waits for the final blow to his existence. We are not fully informed about the intervening events, but are left to assume that he attempts to live honestly and inconspicuously notwithstanding his famous name. Yet it seems problematic to him whether these two, "der große illustre Name" and the "Bettelhaftigkeit" of his real state, are compatible. Are a great name and past glory still a living reality once the present situation no longer bears them out? To make matters worse, the world will not forgo its illusion and tries artificially to restore a situation no longer real. Contarini writes: "Jetzt bin ich ein zitterndes, großartiges Symbol von Dingen, die größer sind als ich selbst." His reaction to the well-meaning intentions of his friends who cling to the past and do not accept his personal solution is a panic-stricken withdrawal, and a

---

[52] The Contarini theme is mentioned in 1903 in the letter to Andrian as part of the original plan for the "Erfundene Gespräche und Briefe". The various fragments were published in 1929 in *Berührung der Sphären*. The Contarini letter has, in this edition, been added to the selection of essays which Hofmannsthal himself had, shortly before his death, suggested to Fischer. The editor remarks: "Aus dem Nachlaß Brief des letzten Contarin (vor 1914)". There is some inner evidence that the "Notizen und Varianten" may have been written at the same time as the essay on Balzac. In both we find the same strange image: in 'Contarini', "Ihr [his ancestors] Blut enthielt die *Metallreflexe* aller dieser Dinge, wie dieses Wasser jene silbernen, ehernen, porphyrenen Schimmer enthält", and in *Balzac*, "weil das Innere der Menschen ein sich selbst verzehrender Brand ist ... ein Glasofen, in welchem die zähflüssige Masse des Lebens ihre Formen erhält ... entzükkend blumenhafte wie die Stengelgläser der Insel Murano, oder heldenhafte, von *metallischen Reflexen* funkelnde, wie die Töpfereien von Derutta und Rhodus." — A changing of hand of the famous Palazzo Ca d'Oro did actually take place. In 1896 Baron Franchetti had bought the Palazzo and we know that Hofmannsthal's friend Hans Schlesinger, the painter, helped Franchetti with the new arrangements for the Palazzo (1899). This may account for Hofmannsthal's special interest in the palace and its story. He himself got to know Franchetti in 1901, and met him again in Venice in 1902.

threat to sever all contacts. Lord Chandos describes from the inside the situation of the poet who gave up writing poetry. Contarini, heir and descendant of a resplendent tradition, defends his withdrawal from his own world and demands that his decision should be respected. Is this not a description of the obstacles which the poet who has suffered bankruptcy encounters from the outside world? For we must remember that young Hofmannsthal liked to see his poetic self under the symbol of the heir, and it would seem that in the disguise of this symbol he is pleading with his friends to allow him to renounce a tradition and a heritage in which he can no longer be himself. A letter from Borchardt gives us a retrospective glimpse of the tensions between him and his well-meaning friends which must have complicated a situation already complicated enough. Not until February 1907 can Borchardt bring himself to admit: "daß es utopisch war, Ihre Entwicklung auf das abstrakte und rein negative Ideal der flawlessness einzuschränken" [53].

Together then these two imaginary letters, both written by noblemen, both written in self-defence, characterise his own precarious situation as a poet at that time.

In looking back upon the essays of his period we can say that they are veiled manifestations of a creative energy which could not, for a while, find an outlet in the directness of an overt lyric form; the reason for this lies in a deep-seated need for greater reality, and this need provides, in the essays, the steady undercurrent of preoccupation.

The tendency towards greater reality is perceptible in his reflections on the lyrical symbol, on the novel and on the dramatist's art. Greater reality is again the watchword of his personal reflections. The thirst for reality is the necessary antidote to the irreality which is inseparable from the state of "Praeexistenz". During that stage, in the exultancy of adolescence, the rich young heir lived on his cultural inheritance; on intellectual and emotional experiences that were part of the climate of the time; on verbal resources that had been pooled and exploited by others before him. Soon the time was to come when he no longer knew what was his nor who he was. The quest for reality

---

[53] *Hugo von Hofmannsthal Rudolf Borchardt Briefwechsel,* Frankfurt a/M., 1954. p. 31.

4*

began. It was a most patient and persistent quest for his own mode of experiencing, and often on levels that could not be verbalised. Only in so far as he was absolutely true to his being and its complex needs could he be sure of avoiding the annihilating threat of inner dissociation and unreality. Only then could he begin to feel wholly integrated again, and able to experience. It is this insight into the precariousness of his inner situation and the process of reintegration that is the thematic link of all "Die Erfundenen Gespräche und Briefe", different as they may be in subject matter and focus of attention.

HUGO VON HOFMANNSTHAL:
DAS BERGWERK ZU FALUN

BY MARGARET JACOBS

By 1899 Hofmannsthal had written dramas which ranged from the meditation on life or art spoken by a number of voices, to the more dramatic piece in which he was concerned to show critical stages of transition in inner experience. He had recently written *Die Frau im Fenster, Der Abenteurer und die Sängerin,* and *Die Hochzeit der Sobeide*—three plays which dealt rather more directly with human relationships as well as with the problematic inner world of the soul, and explored emotion and passion, instead of concentrating on the gains and losses of those in whom they are stultified, like the aesthete, or of those who by-pass them, like the mystic. At certain points in *Die Frau im Fenster* and in *Die Hochzeit der Sobeide* Hofmannsthal even went so far as to present passion in brutal and sensational terms, moving away when he did so from his rarefied lyrical dramas with their atmosphere of feeling once removed. At this stage there were signs of a new realism, and yet this was still clearly the early period of Hofmannsthal's development as a dramatist. After 1900 he was to launch out more boldly and undertake the more dramatic drama, which led him towards the love and intrigue and moral conflict of *Das gerettete Venedig,* and the violence and hysteria of *Elektra* and of *Ödipus und die Sphinx,* in which he pitched emotions at their extremes. After 1900 then, Hofmannsthal's interest in a moral theme still ran side by side with the attraction for him of writers like Breuer and Freud, Nietzsche, Bachofen and Rohde; and in 1904 he was conjuring up on the one hand the moral clarity and moral courage of his Belvidera in *Das gerettete Venedig,* and was evoking on the other hand in his plan for the tragedy *Pentheus,* the fearful non-human cry of the

---

Unless otherwise stated, the E. T. A. Hoffmann passages quoted below are taken from the *Werke,* herausgegeben von Dr. Viktor Schweizer, Leipzig und Wien, 1896 (Bibliographisches Institut), vol. 2, pp. 313—345, *Die Bergwerke zu Falun.*

Bacchae, "das Symbol des Ungeheuern, nicht mehr Bedingten, das der menschlichen Natur als tiefster Kern innewohnt, des Übernatürlichen" [1].

In 1899 itself, when Hofmannsthal was twenty-five years old, he wrote his *Bergwerk zu Falun*, a drama in which there is an unfolding of his tendency towards realism, and at the same time an indication of his interest in strange psychological states, together with a new, more radical view of something which is already familiar to us from his earlier work—the place of inner experience of the mind, soul and imagination in relation to life. In another form he is to raise again the question:

> Tief begreifen und besitzen!
> Hat dies wo im Leben Raum? . . .[2]

When Hofmannsthal outlined his development as a dramatist for Max Pirker in 1921 [3], he saw *Das Bergwerk zu Falun* as part of the first, predominantly lyrical and subjective period which ended in 1899, and as a forerunner of the "Reihe der phantastisch-märchenhaften Dramen" such as *Die Frau ohne Schatten*, to which he gives the date 1912-1914 [4]. *Das Bergwerk zu Falun* was Hofmannsthal's first five-act drama; "ein fünfaktiges märchenhaftes Trauerspiel in Versen" he calls it in a letter of July 1899 to Arthur Schnitzler, adding in the same letter that he has two acts of it nearly ready and that he is enjoying working at this more than anything [5]. By October he has got into deep waters with it and confesses that he has written two useless versions of the third act and has to go back to the second to eradicate what he calls a basic fault in it, without, however, indicating what the fault is. "Wollte ganz aufhören, mich absolut von dem Stoff losmachen. Das war ich aber auch nicht imstande", he writes [6]. In November he is nowhere near finished, has had to re-write the third, fourth and fifth acts completely, and is picking his way amongst the

---

[1] Quoted from the notes for *Pentheus. Ein Trauerspiel in zwei Aufzügen*, D II 525.
[2] *Besitz*, G 516.
[3] A 369 f.
[4] In *Ad me ipsum* Hofmannsthal sees the drama as a work of a transitional stage, v. A 221.
[5] Letter of 20 July, 1899.
[6] Letter of 2 October, 1899 to Arthur Schnitzler.

ruins; the whole thing is resisting him: "Es hat manchmal etwas Teuflisches in seiner trügerischen Lust am Widerstreben, so ein Ding" [7].
Hofmannsthal must have made a distinction in his own mind between the first act and the rest of the drama almost as soon as he had written it, for he allowed Act I to be published for the first time in the following year (1900) [8], whereas other parts of the work were surrendered for publication sporadically between 1900 and 1919, and they arrived on the scene in a totally unexpected order. After Act I, the next act to be published was Act V, in 1908 [9]; then came Act IV in 1911 [10], and Act II together with Act V again in 1918 [11]; the third act, of which Hofmannsthal may have written at least three versions [12], was published for the first time in October 1932 [13], three years after his death. All the five acts came together in the Wiener Bibliophilen-Gesellschaft edition of 1933.

Karl Reuschel in the course of his article 'Über Bearbeitungen der Geschichte des Bergmanns von Falun', published in 1903 [14], refers to Hofmannsthal's version (Act I only), and quotes a communication from the poet, indicating that he felt Act I to have a unity of its own, referring to the source that he used, and to "inner reasons" for not allowing more of the drama to be published:

> Nach freundlicher Mitteilung des Verfassers bildet das im Druck Erschienene nur die ersten drei Szenen (nicht, wie es durch ein

[7] Letter of 10 November, 1899 to Edgar Freiherr Karg von Bebenburg.
[8] *Das Bergwerk zu Falun* in Die Insel, Zweiter Jahrgang, Erstes Quartal, Oktober bis Dezember 1900. The three scenes of Act I are here mistakenly called 'acts'; a complete list of *dramatis personae* for all the five acts is given at the beginning below the title.
[9] *Das Bergwerk zu Falun. Der letzte Akt in* Hyperion I (München 1908).
[10] In the *Almanach der Wiener Werkstätte,* Wien, 1911.
[11] In *Rodauner Nachträge* I, Wien, 1918.
[12] See the letter of 2 October, 1899 to Arthur Schnitzler: "Ich hab' in Vahrn nochmals einen ganz unbrauchbaren 3. Akt gemacht, recht verschieden von dem, den Sie in Ischl gesehen haben, und doch falsch"; also the letter of 10 November, 1899 to Edgar Freiherr von Bebenburg: "Meine große Arbeit, die mich seit dem Sommer beschäftigt, ist nichts weniger als beendet. Ich habe hier sogleich drangehen müssen, den III., IV. und V. Akt völlig umzuarbeiten . . ."
[13] Together with the second, fourth and fifth acts in *Corona* III, (1932/33).
[14] In *Studien zur vergleichenden Literaturgeschichte,* herausgegeben von Dr. Max Koch, vol. III, Berlin, 1903.

Versehen des Setzers oder Korrektors scheint, drei Aufzüge). Diese Auftritte umfassen den ersten Akt eines fünfaktigen Dramas, 'das in sich geschlossene Vorspiel [15], während die folgenden vier Akte zu Falun selbst spielen und das eigentliche Erlebnis des Elis mit der Tochter des Person Dahlsjöh enthalten, bis zu seinem Tod durch Verschüttung am Hochzeitsmorgen'. Weiter berichtet Herr Hugo von Hofmannsthal, was sich aus dem Gedruckten bereits deutlich ergibt: 'Meine einzige Quelle für den Stoff war E. T. A. Hoffmann'. Die Arbeit ist vollendet aber 'aus inneren Gründen' liegen geblieben. Dem Wunsche des Dichters entsprechend, habe ich ihm mein Material über die Bearbeitungen der Geschichte des Faluner Bergmanns überlassen [16], und es steht zu hoffen, daß Hugo von Hofmannsthal, wie er vermutet, ein lebendigeres Verhältnis zu dem Stoffe wieder gewinnt und das ganze Drama der Öffentlichkeit übermittelt [17].

Hoffman's tale, *Die Bergwerke zu Falun,* was the source for Hofmannsthal's drama. It was published in 1819 [18], and was one of the very many versions in the nineteenth century of the fascinating story told by Gotthilf Heinrich Schubert in his *Ansichten von der Nachtseite der Naturwissenschaft* [19]. Schubert tells of the body of a young miner

---

[15] The first act of the drama was published under the title 'Ein Vorspiel' in all the editions of the *Kleine Dramen* and in the 1911 edition of the *Gedichte und Kleine Dramen.*

[16] It is not known whether Hofmannsthal altered any of the four unpublished acts after receiving the material to which Reuschel refers. There seems to be no reason for presuming that he did so.

[17] Reuschel, *op. cit.,* p. 19.

[18] In vol. I of the *Serapionsbrüder.*

[19] D. G. H. Schubert: *Ansichten von der Nachtseite der Naturwissenschaft.* Dresden, 1808, pp. 215 ff. In the eighth lecture Schubert is examining the stage when organic life developed on the earth, and the evidence for the beginnings of human life. He points out that the absence of human remains is not evidence for the absence of human life on the earth at a particular period, since, apart from other considerations, human bodies are more susceptible to decay than those of animals; human bodies which had lain in "Salz- und Gipsauflösungen" possibly for several centuries, dissolved after a few days' exposure to the air, whereas animal remains did not. He continues by relating the story of the miner of Falun: "Auf gleiche Weise zerfiel auch jener merkwürdige Leichnam, von welchem Hülpher, Cronstedt und die schwedischen gelehrten Tagebücher erzählen, in eine Art von Asche, nachdem man ihn, dem Anscheine nach in festen Stein verwandelt, unter einem Glasschrank vergeblich vor dem Zutritt der Luft gesichert hatte. Man fand diesen ehemaligen Bergmann, in der schwedischen Eisengrube zu Falun, als zwischen

which was recovered from the Falun mine in Sweden, perfectly preserved in vitriolated water. When it was brought to the surface, an old woman recognised it to be that of her fiancé, who had died in the mine fifty years before. Obviously moved by the incident, Schubert contrasts the cold stiff body of the youth with the grey old woman, still full of warm love for him.

zween Schachten ein Durchschlag versucht wurde. Der Leichnam, ganz mit Eisen-vitriol durchdrungen, war anfangs weich, wurde aber, so bald man ihn an die Luft gebracht, so hart als Stein. Fünfzig Jahre hatte derselbe in einer Tiefe von 300 Ellen, in jenem Vitriolwasser gelegen, und niemand hätte die noch unver-änderten Gesichtszüge des verunglückten Jünglings erkannt, niemand die Zeit, seit welcher er in dem Schachte gelegen, gewußt, da die Bergchronicken, so wie die Volkssagen bey der Menge der Unglücksfälle in Ungewißheit waren, hätte nicht das Andenken der ehemals geliebten Züge eine alte treue Liebe bewahrt. Denn als um den kaum hervorgezogenen Leichnam, das Volk, die unbekannten jugendlichen Gesichtszüge betrachtend steht, da kömmt an Krücken und mit grauem Haar ein altes Mütterchen, mit Thränen über den geliebten Toden, der ihr ver-lobter Bräutigam gewesen, hinsinkend, die Stunde segnend, da ihr noch an den Pforten des Grabes ein solches Wiedersehen gegönnt war, und das Volk sahe mit Verwunderung die Wiedervereinigung dieses seltnen Paares, davon das Eine, im Tode und in tiefer Gruft das jugendliche Aussehen, das Andre, bey dem Ver-welken und Veralten des Leibes die jugendliche Liebe, treu und unverändert erhalten hatte, und wie bey der 50jährigen Silberhochzeit der noch jugendliche Bräutigam starr und kalt, die alte und graue Braut voll warmer Liebe gefunden wurden." Hülpher is A. A. Hülphers, who wrote a diary of a journey he under-took through the districts of Great Koppar-Berg and Dalarne, whose capital is Falun (*Dagbok öfwer en Resa igenom de under Stora Koppar-Bergs Höfdingdöme lydande Lähn och Dalarne år 1757*, Wästerås, 1762.) On p. 420 Hülphers relates the story of the miner, Mats Israëlsson, who had been in the service of Jon Pers-son, and who had gone down alone in the lift-cage and lost his life in the Mards-kins mine in 1670. Hülphers must have used Bergassessor Adam Leyel's factual, scientific account in the scientific quarterly, *Acta literaria Sveciae Upsaliae publi-cata*, I (1722), 250 ff., which Schubert is presumably referring to with his phrase, "die schwedischen gelehrten Tagebücher"; but Hülphers ignores the report that others besides the old woman (the former fiancée) recognised the body, and Schu-bert shows no signs of knowing this. Cronstedt, whom Schubert mentions, referred briefly to the incident at Falun in his *Mineralogie*, according to G. Friedmann: *Die Bearbeitungen der Geschichte von dem Bergmann von Fahlun*. Berlin, 1887, p. 17. Friedmann gives details of five sources of the story which precede Schubert's account. Besides Leyel (1722) and Hülphers (1762), Friedmann refers to the earliest version of the incident, which is to be found in a quasi-scientific periodical published in Copenhagen, *Nye Tidender om lärde Sager*, No. 29, 20 July, 1720, also to the version of September 1720 in the *Extrait des Nouvelles* (a Danish perio-dical of the same character as *Nye Tidender*), and to an account in a Stockholm newspaper of 28 December, 1749. According to Friedmann, the author of the article in the *Extrait des Nouvelles*, desiring to entertain his readers, began to 'write up' the story ("der Verfasser ... hat offenbar seine Phantasie mitwirken

Hoffmann, using this account, builds up the previous history of the miner, who in his version is first a sailor, Elis [20], born in Nerike, where people are of a melancholy disposition. Elis has lost both his parents and is left helpless and wretched, "einsam wie auf ein ödes Riff verschlagen" [21]. He follows the advice of the old ghost-miner, Torbern, and goes to Falun, after dreaming of the magical realm below the ground where the majestic Bergkönigin appears to him. In Falun he becomes a miner and falls in love with Ulla, the daughter of his rich employer, but he feels that his real self belongs with the powerful queen in the mine. He suffers from delusions, thinking that he is discovering rich seams and bringing up worthless stones. On his wedding morning, in his madness, he disappears to fetch from the mine the blood-red jewel, almandine, for Ulla's wedding-gift, and is never seen alive again.

lassen", *loc. cit.*, p. 10), and it is interesting to note that this happened so early—in the year after the body was discovered, and two months after the first brief report in *Nye Tidender*. The authors of the accounts in *Nye Tidender* and the *Extrait des Nouvelles* both refer to a dispute which arose when there were various claimants for possession of the body, which was ultimately granted to the old woman who had been engaged to the miner. *Nye Tidender* reports her statement that if the medical faculty wanted the body, they would have to buy it from her. The *Extrait des Nouvelles* reports that she actually sold the body to the medical faculty for 500 crowns. Hülphers on the other hand says that the old woman demanded to be allowed to bury the body. Schubert bases his account mainly on Hülphers, and so the touch of cold realism does not appear in his account. The history of the various versions of the story makes a fascinating study for anyone who is interested in the process by which actual events find their way into literature. The Schubert account was printed in the April number of the periodical *Jason* for 1809, together with a request for poetic treatment of the subject. The first response to this came in the following year, with an undistinguished poem by Theodor Nübling (Friedmann, *op. cit.*, pp. 19 ff.) and the Schubert passage continued to be a source for poetry, narrative prose, opera and drama throughout the nineteenth century. For an account of the large number of nineteenth century literary productions which are based on the story, see Friedmann and Reuschel.

[20] Elis is a common Swedish Christian name. Curt von Faber du Faur in his article, 'Der Abstieg in den Berg. Zu Hofmannsthals *Bergwerk zu Falun*', *Monatshefte*, January 1951, suggests that Hoffmann may have arrived at the name 'Elis' by transposing the letters in the name of the real miner, Israëlsson; he also suggests that the Christian name of the real miner, 'Mats' (an abbreviation of 'Mathias') gave Hoffmann the idea of turning the miner into a sailor (Mat), and of building up a previous seafaring history for him. For the sources of the other names which Hoffmann's story and Hofmannsthal's drama have in common, see Faber du Faur's article. For 'Agmahd', see p. 75 of the present article.

[21] E. T. A. Hoffmann, p. 317.

The walls of the mine have collapsed and buried him. In a brief closing section, Hoffmann tells of the recovery of the body intact fifty years later, and of Ulla's recognition of her lost fiancé. She breathes out her life over his body.

The story is told by Theodor in Hoffmann's collection, *Die Serapionsbrüder*, and is given a kind of epilogue by Cyprian in the following words:

> Wie oft stellten Dichter Menschen, welche auf irgend eine entsetzliche Weise untergehen, als im ganzen Leben mit sich entzweit, als von unbekannten finstren Mächten befangen dar. Dies hat Theodor auch gethan, und mich wenigstens spricht dies immer deshalb an, weil ich meine, daß es tief in der Natur begründet ist. Ich habe Menschen gekannt, die sich plötzlich im ganzen Wesen sich veränderten, die entweder in sich hinein erstarrten oder wie von bösen Mächten rastlos verfolgt in steter Unruhe umhergetrieben wurden und bald dieses, bald jenes entsetzliche Ereigniß aus dem Leben fortriß [22].

Hoffmann has merely set side by side the two worlds to which Elis is drawn and has not related them to each other. Elis's other self, which belongs to the Bergkönigin, seems to have been imposed upon him, and Hoffmann has not conveyed to us that Elis is "im ganzen Leben mit sich entzweit", but rather that he is a young man who, after the death of his mother, is suffering from a normal and understandable sorrow and depression, touched with self-pity, and whose child-like, pious nature keeps reasserting itself. There is also a straining after effect in the tale, and this is particularly noticeable in the use of excessive adjectives and in the repetition of certain formulae for emotion. Other faults are a tendency to weak sentimentality, the somewhat confusing characterisation of Torbern, and the incongruous idyllic ending of the story. In spite of certain compelling passages, such as the description of Elis's first view of the mine and the miners at Falun, which inspire him with horror, and the meeting with Torbern down in the mine, it must be admitted that this is one of the weaker tales of Hoffmann. But the story might well have attracted Hofmannsthal because of the juxtaposition of two worlds.

[22] E. T. A. Hoffmann's *Gesammelte Schriften*, Berlin, 1871. Vol. I, p. 200.

We know from Hofmannsthal's earlier work that he was acutely aware of a moral world as well as of a mystical, poetical, spiritual one. It is the romantic apprehension of divided worlds which draws him, and his shaping of the story shows a modern, complex, sensitive imagination appropriating romantic symbolism. Hofmannsthal's deep awareness of a subtle antagonism between an ambivalent spiritual realm and the claims of human responsibility and love emerges through the source and effects a remarkable transformation, but a certain embarrassment for the reader arises from the fact that Hofmannsthal is using apparently old-fashioned romantic symbols, so that one is at first tempted to think that he has just stepped back into the early nineteenth century, and imposed his own refinements on a late romantic tale. This is not so [23], but on the other hand one would hesitate to claim that Hofmannsthal has made it completely clear what he is about in this drama. One has to take into account the restrictions imposed by the source, and not be too ready to assume that he knew exactly where this story was leading him and was working on a symbolic scheme already conceived as a kind of 'Total-idee'. Hofmannsthal found himself exploring a highly personal spiritual situation, which revealed itself more clearly to him as he handled his source-material. Whether one should go further and suggest that he then found the whole thing so embarrassing in its implications that he would only allow the first part of the exploration to be published is a delicate question [24].

Hofmannsthal uses the main outline of Hoffmann's story, dramatizing with skill carefully selected material from it, taking over and transforming key ideas and motives, with the result that he has absorbed the source into a totally different atmosphere. The following passages make the point clear. Hoffmann's Elis is telling the old miner the story of his misfortune:

[23] Olga Schnitzler records an interesting remark of Hofmannsthal's in her essay, 'Der junge Hofmannsthal', *Die Neue Rundschau*, LXV (1954), 519: "Hofmannsthal ist gezwungen 'sich seine Welt in die Welt einzubauen'. Und doch weiß er mit immer wieder aufgestörtem Sinn: 'Wir sind zu kritisch, um in einer Traumwelt zu leben wie die Romantiker; mit unseren schweren Köpfen brechen wir immer durch das dünne Medium wie schwere Reiter auf Moorboden.'"

[24] Perhaps this is what is implied by Hofmannsthal's reference to "innere Gründe" which caused him to put the drama aside.

Denn Seemann habe er doch nun einmal, von Kindesbeinen an dazu bestimmt, bleiben müssen, und da habe es ihm ein großes Glück gedünkt, in den Dienst der Ostindischen Kompanie treten zu können. Reicher als jemals sei diesmal der Gewinn ausgefallen, und jeder Matrose habe noch außer dem Sold ein gut Stück Geld erhalten, so daß er, die Tasche voll Dukaten, in heller Freude hingelaufen sei nach dem kleinen Häuschen, wo seine Mutter gewohnt. Aber fremde Gesichter hätten ihn aus dem Fenster angeguckt, und eine junge Frau, die ihm endlich die Thür geöffnet, und der er sich zu erkennen gab, habe ihm mit kaltem rauhen Ton berichtet, daß seine Mutter schon vor drei Monaten gestorben, und daß er die paar Lumpen, die, nachdem die Begräbniskosten berichtigt, noch übriggeblieben, auf dem Rathause in Empfang nehmen könne. Der Tod seiner Mutter zerreiße ihm das Herz, er fühle sich von aller Welt verlassen, einsam wie auf ein ödes Riff verschlagen, hülflos, elend. Sein ganzes Leben auf der See erscheine ihm wie ein irres, zweckloses Treiben, ja, wenn er daran denke, daß seine Mutter, vielleicht schlecht gepflegt von fremden Leuten, so ohne Trost sterben müssen, komme es ihm ruchlos und abscheulich vor, daß er überhaupt zur See gegangen und nicht lieber daheim geblieben, seine arme Mutter nährend und pflegend [25].

Hofmannsthal has made drama out of the material of this narrative passage:

ILSEBILL

Es ist gar lang her, daß du fort warst.

ELIS

mit künstlicher Gelassenheit

Ja, ja. Die Mutter muß jetzt so was sein,
Wie da an meinem Stiefel hängt. Und ist
Nicht etwa schnell gestorben ...

ILSEBILL

nickt

Deine Mutter.

[25] E. T. A. Hoffmann, p. 317.

ELIS

Und da wir gingen, war sie aus dem Zeug
Wie du und ich, nur besser. Ihre Augen
So rein, ihr Mund viel frischer wie der deine.
Drei Jahr sind freilich eine lange Zeit.

ILSEBILL

Und du hast's nicht gewußt?

ELIS

anscheinend gleichmütig, mit der Ironie tiefsten Schmerzes

Nein, nein, o nein.
Erst beim Anklopfen. Erst hab ich gemeint,
Es ist ein falsches Haus. Es steht ein Ofen,
Wo sonst ihr Bette stand; und wo ihr Leib
Erkaltete im Tod, da wärmt ein Hund
Den seinen. Und dem Kirchspielschreiber Niels
Hab ich geschrieben, daß er mir das Amt
Ansagt, wo ich die Sachen holen kann,
Wenn was geblieben ist, wie man so schreibt:
Nach Abzug der Begräbniskosten.

Starrt vor sich hin.

ILSEBILL

wischt sich die Augen

Elis! [26]

ELIS

Den Star hat mirs gestochen, und mir kehrt
Das Leben wie ein Wrack sein Eingeweide zu [27].

The simple ingenuous outpourings of the young man who is relieved
to find a sympathetic listener, give place in Hofmannsthal's version to
harshness, reticence and surface indifference, which hide deep suffering
and emotional tension. After holding back emotion by the device of
a deliberately prosaic style, Hofmannsthal suddenly releases it in a
fine, powerful metaphor, heightening Hoffmann's image of the barren

[26] G 330-331.
[27] G 334.

reef to that of life as a gaping wreck. (The effective device of retaining emotion and keeping the dialogue in a low key, and then releasing it in moments of crisis in a passage of concentrated and complex poetic language is repeated throughout the drama.)

In the following parallel, Hofmannsthal has seized on the rhythmic quality of Elis's lament in the original and has elaborated it. This is a good example of his typical use of repetition, alliteration and assonance to give a stylised effect:

'Ach', erwiderte Elis, 'ach, daß niemand an meinen Schmerz glaubt, ja daß man mich wohl albern und thöricht schilt, das ist es ja eben, was mich hinausstößt aus der Welt. — Auf die See mag ich nicht mehr, d a s Leben ekelt mich an' [28].

ELIS

Mir ist übel,
Die Landluft widert mir, mir widert Seeluft.
Mir ist das Bett verleidet und der Becher;
Wenn ich allein bin, bin ich nicht allein,
Und bei den andern bin ich doppelt einsam [29].

The third example shows Hofmannsthal selecting what are for him the most telling motives from Torbern's long exhortation to Elis to leave the sea and become a miner, and from Elis's response:

'Ich höre Euch', sprach der Alte, als Elis schwieg, 'ich höre Euch mit Vergnügen reden, junger Mensch, so wie ich schon seit ein paar Stunden, ohne daß Ihr mich gewahrtet, Euer ganzes Betragen beobachtete und meine Freude daran hatte. Alles, was Ihr thatet, was Ihr spracht, beweist, daß Ihr ein tiefes, in sich selbst gekehrtes, frommes, kindliches Gemüt habt, und eine schönere Gabe konnte Euch der hohe Himmel gar nicht verleihen. Aber zum Seemann habt Ihr Eure Lebetage gar nicht im mindesten getaugt. Wie sollte Euch stillem, wohl gar zum Trübsinn geneigten Neriker (daß Ihr das seid, seh' ich an den Zügen Eures Gesichts, an Eurer ganzen Haltung), wie sollte Euch das wilde, unstete Leben auf der See zusagen? Ihr thut wohl daran, daß Ihr dies Leben aufgebt für immer. Aber die Hände werdet Ihr doch nicht in den Schoß

---

[28] E. T. A. Hoffmann, p. 318.
[29] G 337.

legen? — Folgt meinem Rat, Elis Fröbom! geht nach Falun, werdet ein Bergmann. Ihr seid jung, rüstig, gewiß bald ein tüchtiger Knappe, dann Hauer, Steiger und immer höher herauf. Ihr habt tüchtige Dukaten in der Tasche, die legt Ihr an, verdient dazu, kommt wohl gar zum Besitz eines Bergmannshemmans, habt Eure eigne Kuxe in der Grube. Folgt meinem Rat, Elis Fröbom, werdet ein Bergmann!'
Elis Fröbom erschrak beinahe über die Worte des Alten. 'Wie', rief er, 'was ratet Ihr mir? Von der schönen, freien Erde, aus dem heitern, sonnenhellen Himmel, der mich umgibt, labend, erquickend, soll ich hinaus — hinab in die schauerliche Höllentiefe und dem Maulwurf gleich wühlen und wühlen nach Erzen und Metallen, schnöden Gewinns halber?' [30]

PETER

Du willst nicht mit? Du bist ja gar kein Seemann,
Hätt ich ein Schiff, mir tät es grausen, grausen,
Dich mitzunehmen, dich.

ELIS
sieht einen Augenblick ihm ins Gesicht, dann zu Boden
Das kann wohl sein,
Daß ich kein Seemann mehr bin, kurzer Peter!

PETER
zornig, daß ihm Elis nicht widerspricht
Ein Maulwurf bist du, weiter nichts!

Links vorne ist unscheinbar der alte Tobern aufgetreten. — Er ist ein kräftiger, etwas gebeugter Mann, dem Ansehen nach kaum siebzig. Trägt altertümliche Bergmannstracht, völlig abgetragen und verschossen. Hat blutumränderte merkwürdige Augen. Steht dort in der linken Ecke, an den Zaun gelehnt, von niemandem beachtet, und läßt seine Augen auf Elis ruhen.

ELIS
sieht Peter groß an
Ja, Peter,
Das kann schon sein. Mir ist, du hast ganz recht.
Das ist nicht dumm, was du da sagst. Mir wär
Sehr wohl, könnt ich mich in die dunkle Erde
Einwühlen. Ging es nur, mir sollt es schmecken,
Als kröch ich in den Mutterleib zurück [31].

[30] E. T. A. Hoffmann, pp. 319 f.
[31] G 342.

The sympathetic statement "Aber zum Seemann habt Ihr Eure Lebetage gar nicht im mindesten getaugt" becomes the sharp accusation by
Peter, to which he adds the insulting comparison with the mole; this
is at the same time Torbern's cue, and the spring which releases Elis's
hidden desires.

Hoffmann's Elis runs mad. The possibility that the reader might interpret Elis as a psychological case of delusion and madness in Hoffmann's sense is firmly eliminated by Hofmannsthal [32]. He also omits
Hoffmann's concluding episode—the little scene of reunion which is
so touching as Schubert tells it. The drama is then of special interest in
that it is the first completed work [33] on the basis of this material which
leaves aside the final incident in the original account—that is the
reunion of the old woman and her dead fiancé—an incident which
appealed strongly to all the poets and would-be poets who worked up
the story in the nineteenth century [34]. The miraculous restoration to
the old woman of her former love with his youth and beauty unim-
paired, had already moved Schubert to eloquence, and poet after poet
attempted to extract the last ounce of sentiment from this moving
little scene. There are poems on this subject as sentimental as Tennyson's 'Tomorrow' [35]—for instance Friedrich Rückert's 'Die goldene
Hochzeit'—and there is too on this subject one of the finest poetic
realist tales of the nineteenth century, Johann Peter Hebel's *Unver-
hofftes Wiedersehen*, with its magnificent conclusion. Hofmannsthal's
Elis, however, does not reappear. For Hofmannsthal it is not the long

---

[32] Hofmannsthal does this by making Anna see and understand Torbern in Act IV,
and by letting the grandmother resign herself to Elis's inevitable end in Act V.

[33] Wagner's opera *Die Bergwerke zu Falun* (based on Hoffmann's story) was also
to omit the final episode and end with the death of Elis and the collapse of Ulla;
it was begun in March 1842, but did not get beyond the planning stage.

[34] For example, Theodor Nübling's poem, printed in the *Morgenblatt* of 22 September, 1810, quoted by Friedmann, *op. cit.*, pp. 19 f.: "Willkommen, mein Trauter!
das Schicksal gab / Dich mir wieder, die Ruh' zu bereiten. / Auf dem Kirchhof,
zu deiner Eltern Grab, / Will die redliche Braut dich begleiten, / Auch konnte
dein Schlummer im Schachtengrund / Nicht lösen den heiligen Eid und Bund; /
Was die Liebe schwur und das Herz gebot, / Das trotzt dem Moder, das trennt
kein Tod!"

[35] The material and the theme of this poem are strikingly similar to those of the
German poems; it is about old Molly, who was reunited to her fiancé after he
had been preserved for forty years in a peat-bog.

5

patience of love which is important, but the idea that the miner is for long years untouched by the ravages of time. He dwells on the escape from transitoriness and decay into a timeless realm, and this characteristic idea dominates his presentation of the supernatural elements. Hofmannsthal's imagination dwells on the love which must fail, and the scenes in Falun are unlike anything we have seen before in his work, and deserve more attention than has usually been accorded to them.

The dialogue between Elis and Anna is realistic and compelling, whereas the scenes of family life are more remote. Hofmannsthal writes these scenes in a lingering leisurely way in the second act, as if he had to make this picture of a family real to himself by exploring the figures one by one. As in the earlier plays, he makes the very young and the very old more convincing than the wan character from middle life. The dialogue between Anna and the child, building up atmosphere for Elis's arrival at the house, is a little masterpiece, and the portrait of Anna herself is delicately and sensitively drawn. The young girl's beautiful modesty and naiveté is thrown into relief by the aged wisdom of her grandmother, the precociousness of her brother, Christian, and the weary resignation of her father. It is really Anna who suggests the simple delights of contented love. Otherwise the Dahlsjöh family, with the exception of Anna, tends to become 'voices' for the meditations on aspects of life, on its transitoriness, on success and failure, on moral experience, and on the bond between the generations. Here is something which recurs in Hofmannsthal's early work—the passage which is almost too allusive and meditative for the stage; as when the blind grandmother comforts her despondent son:

> Hast du
> Noch nicht gefühlt, wie alles sich verzweigt?
> Wer ist denn stark, wer ist denn schwach? Mein Sohn,
> Sieh, wie ich jung war, dünkt mich jetzt, ich war
> Ganz Sehnsucht, nichts als ein beseeltes Auge.
> Mit meinen Augen sog ich wie im Traum
> Die Welt in mich hinein, von innen trat
> Die Seele an dies Fenster, und dein Vater
> Liebte mich um nichts andres auf der Welt.
> Nun starben mir die Augen ab — und ich
> Bin drum nicht minder ganz: im Innern drängt

Sich ein Gewinde, ein Gewühl empor,
Verbunden alles wie in Blumenketten.
Dich und die Kinder und die nicht mehr sind,
Ihr aller Schicksal fühle ich in Einem,
Wie wenn die Hände Blüten und Gezweige
Von einem Strauch betasten. Alles blüht!
Aufwachsen laß die Kinder, häng dein Herz
Nicht an dein Haus, hängs nicht an dein Gewerb:
Du kannst das Glück nicht in verschlossnen Höhlen
Dir halten, denn es atmet nur im Flug! [36]

Here Hofmannsthal's attempt to move towards more natural dramatic speech has resulted in flatness, and one cannot help feeling that these things have been better said in the poems. His problem here seems to be that his starting-point is still lyrical experience instead of human relationships, and the establishing of a dramatic relationship between characters is still a difficulty. Much more successful are the long scenes which explore with impressive and painful effect the frustration of the love between Elis and Anna. These scenes contain a dramatic force and urgency which arises, strangely, not from the passion of love itself, but from the fear of remaining unloved and from the fear of losing the beloved. There are no parallels to these passages in Hoffmann, and one feels that they may be particularly personal to Hofmannsthal. Elis comes to Falun and sees in Anna's life the sweet regularity of passing time and ordinary human experience from which he knows he is to be excluded. This awakens in him the terrible fear of being obliterated from human memory, and dramatic significance is at once established. Two lives suddenly become dramatically involved with each other:

Jetzt steht die Tür von deiner Kammer offen:
Da wirst du leben drin und deine Tage,
Die werden kommen und vorüberrinnen
So wie der Brunnen draußen, hör nur, hör.
Und Nächte auch, erst solche wie bisher,
Dann eine, wo du liegst und glühst im Dunkeln,
Weil der im Dunkeln steht, dem du gehörst . . .
Doch vorher noch so viel: des Kuckucks Ruf
Wird durch den Abend dringen, weit herab,

[36] G 377.

5*

Weit hin, nur nicht hinunter, Stürme werden
Am Fenster rütteln, sanfte Regenbogen
Aufsteigen aus den Schluchten, immer wirst du
Die Glocken läuten hören, Anna, Anna, —
Ich will nicht ganz vergessen sein hier oben! [37]

Anna begins to know that she loves and to fear its loss at the same point in the drama, and Elis is most moving in his appeal for love when Anna is already out of reach. They are cheated of their confession of love to one another by the magic which draws Elis to the mine so that he wastes his tenderness on Agmahd, the shadow of Anna [38]. There is a deep pathos in all this, but not tragedy, because love has been frustrated all along. Hofmannsthal has established the character of Anna so finely that it is a disappointment to see her fail and capitulate in sad humility before unknown powers. She, like Elis, ceases to be real in Act V, which is an ending strangely mechanical and lacking in emotion. Hofmannsthal turns it into a kind of dream, where people move as shadows in a mournful dance whose pattern has been determined for them. The madness of Gretchen or Ophelia, the proper conclusion for suffering imposed by the Faust or Hamlet figure, is perhaps being deliberately avoided by Hofmannsthal for the obvious reasons. So love fails to save the magician, but this is not tragedy.

The central difficulty of interpretation arises from the character of Elis and from his strange experience. His radical and morbid rejection of life at the beginning of the drama contrasts with the romantic melancholy of Hoffmann's central character. Hofmannsthal drives Elis into a state of nihilistic feeling which is dangerous and vulnerable, and makes him harsh and almost repulsive, with deep hidden emotions but no apparent refinement of mind and feeling. Here is a character to whom no parallel can be supplied from the earlier works, a figure suggested to Hofmannsthal by his source which already contains, as an addition to the Schubert version of the story, the motives of suffering and of rejection of life, but in a plaintive and muted key.

[37] G 397.
[38] Agmahd is a spirit who reflects Elis's secret affections, v. G 363. Compare the Efrit in *Die Frau ohne Schatten* who mirrors for the Färberin the lover whom she secretly longs for.

Hofmannsthal changes and elaborates them; he reveals an Elis who in his sombre and introverted brooding is almost neurotic. But Elis's broodings in his half-conscious state provide a remarkably complex passage of haunting poetry, part meditation and part incantation. Elis desires to burrow into the earth as if into his mother's womb, and aware of his body as compounded of the same stuff as earth and stars, he longs to return to communion with earth-bound creatures, with the sparkling mystery of dark nature away from the darkness of the bright world. (The passage has many examples of this kind of paradoxical image.) The meditation then develops into an incantatory fantasy of invading the inner chamber where his parents sleep in the ground, and joining himself in substance to the secret veins, sparkling roots, and red jewels of the earth, his own heart glowing red with the unsleeping glow of precious stone:

> Haus, tu dich auf! gib deine Schwelle her:
> Ein Sohn pocht an! auf tu dich, tiefe Kammer,
> Wo Hand in Hand und Haar versträhnt in Haar
> Der Vater mit der Mutter schläft, ich komme!
> Entblößt euch, ihr geheimnisvollen Adern,
> Ausbluten lautlos sich die meinen schon!
> Mein Haar sträubt sich vor Lust, bei euch zu sein,
> Ihr Wurzeln, die ihr an dem Finstern saugt,
> Euch funkelnd nährt aus jungfräulicher Erde!
> Mein Herz will glühn in einem Saal mit euch,
> Blutrote Funkelsteine, hocherlauchte,
> Schlaflose Lampen, täuscht mich nicht, ich seh euch,
> Ich seh euch glühen wie durch fahles Horn,
> Versinkt mir nicht, ich halt euch mit der Seele! [39]

[39] G 344. It is interesting to compare and contrast the passages in Hoffmann's story which provide the starting-point for Hofmannsthal's ideas: "Gestein war das nämlich, was er erst für den Wolkenhimmel gehalten. Von unbekannter Macht fortgetrieben, schritt er vorwärts, aber in dem Augenblick regte sich alles um ihn her, und wie kräuselnde Wogen erhoben sich aus dem Boden wunderbare Blumen und Pflanzen von blinkendem Metall, die ihre Blüten und Blätter aus der tiefsten Tiefe emporrankten und auf anmutige Weise ineinander verschlangen. Der Boden war so klar, daß Elis die Wurzeln der Pflanzen deutlich erkennen konnte, aber bald immer tiefer mit dem Blick eindringend, erblickte er ganz unten — unzählige holde jungfräuliche Gestalten, die sich mit weißen glänzenden Armen umschlungen hielten, und aus ihren Herzen sproßten jene Wurzeln, jene Blumen und Pflanzen empor, und wenn die Jungfrauen lächelten, ging ein süßer Wohllaut

The instinctive desire in Elis to return to the womb, to penetrate the earth and to join his parents in their sleep of death is combined with a mystical impulse to partake of nature's existence; the journey home, as it were, is then transformed into action; Elis sinks down through the earth into an enclosed chamber, the deeper level of his own being from which the dream has sprung, and finds there something new and unexpected—he finds, not the dead, nor living nature, but a being who represents pure spirit. The psychological dilemma changes to a spiritual one, and Elis becomes a victim of the ambivalent superior powers of the soul [40]. We are to understand that it is to this other realm of pure spirit that Elis penetrates; he is never drawn back to his original fantasy. The difficulty here is that the character established by Hofmannsthal at the beginning of the drama in realistic terms is drawn over at this point into a symbolic world which has more to do with Hofmannsthal's own inner problems than with Elis's dilemma. There is, then, in the first act of the drama, a psychological pattern of emotional crisis, rejection of life, and regression; at the same time

durch das weite Gewölbe, und höher und freudiger schossen die wunderbaren Metallblüten empor. Ein unbeschreibliches Gefühl von Schmerz und Wollust ergriff den Jüngling, eine Welt von Liebe, Sehnsucht, brünstigem Verlangen ging auf in seinem Innern. 'Hinab — hinab zu euch', rief er und warf sich mit ausgebreiteten Armen auf den kristallenen Boden nieder." (E. T. A. Hoffmann, p. 322.) The red jewels have their parallel in Hoffmann's "funkelnder Almandin", which Elis goes to find on the morning of his wedding-day. His words to Ulla are: "Er ist schöner als der herrlichste blutrote Karfunkel, und wenn wir in treuer Liebe verbunden hineinblicken in sein strahlendes Licht, können wir es deutlich erschauen, wie unser Inneres verwachsen ist mit dem wunderbaren Gezweige, das aus dem Herzen der Königin im Mittelpunkt der Erde emporkeimt." (E. T. A. Hoffmann, p. 342.) This passage in its turn may well be based on certain motives from Ludwig Tieck's Der Runenberg, especially Christian's discovery of the "magische Tafel mit den farbigen Edelgesteinen" which his father describes as "blutdürstig, wie das rote Auge des Tigers", and which corresponds to the „magische Figur" within Christian, representing his other, enchanted self.

[40] The Freudian significance of this passage has been explored in an article by Dr. Emil Lorenz: 'Die Geschichte des Bergmanns von Falun vornehmlich bei E. T. A. Hoffmann, R. Wagner und Hugo von Hofmannsthal', Imago, Jahrgang III (1914). It appears that Lorenz only knew the first act of Hofmannsthal's drama. The effect of the Freudian interpretation is to reduce all three versions to a common denominator in a basic scheme of infantile fixation, supplanting of the father and incestuous relationship with the mother-figure (Bergkönigin). Lorenz does not set out to explore the complexity of the language and of the ideas, and the distinctions between the three versions as literature.

there are the mythological associations of the mother, chthonic regions, and death which can be a new form of life. So far the character of Elis is a unity, and there is no contradiction between the realistic and the symbolic. But the scene of Elis's introversion is more complicated than this; it contains the symbolism of a relationship with pure timeless being which can only be interpreted by reference to certain personal problems of Hofmannsthal. The result is that Elis as a character is made to bear too heavy a burden of symbolism. It would seem that Hofmannsthal pursues a number of ideas as they are suggested to him by his source, and finally settles down with the problem which has engaged his thoughts most deeply, because it has arisen from his own early experience. So Elis's "Zauberwort" is followed by what one might call a spiritual seduction scene in the realm below the ground. Elis, bewildered and blindly groping for the meaning of his experience, struggling against his feeling of horror, is gradually led to prostrate himself at the feet of the Bergkönigin.

There is a remarkably different earlier version of this scene [41]. Here the domain of the Bergkönigin is inhabited by groups of figures who belong to an age that is long past; it is a realm of the dead enslaved to a bright enchantress. Elis, after penetrating into the earth is quickly and securely claimed by this supernatural world. The second version confines the servants of the Bergkönigin to Torbern and Agmahd and employs them in the long process of awakening the spirit and magician in Elis who has to be led to an understanding of the spirit-life outside time. Most remarkable amongst the contrasts with the first version of the scene is the fact that Elis is overcome with mingled horror and fascination at the sight of the Bergkönigin. Instead of the words "und nicht einmal schaudert" [42] of the earlier version, there is a persistent reiteration of the horror motive: "Mir grauts vor dir", "mir schauderts bis ins Mark", "Was zuckst du? Grauts dich so?", "Graut dir, daß ich schon war bevor du warst" [43]? Elis shudders before the vision of pure

---

[41] First published by H. Steiner in *Die Neue Rundschau*, 1950, it is to be found in D IV 500 ff. H. Steiner in his note in the *Neue Rundschau*, p. 179, indicates that it was written shortly before the version in G, and in D IV 512, he calls it "die Frühfassung der Bergszene".

[42] D IV 508.

[43] G 354 f.

timeless spirit, and the Bergkönigin, in her turn, is horror-struck at the spectacle of human life and death:

> Mich dünkt, ich stürb vor Graun, müßt ich so leben
> Hervor aus einem Leib, hinab zu Leibern.
> Und wenn ich eurer einen atmen seh,
> Werd ichs nicht los, mir ist, als müßt an ihm
> Noch hängen Ungewordnes und Verwestes,
> Als wär er nie allein, wo er auch geht und steht [44].

Both expressions of horror are in fact personal confessions of Hofmannsthal. There is evidence here on the one hand of the strange pang which Hofmannsthal felt when he meditated on the relationship of human beings to each other in birth and death, and on the other hand of his deep fear of becoming inhuman, of failing in his contact with the world and which reality; and this fear is at the same time associated with the experiences of the mind and of the imagination which have a magical fascination—such as mystical experience, and indeed the experience of being a poet.

It is interesting that Keats helped Hofmannsthal to exorcise these fears, as we see from the letter to Stephen Gruss of 23 January 1907:

> Dein Rückblick auf unsere Kinderjahre hat mich in manchem Punkt recht gerührt . . . Manches, was Du über meine spätere Entwicklung sagst—eben über jene Phase, die uns auseinanderbrachte—, hätte mich vielleicht noch vor fünf Jahren verstimmt oder beunruhigt. Seitdem ich aber über Dreißig bin, Frau und Kind habe und mich dabei innerlich ebenso jung fühle als je und mit einer noch stärkern freudigen und fröhlichen Grundstimmung als damals vor 15 Jahren, — seitdem weiß ich auch, weiß es aus mir und aus Dokumenten, die ich nun verstehen gelernt habe, daß die sonderbare, fast unheimliche seelische Beschaffenheit, diese scheinbar alles durchdringende Lieblosigkeit und Treulosigkeit, die dich an mir so sehr befremdet und mich manchmal so sehr geängstigt hat — der 'Tor und Tod' ist nichts als ein Ausdruck dieser Angst —, daß diese seelische Beschaffenheit nichts andres ist, als die Verfassung des Dichters unter den Dingen und Menschen. Der schöne Brief von Keats, der neuerdings vielfach in gelehrten Werken zitiert wird, . . . der Brief mit den merkwürdigen Klagen über das Chamäleondasein des Dichters ('he has no identity:

---

[44] G 355. Cf. 'Terzinen I, Über Vergänglichkeit', G 17.

he is continually in for, and filling, some other body.—It is a wretched thing to confess, but it is a very fact, that not one word I ever utter can be taken for granted as an opinion growing out of my identical nature. How can it, when I have no nature?' usf. usf.). Dieser Brief hat mich sehr entlastet, als er mir vor Jahren das erstemal in die Hand kam. Ein Dichter zu sein, ist eine Sache, gegen die man sich nicht helfen kann. Aber es wäre mir leid, wenn ich deswegen kein Mensch wäre (woran ich jetzt nicht mehr zweifle, hatte aber etwas böse Phasen mit diesem Zweifel) [45].

We may compare with this a statement in the letter to Rudolf Borchardt of 11 July 1912, the year in which Hofmannsthal began serious work on the libretto Die Frau ohne Schatten, where love and marriage triumph over daemonic magic:

> Einsam bin ich, wie jeder Mensch meiner, unserer Art es ist. Manches in meiner Natur läßt mich die auferlegte Einsamkeit leichter tragen, als andere sie getragen haben. Denn ich habe darüber daß ich ein Dichter bin, nicht aufhören müssen ein Mensch zu sein, das ist mein unermeßliches Glück — und der Mensch in mir ist nicht einsam, ist reich an Freundschaft, an Liebe und fast über sein Vermögen beglückt. Der Dichter aber ist einsam, wie sollte er es anders sein ...

Hofmannsthal's fear that by being a poet he might cease to be a human being was ultimately allayed by the realisation that his apparent inadequacy in human relationships did not imply a moral defect or a lack of moral integrity, and by the experience of becoming a husband and father. "Ein Mensch zu sein" seems to mean for Hofmannsthal the ability to develop and mature in one's relationships with

---

[45] It is interesting to note Hofmannsthal's misinterpretation of this letter from Keats to Richard Woodhouse of 27 October, 1818. Keats is in fact not referring to a condition of 'Lieblosigkeit' and 'Treulosigkeit', but to one of general love and participation, as this passage from the same letter shows: "As to the poetical Character itself (I mean that sort of which, if I am any thing, I am a Member; that sort distinguished from the wordsworthian or egotistical sublime; which is a thing per se and stands alone) it is not itself—it has no self—it is every thing and nothing—It has no character—it enjoys light and shade; it lives in gusto, be it foul or fair, high or low, rich or poor, mean or elevated—It has as much delight in conceiving an Iago as an Imogen. What shocks the virtuous philosopher, delights the camelion Poet." Dr M. E. Seaton has pointed out to me that Keats' The Poet. A Fragment (1818) illuminates the letter, and the poem brings out very clearly the difference in the mind of Keats and of Hofmannsthal on this matter.

other people and in the experience of love, also perhaps the "vivre simplement et tranquillement" of Pascal [46].

The consideration of Hofmannsthal's personal dilemma, his fear of failure in love and humanity, brings us back to the question of the spiritual dilemma represented by Elis's relationship with the Bergkönigin, to which it is ultimately the key. The figure of the Bergkönigin is not borrowed from Hoffmann's tale [47]. She is described as bathed in her own light, muted to a soft luminousness by the veil which covers her completely from crown to toe—presumably the veil of mystery. She trembles faintly like a flower on a tall stem. At this point it is necessary to refer to a fragmentary plan for a work called *Jupiter und Semele* (1901) [48], in which Hofmannsthal was to portray a poet and his two loves, a human being and a supernatural creature, his muse, to whom he devotes his finer energies. A note on the poet's muse runs like this: "Ob nicht als seine Geliebte die Muse einzuführen wäre, eine Gestalt ähnlich der geheimnisvollen Königin in 'Idyll of the White Lotus'." *The Idyll of the White Lotus* was first published in 1884 [49]. A certain Mabel Collins [50] claimed to have "arrested the thinking principle of her brain" to receive it from the astral forms of a number of priests of ancient Egypt [51]. It is not the story of a miner, nor of a poet, but of a young initiate into the mysteries of the human soul, the battleground for light and darkness, spiritual truth and physical desire. He meets "Our Lady of the Lotus" who is flower-like,

---

[46] A 13.

[47] E. T. A. Hoffmann, p. 322: "Elis gewahrte neben sich den alten Bergmann, aber sowie er ihn mehr und mehr anschaute, wurde er zur Riesengestalt, aus glühendem Erz gegossen. Elis wollte sich entsetzen, aber in dem Augenblick leuchtete es auf aus der Tiefe wie ein jäher Blitz, und das ernste Antlitz einer mächtigen Frau wurde sichtbar." Later, when Elis surrenders to the magic, he sees "das hohe Antlitz der mächtigen Königin" (p. 338).

[48] D II 504 f.

[49] Reeves and Turner were the publishers. I have seen copies dated 1890 and 1896. It is a theosophical tract of no literary value.

[50] Mabel Collins published a number of novels towards the end of the nineteenth century. With Mme. H. P. Blatavsky she edited the first three volumes of *Lucifer. A Theosophical Magazine* (later known as the *Theosophical Reviews*) between September 1887 and February 1889.

[51] Mabel Collins, *The Story of Sensa. An Interpretation of the Idyll of the White Lotus*. London, Theosophical Publishing Society (undated), pp. 3 f.

whose face dazzles him, who is full of light and illuminated by her own radiance [52]. According to Mabel Collins, the Lotus-queen is the young initiate's own divine nature [53]. He also meets an evil queen clad in a dark veil which is a garment of snakes, and holding a light which makes nothing else visible. Her face, when she draws back the veil, inspires horror and loathing in the youth. The servants of this queen have to renounce their humanity in order to serve her; their hearts become hard and their faces like stone [53a]. This queen represents the youth's evil nature [53b]. To which of the two queens Hofmannsthal is referring in his note on the poet's muse is not clear. Possibly he is thinking of features and influences which belong to both. The name of the wicked priest in the *Idyll*, who renounces his humanity, is Agmahd, and this name must have caught Hofmannsthal's imagination at once, since he uses it for the boy-spirit who serves the Bergkönigin. This proves that Hofmannsthal had read the *Idyll* before he wrote the *Bergwerk*, and it seems that both the queens in the theosophical tract may have influenced his conception of the Bergkönigin [53c].

It is of course tempting to assume that the Bergkönigin represents simply Elis's superior transcendental self in a positive sense, that part of the self which partakes of absolute existence, outside time and space. The Bergkönigin reminds us of the veiled goddess of the 'Hyacinth und Rosenblüte' Märchen in Novalis's *Lehrlinge zu Sais*, and in fact in 1900 Hofmannsthal began a story called *Das Märchen von der verschleierten Frau* [54] which bears a strong resemblance in the most important motives to the *Bergwerk*, and in which the miner bears

---

[52] *The Idyll of the White Lotus.* London, 1896. pp. 12, 35, 55.
[53] *The Story of Sensa*, p. 41.
[53a] *The Idyll of the White Lotus*, pp. 23 ff., 70 ff., 74, 77 f., 96, 114.
[53b] *The Story of Sensa*, pp. 15, 40 f.
[53c] I am indebted for this point on the possible influence of both queens, to Mr. Michael Hamburger's article, 'Hofmannsthals Bibliothek', *Euphorion*, LV (1961), 59.
[54] *Die Erzählungen*, pp. 76 ff., first published in *Corona*, 1939. In this story, which remained a fragment, the Bergmann, Hyacinth, leaves his wife and child to go in search of the mistress of his soul (p. 81); the "geheime Tür ins Innere" (p. 79) does not lead him out of life for good, but back to his wife and his home (cf. the return of Hyacinth to Rosenblüte in the Märchen which Novalis incorporates into the *Lehrlinge zu Sais*). Here Hofmannsthal is approaching a solution in which he attempts to combine his two worlds and bridge the gap between the deeper self and life. He was very susceptible to the idea of a cyclical pattern

the name Hyacinth. However, it is clear that we must distinguish between the ideas of the *Lehrlinge zu Sais* on the one hand, and those of Hofmannsthal's drama on the other. The veiled goddess in the *Lehrlinge zu Sais* is at once the ideal goal and the earthly beloved. The Bergkönigin is alien to humanity and draws men away from it. She is an ambivalent figure. We must then avoid calling, for a final solution, on those poetic-philosophical ideas of the transcendental self into which Novalis's 'magischer Idealismus' and all kinds of mystical exploration of the self in Eastern and Western literatures has initiated us. Otherwise we shall over-simplify and find ourselves saying: Hofmannsthal tells us in this drama that the mind can only achieve the purest and most beautiful acts of contemplation or mystical concourse with the universe when it is out of touch with life and reality as we normally know it. This kind of statement does not take us far enough. The other temptation is to regard the play simply as another treatment of the theme of life and art. The artist can be said to transcend time, as does Elis, and Hofmannsthal with his circle of friends was exercised by the problem raised in Ibsen's drama, *When we Dead awaken* [55], that is, the betrayal of life and love for the sake of art. Instead of Novalis's thought on poets, "Freie Gäste sind sie, deren goldener Fuß nur leise auftritt" [56], we have Elis's agonised cry, "Ich bin ein Gast, ein schauerlicher Gast!" [57]. We may say that legitimate magic, to which poetry belonged for Novalis, is for Hofmannsthal shadowed by daemonic suggestions, and the poet—if Elis does symbolise the poet—is a doubtful figure. But this is again only a partial interpretation.

It must be admitted that some of the scattered comments on the *Berg-werk* in the later document *Ad me ipsum* appear to lead in the direction of the above interpretations. In *Ad me ipsum* Hofmannsthal sees

in experience, see the letter to Georg Freiherr zu Franckenstein of 1 August, 1903. We also know that Hofmannsthal felt an affinity with Novalis: "Mit Novalis hat mich immer ein brüderliches Gefühl verbunden." (*Die Neue Rundschau*, 1954, p. 357.) For the relationship between *Das Bergwerk zu Falun, Das Märchen von der verschleierten Frau*, and *Die Frau ohne Schatten*, see Belma Çakmur, *Hofmannsthals Erzählung Die Frau ohne Schatten*, Ankara, 1952, pp. 243 ff.

[55] *Die Neue Rundschau*, 1954, pp. 526 f.
[56] Novalis, *Heinrich von Ofterdingen*, Ch. VI.
[57] G 440.

the drama as an attempt to return to the "höchste Welt, deren Bote der Tod" [58], in a cryptic note associates Elis with the idea of the transcendental self [59], and brackets together *Der Kaiser und die Hexe* and *Das Bergwerk zu Falun* as "Analyse der dichterischen Existenz" [60]. But these notes do not take us very far. To be distinguished from them are the comments to which a special significance attaches, since they suggest strongly the ambivalence, and even the negative interpretation of Elis Fröbom's supernatural experience. Hofmannsthal sees Elis as an illustration of the statement, "Wer sich der Introversion unterzieht ... gelangt an einen Punkt, wo sich zwei Wege trennen" and adds in parenthesis his own comment, "Bild des Abgrundes, des Scheideweges" [61].

Hofmannsthal is quoting here from Herbert Silberer's *Probleme der Mystik und ihre Symbolik* [62]; if Elis is to be taken as an illustration of

[58] A 214 f.

[59] A 226.

[60] A 223.

[61] A 215.

[62] Published in Vienna in 1914. I have been unable to obtain a copy in German and have used the translation by Smith Ely Jelliffe, New York, 1917. Silberer examines alchemical and mystical sources, dreams and myths, and produces a psychoanalytical interpretation of the symbols (resting mainly on Freud and Jung), comparing this with natural philosophic interpretations on the one hand, and the anagogic, i.e. hermetic religious interpretation on the other. He operates with the Jungian term 'introversion', meaning the withdrawal of interest from the outer world and the search for the joys that can be afforded by the inner world. Hofmannsthal drew his quotation from the first section of Part III, a section dealing with introversion and regeneration. The relevant passage opens the discussion of the effects of introversion, and in the English translation runs as follows: "Introversion is no child's play. It leads to abysses by which we may be swallowed up past recall. Whoever submits to introversion arrives at a point where two ways part; and there he must come to a decision, than which a more difficult one cannot be conceived. The symbol of the abyss, of the parting of the ways, both were clearly contained in our parable. (Silberer is referring to the hermetic parable with which he opens the book). The occurrence of the similar motive in myths and fairy-tales is familiar. The danger is obvious in that the hero generally makes an apparently quite trivial mistake and then must make extraordinary efforts to save himself from the effects of these few trivial errors. One more wrong step and all would have been lost. Introversion accordingly presents two possibilities, either to gain what the mystic work seeks, or to lose oneself. In introversion the libido sinks into 'its own depths' (a figure that Nietzsche likes to use), and finds there below in the shadows of the unconscious, the equivalent for the world above which it has left, namely the

Silberer's argument at this point, then the implication must be that he has lost his way in the mine of the self, the "Abgrund", and has failed to find the path back into life. The suggestion that the Bergkönigin represents something dangerous is to be found in the description of *Die Frau ohne Schatten* as the "Umkehrung der Motive von 'Kaiser und Hexe' und 'Bergwerk': die Liebe zu einem Dämon wird hinaufgeläutert zur Liebe zu einem menschlichen Wesen, anstatt zu dieser in Antithese zu stehen" [63], and in the note on what Hofmannsthal calls the "Grundproblem": "Das Über-ich . . . als dämonische Mächte welche über die Seele verfügen wollen" [64]. And further there is the conception of the dichotomy between life and art in the often-quoted note: "Im 'Bergwerk' ist jenes gewaltig Hinüberziehende (das die Seele dem Leben entfremdet) erst wirklich gestaltet: das Reich der Worte worin alles Gegenwart. — Das Ganze drückt den Versuch der Seele aus, der Zeit zu entfliehen in das Überzeitliche . . ." [65]. This second group of notes from *Ad me ipsum* sheds more light on the drama.

world of phantasy and memories, of which the strongest and most influential are the early infantile memory images. It is the child's world, the paradise of early childhood, from which a rigorous law has separated us. In this subterranean realm slumber sweet domestic feelings and the infinite hopes of all 'becoming'. Yet as Mephistopheles says, 'The peril is great'. This depth is seducing: it is the 'mother' and—death. If the libido remains suspended in the wonder realm of the inner world the man has become but a shadow for the world above. He is as good as dead or mortally ill; if the libido succeeds however in tearing itself loose again and of pressing on to the world above, then a miracle is revealed; this subterranean journey has become a fountain of youth for it, and from its apparent death there arises a new productiveness." *Op. cit.* pp. 269 ff. This passage explains Hofmannsthal's note in *Ad me ipsum:* "Die Introversion als Weg in die Existenz. (Der mystische Weg.)"—a note which must refer to the successful outcome of introversion, as contrasted with 'losing oneself'. Hofmannsthal sees statements in the passage from Silberer as relevant to Elis, and it is clear that for Silberer, as for Jung, Elis would be an example of one who has lost himself in introversion. We still have to face the problem of the meaning of what Elis found when he descended into the depths of the self, and Silberer's chapter on introversion does not provide the clue. Jung would certainly have used the term 'anima' to describe the Bergkönigin, but to indicate that she is the 'soulimage' does not solve the problem of what this particular manifestation of the anima meant for Hofmannsthal.

[63] A 218 f.
[64] A 219.
[65] A 241. That Hofmannsthal is here referring to poetry is I think clear, cf. "Poesie als Gegenwart. Das mystische Element der Poesie: die Überwindung der Zeit" (*Andreas oder Die Vereinigten*, E 201.)

When we look at the *Bergwerk* as a whole we note that after the first act the ecstasy and emotion associated with the Bergkönigin fade and die, giving way to a mechanical repetition of the motives of spiritual power in a timeless world, which have already been exploited fully in the first act. There is a constant repetition, but no development of these, and the spirit-realm looks very different once life begins to state its claims from Act II onwards, so that each time Elis's spiritual destiny is rehearsed, Hofmannsthal makes clearer the antagonism between this experience and the sweetness and promise of human life. The vision of Elis's spiritual destiny gradually loses its positive meaning for Hofmannsthal and for his readers, and becomes more and more distasteful. The Bergkönigin is the one figure which could mean an ecstatic experience of the mind and spirit, caught away from the dumb ache of human existence to a realm where it meets its more powerful potentialities, and, significantly, she does not appear after the first act: she merely sends her far less prepossessing messengers, Agmahd and the ugly and inhuman Torbern, who prefigures Elis's fate.

The *Bergwerk* is for Hofmannsthal an exploration and a discovery; it leads him to suggest in symbolic form, not only the antagonism between spirit and life, in which the dichotomy between art and life may be included, but also the fascination and horror of a mind descending to a mysterious region of itself, to the mine or abyss of the self, where anonymous experience may prove to be divine or devilish, and end in a terrible limbo or in annihilation. Hofmannsthal is exploring the "tiefsten Tiefen des zweifelhaften Höhlenkönigreiches 'Ich'" [66] over which his mind is to hover again as he plans his character Sigismund for *Der Turm*. "Keiner wird, was er nicht ist" [67], says Torbern. "Es schläft in euch. Doch ahnt ihr's nicht" [68], says the Bergkönigin. What is this secret self? In Elis lies, not the blue flower of Novalis, nor the golden flower of the Chinese mystics, nor the white lotus of Egypt, but that ambivalent realm of unattached spiritual power which is a source of revelation and a hindrance to life. And yet Elis feels that he is responding to something outside himself, for the higher self may

[66] Quoted from the undated letter to Hermann Bahr, *Briefe 1900—1909*, p. 155.
[67] G 349.
[68] G 360—361.

appear as daemonic powers waiting to take possession of the soul [69]. The Faustian echoes [70] in the drama must all be related to Hofmannsthal's difficult, personal intimations of depths in the self which seem to contain the fearful and the beautiful outside any known frame of reference—intimations of a powerful inner world, exclusive and outside living human relationships, but also out of touch with God and nature; to enter it is to find oneself in communion with a goddess-daemon who is nameless [71].

---

[69] Cf. A 219.

[70] For example, Elis's relationship with Anna is a part of his destiny which has to be fulfilled, and she, like Gretchen, must be destroyed. To Torbern Elis cries: "Du fürchterlicher Knecht, was führtest du / Mich her, hier her? Konnt ich nicht diese Frist / In der Einöde hausen? Konnt ich nicht / Mich aus der Wildnis dort hinunter wühlen?/Was mußt ich her und dies Geschöpf verderben?" G 444.

[71] Walther Brecht in his article, 'Über Hugo von Hofmannsthals "Bergwerk zu Falun"', Corona, III, 2, 1932, pp. 211 f. records that Hofmannsthal chose three mottoes for his drama in 1899, although none of them were printed with it. (Brecht does not give their sources.) They are, "The sad rhyme of the man who proudly clung / To his first fault, and withered in his pride"; then, "Könnt ich Magie von meinem Pfad entfernen"; and finally, "Entzieh dich nicht dem einzigen Geschäfte: / Vor dem dich schaudert, dieses ist das deine". The second motto, from Faust. Zweiter Teil, reinforces the negative interpretation of the Bergkönigin. The third is the first two lines from Hofmannsthal's Inschrift (G 78), but with different punctuation from that in the Gedichte und lyrische Dramen (1946 and 1952 editions). Inschrift in these editions is punctuated as follows: "Entzieh dich nicht dem einzigen Geschäfte! / Vor dem dich schaudert, dieses ist das deine: / Nicht anders sagt das Leben, was es meine, / Und schnell verwirft das Chaos deine Kräfte." Brecht interprets the 'Geschäft' as 'introversion' and 'poetry', but there is reason to believe that 'Geschäft' could also be interpreted as 'life' or 'love'. Brecht cursorily dismisses the first motto — "das ist bewußt noch halb von außen gesehen", p. 211 — because he is rather more inclined to the positive than to the negative view of Elis's experience, although he vacillates in his article between the two. The source of this motto appears to be Browning's Paracelsus, ll. 527 f.: "The sad rhyme of the men who proudly clung / To their first fault, and withered in their pride". Browning gives these lines in quotation marks as the conclusion of the parable told by Paracelsus to Festus. The parable points to the blindness of men who refuse to accept an alternative point of view and cling to a false goal. Paracelsus, a Faustian character, has pursued knowledge detached from love, and has to learn to know through love; he sees his error in the end. Perhaps Hofmannsthal thought of using the quotation to indicate Elis's failure to pursue the superior goal—the goal of human love. Hofmannsthal quoted Browning in the diaries as early as 1894 (A 109), and Mr. Michael Hamburger has seen in Hofmannsthal's library the copies of Browning's poems which he read repeatedly, and in which Paracelsus is contained.

Carl Burckhardt records some words of Hofmannsthal when they were together in Sicily, in Palermo, probably in the year 1924:

> Eines Morgens standen wir vor dem Eingang der palermitanischen Kapuzinergruft. 'Ich gehe hinein', sagte Hofmannsthal, 'dort liegen sie alle, schön erhaltene Mumien in ihren Uniformen und Fräcken.' Ich weigerte mich mitzukommen; später, auf der Fahrt nach Segesta, zwischen den blühenden wilden Geranien, auf damals noch staubigen Wegen, fragte er: 'Das ist Ihnen zuwider oder unheimlich, jene Gruft? Mich aber beruhigt es, diese vielen, jetzt so würdigen Männer, die ihr Leben hinter sich haben und in ihren Nischen liegen, geordnet in der trockenen Luft ihrer Heimat; einst haben sie sich gekannt, haben sie geredet und gestritten, nun sind sie ruhig, ihre eigene Epoche, die sie einst so ernst genommen haben, ist vorüber, jetzt schweigen sie. Nein, ich könnte dort Tage verbringen, meditieren oder auch Lustspiele schreiben; das Grauen, das wirklich Unheimliche ist anderswo, ist in uns selbst, die größte Wirklichkeit, die erhabenste und die gefährlichste, die der Himmel wie der Höllen, bauen sich aus einer Substanz auf, die in uns selber ist, das Nichts aber beginnt dort, wo wir diese unsere schöpferischen Vorstellungen wegwerfen' [72].

In the *Bergwerk* the poetic fiction of a daemonic realm serves a personal myth in which the soul bears in embryo its own fetish, divinity or devil. The Bergkönigin is a symbol for experiences which seemed to imply for Hofmannsthal on the one hand a transcending of ordinary human life, and on the other hand a failure in human relationships and human love. The clue to them lies in Hofmannsthal's sense that mystical feeling can be an indulgence of self, and in his understanding of the imaginative processes and of poetry as that which separated him from other men, instead of drawing him closer to them. The symbolism of the drama has then to be interpreted by reference to Hofmannsthal's own personal problems as a man and as an artist, and the conclusion he gives to it indicates that he has outgrown the work as he has written it. At the end of the fifth act Hofmannsthal is impelled to express a warning, not against dark powers as we should find them in folk fairy-tale, nor against the dark power of the Christian devil, but against "das fürchterliche Unbegreifliche" [73] in his own personal sense.

[72] *Die Neue Rundschau*, 1954, pp. 349 f.
[73] G 448.

6

Thus, in spite of the fact that there is no frame of reference for this work in any accepted absolute scheme, Hofmannsthal makes his simple onlookers in the final scene sense disaster, and sing their hymn to God for the protection of the miner against "Die Kräfte, so im Dunklen sind", and for his return to the embrace of human love:

> Der Bergmann fährt in finstern Schacht,
> Daraußen läßt er Weib und Kind.
> Es rührn ihn an mit großer Macht
> Die Kräfte, so im Dunklen sind.
>
> Herr! nimm ihn Du in Deinen Schutz—
> Sonst ist ihm schnell sein Sinn verwirrt, —
> Daß er, ein Mensch, mit Ehr und Nutz
> Dem Finstern wiederum entwird,
>
> Daß er an seines Hauses Schwell
> Sich nicht erst lang besinnen muß,
> Mit unverstörter Seele schnell
> Sich freu an Menschenblick und -kuß.

In other words, what shall it profit a man, if he shall gain his own soul, and lose the whole world?

FROM HIGH LANGUAGE TO DIALECT
A STUDY IN HOFMANNSTHAL'S CHANGE OF MEDIUM

BY J. B. BEDNALL

I

> Hier ist eine höfliche Andeutung ebensoviel wert wie
> drüben ein Messerstich in die Rippen.
>
> *Cristinas Heimreise* [1]

One of the things about Hofmannsthal which every student has to
know is that, while still in his teens, he wrote a certain amount of
high-class lyric poetry, and that then something seems to have gone
wrong, as a result of which he hung up his singing-robes behind the
kitchen door and turned to writing plays and libretti instead. The more
deeply instructed will also be able to explain that, in some curious
way, the cause of the whole trouble appears to have been a growing
consciousness that the very tools of his trade—words—were somehow letting him down. It is all true as far as it goes; but Hofmannsthal scholarship has gone further; words do not let *us* down. We have
ready-made labels for the phases and causes of the whole long-drawn-
out process. "Der Anfang ist pure Magie" [2], says Hofmannsthal;
"Präexistenz", we chorus; the person of the author seems to lurk just
out of sight in his works: "Ichverschwiegenheit", we say (after Broch);
in 1902, a year of particularly acute doubts and depression, an essay
is written which fixes once and for all in words an aspect of the problem: "Chandos-Krise", we say. There is an irony in all this which
would have appealed to Hofmannsthal himself, the more so since he
personally supplied many of the terms with which we etherize our
specimen. And when we do not etherize, we etherealize. It is fatally
attractive to pluck pregnant obscurities from diaries, the *Buch der
Freunde* and *Ad me Ipsum* and work them up into a fragrant mystical

---

[1] L I 177.
[2] A 238.

6*

nosegay to tease our readers out of thought: whether many new insights are gained by reshuffling the same old pack of abstractions is more doubtful. "Mir ist manchmal, als ob alle Worte, die's gibt, nur dazu da wären, daß man sich damit verwirrt" [3], says Silvia. And yet, if we are to have any critical basis at all for interpretation and evaluation, we cannot ignore the hints Hofmannsthal provides for us; we are obliged to pick our way through this perilous terrain and familiarize ourselves with its topography and terminology. In such a process, distinctions are more important than apparent similarities. "Ja, auf die Goldwaage legt die Welt ihre Wörter nicht" [4], says Mme. Laroche earlier in the same play. We should take the hint.

I have tried to adopt this attitude in putting together the present essay, which is an attempt to take a steady look at some of the factors involved in Hofmannsthal's abandonment of lyric poetry for dialect comedy, a sort of prolegomenon or theoretical basis for evaluation of his writings in his native tongue, a tongue we could call Austrian German or just plain Austrian; which he himself called "österreichischer Dialekt", and which the philologist—amongst others—tends to call sub-standard German. The last-named, of course, means nothing derogatory by his "sub-standard": Austrian is clearly not standard German, and since his fondness for scaling his material moves the philologist to place it in some sort of spatial relationship to the standard, it clearly has to be 'sub' rather than 'super'. Others—mainly Germans—feel that Austrian is sub-standard in a quite different sense. The mere fact that Hofmannsthal should have chosen to employ it condemned him in some eyes: in Gundolf's, for example, who fancied that he had despatched and interred the traitor when he expressed the rhetorical hope: "[Borchardt] wird wohl jetzt selbst nicht mehr frivol genug sein, den heutigen Hofmannsthal der Dialekt-Komödien und Opern-Texte der deutschen Jugend als Meister und Vorbild zu preisen" [5]. Borchardt need not have let this anger him: it is not Hofmannsthal whom posterity has buried. There is little one can do about this kind of prejudice except shrug one's shoulders and regret that the

[3] L II 94.
[4] L II 68.
[5] Quoted in: *Der Briefwechsel Hugo von Hofmannsthal—Rudolf Borchardt.* Frankfurt a. M., 1954, p. 227.

persons concerned have no *Organ* for the flavour and potentialities of Austrian as an aesthetic medium.

Scarcely less insensitive is that inner rejection which goes with a sentimental attachment to things Austrian and seems to be based on an epicurean appreciation of the consoling and relaxing surface aspects of the national character and culture; a rejection which fastens on words such as "frühgereift und zart und traurig . . . halbes, heimliches Empfinden" [6] as if they explained the whole of the *res austriaca*. The ambivalence of the attitude is well illustrated in the letter Stefan George wrote to Hofmannsthal congratulating him on having escaped the baneful influence of Vienna: "In Ihrem engeren land jedoch (dessen verhältnisse wie Sie vielleicht einmal erfahren werden ich besser weiß als Sie ahnen und das ich sehr 'liebe) weht ein müder verlassener zug und Ihre ganze dortige jugend hat etwas rückgratloses bei äußerlicher überbildung und gefällt sich [in] einer äußerlichen süßlichen verkommenheit" [7]. He did not post the letter, in an access of tact as welcome as, we feel, it must have been rare. Emil Staiger shows a truer appreciation when he speaks of "der österreichische Geist, der vornehme, der Unergründliches gern in gefällige Anmut verbirgt und, wenn er nur erheitert, auf ein tieferes Verstehen mit einem Lächeln je und je verzichtet" [8].

It is with reluctance that one speaks, in these positivist times, of the spirit of a language. But one is forced to describe one's experience in some such terms when listening to Austrian used creatively in the way Hofmannsthal could use it. I say: 'used creatively'. There are few writers Hofmannsthal himself would concede to be "Austrian" in the full sense [9], but a host of others better described as *Heimatdichter* who use more or less faithful approximations to some local dialect. Every language, no matter how geographically restricted, has overtones and associations for those who have created it as an instrument of communication—its present is redolent of its past; but a distinction has to be made between the use of a language for reasons of realism,

---

[6] G 44, 45.

[7] *Der Briefwechsel zwischen George und Hofmannsthal.* Düsseldorf, 1953, p. 257.

[8] *Meisterwerke deutscher Sprache.* Zürich, 1948, p. 259.

[9] cf. letter (22 March, 1922) to S. Fischer, *Die Neue Rundschau*, 1954, p. 398.

sentiment or even some sort of *Blut und Boden* local patriotism on the one hand, and the deliberate exploitation of its expressive possibilities for an aesthetic end. This latter is Hofmannsthal's practice. It should further be noted as an empirically verifiable fact that great master-pieces are not written in the dialect of Hintertupfingen im Niederen Zillertal, for the simple reason that it lacks historico-cultural ampli-tude; whereas Austrian German—a dialect amalgam of South Bava-rian and High German with Slav, Romance und Magyar elements—for all its subtle social and professional variations *is* a *Kultursprache,* a uniquely rich medium of communication, a mediator of the culture which produced it and which it produced—and as perishable as that cul-ture. "Vielleicht", says Staiger, in elegiac mood, of *Der Schwierige,*"wird eines Tages seine leise Sprache unhörbar, und ratlos legen spätere Ge-schlechter dieses Ding beiseite" [10]. Perhaps that day has already arrived, as Hofmannsthal foresaw. There remains, however, the con-soling task of making a study of how he used it, and how he came to use it; a task in which the literary historian must take care to equip himself equally with knowledge of and sympathy for his subject: the Austrian thing. "Quid faceret eruditio sine dilectione?" asks St. Ber-nard. "Inflaret. Quid, absque eruditione dilectio? Erraret."

II

Moi! moi qui me suis dit mage ou ange, dispensé de toute morale, je suis rendu au sol, avec un devoir à chercher, et la réalité rugueuse à étreindre! Paysan!

Rimbaud: *Une Saison en Enfer*

A term frequently employed to describe the attitude to and experience of the world revealed in Hofmannsthal's lyric poems and playlets is "mysticism". We have his own authority for its use. In *Ad me Ipsum* he speaks of the two ways to existence as: "Die Introversion als Weg in die Existenz. (Der mystische Weg)", and "Der Weg zum Sozialen als Weg zum höheren Selbst: der nicht-mystische Weg" [12], and these are only two key passages among many similar exercises in self-analysis scattered throughout his writings. The term has certain obvious

[10] *op. cit.,* p. 259.
[11] *Oeuvres.* Paris, 1937, p. 307.
[12] A 215, 217.

advantages, as well as being of a kind likely to recommend itself to critics living in an age of do-it-yourself mysticism when a dose of mescalin, a nibble at the appropriate mushroom or a glance at a manual of Zen Archery have placed the Dark Night of the Soul within the reach of all, without the discomfort and inconvenience of that Dark Night of the Senses which, so the masters tell us, ought properly to precede it. The difficulty arises when one seeks a definition of mysticism comprehensive enough to have some generic usefulness without being so attenuated as to lose its cutting edge. There is an added complication in the fact that, as one would expect, Hofmannsthal himself uses it in a variety of different senses; Werner Metzeler distinguishes three such: "1. 'mystisch' im Sinne von 'geheimnisvoll' . . . 2. 'mystisch' im Sinne von 'rauschhaft' . . . 3. 'mystisch' als Umschreibung dafür, daß man sich einer höchsten Welt angehörig fühlt" [13]. Metzeler has to concede: "Die drei Bedeutungsnuancen des Begriffs 'mystisch', die sich in Hofmannsthals Schaffen nachweisen lassen, gehen häufig ineinander über . . ." [14] whilst nevertheless (and very properly) defending their usefulness. It is the third category, however—it could, for the sake of brevity, be described as the unitive experience—which needs closest definition; and certain essential distinctions must be made about the nature of the unitive experience itself, since it is his insight into these distinctions which proved crucial for Hofmannsthal's own development.

Setting aside for the moment the two other categories (of which the first refers to what is really no more than a handy epithet, whilst the second—with its Nietzschean overtones—denotes that dionysian striving for union through sensual intoxication which Hofmannsthal certainly treated at length, but which can hardly be said to have been a major factor in his own experience), I shall define mysticism as a transconceptual experience of union with the ultimate ground of being, and then distinguish two main types: the theistic and the pantheistic, according to whether the mystic experiences the world as created and contingent (ontological dualism, the metaphysical position of Judaism, Christianity and Islam) or as self-contained and possibly

[13] *Ursprung und Krise von Hofmannsthals Mystik*. München, 1956, pp. 18—22.
[14] *ibid.*, p. 23.

self-explanatory (idealist or materialist monism, an attitude common to Eastern religions).

Since the mystical experience is by definition inexpressible in conceptual terms, it will be difficult to determine from the mystic's utterances to which of the two categories his experience properly belongs, whatever his formal beliefs may be. For mystics, words are the great trap. If they would speak of their experiences, they must employ metaphor; and thus it happens that the rapturous imagery in which, say, Angelus Silesius celebrates the *unio mystica* comes to be misinterpreted as a formal belief that the Ancient of Days and Johannes Scheffler are consubstantial. The distinction which must be grasped is that between the attitudes of theistic and pantheistic mysticism; whatever their validity as metaphysical positions may be, we must concede that, if words mean anything at all, we are faced with two quite distinct types of experience. In theistic mysticism (as found principally among Christians and Sufis [15]) the individual is conscious of an affective union with a completely transcendent being—absolute otherness—who is recognized as the ground of all that is; a union in which the human personality is preserved distinct whilst yet being completely transformed, for the eternal instant of the experience, into the object of its love. Such mystics insist that their moments cannot be commanded, but are a free gift for which one must exercise oneself by prayer and a careful exercise of the precepts of justice and charity; this involves a recognition of the social order and the claims (as well as the existence!) of other people, an insistence upon love as the root of moral behaviour, and an uncompromising assertion of the impossibility of self-transcendence without the aid of grace.

Pantheistic mysticism takes two forms, which are closely linked. In one, the individual's ecstatic experience is such that he can truly be said to stand outside himself—"JE est un autre", says Rimbaud [16]; he no longer feels himself to be finite and contingent, but is aware of that within the ground of his own being which is identical with the eternal

---

[15] It is worth noting that when Hofmannsthal quotes a Sufi mystic, it is the affective nature of the doctrine which appeals to him: "Wundervolles Wort des Dschellaledin Rumi, tiefer als alles: 'Wer die Gewalt des Reigens kennt, fürchtet nicht den Tod. Denn er weiß, daß Liebe tötet.'" (In the essay *Sebastian Melmoth* of 1905, P II 138.)

[16] In the celebrated letter to Paul Demeny of 15 May, 1871.

stuff of the universe. The classical expression of this experience is the upanishadic identification of ātman with Brahman, the inmost self of the individual with the inner reality of the world; but (as Mr. Aldous Huxley has been at pains to show) [17] it is found in all places and at all times as a constant factor in human experience. Sometimes, not always, the mystics—if such they can be called, for it appears that quite ordinary people can be taken unawares by these fits of alienation—apply the label "God" to the all-embracing oneness of which they become overwhelmingly conscious.

The other form of pantheistic experience is that in which one becomes so intensely aware of the individuality and ontological uniqueness of other things—trees, chairs, people—that one flows out into them, as it were, lives with their life as long as the mood lasts, and is, in one's turn, invaded by them. (The parallels with the experiences described in Hofmannsthal's lyric poetry are obvious here). At other times, however, the world of outside things appears hostile, frightening; the individual is helpless, metaphysically isolated, menaced. It has been pointed out that such experiences correspond very closely with the two phases of the manic-depressive psychosis; they are symptoms of acute schizophrenia; and they can be induced by drugs [18]; there is a link here with the second (dionysian) connotation listed by Metzeler in Hofmannsthal's use of the word "mystisch". William James, who recorded many interesting examples of the phenomenon, delivered judgment against indulgences of this kind as not being consistent with what he called the "religion of healthy-mindedness" [19]. The important characteristic of both these pantheistic types of unitive experience is the individual's sense of complete freedom from any kind of moral obligation: even the *tat tvam asi* of the *Chandogya* Upanishad, which became so important for Schopenhauer's ethic of compassion, depends in the last resort upon a self-regarding consideration for others; and this is the sense in which Hofmannsthal used the phrase in 1891 when reviewing Amiel's *Fragments d'un journal intime* [20].

[17] In: *The Perennial Philosophy*. London, 1946.
[18] cf. Aldous Huxley: *The Doors of Perception*. London, 1954.
[19] *The Varieties of Religious Experience*, 1902. The significance of James's attitude for Hofmannsthal at this time should not be overlooked.
[20] P I 24. Incidentally, Amiel's *Journal* records unitive experiences of the pantheistic type [cf. *Journal*, I (Geneva 1919), 49, a passage quoted by W. James].

The relevance of the above distinctions to Hofmannsthal's case should be clear. Prescinding for the moment from the para-mystical experiences associated with lyric creation, one can say with confidence that upon the purely abstract level of personal convictions Hofmannsthal's growing acceptance of a traditional Christian standpoint, with its doctrines of divine transcendence, grace and love of one's neighbour, would inevitably cause the amoral egocentric universe of the pantheistic mystic to appear suspect, whilst his unitive experiences would seem explicable in non-metaphysical terms. By the same token, the ethical and institutional tendencies of theistic mysticism will increasingly appear as the mystical norm.

The difficulties inseparable from this type of subject are multiplied when one comes to consider the poetry of mystics and what is sometimes called mystical poetry, but which upon closer analysis is seen to contain a wide range of experiences of the pantheistic type, from the nature-mysticism of Wordsworth to the ecstasies of Rimbaud, a scale upon which Hofmannsthal with his rather more discreet moments may be thought of as coming halfway. What should be clear from the outset is that it is not necessary to make any lengthy excursion into the realm of spiritual semantics to see that the experience of the poet and the experience of the mystic, even though the former may *be* a practising mystic, are not identical. Otherwise one would be forced to assert that the poem itself is the mystical experience, which presumably can be communicated to and vicariously enjoyed by the reader; whereas, in fact, the greatest mystical poets (one may take St. John of the Cross as an example) insist that when they write their mystical experience becomes the basis of their aesthetic experience. And it is this that they communicate. In aesthetic terms, there is no generic difference between what they *make* of their experience of the One and what another poet *makes* of his experience of an old boot: the difference lies in the nature of the mystical and the poetic experience themselves.

This point having been made, however, it must be conceded that mystical and poetic experience show such striking similarities both in their mode of operation and (in so far as the mystic is moved to communicate his experience) in the effects they produce, that parallelisms, cross-fertilizations and even mistaken identifications can hardly fail to arise, particularly with lyric poets of a certain type. The key word here is "identification", because this is the characteristic mode of all contacts between the self and the non-self (to use as general a term as possible for extra-mental reality). Mysticism and magic both aim at identification, the one for the sake of love, the other for the sake of power; the identification sought is a real one. Abstract thought and poetry, on the other hand, depend upon an ideal identification; with the one, the intellect's grasp of an extra-mental existent issues in a concept, whilst with the other the subjectivity of the poet submits to its intuition of things in themselves and their interrelationships; it is a dark [21], pre-conceptual knowledge through the medium of creative emotion, and issues in an aesthetic act. "Die Poesie löst fremdes Dasein im eignen auf", says Novalis [22].

It is evident that the analogy between the two types of identification with which we are primarily concerned (the magico-mystical and the poetic) will be most clearly marked, and will give rise to the greatest emotional confusion, in the case of the lyric poet, if one recollects that, of all literary forms, the lyric is that in which subject and object are fused in an instant of timeless contemplation [23]. Moreover, there is more than one kind of lyric poet. "We should certainly distinguish two types of poets", says René Wellek, "the objective and the sub-jective: those who, like Keats and T. S. Eliot, stress the poet's 'nega-tive capability', his openness to the world, the obliteration of his concrete personality, and the opposite type of the poet, who aims at displaying his personality, wants to draw a self-portrait, to confess, to express himself" [24]. Whether or not we are prepared to accept Wellek's (and Keats') two categories as exhaustive, there can be no denying the existence of the Keatsian type of poet, nor can we afford to overlook the fact that Hofmannsthal accepted Keats' definition as being true of his own poetic temperament. He wrote to Stephan Gruss

---

[21] Hence the importance of the symbol "night" for the Romantics, who pioneered the exploration of the creative self; cf. Albert Béguin: *L'Âme romantique et le Rêve*, Cahiers du Sud, Marseille, 1937.

[22] *Fragmente* 1190.

[23] "[Der Dichter] ist es, der in sich die Elemente der Zeit verknüpft. In ihm oder nirgends ist Gegenwart." (P II 282).

[24] Austin Warren and René Wellek: *Theory of Literature*. London, 1955, p. 71.

in 1907: "[Ich weiß], daß die sonderbare, fast unheimliche seelische Beschaffenheit, diese scheinbar alles durchdringende Lieblosigkeit und Treulosigkeit, die dich an mir so sehr befremdet und mich manchmal so sehr geängstigt hat — der *Tor und der Tod* ist nichts als ein Ausdruck dieser Angst — daß diese seelische Beschaffenheit nichts andres ist, als die Verfassung des Dichters unter den Dingen und Menschen. Der schöne Brief von Keats ... mit den merkwürdigen Klagen über das Chamäleondasein des Dichters ('he has no identity: he is continually in for, and filling, some other body.—It is a wretched thing to confess, but it is a very fact, that not one word I ever utter can be taken for granted as an opinion growing out of my identical nature. How can it be, when I have no nature?' usf. usf.) Dieser Brief hat mich sehr entlastet, wie er mir vor Jahren das erstemal in die Hand kam" [25].

Given this close correspondence between the states of mystical contemplation and lyrical creation, the question arises as to whether the experiences described by the poet of negative capability, supersensitive as he is to the invasion of outside things, are any different in kind from the experiences which I have placed in the category of pantheistic mysticism. Certainly, the world of Hofmannsthal's *Präexistenz* seems to correspond at all points, a world described, in so far as words can convey anything at all, by Lord Chandos:

"Mir erschien damals in einer Art von andauernder Trunkenheit das ganze Dasein als eine große Einheit: geistige und körperliche Welt schien mir keinen Gegensatz zu bilden, ebensowenig höfisches und tierisches Wesen, Kunst und Unkunst, Einsamkeit und Gesellschaft; in allem fühlte ich Natur, in den Verirrungen des Wahnsinns ebensowohl wie in den äußersten Verfeinerungen eines spanischen Zeremoniells; in den Tölpelhaftigkeiten junger Bauern nicht minder als in den süßesten Allegorien; und in aller Natur fühlte ich mich selber ... Das eine war wie das andere; keines gab dem anderen weder an traumhafter überirdischer Natur, noch an leiblicher Gewalt nach, und so gings fort durch die ganze Breite des Lebens, rechter und und linker Hand; überall war ich mitten drinnen, wurde nie ein Scheinhaftes gewahr: Oder es ahnte mir, alles wäre Gleichnis und jede Kreatur ein Schlüssel der anderen ..." [26]

[25] *Briefe 1900—1909.* Wien, 1937, pp. 253—254.
[26] P II 10—11.

It is sweet, while it lasts, "Immer frisch auf Traumglück auszugehen/ Und zu schwanken auch in Traumgefahr." There is hardly a one amongst mystics of the pantheistic type who did not at some time suffer from a bad conscience. Some—Baudelaire, for instance— roundly declared that their experiences were a contact with evil [27]. This is a recurrent attitude which is notably absent from theistic mysticism. All charms fly at the mere touch of cold philosophy, and as the heir to a centuries-old German intellectual tradition Hofmannsthal was peculiarly vulnerable. The attack when it came was from three quarters: from his reflections upon the mystical tradition in general and his own experiences in particular; from the post-Kantian thought of the nineteenth century; and from life itself. "Die Menschen suchen ihre Seele und finden dafür das Leben" [28]. In each case, despair of language is the consequence.

It is clear that for the pantheist an experience of transcendent being will come as something of a shock, bringing as it does considerations of the knowability and utterability of that being, and a whole new range of ethical perspectives and imperatives. But there is that in the main tradition of Western mysticism, particularly that apophatic stream, tinged with neo-platonism, which derives from St. Gregory of Nyssa, which also appears to command to silence. "Ah, Lord God! behold I cannot speak", says Jeremiah [29]. In this case the mystic's experience reveals to him the complete helplessness of human language in the face of transcendent reality, and he indulges in gestures of rhetorical despair at the mere idea of capturing the infinite in a concept. From doubts of this kind, the step to a complete denial of the ability of language to put us in contact with extra-mental reality is not a far one.

But if theistic mysticism tends to issue in silence, the lyric poet who conceives a doubt as to the validity of his unitive experiences, or who questions the morality of indulgence in them, will *a fortiori* tend to

[27] The *locus classicus* for this belief is probably in Porphyry's life of Plotinus; the latter was inspired by a higher daemon, says Porphyry, and at the moment of his death this daemon, in the form of a serpent, glided under the bed on which he was lying, and into a hole in the wall (II, 25).

[28] A 117.

[29] Jer. I, 6.

suspect the linguistic medium in which he works. Certainly, Hofmannsthal himself, in retrospective self-analysis, came to view his *Präexistenz* as a concomitant of the lyrical state, and something of a psychosis to boot [30]. He made Balzac prophesy: "Um 1890 werden die geistigen Erkrankungen der Dichter, ihre übermäßig gesteigerte Empfindsamkeit, die namenlose Bangigkeit ihrer herabgestimmten Stunden, ihre Disposition, der symbolischen Gewalt auch unscheinbarer Dinge zu unterliegen, ihre Unfähigkeit, sich mit dem existierenden Worte beim Ausdruck ihrer Gefühle zu begnügen, das alles wird eine allgemeine Krankheit unter den jungen Männern und Frauen der oberen Stände sein" [31]. He calls the condition an illness. The unitive experience, called into doubt, ceases to be creative. "Der Dichter, aus jener höchsten Welt (deren Bote der Tod) herausgefallen" [32].

III

Wenn wir was reden, Livio, tauschen wir
Nur schale, abgegriffne Zeichen aus ...

Der weiße Fächer [33]

If such difficulties may be thought of as constituting an assault upon the private aspect of language, that is to say, upon words as the medium through which creative intuition can issue in an aesthetic act (a fate which, though it may be common to many poets, is personal to each), there is a further dilemma in which Hofmannsthal, as a *fin de siècle* writer, was inevitably involved: the modern breakdown of language in its social aspect as a system of signs mediating the human community's apprehension of reality. Ever since Descartes locked us up in our own minds, and Kant threw away the key, we have been suffering from an acute phase of the chronic antinomy: how can a concept, which is a fixed and lasting thing, be appropriately applied to that restless kaleidoscope which is the sensible appearance of phenomena? The problem is a serious one, for the poet no less than for the philosopher. Can a word do more than stick a convenient label

[30] cf. Mr. Michael Hamburger's remarks in: *Hugo von Hofmannsthal—Poems and Verse Plays*. Bollingen Institute, New York, 1961, p. xxxii.
[31] P II 48.
[32] A 223.
[33] G 225.

on the thing? How can it claim to lift the thing out of that Heraclitean flux [34] which is the world we live in, when the thing changes and crumbles even as we look at it and seek to capture it?

> Mir ist zumut,
> daß ich die Schwäche von allem Zeitlichen recht spüren muß,
> bis in mein Herz hinein,
> wie man nichts halten soll,
> wie man nichts packen kann,
> wie alles zerlauft zwischen den Fingern,
> alles sich auflöst, wonach wir greifen,
> alles zergeht wie Dunst und Traum [35].

Is the word with which we seek to describe it any more than a half-truth, and thus a lie? And do not words, because of their permanence, seek to endow the thing with a false eternity, leading to a further divorce from reality? That is the problem; let us quick-freeze it and retain its flavour: it is epistemological. That Hofmannsthal not only pondered it deeply on an abstract level, but also lived it through his art, is a fact that admits of no question. Paul Requadt has shown how his reading of Nietzsche, and through him of Lichtenberg, gave him an early experience of sceptical nominalism [36]. It would be instructive, too, to know the extent of Hofmannsthal's readings in Francis Bacon, and particularly whether he ever studied *The Advancement of Learning*. Certainly, there are suggestive parallels between Bacon's nominalistically-inclined enumeration of the sources of error in the human intellect—"idols" he calls them—and Hofmannsthal's own remarks on the subject. Bacon's idols are those of the tribe, the cave, the market, the theatre and the schools, corresponding to tendencies to error inhering respectively in human nature, individual human beings, human language, received systems of thought and blind conformity to dialectical rules. It is the *idola fori* which concern us particularly, of course. Errors through human language can arise, says Bacon, either because words can be used to refer to things which do not exist

---

[34] cf. J. Sofer: 'Die Welttheater Hugo von Hofmannsthals und ihre Voraussetzungen bei Heraklit und Calderon'. *Vorträge und Abhandlungen der österreichischen Leogesellschaft*, XXXVII (Wien 1934), 12—20.

[35] L I 333.

[36] In: 'Sprachverleugnung und Mantelsymbolik im Werke Hofmannsthals'. *Deutsche Vierteljahrsschrift*, XXIX (1955), 255—283.

(abstracts, imaginary creatures), or because they do not adequately describe—exhaust the essence—of the thing to which they refer [37]. It is of more than passing interest that Hofmannsthal uses the same terminology in a diary entry which appears to date from December 1893: "Götzendienst, Anbetung eines eidolon, Sinnbildes, das einmal für einen Menschen lebendig war, Mirakel gewirkt hat, durchflammende Offenbarung des göttlichen Geheimnisses der Welt gewesen ist; solche eidola sind die Begriffe der Sprache. Sie sind für gewöhnlich nicht heiliger als Götzenbilder, nicht wahrhaftiger 'reich' als eine vergrabene Urne, nicht wahrhaftiger 'stark' als ein vergrabenes Schwert" [38]. The difference between the two positions is one of emphasis: Bacon views such idolatry as endemic in human language, Hofmannsthal is concerned with a contemporary dilemma; in a deeper analysis, however, the one is reducible to the other. For both men, too, the goal of human striving must be the transcendence of innate and environmental limitations: "Fünf Schicksale leiten den Menschen: seine geistige Natur, sein Körper, sein Volk, seine Heimat, die Sprache: sich über alle fünf zu erheben, ist das Göttliche" [39]. If one attempts a comparison between Bacon's five idols and Hofmannsthal's five destinies, the followings scheme emerges: Tribe = geistige Natur, Cave = Körper, Market = Sprache; Theatre and Schools are then loosely correlated with Volk and Heimat as referring to concentric environmental circles. In the absence of direct evidence, one can only speak of suggestive affinities; but even such affinities with the thought of a thoroughgoing nominalist like Bacon throw light on the essentially epistemological nature of this aspect of Hofmannsthal's linguistic problem.

The extent to which Hofmannsthal was influenced by his absorption of the critical theories of knowledge current since the sixteenth century can best be seen from the scattered remarks in his diaries and the *Buch der Freunde;* in his literary works he depicted and pondered the effects. Sometimes the reference is direct, sometimes oblique, as one

---

[37] *The Advancement of Learning,* ed. Spalding. London, 1857, III, 396—397; also in the *Novum Organon,* Partis Secundae Summa digesta in Aphorismas, XLIII, LIX—LX.

[38] A 105—106.

[39] A 37.

would expect from a poet whose browsings in philosophy were eclectic rather than systematic, designed to confirm what his sensibility told him about the world he lived in, rather than to direct and mould that sensibility. Sometimes we find echoes, sometimes only echoes of echoes [40], but a consistency of experience emerges nevertheless. Of the Heraclitean flux he says: "Der Geist besiegt die Materie. Ihre stärkste Waffe im Kampf mit ihm ist ihre Flüchtigkeit" [41]. There is clear evidence of Cartesian dualism in remarks such as: "Die Ideen sind vermöge der Realitäten für uns existent (= für uns geweckt, entbunden, weil in uns wie Granatapfel all in eins), aber nicht in den Realitäten zu finden" [42], or: "Die Welt der Worte eine Scheinwelt, in sich geschlossen, wie die der Farben, und der Welt der Phänomene koordiniert" [43]. He quotes Blake: "Generelle Kenntnis ist entfernte Kenntnis, das Wissen besteht aus Einzelheiten, ebenso wie das Glück" [44]. While accepting, however, many of the attitudes of a critical philosophy, Hofmannsthal could not feel at ease with the *Weltgefühl* it produced, particularly since this ran counter to his own poetic intuitions of the nature of outside reality. He was inclined to view the Germans as peculiarly prone to the corrosive influence of epistemological scepticism: "Nicht durch den kategorischen Imperativ, den man immer im Munde führt, hat Kant auf ganze Generationen gewaltig gewirkt, sondern durch den Kritizismus, in dem das scheue, weltlose der Deutschen seinen abstrakten Ausdruck fand" [45]. The result: "Der Deutsche hat eine ungeheure Sachlichkeit und ein sehr geringes Verhältnis zu den Dingen" [46].

There could hardly be a clearer statement than this of the effect upon our culture of the spread of critical theories of knowledge. A wedge has been driven between the individual and the outside world, in which he now feels himself a stranger. Many modern poets have

---

[40] cf. the Kantian tone of: "Wie der innerste Sinn aller Menschen Zeit und Raum und die Welt der Dinge um sie her schafft, so ... usw." (P II 283).

[41] A 40.

[42] A 124—125.

[43] A 119.

[44] A 45.

[45] A 47.

[46] A 58.

explained the phenomenon in terms of the human condition after the loss of primal innocence [47]—an event which is sometimes accepted literally, more often viewed as man's groping intuition or allegorical interpretation of the disruptive effects of individuation: hypertrophy of the rational faculty at the expense of non-conceptual forms of cognition. Hofmannsthal has his own version of it: "Unsern Blicken ist Vollkommnes seit dem Tag des Sündenfalls verborgen" [48]. The theory is unhistorical. Whatever the truth may be about man's awareness through the ages of the tension between abstraction and intuition (and it seems to be pretty ancient: "And now the wild creatures had all fled away; Enkidu was grown weak, for wisdom was in him, and the thoughts of a man were in his heart" [49]), the fact remains that our modern dissociation of sensibility seems as much as anything the result of a lack of balance between the rational and intuitive faculties caused, not by the very existence—it would be a bold man who maintained that we could do without it and remain human—but by the malfunction of the power of abstractive cognition. The thought is no longer felt to unite the existence of the thinker with that of the thing; it does not grasp the essence of the thing; instead, it identifies it by its sensible appearance. Abstract knowledge which has thus abandoned its true vocation—that search for the inner nature of things and their relationships which leads to wisdom—celebrates triumphs of its own. The physico-mathematical classification of phenomena which is made possible by the shuffling of lifeless abstractions has led to a staggering conquest of the material world, to a peremptory use of things which, because they are not truly known, is an abuse. It is left for the poets to attempt reparation; and this they can do because their intuitive knowledge is true knowledge.

Hofmannsthal expressed his realization of the dilemma in many places and in many forms: in his frequent adverse comments on "der wissenschaftliche Geist"; in his own abandonment of a projected university career; in linguistic matters: "Diejenigen, welche alle Sprachen

[47] Kleist was one of the earliest (in *Über das Marionettentheater*), and only recently Mr. William Golding has told us that that is what his *The Inheritors* is about.
[48] 'Ghasel I', G 488.
[49] *The Epic of Gilgamesh*, English version by N. K. Sandars. Penguin Books, 1960. p. 63.

so lehren, als ob sie tot wären, nennt man Philologen" [50]; in the men of learning in his plays. But the analysis went deeper: "Es war eine unerhörte Herrschaft über die Natur. Der alte Kampf mit der Natur schien ausgekämpft. Technisch ausgebeutet als der Sklave lag die Natur da, nicht als Dämon, als geheimnisvoller Lehrer, als gigantischer Feind ... [das] Resultat der gesamten Weisheit und Wissenschaft unserer Tage ... Das tausendfache internationale Ich, dieses europäische Wesen, für das diese ganze Maschine lief, es war nicht gewaltig. Diese berauschende Eroberung des Geistes hat sein Leben nach innen umgestaltet mit der Gewalt einer Elementarkatastrophe. Sie hat uns fast mehr zermalmt als vordem unsere Ohnmacht gegen die Natur" [51]. His analysis of the effects of this situation, and its cause, is incisive: "Eine verzehrende Ironie [ist] über all unser Tun gekommen. Eine Kritik, die alles ergriff, nach innen. Zweifel an der Möglichkeit, mit der Sprache etwas vom Weltstoff fassen zu können. Sprachkritik als Welle der Verzweiflung über die Welt laufend: als jene Seelenverfassung, die sich ergeben hatte, *weil nicht Wahrheit sondern Technik das Ergebnis des wissenschaftlichen Geistes gewesen war*" [52].
I said that poets retain their intuitions of reality. But they, too, are the victims of their age when it comes to expressing what they know. They suffer from the depreciation of mythical and symbolical interpretations of existence, that fragmentation of the collective consciousness which is the price we pay for technological mastery. But words themselves betray them. Cut off from their rootedness in things, words become opaque. "Die Worte haben sich vor die Dinge gestellt" [53]. When the process of doubt began in Hofmannsthal, it was, characteristically, with abstract value-judgments that it began, spreading finally to the whole of the vocabulary in which his lyrical unitive experience had been expressed. As early as 1896, six years before the Chandos letter, he wrote to Stefan George: "für wessen Dichtungen vermöchte ich mit Zuversicht und Glauben einzutreten, solang ich, an mir selber irre, erst von jedem neuen Tag schwankend und ängstlich die Bestätigung erwarten muß, daß ich überhaupt die Worte, mit denen wir

---

[50] P I 349.
[51] P III 376.
[52] *ibid.* My italics.
[53] P I 265.

Werthe bezeichnen, in den Mund zu nehmen nicht völlig unberechtigt
bin ..." [54]. These are words echoed by Lord Chandos: "Die abstrakten
Worte, deren sich doch die Zunge naturgemäß bedienen muß, um
irgendwelches Urteil an den Tag zu legen, zerfielen mir im Munde
wie modrige Pilze" [55]. Such doubts about words as signs will inevitably
react powerfully with malaise in the private (creative) use of
language, the more so since both involve a direct conflict with that
sovereign freedom in the use of words which is a prerequisite of lyrical
activity. It is not merely that a poet is liable to be hamstrung if his
resolutions are sicklied o'er with the pale cast of thought; at a much
profounder level, a nominalistic attitude is inimical to that epistemological realism which, consciously or unconsciously, is the characteristic
mode of the poet's intuition of the real nature of the world. Nominalism tends to eternalize the sensible appearance of things, whereas the
poet is conscious of nothing more urgently than the peremptory
claims upon him of things in their particularity, their ontological
uniqueness; a reality bearing in upon him ("instressing", Hopkins
would say) which is the ground and substratum of that changing
exterior mediated by the senses. "Niemals setzt die Poesie eine Sache
für eine andere", says Gabriel in the *Gespräch über Gedichte*, "denn es
ist gerade die Poesie, welche fieberhaft bestrebt ist, die Sache selbst zu
setzen, mit einer ganz anderen Energie als die stumpfe Alltagssprache,
mit einer ganz anderen Zauberkraft als die schwächliche Terminologie
der Wissenschaft. Wenn die Poesie etwas tut, so ist es das: daß sie aus
jedem Gebilde der Welt und des Traumes mit durstiger Gier sein
Eigenstes, sein Wesenhaftestes herausschlürft, so wie jene Irrlichter im
Märchen, die überall das Gold herauslecken. Und sie tut es aus dem
gleichen Grunde: weil sie sich vom Mark der Dinge nährt, weil sie
elend verlöschen würde, wenn sie dies nährende Gold nicht aus allen
Fugen, allen Spalten in sich zöge" [56].
The power which drove Hofmannsthal out of his primal Eden was
what William Rey has called "Die Drohung der Zeit" [57]. Time is the

---

[54] 13 October, 1896. *op. cit.*, pp. 112—113.
[55] P II 13.
[56] P II 99.
[57] 'Die Drohung der Zeit in Hofmannsthals Frühwerk'. *Euphorion*, XLVIII (1954),
280—310.

measure of mutability; and nothing is more patent than Hofmannsthal's oppressive awareness of the transience of earthly things:

> Dies ist ein Ding, das keiner voll aussinnt,
> Und viel zu grauenvoll, als daß man klage:
> Daß alles gleitet und vorüberrinnt [58].

His very first playlet, *Gestern*, is an ironic comment upon the failure
of his hero to come to terms with this basic fact. The awareness of
time is a threat at all the levels we have so far been considering; in the
words of Lord Chandos: "Allmählich aber breitete sich diese Anfech-
tung aus wie ein um sich fressender Rost" [59]. For the neoplatonic
mystic whose gaze is fixed on the eternal and unchanging essences, it
is a confirmation that he is right in turning away from a world of
shadows; there is an echo of this in the text from St. Gregory of Nyssa
with which Hofmannsthal prefaced *Ad me Ipsum:* "Er, der Liebhaber
der höchsten Schönheit, hielt was er schon gesehen hatte für ein Ab-
bild dessen, was er noch nicht gesehen hatte und begehrte dieses selbst,
das Urbild, zu geniessen" [60]. But a sense of time is equally fatal to
unitive experiences of the pantheistic type; it breaks the charmed
circle of inner and outer being; the *Priesterzögling*, "ganz gebrochen
von dem Begriff der Zeit" [61], is turned out of the temple into the
street. An experience of time is one thing, an acceptance of its implications is another. To accept is to bind oneself, to have a fate; and this,
for the lyric poet, can lead to crisis: "Der lyrische Dichter hat kein
Schicksal", says Emil Staiger. "Dort, wo das Schicksal, der Widerstand
eines fremden Daseins einsetzen könnte, hört sein Dichten jeweils
auf" [62].
Even more destructive, however, is the impact of an awareness of
change upon an epistemology of a nominalist cast. The concepts which
are meant to link us with reality are torn loose from things and seek
to impose a false eternity upon them. This is the situation depicted in
Das Bergwerk zu Falun: "Im *Bergwerk* ist jenes gewaltig Hinüber-

---

[58] G 17.
[59] P II 13.
[60] A 214.
[61] D III 491, 493.
[62] *Grundbegriffe der Poetik*. Zürich, 1946. p. 88.

ziehende (das die Seele dem Leben entfremdet) erst wirklich gestaltet: das Reich der Worte worin alles Gegenwart. — Das Ganze drückt den Versuch der Seele aus, der Zeit zu entfliehen in das Überzeitliche. Worte reißen das Einzelne aus dem Strom des Vergehens, vergegenwärtigen = verewigen es" [63].

It would, I think, be true to say that the remainder of Hofmannsthal's life was an endeavour to come to terms with the problem of time and eternity. The corrosive effect of time was a permanent threat: it was the meaning and possibility of eternity which had first to be thrashed out, starting with that painful process which led from the testing and rejection of a false notion of eternity as time open at both ends to that transcendence of change which can be achieved by the acceptance of a fate and metamorphosis through love. It is at this point that moral considerations occur and gradually assume a dominant role. To cling obstinately to one's magic powers over language is to incur guilt: "Die magische Herrschaft über das Wort das Bild das Zeichen darf nicht aus der Praeexistenz in die Existenz hinübergenommen werden" [64]. The greatness of the temptation, however, cannot be overestimated. In a world which has abandoned the rational search for that wisdom towards which the poet innately tends, he will feel inescapably drawn to the only practical identification apparently left to him: "binden mit dem Schattenbande" [65]; in doing so, poetry is but remaining true to the essential practicality of its own nature: "Magie ist Weisheit, praktisch geworden. Auch unbewußte Weisheit kann praktisch werden. (Für gewöhnlich wird nur das Praktischwerden des Verstandes wahrgenommen.)" [66]. But poetry will then be guilty of *felo de se* through aesthetic pride; "den Dingen ihre Seele abgewinnen, in ihre Blutwärme untertauchen, *aus ihnen mit den Augen ihrer Liebe herausschauen: das ist zugleich alle Poesie*" [67]: if the poet forgets his place as "der lautlose Bruder aller Dinge" [68] this power becomes forfeit.

The path that must now be trodden is what he describes (in Kleistian terms) as "der nicht-mystische Weg. a) durch die Tat, b) durch das Werk,

---

[63] A 241.
[64] A 215—216.
[65] G 74.
[66] A 38.
[67] A 108. My italics.
[68] P II 282.

c) durch das Kind" [69]. What must be avoided (although speech is "*das soziale Element*" [70]) is what he calls "ein Zu-viel im Reden ... Es ist, nach der Einsamkeit der Praeexistenz, die leidenschaftliche Vorwegnahme des Sozialen, bis zum Frevelhaften, auch ein Verwischen der Grenze zwischen Phantasie und Wirklichkeit, also Lüge" [71]. We have reached a situation in which society is filled with a metaphysical disgust in the presence of fine speech: "Die Leute sind es nämlich müde, reden zu hören. Sie haben einen tiefen Ekel vor den Worten" [72]. Words used thus now become instruments of magic aggression:

> alle Worte sind
> wie Wellen, die nach vorwärts wollen, alle
> sind voller Fieber, alle jagen, alle
> ergreifen ihre Beute, alle fassen
> ein Lebendes um seinen Hals, sie schlagen
> die Zähne in ein Lebendes, das flieht
> und fliehend doch sich gibt ... [73].

The only morally acceptable attitude is to seek contact with the outside through a humble acceptance of obligations (things which bind) and, for the rest, to remain silent, either in proud defiance like the last Contarin ("die zusammengepreßte Kraft des Schweigens" [74]) or the more hopeful (although still aristocratic) humility of Chandos, who has intuitions of a way out: "Es ist mir ... als könnten wir in ein neues, ahnungsvolles Verhältnis zum ganzen Dasein treten, wenn wir anfingen, mit dem Herzen zu denken" [75]. Hofmannsthal says of Chandos that his is "die Situation des Mystikers ohne Mystik" [76]; but it is clear from the experiences Chandos describes that he has, in fact, merely abandoned one kind of (pantheistic) mysticism for a practical but ultimately no less traditional type which seeks its experience of the transcendent concurrently with a loving acceptance of the ordinary and everyday. There is a further hint of this in the story Hof-

[69] A 217.
[70] A 231.
[71] *ibid.*
[72] P I 265.
[73] D II 540.
[74] E 88.
[75] P II 18.
[76] A 215.

mannsthal recorded about St. Teresa, who felt an ecstasy coming on while she was frying some fish, but only allowed herself to be enraptured in so far as was consistent with the claims of good cooking [77]. Whether or not he made a conscious distinction between the various mystical tendencies which may be observed in his work, there is no doubt that in his increasing acceptance of traditional Christian themes as embedded in morality and mystery, and in his breaking out of the charmed circular time of his pantheistic experiences in order to attain the linear time of Christian theology with its eschatological implications, he was undergoing a spiral development which ultimately led him back to the acknowledgment (although hardly the practice, as far as we can tell) of the classic forms of theistic mysticism.

IV

Kann wohl den Wert eines Menschen
jemand kennen, der nicht in der Welt
Hitze und Kälte erlitten hat?

Buch der Freunde [78]

I said that the third attack upon the state of *Präexistenz* came from life itself. The very name he applies—in retrospect—to that state, speaks of it as something provisional and, by implication, invalid. It can be established by comparing the course of his mental development with that of his personal career that the heavier the claims life made upon him, the further he was forced to move away from his early paradise. He put it quite simply in a letter to Rudolf Alexander Schröder: "Ich glaube die beängstigende nun seit fast zwei Jahren ... anhaltende Erstarrung meiner produktiven Kräfte auch so auffassen zu sollen: als den mühsamen Übergang von der Produktion des Jünglingsalters zu der männlichen ..." [79]. *Der weiße Fächer,* written five years earlier, already expressed his ironic realization

Daß Jugend gern mit großen Worten ficht
Und doch zu schwach ist, nur dem kleinen Finger
Der Wirklichkeit zu trotzen [80].

[77] A 187.
[78] A 23.
[79] 14 February, 1902. *Briefe 1900—1909*, p. 67.
[80] G 221.

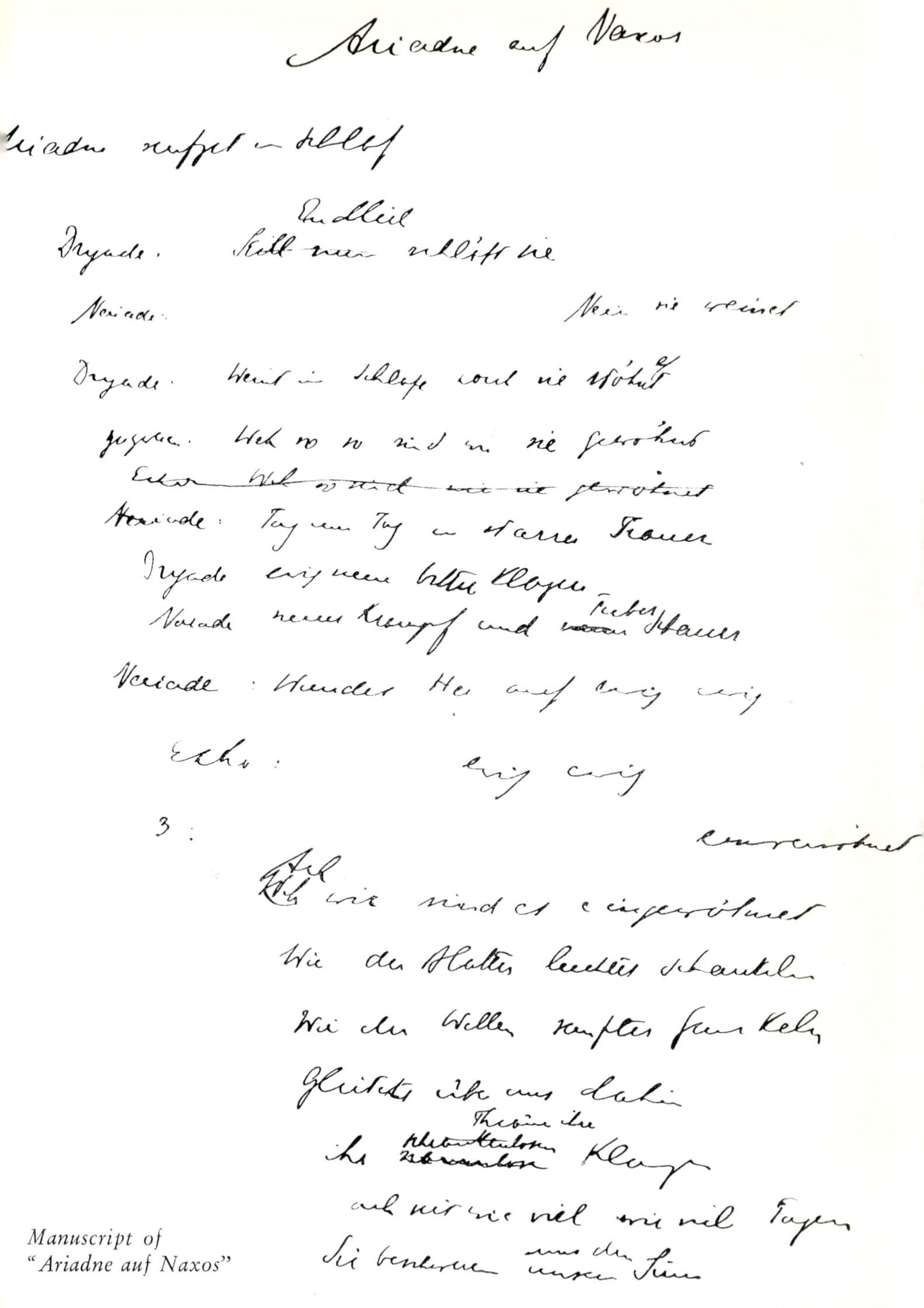

Manuscript of
"Ariadne auf Naxos"

Alexander Moissi in " Jedermann". 1920

Josef Kainz in "*Abenteurer und Sängerin*". *1899*

Hofmannsthal Exhibition at Institute of Germanic Studies

The process he underwent was more than a simple matter of education: there was little lacking in Loris either of intellectual penetration or of aesthetic sensibility; moreover, it is worth mentioning at this point that he never lost his facility in the use of words [81], which come easily to young men anyway. What he did lose was the experience which could only be transmuted into lyric poetry. The metamorphosis he had to undergo was nothing less than the discovery of himself as a human being; and in discovering himself as a human being he discovered himself as an Austrian.

It is instructive to take soundings of his mental processes at moments of critical encounter with the outside world. Such a moment was, for example, his first meeting with Stefan George, which led, as far as we can gather, to something like a foolish challenge from George and the protective intervention of Hofmannsthal's father. Despite their mutual respect in literary matters, and a certain community of literary ideals, it is fairly clear that the real cause of the trouble was an incompatibility of temperament which arose as much from national as from personal characteristics. This is a factor which emerges on occasion during the whole of their fifteen years' correspondence. Hofmannsthal reacted against the assertive self-confidence and (ultimately) the hieratic exclusiveness of George, whilst the latter, for all his protestations to the contrary, sensed in Hofmannsthal too much of that Viennese willingness to compromise which he secretly rejected. It is significant that many misunderstandings arise when Hofmannsthal is doing his military service with the cavalry, and allows a few unseemly remarks to slip about life and art: Would George care to meet his friend Graf Schönborn, who would give him "einen schönen Begriff vom öster-reichischen Wesen . . . Er gehört völlig dem Leben an, keiner Kunst" [82]. George was shocked by the blasphemy: "wer gar keiner kunst ange-hört, darf sich der überhaupt rühmen dem leben anzugehören?" [83] It is at such times, too, that Hofmannsthal's letters reveal a colloquial tinge otherwise totally lacking in the rather strained style he usually maintained when writing to George. He writes from manoeuvres in

[81] Best seen in the eloquence of his prose writings.
[82] 13 March, 1896. *op. cit.*, p. 86.
[83] 21 March, 1896. *ibid.*, p. 87.

Galicia: "Ich hoffe, etwas in Prosa schreiben zu können, aber erzwingen kann ichs ja nicht, und wenn ichs verspreche wird es sicher unmöglich. Liegen hab ich *nichts*" [84]. The same sort of situation provokes the comment on a book about Böcklin: "Nur bin ich zu tief im Leben befangen, um an dergleichen Spiegelung der Spiegelung viel Gefallen zu finden" [85]. Such lapses must have afforded George a disturbing insight into the unregenerate nature of the partner with whom he had hoped to exercise "eine sehr heilsame dictatur" [86] in literary matters.

A characteristic document of these years is the *Brief an Richard Dehmel*. In this he describes how, when he is out exercising with the dragoons, shapes, scents and colours flash by him, only to leave him, when he returns tired at night, devoid of any sense of reality, even of the power to think. He rides like Chandos, his eye roving in the hope of lighting upon some poor everyday thing of earth which will become the vessel of a revelation to him; and perhaps, on a more mundane level, one can say that there is nothing like tired muscles for dispelling solipsist suspicions that the world is a mere extension of one's own ego. This is ironically anticipated by the Smith's remark in *Idylle:*

> Den Sinn des Seins verwirrte allzuvieler Müßiggang
> Dem schön gesinnten, gern verträumten Kind, mich dünkt [87].

Now, learning the cavalryman's trade on the empty plains of Göding, he notes in his diary: "Die Elemente. Der beschwerliche Staub, die mühseligen Steine, die traurigen Straßen, die harten Dämme, die Tücken der Pferde und des eigenen Körpers." Then he looks back on his previous existence and records, amid the stamping of the horses and the snores of the dragoons: "Zwei große Epochen: die schweifende, die absichtliche; erstere gebraucht in einer dumpfen Antizipation die späteren termini voraus. — Erstere hat etwas von Kinderkomödie; leichtfertiger Gebrauch der Worte Glück, Ich, Menschen. — Leichtfertige Opposition, allmähliche Einsicht in den Wert des Bestehenden.

---

[84] 6 May, 1896. *ibid.*, p. 95.
[85] 25 October, 1895. *ibid.*, p. 80.
[86] May 1902. *ibid.*, p. 150.
[87] G 58.

— Der Übergang bei mir Edgar, Militärjahr, neue Berufswahl" [88] —
thoughts provoked by *Wilhelm Meisters Lehrjahre,* but applied to
himself.

As a final example of the change in attitude brought about by the
impact of outside things, it should be recalled that the year 1902, the
year we have been conditioned to think of as fraught with crisis for
Hofmannsthal, was also notable for the pressure of domestic circumstances. He speaks of financial difficulties; it is also the year in which
his first child was born (few things impress a man more with a sense
of his own responsibilities), and the year in which the death of his
grandmother occurred, "mit welcher meine Kindheit aufs innigste
verflochten war" [89]. The figure of the grandmother in his plays, a sort
of embodied affirmation of the life-force, reveals her importance for
him. So in 1902 fate seems to have drawn a line under his early life.
The way forward lay in the acceptance of a humbler mission, using
traditional means. What remained to be discovered was that those
means—and particularly the medium of dialect—would ultimately
prove no less effective for creative communication than those he had
been compelled to renounce.

V

Seldom, very seldom, does complete truth belong to
any human disclosure; seldom can it happen that something is not a little disguised, or a little mistaken; but
where ... though the conduct is mistaken, the feelings
are not, it may not be very material.

Jane Austen: *Emma*

A lyric poet in whom temperament combines with environment to
produce linguistic doubts will either seek a way out through new
patterns of relationships, or else he will fall silent. Hofmannsthal
perceived the first possibility: in *Ein Brief* Chandos says he will never
write again, "weil die Sprache, in welcher nicht nur zu schreiben, sondern auch zu denken mir vielleicht gegeben wäre, weder die lateinische
noch die englische noch die italienische und spanische ist, sondern eine
Sprache, von deren Worten mir auch nicht eines bekannt ist, eine
Sprache, in welcher die stummen Dinge zu mir sprechen, und in welcher

[88] A 126—127.
[89] To George, 27 August, 1902. *op. cit.,* p. 167.

ich vielleicht einst im Grabe vor einem unbekannten Richter mich ver-
antworten werde" [90]. But this is about the thing; it is not the thing
itself. For a time, the poet can feed on his own dilemma, but then he
must develop or desist. Richard Brinkmann puts it well: "Indem sie
ihre Fragwürdigkeit ausgesprochen hat, muß sie notwendigerweise —
als lyrische Sprache wenigstens und Sprache des Ausdrucks — verstum-
men ... Hofmannsthals Weg aus dem Dilemma führte nicht zu neuen,
mehr oder weniger abstrakten Beziehungssystemen der Worte, kraft
derer sie als neue Form der Lyrik neue Aussagekraft gewinnen könnten, wie das seit dem Expressionismus moderne Lyriker in mancherlei
Spielarten versucht haben. Als Dichter konnte Hofmannsthal seiner
ganzen Art und seiner Grundkonzeption und Grundüberzeugung ge-
mäß nichts anderes tun, als die Sprache als Medium, als Realisierung,
als Realität der Verknüpfung, der Gewinnung des Sozialen gelten zu
lassen und zu gestalten" [91]. In turning thus to the theatre, as Brinkmann implies, Hofmannsthal was doing no more than follow his own
natural inclinations as a Viennese writer. As early as 1893 an entry
in his diary indicates the aspects under which his use of dialect comedy
must be considered: "Für mich: Bedürfnis nach lebendiger Tatsächlich-
keit drängt zum Volksliedton, zum Drama" [92]. Whilst struggling
through the dark summer of 1902—and writing *Ein Brief*—Hofmannsthal can be observed, in his correspondence with George, pon-
dering on Goethe's use of the *Volkston:* "Auch mir erscheint der volks-
thümelnde Ton als einer der schlimmsten Verirrungen unserer Vor-
gänger: und doch wenn ich bedenke, wie ihn Goethe gleichsam als
Hirtenpfeife brauchte, wenn ich Uhland, Mörike bedenke, werde ich
schwankend ..." [93]. *Volkston* in lyric poetry and dialect on the stage
are not the same thing; but the drift of his thought is unmistakeable.

In this connection, there is no more revealing poem in the whole
corpus than 'Des alten Mannes Sehnsucht nach dem Sommer', written
in 1907, when the changeover was almost complete. The first few lines
will suffice:

[90] P II 22.
[91] 'Hofmannsthal und die Sprache'. *Deutsche Vierteljahrsschrift*, XXXV (1961), 80.
[92] A 102.
[93] 24 July, 1902. *op. cit.*, p. 166.

Wenn endlich Juli würde anstatt März,

Nichts hielte mich, ich nähme einen Rand,

Zu Pferd, zu Wagen oder mit der Bahn

Käm ich hinaus ins schöne Hügelland [94].

One's first impression is probably of the tension between the stilted subjunctives ('würde', 'hielte', 'nähme') and the colloquialisms (the unusual UG idiom 'einen Rand nehmen', the 'mit der Bahn'); then the flavour of 'mit der Bahn' suddenly registers: not 'Eisenbahn', but most likely the tram that ran out to the *Wienerwald*, "das schöne Hügelland". The remainder of the poem confirms the impression: this *Gestalt* is that of an old man from the *Vorstadt* dreaming of a trip out to the end of the line—on the old steam-tram to Rodaun, perhaps, where the woods and hills begin? The poem is still successful in communicating a lyrical experience; but the contrast—and conflict—between the two levels of language reveals the incursion of a dramatic element derived not merely from the convention of the speaking mask, but also from a concretized spirit of place.

One has to look hard to discover much trace of Austrian in the prose and verse of his early years. One finds an occasional hint of more southern German usage in a gender, a word-order or an intrusive article. The demands of theatrical realism cause him, in *Das Bergwerk zu Falun*, to make his nordic sailors talk with an unmistakeable southern accent: "Ich möcht ein bissl noch was andres haben/Als fades Bier und die paar Mädel da" [95] (which sounds a little strange in blank verse). The series of verse tragedies which form an intermediate stage in his production exclude dialect by their nature; not until the *Vorspiel für ein Puppentheater* of 1906 is a deliberate attempt made at a pastiche of the old comedy of the *Vorstadt*, with the comic exchanges between the Poet (here ironized) and the Old Woman: "Fremd und einsam", he declaims in agony, "einsam und verhöhnt, verhöhnt und umlauert! o Welt, Welt!" "A Geld?" she replies in the best tradition of Kasperle, "ja das ist was Schön's. Das

---

[94] G 29.
[95] G 341; cf. Walther Brecht: 'Über Hugo von Hofmannsthals *Bergwerk zu Falun*'. *Corona*, III (1932), 226: "Die Mundart klingt stark an, mit ihrer spezifischen Seelenfarbe".

möcht i freili a, je je!"[96] He employed the same technique with virtuosity ten years later in his Raimund phantasy *Der Sohn des Geisterkönigs;* but in the meantime he had conceived and in some cases executed no less than five comedies, in all of which dialect plays some role (*Silvia, Cristina, Der Schwierige, Der Rosenkavalier* and *Lucidor*—which later became *Arabella*), as well as *Jedermann,* his first morality[97].

Since the publication in 1960 of all the notes and fragments which compose *Silvia im 'Stern'* we have a much clearer idea of what the play was intended to look like. Its present interest—apart from the fact that he seems to have designed it as a vehicle for the theatrical projection of his musings upon the problem of *Erkenntniszweifel,* from some form of which all the main characters are suffering—is that Hofmannsthal employs in it a range of dialect not found anywhere else outside of *Der Rosenkavalier.* It is difficult, since the play is a fragment, to assess whether this is dictated by anything more than the demands of realism; what cannot be doubted is the loving virtuosity with which it is done.

There is a point at the end of Act I in *Der Rosenkavalier* when the Marschallin reflects on time and the approach of old age:

> Das alles ist geheim, so viel geheim.
> Und man ist dazu da, daß mans ertragt.
> Und in dem 'Wie' da liegt der ganze Unterschied[98].

Edgar Hederer comments: "Die Wiener Mundart, die sie nie ganz aufgibt, das Geheimste zu sagen, ist die Mundart ihres Herzens"[99]. The same must have been true of Hofmannsthal. From all the many-faceted recollections of him as a person which are gathered into Fiechtner's book[100], one habit emerges with great clarity: he spoke his

---

[96] D II 494.

[97] cf. his remarks to Strauss: "Dieser Stoff [*Jedermann*] formt sich mir unwiderstehlich zu einer Szenenfolge ziemlich realen Gepräges um, in Prosa, ja im Wiener Dialekt will es sich gebärden" (27 April, 1906); "Meine ... im österreichischen Dialekt geschriebene Komödie [*Silvia*]" (18 October, 1908); both in: *Richard Strauss und Hugo von Hofmannsthal, Briefwechsel.* Zürich, 1954, pp. 18 and 43.

[98] L I 331.

[99] In: *Hugo von Hofmannsthal.* Frankfurt a. M., 1960. p. 221.

[100] H. A. Fiechtner: *Hugo von Hofmannsthal. Die Gestalt des Dichters im Spiegel der Freunde.* Wien, 1949.

Kavalierswienerisch with pleasure and defiance. That he should have had a good ear for the dialects of other classes and nationalities is only to be expected in a man with his gift for languages. When it was a question of obtaining an authentic effect in dialogue, he was implacable, as can be seen from the reproaches he addressed to Strauss when the latter, in his slapdash way, put an 'e' on Theres' [101] (just what subtleties he can achieve by the use or omission of an 'e' can be seen from a close study of the state of mind Hans Karl in *Der Schwierige* reveals, according to whether he says "ich habe" or "ich hab"). He instructed Strauss: "Alles kostet mich genau die gleiche Konzentration — eine Zeile von Aithra oder eine von Waldner — und die Zeile 'Leopold, i zahl, i geh' ist im Grunde nicht schwerer und nicht leichter zu erfinden als 'Gewogene Lüfte, führt uns zurück!'" [102] There is more than just a conscientious devotion to his trade in such an attitude; implicit in it is Hofmannsthal's belief that the dialect can be used to communicate an experience for which no other form of words would be adequate. In *Der Rosenkavalier* this has been achieved: "Diese Sprache ist es, welche dieses Libretto zum unübersetzbarsten in der Welt gemacht. Außerordentlich geschickte Federn haben sich bemüht, es ins Englische, Französische und Italienische zu übertragen. Aber die Figuren, aus dem Element dieser Sprache genommen, nehmen etwas Kaltes an, sie stehen in viel härterer Kontur gegeneinander. Es fehlt der zarteste Teil der Modellierung, durch welche die Lebensluft eines Stückes entsteht" [103].

Hofmannsthal has now reached a point at which it is no longer admissible to dismiss his Austrian as a mere concession to the demands of stage realism and local colour: he asserts in the above passage that the configuration of the characters depends directly upon the language in which they express themselves; in other words, unless one is sensitive to the subtle gradations of utterance employed, one will miss the ironic

---

[101] "Eine Anzahl kleiner, aber mich sehr störender, *anscheinend* zufälliger Alterationen des Wienerischen (z. B. Therese anstatt Theres', was im Munde Octavians ganz *unmöglich*) müssen ... getilgt werden. Ihnen scheinen diese Silben und Buchstabenverbindungen gewiß minimal, für mich sind sie so störend, wie es für Sie wäre, wenn man Ihnen in der Partitur Noten verändern würde." (14 July, 1910. *op. cit.*, p. 81).

[102] 13 July, 1928. *ibid.*, p. 559.

[103] P IV 430.

112

tensions through which comedy presents its comment on the dilemma of human attempts at communication—presents them, and reconciles them by transcending the whole tangle of mutual incomprehension. "Das Element der Komödie ist die Ironie ... die wirkliche Komödie setzt ihre Individuen in ein tausendfach verhäkeltes Verhältnis zur Welt, sie setzt alles in ein Verhältnis zu allem und damit alles in ein Verhältnis der Ironie" [104]. This web of relationships which Hofmannsthal spins between his characters depends not only on fine shades of individual, but also of social speech: "Im Reden der Charaktere sehe ich die eigentliche dichterische Kreation. Wie sie reden, wie ihre Diktion steigt und sinkt — darin ist mir das Mittel gegeben, diese Charakteristik wahrhaft lebendig zu machen, auch vieles kaum direkt aussprechbare *zwischen* den Figuren fühlen zu machen" [105].

It should be clear by now that in order to fulfil his requirements Hofmannsthal needed not only an Austrian milieu but also the language in which that milieu could be projected: neither would suffice alone. In the idiom of Vienna he believed he had found just such a uniquely flexible instrument: "Die österreichische Umgangssprache ist auch heute ein Ding für sich; aber vor hundert Jahren war dieses Ding noch konkreter und besonderer als heute. Es war sicher unter allen deutschen Sprachen die gemengteste: denn es war die Sprache der kulturell reichsten und vermischtesten aller Welten. Wir haben eine Diplomatensprache und wir hatten sie ganz anders; wir hatten und haben eine Militärsprache. Aber wir hatten und haben neben der bürgerlichen eine aristokratische und neben der Sprache der Innern Stadt eine Vorstadtsprache; und dies wieder ist nicht gleich der Sprache der Ortschaften rings um Wien, ganz zu schweigen vom flachen Lande. In den Vorstädten aber wieder hat es in früherer Zeit scharfe dialektische Sprachgrenzen gegeben, und so im Gesellschaftlichen ..." [106]. "Der immer sehr wache und schnelle Sinn des Publikums für diese Nuancen hat der [Wiener] Bühne einen großen Reichtum gegeben: denn die mimischen Differenziertheiten der Stände gehen Hand in Hand mit

[104] P IV 40; cf. the comment on *Ariadne:* "So sind die beiden Seelenwelten im Schluß ironisch verbunden, wie sie eben verbunden sein können: durch das Nichtverstehen". (P III 140).
[105] To Strauss, 13 July, 1928. *op. cit.*, p. 559.
[106] P III 199.

den sprachlichen ..." [107] It is hardly necessary to dilate upon the limitations which such a choice of milieu places upon a dramatist, limitations which Hofmannsthal was prepared to accept for the sake of the opportunities of expression it afforded. Only in a play where this gay social tapestry could be unfolded would communication be truly established; only in a comedy where the spatial element of personal and social relationships would form a continuum with the historical perspectives of the great Austrian past; only in *Der Rosenkavalier*, in fact, in *Ariadne auf Naxos*, in *Der Schwierige*, *Der Unbestechliche* and *Arabella* (to which one must add *Cristina* and the *Silvia* torso); and of these, three are written for music [108]. Elsewhere, if dialect is used, we may expect to be conscious of a disharmony between the form and the medium in which it is expressed, although even in such cases important things may be missed if we do not keep our ears pricked for what the dialect has to tell us [109].

"Man kann sich kein Milieu erschaffen, wie man sich keine Heimat machen kann" [110]. Hofmannsthal wrote this in 1891; but his real discovery of his own fatherland was a slow process which reached its culmination during the Great War when, under the pressure of a culturo-historical catastrophe which threatened disintegration to that bruised relic of the European past which was Austria-Hungary, he came to realize what quality it was in his own people which distinguished them from their German allies, and how that quality could still express itself creatively in his art. "Darüber, wo das Wirkliche zu finden ist, hat uns vielleicht der Krieg einen Fingerzeig gegeben. Das muß doch das Wirkliche sein, wo die größte, unbedingteste, innerste,

---

[107] A 268.

[108] Although Borchardt was prepared to maintain that *Der Rosenkavalier* at least could dispense with music: "Ich kenne auch die Musik der Lysistrata und der Vögel nicht und habe nie nach ihr verlangt." (23 July, 1911. *Briefwechsel Hofmannsthal Borchardt*, p. 46).

[109] cf. J. Nadler on *Der Turm* in: 'Hugo von Hofmannsthals Ausklang'. *Hochland*, XXVI, ii (1929), 620: "Das schwebt und braust und flackert vom Ungewissen ins Ungewisse, doch dem Ohr vorüberklingend wie Sage und Legende — wenn man das rechte Wort überhört. Und dieses rechte Wort fällt mit dem ersten, das in dieser Tragödie gesprochen wird: 'Rekrut, hierher!' Dieser Wachkommandant Olivier und seine Leute, man hört und sieht es ihnen an, das sind ja österreichische Soldaten."

[110] P I 19.

8

lauterste Kraft ist. Sie ist beim Volk . . . In den Naturtiefen, in denen das Volk west, gleichwie in jenen dunklen Tiefen des Individuums wo zwischen Geistigem und Leiblichem eine fließende Grenze aufgerichtet ist, dort ist nicht Reflexion und Erkenntnis zu Hause. Nur wollend und glaubend kann die österreichische Idee erfaßt werden . . ." [111] In this union of simple faith with an unsapped will lay Hofmannsthal's hope of a way around the barrier of silence imposed by our divorce from ontological living: "Stummes Dulden und Tun. Frömmigkeit. Idealismus und Realismus dagegen kraftlose Wörter: Gott erkennen im Wirbel der Technik. Urkräfte geweckt: das Volk" [112]. These are ideas which find their clearest formulation in the scheme he drew up in 1917: *Preuße und Österreicher*. One statement here is of particular relevance: the one which attributes to the Austrian in general what he had previously found typical of himself as a lyric poet: "Hineindenken in andere bis zur Charakterlosigkeit" [113]. The wheel has come full circle. The poet's gift of empathy, which had deserted him, is now metamorphosed into a social characteristic capable of dramatic projection through the social medium: dialect. "Der Österreicher hat unendlich viel mehr geselligen Sinn als der nördliche Deutsche, mehr Sinn für das, was zwischen den Menschen liegt, ein unvergleichlich feineres Gefühl für die Nuance" [114].

That the speech of Austrians was so apt a medium for creative communication on the highest level is directly attributable to the unity in diversity which made up the Austrian *res*: a sense of continuity with the past, and of the past in the present; an understanding of the realities of earthly existence based on suffering and acceptance rather than action and dialectic; a still unfragmented social structure in which the high and the low were close to one another in *Weltgefühl;* an insight, above all, into the ineluctable fact of time, and the graceful acceptance of the need to let go of what one may not cling on to without guilty self-assertion. These are the things Hofmannsthal found when he chose the non-mystical way through "Werk, Tat und Kind", the 'social' way. If time was the enemy who threatened to turn pre-

---

[111] P III 348—349.
[112] P III 381.
[113] P III 409.
[114] A 268.

existence into the rigidity of a false eternity, time could also be overcome by accepting a habit of mind, moulded by centuries of patient
experience, which had triumphed over it. "Bei keinem Volk [ist] so
viel von der Zeit die Rede, als bei den Deutschen; sie ringen um den
Sinn der Gegenwart, uns ist er gegeben. Dies Klare, Gegenwärtige ist
am schönsten im österreichischen Volk realisiert, unter den oberen
Ständen am schönsten unter den Frauen" [115]. The use of Austrian
would enable Hofmannsthal to preserve his instinctive aversion from
stage dialectic — "Die fälschende Gewalt der Rede geht so weit, daß
sie den Charakter des Redenden nicht nur verzerrt, sondern geradezu
aufhebt. Die Dialektik drängt das Ich aus der Existenz" [116]. The failure
of the lyrical mood led to silence: on the stage he could circumvent
silence by mixing communication through shifting configurations of
characters with speech which, in its purest form as in *Der Schwierige*,
communicates by its hints, its reticences, its renunciation of wounding
dialectic, its *Anstand:* "Über den Wiener Dialekt. Das Schöne davon:
das Maßvolle" [117].
A demonstration of just how Hofmannsthal uses dialect to obtain
the effects he aims at would, of course, involve a close interpretative
analysis of the relevant plays; a lengthy, though rewarding task. It
would show, I think, just how right he was when he said, "Uns ist der
Sinn der Zeit gegeben." The main characteristics of his language can,
however, be indicated here. On the social plane, the symbiosis of high
and low is nowhere better indicated than in their mutual use of dialect
peculiarities which in any other setting would be grotesque. That
Edine and Crescence, for example, should feel no less than their
servants that certain prepositions govern the accusative rather than the
dative on occasion ("Edine: 'Ich les doch die Bücher von die Leut';
Crescence: 'Dazwischen bet ich die ganze Zeit zu die vierzehn Not-
helfer'" [118]) is not a sign of faulty education: these things are normal
in the appropriate context. Historical perspectives (and the tension
between the past and the present) are indicated by the fluctuating use
of archaic forms (of address, for example), whilst the ambiguous

[115] P III 257.
[116] P IV 458.
[117] A 233.
[118] L II 341, 429.

8*

epistemological predicament of the individual—now thinking and experiencing through social media, now hiding within the confines of his own personality—is subtly indicated by the use of or abstention from *Fremdwörter*, themselves an indicator of racial and cultural complexity. These are things that only Austrian can do. It can also make subtle communication through that avoidance of involved syntactical structures which more than anything else speaks of a tactful reluctance to commit verbal assault and is an implicit recognition that dialectic lets the real stuff of life slip through its nets; without surrendering its prerogative and obligation of silence and *Anstand* it can, in the theatre, point a contrast with the over-articulate, over-articulated utterances of the masterful ones who are cut off from reality yet fight on with the mournful magic of their invalid verbal eternities. In parataxis and anacoluthons Hofmannsthal's Austrian expresses the hesitations and *Hemmungen* of an individual faced with the multiplicity of phenomena and the indecent necessity of choice; in the fine shadings of the all-pervasive particle *halt* lies a fatalistic acceptance of this predicament; and in the use of the perfect rather than the imperfect time is given its due as the universal solvent; accepted, and thus overcome [119].

Kleist said that we must eat a second time of the fruit of the tree of knowledge: we must eat forgetfulness. For Hofmannsthal, too, the only way of repairing the damage caused by our second Fall—the fragmentation of modern consciousness—was transcendence of our predicament by a return to the state of innocence, as symbolized for him by the wonder and simple faith of a child—all the things summed up in the figure of the *Kinderkönig* in *Der Turm*. He felt that he had found reserves of such childlike simplicity in his own people; and one of the most lasting impressions left by his characters is that of naive

---

[119] "Daß die verbindliche Umgangssprache Österreichs, das Wienerische, kein Imperfektum kennt, mag es mit anderen Dialekten und Sprachen gemein haben. Bedeutsamer ist, daß sich der Wiener auch dann der Mitvergangenheit enthält, wenn er sich infolge ungünstiger Bedingungen des Schriftdeutschen oder gar des Hochdeutschen bedienen muß . . . denn was nicht unmittelbare Gegenwart ist, ist in Wien auch schon der Vergangenheit anheimgefallen, wird schon ein wenig ungewiß, ist unbestimmbar geworden, ist endgültig vorbei . . . Aber weil ihm die Gegenwart so schnell zur Vergangenheit wird, bleibt ihm wiederum die Vergangenheit etwas sehr Gegenwärtiges." — Jörg Mauthe: *Wien für Anfänger*. Zürich, 1959. pp. 12—13.

wonder in the face of a reality which may be strange and sometimes frightening, but is not meaningless. It is not the 'was' of rational enquiry, but the 'wie', spoken sometimes in childlike perplexity:

> Aber wie kann das wirklich sein,
> daß ich die kleine Resi war
> und daß ich auch einmal die alte Frau sein werd! . . .
> Wie kann denn das geschehen?
> Wie macht denn das der liebe Gott? [120]

and sometimes in wondering acknowledgment of another *fait accompli* that a mysterious world has presented: "Wie du das sagst!"—a phrase which recurs throughout Hofmannsthal's works [121]. And it is the 'wie' of the aesthetic gesture which such characters represent that makes them into an aesthetic (and so by definition trans-conceptual) experience; they exist only in the medium of the language they speak, which must therefore be part of the totality of that experience. The achievement was a unique one, possible only to a man who had lived through the existential and epistemological crisis of his own art, his own country, his own age; and no prodigies of archaeological empathy will produce a single living line in the same idiom. Nor is it an achievement which imposes itself on anyone who has an adequate knowledge of that idiom, and no more:

> Geheimnis ist der Schönheit schönstes Kleid:
> ihr solltet immer nur in Larven gehn,
> und euer Geist sollt was Verborgnes sein
> und sich dem Blick nur geben, der schon liebt [122].

The medium of ethical self-transcendence and re-integration is also the medium of aesthetic participation in the struggle; an effort of goodwill is demanded. But: "Was einem vom Herzen kommt", says Cristina, "dabei vergibt man sich nichts" [123].

---

[120] L I 330.

[121] First used, as far as I can detect, in *Das gerettete Venedig*, D II 91, a transitional play with strong colloquial elements, particularly in the prose passages. There is more than a touch of the traditional Viennese servant-figure in the Haushofmeister.

[122] D I 277.

[123] L I 253.

HUGO VON HOFMANNSTHAL IN ENGLAND AND AMERICA

A BIBLIOGRAPHY

The following survey of works by and on Hugo von Hofmannsthal published in English-speaking countries constitutes, as far as we can see, the first major attempt at collecting such information. We therefore present it with due reservations and with no claim to an exhaustive treatment of the subject, especially as far as American publications are concerned. We hope, however, that no item of importance has escaped our attention.

It was not deemed necessary to record every chance reference to Hofmannsthal. Yet entries in general books of reference are given, however short, because the inclusion of Hofmannsthal's name in such works is, to some extent at least, a measure of his reception at the time of their publication.

Work by British or American writers published in Austria or Germany has been included as well as work by Austrian or German writers published in Great Britain or America. Programme and record sleeve notes have been disregarded.

Entries are confined to essential bibliographical data though critical references are occasionally quoted if of historical interest. Abbreviations referring to titles of periodicals are those adopted in *The Year's Work in Modern Languages*.

Acknowledgements for help are due to Dr. Mary E. Gilbert, Michael Hamburger, M. A., Dr. K. G. Knight and to B. Keith-Smith, B. A. who is preparing a comprehensive bibliography on Hofmannsthal which is to supersede the 1936 bibliography by Karl Jacoby.

31 December 1961   R. Pick
                                                Ann C. Weaver

CONTENTS

122

WORKS PUBLISHED IN AMERICAN JOURNALS DURING THE
AUTHOR'S LIFETIME

1 HOFMANNSTHAL, HUGO VON: Vienna Letter. *The Dial*, LXXIII, ii, 206. 1922.

2 HOFMANNSTHAL, HUGO VON: Vienna Letter. *The Dial*, March 1923, 281.

3 HOFMANNSTHAL, HUGO VON: Vienna Letter. *The Dial*, September 1923, 271.

4 HOFMANNSTHAL, HUGO VON: Eugene O'Neill. *The Freeman*, 23 June, 1923. New York.

5 SAYLER, O. M. [Ed.]: Max Reinhardt and his Theatre. New York, *Brentano's*, 1924. Chapters II, VI and part of XVI written by HvH.

POETRY AND PROSE IN ANTHOLOGIES

a) German

6 BERN, MAXIMILIAN [Ed.]: The German Lyric since Goethe. An anthology. London, *Hachette*, 1926. [HvH: pp. 262—263, 'Erlebnis' and 'Die Beiden'.]

7 BITHELL, JETHRO [Ed.]: An Anthology of German Poetry 1880—1940. London, *Methuen*, 1941. [HvH: pp. 87—91, 'Vorfrühling', 'Die Beiden', 'Manche freilich...', 'Ballade des äusseren Lebens', 'Terzinen über Vergänglichkeit'.]

8 CLOSS, AUGUST and WILLIAMS, T. PUGH [Ed.]: The Harrap Anthology of German Poetry. London, *Harrap*, 1957. [HvH: pp. 493—497, 'Ballade des äusseren Lebens', 'Die Beiden', 'Manche freilich...' and an extract from 'Der Tor und der Tod'.]

9 FIEDLER, H. G. [Ed.]: The Oxford Book of German Verse. *Oxford University Press*, 1927 (2nd edition). [HvH: pp. 543—545, 'Vorfrühling', 'Die Beiden', 'Manche freilich...'.]

10 FIEDLER, H. G. [Ed.]: The Oxford Book of German Prose. *Oxford University Press*, 1943. [HvH: pp. 614—618, 'Schöne Sprache'.]

11 FORSTER, LEONARD [Ed.]: The Penguin Book of German Verse. Harmondsworth, *Penguin Books*, 1957. [HvH: pp. 394—398 with prose translations, 'Die Beiden', 'Terzinen über Vergänglichkeit', 'Eigene Sprache', 'Manche freilich...', 'Lebenslied'.]

12 ROSE, W. [Ed.]: A Book of Modern German Lyric Verse. 1890—1955. Oxford, *Clarendon Press*, 1960. [HvH: pp. 57—63, 'Vorfrühling', 'Erlebnis', 'Die Beiden', 'Ballade des äusseren Lebens', 'Terzinen über Vergänglichkeit', 'Manche freilich . . .'.]

b) English

13 BITHELL, JETHRO [Ed.]: Contemporary German Poetry. Selected and translated by Jethro Bithell. London, *Scott*, 1909. [HvH: pp. 92—97, 'Die Beiden', 'Ballade des äusseren Lebens', 'Manche freilich . . .', 'Erlebnis', 'Dein Antlitz . . .', 'Terzinen über Vergänglichkeit'. "The best known of the difficult poets of the circle of the *Blätter für die Kunst* is HvH."]

14 BROICHER, DAISY: German Lyrists of Today. Done into English verse. London, *Mathews, Vigo Cabinet Series*, 1909. [HvH: pp. 44—51, 'Vorfrühling', 'Erlebnis', 'Wir gingen einen Weg . . .', 'Dein Antlitz . . .', 'Die Beiden'. "HvH has already attained a universal reputation by his numerous plays."]

15 FLORES, ANGEL [Ed.]: An Anthology of German Poetry from Hölderlin to Rilke. In English translation with German originals. New York, *Doubleday, Anchor Books*, 1960. [HvH: pp. 323—337, 'Erlebnis', 'Reiselied', 'Lebenslied', 'Dein Antlitz . . .', 'Ballade des äusseren Lebens', 'Terzinen über Vergänglichkeit', 'Manche freilich . . .', 'Unendliche Zeit', 'Der Jüngling in der Landschaft', 'Ein Knabe'. Translated by Alfred Schwarz, Michael Hamburger, Dwight Durling, Herman Salinger and Vernon Watkins.]

SELECTIONS FROM WORKS IN TRANSLATION

16 ANON: Selections from HvH. *Harvard Advocate*, CXXVIII, 24, 1942.

17 ANON: 'Colours'. Extracts from the Letters of a Man who Returned, by HvH. [Based on: Selected Prose, New York, 1952]. In: Drawings and Watercolours by Vincent van Gogh. A selection of thirty-two plates in colour with notes by Douglas Cooper. New York, *Macmillan Co.;* Basel, *Holtim*, 1955. pp. 5—7.

18 FRANCKE, KUNO and HOWARD, W. G. [Ed.]: The German Classics of the 19th and 20th Centuries. New York, *German Publishing Society*, 1913/1915. [HvH: 17 extracts translated. See also separate entries: 'Death and the Fool', 'The Death of Titian' and 'The Marriage of Sobeide'.]

19 HAMBURGER, MICHAEL [Ed.]: Poems and Verse Plays of HvH.
    Bilingual Edition. Introduced by editor. With a Preface by T. S. Eliot.
    London, *Routledge and Kegan Paul;* New York, *Pantheon Books*
    for Bollingen Foundation, 1961. Reviewed: *Times Literary Supple-*
    ment, 20 October, 1961; *Kenyon Review,* XXIII, 721—724, 1961.

20 HOTTINGER, MARY and STERN, TANIA and JAMES: Selected
    Prose of HvH, translated. Introduced by Hermann Broch (Trans-
    lated by James Stern from article in: *Neue Rundschau,* LXII, 1951.
    This later incorporated as Chapter III in long essay on HvH in
    Broch's 'Gesammelte Werke. Essays' Bd. I, 43—182. Zurich, 1955).
    London, *Routledge and Kegan Paul;* New York, *Pantheon Books*
    for Bollingen Foundation, 1952. Reviewed: E. Sackville-West, *New*
    Statesman, XLIV, 722—723, 1952; *Times Literary Supplement,*
    12 December, 1952.

21 STORK, CHARLES WHARTON: The Lyrical Poems of HvH.
    Translated from the German with an introduction. New Haven,
    Yale University Press; Oxford University Press, 1918. Reviewed:
    MLR, XIV, 352, 1919.

22 WARNER, C. D. [Ed.]: Library of the World's Best Literature,
    Ancient and Modern. New York, *Warner Library Co.,* 1917/1918
    (2nd edition). [HvH: 8 extracts translated. See also separate entry:
    'The Adventurer and the Singer'.]

SINGLE WORKS
Texts or Editions; Translations; Critical Appraisals

Der Abenteurer und die Sängerin
23 MORGAN, B. Q.: 'The Adventurer and the Singer'. Translated. In:
    Library of the World's Best Literature. Ed. C. D. Warner. Vol. VIII.
    New York, *Warner Library Co.,* 1917/1918.

Die ägyptische Helena
24 KALISCH, ALFRED: 'Helen in Egypt'. Opera in two acts by HvH.
    Translated with the original German text. Berlin, *Fürstner;* New
    York, *Ricordi & Co.,* 1928.

Alkestis
25 WELLESZ, EGON: 'Alkestis'. Drama in einem Aufzug nach Euripides
    [German version by HvH]. Bearbeitung für die Opernbühne und
    Musik von Egon Wellesz. op. 35. New York, Vienna, *Universal-*
    Edition, 1923.

26 BUTLER, E. M.: Alkestis in Modern Dress. *Journal of the Warburg Institute*, I, i, 46—60, 1937. [Very brief reference to HvH.]

27 WELLESZ, EGON: Essays on Opera. Translated from the German by Patricia Kean. London, *Dobson*, 1950. Chapter VIII: 'Alkestis' pp. 145—152.

Andreas oder die Vereinigten

28 HOTTINGER, MARIE D.: 'Andreas or the United'. Being fragments of a novel by HvH, translated with an introduction. London, *J. M. Dent & Sons*, 1936.

Arabella

29 GUTMAN, JOHN: Richard Strauss. 'Arabella'. A lyrical comedy in three acts by HvH. English text. Libretto. New York, *Boosey & Hawkes*, 1955.

30 MANN, WILLIAM: Two of Strauss's Later Operas ['Arabella' and 'Capriccio'], *Opera*, IV, 523—529, 1953.

31 MASUR, GERHARD: HvH's 'Arabella' [An article]. *American-German Review*, XXII, vi, 24—26, 1956.

Ariadne auf Naxos

32 KALISCH, ALFRED: 'Ariadne on Naxos'. Opera in one act by HvH. Translated. Berlin, *Fürstner*, 1913. New version printed in 1922, reprinted in 1924.

33 HEYWORTH, PETER: Richard Strauss in Vienna. Review of 'Ariadne on Naxos' at Sadler's Wells. *The Observer*, 12 February, 1961.

34 WINDER, MARIANNE: The Psychological Significance of HvH's 'Ariadne auf Naxos'. *GLL* (NS), XV, i, 100—109, 1961.

Ballade des äusseren Lebens

35 HAGGARD, STEPHEN: 'Ballad of the Outward and Visible Things of Life'. From the German of HvH. In: The Unpublished Poems of Stephen Haggard. With a Preface by Christopher Hassall. *Salamander Press*, 1945. p. 36.

36 HAMBURGER, MICHAEL: 'Ballad of the Outer Life', translated from HvH. *New Statesman & Nation*, XLI, 656, June 1951.

37 MUENSTERBERG, MARGARETE: 'Ballad of the Outer Life', translated. In: A Harvest of German Verse, p. 215. New York, *Appleton*, 1916.

Die Beiden

38 ANON: 'The Two'. A poem, translated. *Poet Lore*, XXIII, 444, 1912.

———

39 JÀSZI, ANDREW O.: Expression and Life in HvH's 'Die Beiden'. GQ, XXVI, 154—159, 1954.

Das Bergwerk zu Falun

40 FABER DU FAUR, CURT VON: Der Abstieg in den Berg. Zu HvHs 'Bergwerk zu Falun'. *MDU*, XLIII, 1—14, 1951.

Brief des Lord Chandos

41 ANON: 'The Letter' translated from 'Brief des Lord Chandos'. *Rocky Mountain Review*, VI, 1, 3, 11—13, 1942.

42 SCHULZ, H. STEFAN: HvH and Bacon: The Sources of the Chandos Letter. *Comparative Literature*, XIII, i, 1—15, 1961. Oregon.

Buch der Freunde

43 ANON: 'From the Book of Friends', an excerpt translated from 'Buch der Freunde'. *Dial*, LXXIII, 23—24, 1922. Chicago.

Cristinas Heimreise

44 HOUSE, ROY T.: 'Cristina's journey home'. Translated from 'Cristinas Heimreise'. Boston, *Badger*, 1916. Reprinted in: Poet Lore Plays, vol. XXVIII, 129—186. Boston, *Badger*, 1917.

———

45 NAUMANN, WALTER: 'Cristinas Heimreise' und ihr Vorbild. *MLN*, LIX, ii, 104—106, 1944.

Der Dichter und diese Zeit

46 LEWISOHN, L.: Excerpts from 'Der Dichter und diese Zeit', translated. In: Modern Book of Criticism, pp. 65—74. New York, *Boni and Liveright*, 1919.

Elektra

47 DICKINSON, T. H. [Ed.]: 'Electra'. Translated. In: Chief Contemporary Dramatists, 3rd series. Boston, *Houghton Mifflin*, 1930.

127

48 KALISCH, ALFRED: 'Elektra'. Tragedy in one act by HvH. Translated. Berlin, *Fürstner*, 1910.

49 MASON, CHARLES T.: 'Elektra'. Translated. Berlin, *Fürstner;* New York, *Steinway & Sons*, 1909.

50 SYMONS, ARTHUR: 'Elektra'. Translated. New York, *Brentano's*, 1908. [First performance in English: 19 September, 1908 in Edinburgh under the direction of Mrs. Patrick Campbell.]

51 BUTLER, E. M.: HvH's 'Elektra': A Graeco-Freudian Myth. *Journal of the Warburg Institute*, II, ii, 164—175, 1938.

52 CARNER, M.: 'Elektra' in Perspective. *Time and Tide*, XXXIV, 721 ff., 1953.

53 CORRIGAN, ROBERT W.: Character as Destiny in HvH's 'Electra'. *Modern Drama*, II, 17—28, 1959.

54 DIECKMANN, LISELOTTE: The Dancing Electra. *Texas Studies in Language and Literature*, II, 3—16, 1960.

55 MANN, WILLIAM: An Introduction to Strauss's 'Elektra'. *Opera*, IV, 266—273, 1953.

56 SHAW, BERNARD: How to Become a Musical Critic. London, *Rupert Hart Davis*, 1960. Ed. with an introduction by Dan H. Laurence; pp. 257—267 refer to an exchange of open letters to *Nation* by Shaw and Ernest Newman following reviews of 'Elektra' by Newman (26 February, 1910) and W. H. Massingham (26 March, 1910).

57 SHAWE-TAYLOR, DESMOND: Bernard Shaw's Other Island. *Sunday Times*, 12 February, 1961. [Account of exchanges between Shaw and Ernest Newman on subject of 'Elektra'.]

Das Erlebnis des Marschalls von Bassompierre

58 COHN, HILDE D.: 'Das Erlebnis des Marschalls von Bassompierre'. HvHs Nacherzählung verglichen mit Goethes Text. *GR*, XVIII, 58—70, 1943. [See also No. 96]

Der Ersatz für die Träume

59 ANON: 'A Substitute for Dreams', translated from HvH. *London Mercury*, IX, 177—180, 1923.

Essays

60 GILBERT, MARY E.: HvH. Selected Essays. Oxford, *Blackwell,* 1955. Reviewed: *ML,* XXXVII, 37, 1955; Margaret McHaffie, *MLR,* LI, 144, 1956; A. R. Robinson, *GLL* (NS), IX, 234 ff., 1955/56.

61 COHN, HILDE D.: Loris, die frühen Essays des jungen HvH. *PMLA,* LXIII, iv, 1294—1313, 1948.

62 EXNER, R.: Probleme der Methodik und der Komposition in den Essays von Thomas Mann und HvH. *GQ,* XXX, 145—157, 1957.

Die Frau im Fenster

63 BOAS, HARRIET BETTY: 'Madonna Dianora', a Play in Verse. Translated from 'Die Frau im Fenster'. Boston, *Badger,* 1916. Reprinted by *Four seas co.,* Boston, 1919.

64 SHAY, FRANK [Ed.]: 'Madonna Dianora'. Translated from 'Die Frau im Fenster'. In: Fifty Contemporary One-Act Plays. Cincinnati, *Stewart & Kidd,* 1920.

Die Frau ohne Schatten

65 ANON [Edition]: 'Die Frau ohne Schatten'. Oper in drei Akten von HvH. Musik von Richard Strauss. London, *Boosey & Hawkes,* 1943.

66 NAUMANN, WALTER: Die Quelle von HvHs 'Frau ohne Schatten'. *MLN,* LIX, 385—386, 1944.

67 SACKVILLE-WEST, E.: Strauss, HvH and 'Die Frau ohne Schatten' [Article with illustrations]. *Opera,* IV, 725—732, 1953.

68 STEINER, HERBERT: 'Die Frau ohne Schatten' [An article]. *MDU,* XXXVII, 99—101, 1945.

Das gerettete Venedig

69 WALTER, ELISABETH: 'Venice Preserved'. A tragedy in 5 acts by HvH. Authorized translation from the German. In: Poet Lore Plays, Series 2, XXVI, v, 529—643. Boston, *Badger,* 1915.

70 WINTHER, FRITZ: 'Das gerettete Venedig', eine vergleichende Studie. *University of California Publications in Modern Philology,* III, ii, 87—246, 1914. [Compares Otway, La Fosse and HvH.]

Gespräch der Tänzerinnen (Furcht)

71 STERN, JAMES: 'Conversation of the dancers'. Translated. *Partisan Review*, XVI, 498—504, 1949.

Griechenland

72 ANON: 'Greece'. Translated from the first part of the introduction to Hans Holdt's 'Griechenland', 1923. *Criterion*, II, 95—102, 1923.

73 HAMILTON, L. [?]: 'Greece'. Translation of introduction by HvH to 'Picturesque Greece' ed. by Hans Holdt. London, "The Studio Ltd.", 1928?

Die Hochzeit der Sobeide

74 MORGAN, B. Q.: 'The marriage of Sobeide'. Translated. In: The German Classics of the 19th and 20th Centuries. Ed. Kuno Francke and W. G. Howard, XX, 234 ff. New York, *German Publishing Society*, 1913—1915.

Idylle

75 ANON: 'Idyll'. Translated. *Drama*, XXVI, 169—175, March 1917. Chicago.

76 SCOTT, M.: 'Idyl'. Translated. *Poet Lore*, LII, ii, 141—148, 1946.

Die Ironie der Dinge

77 ANON: 'The Irony of Things', translated from HvH. *London Mercury*, IX, 175—177, 1923.

Jedermann

78 JACOBS, MARGARET [Ed.]: 'Jedermann. Das Spiel vom Sterben des Reichen Mannes'. With notes and bibliography. London, *Nelson's German Texts*, 1957.

79 ANON [M. E. Tafler?]: 'The Salzburg Everyman'. The Play of the Rich Man's Death. An English translation of HvH's 'Jedermann' as acted before the cathedral at Salzburg. Salzburg, *M. Mora Verlag*, (1911?).

80 JONES, T. GWYNN: 'The Theatre of the World'. A morality play translated from HvH's 'Jedermann'. Published by the *Welsh National Theatre*, Plas Newydd, Llangollen, 1936. [Also translated into Welsh by same translator in 1933.]

81 STERLING, GEORGE: 'The Play of Everyman'. Based on the old English morality play; new version by HvH set to blank verse by George Sterling in collaboration with R. Ordynski. San Francisco, *Robertson*, 1917. Revised and published on the occasion of its presentation in the Hollywood Bowl, September 1936. California Festival Edition.

82 TAFLER, M. E.: 'The Salzburg Everyman'. The play of the rich man's death as acted before the cathedral at Salzburg. Translated. Salzburg, *M. Mora Verlag*, 1929. [Reprint of anon. translation, 1911?]

83 ANON: The Beggar's Role [An article on 'Everyman']. *Nation*, XXXI, 735—736, 1922.

84 ADOLF, HELEN: From 'Everyman' and 'Elckerlijc' to HvH and Kafka. *Comparative Literature*, IX, 204—214, 1957. Oregon.

85 NEIGHBOUR, O. W.: Frank Martin: Sonata da chiesa. Six monologues from HvH's 'Jedermann'. *Music and Letters*, XXXV, i, 70—71, 1954.

86 SHIPP, H.: Martin Harvey comes to Town. 'Via crucis' at the Garrick Theatre. [HvH's 'Everyman']. *English Review*, XXXVI, 265—268, 1923.

87 YOUNG, S.: 'Jedermann', German Vision. *New Republic*, LIII, 164, 1953. New York.

Die Josephslegende

88 KALISCH, ALFRED: 'The Legend of Joseph'. Plot by Harry Graf Kessler and HvH. Translated. Berlin, *Fürstner*, 1914.

Das kleine Welttheater

89 STEINER, HERBERT: Zu HvHs 'Kleinem Welttheater'. *MDU*, XXXV, 224—225, 1943.

Lucidor

90 BURKE, KENNETH: 'Lucidor', characters for an unwritten comedy, by HvH. Translated. *The Dial*, LXXIII, 121—132, 1922.

Oedipus und die Sphinx

91 REY, WILLIAM H.: Geist und Blut in HvHs 'Oedipus und die Sphinx'. *GQ*, XXXI, 84—93, 1958.

Prolog zu dem Buch 'Anatol'

92 BLAKEMORE, TREVOR: 'The Prologue to Anatol'. Rendered into English Verse. Published with a translation of Schnitzler's 'Liebelei' ['Playing with Love'] by P. Morton Shand. London, *Gay & Hancock Ltd.*, 1914. Shand: [Prologue] ... "incorporated in order to introduce to English readers the verse of the greatest living poet writing in the German language."

Prolog für ein Puppentheater

93 LOVING, PIERRE: 'Prologue for a Marionette Theater'. Englished by Pierre Loving. In: Pierre Loving, Ten minute plays, pp. 15—24. London, New York, *Brentano's*, 1924.

Reitergeschichte

94 CREIGHTON, BASIL: 'Cavalry Patrol' translated from 'Reitergeschichte'. In: Tellers of Tales. 100 Short Stories. Ed. by W. Somerset Maugham, pp. 860—867. New York, *Doubleday, Doran*, 1939.

95 GILBERT, MARY E.: HvHs 'Reitergeschichte' — Versuch einer Interpretation. *Deutschunterricht*, VIII, iii, 101—112, 1956.

96 GILBERT, MARY E.: Some Observations on HvH's Two Novellen 'Reitergeschichte' and 'Das Erlebnis des Marschalls von Bassompierre'. *GLL* (NS), XI, 102—111, 1957/58.

Der Rosenkavalier

97 KALISCH, ALFRED: 'The Rose-Bearer'. Translated from 'Der Rosenkavalier'. Berlin, *Fürstner*, 1912. Also Vocal Score, copyright 1911. The latter reprinted in 1939 by *Fürstner*.

98 JOUBERT, M.: The Librettist of 'Rosenkavalier'. *Times Literary Supplement*, 1927, pp. 381—382.

99 ROSE, MICHAEL: 'Der Rosenkavalier'. Extracts from letters between Strauss and HvH during composition of the opera. Selected by Michael Rose. With illustrations. *Opera*, X, 356—362, 1959.

Das Salzburger grosse Welttheater

100 BERGSTRÄSSER, ARNOLD: The Holy Beggar: Religion and Society in HvH's 'Great World Theatre of Salzburg'. *GR*, XX, 261—286, 1945.

101 BEST, A. J.: The Mystery Play in a Leeds Church. [Review of production of HvH's 'Great Theatre of the World'] *Spectator*, CXXXII, 80, 1924.

102 ELLIS, ADA M.: Language and Style in 'Das Salzburger grosse Welttheater' by HvH. *M. A. Thesis*. Manchester, 1952.

103 WELLESZ, EGON: HvH's 'Das Salzburger grosse Welttheater' [Description of production]. *Musical News and Herald*, XLIII, 190, 1922.

Der Schwierige

104 COHN, HILDE D.: Die beiden Schwierigen im deutschen Lustspiel. Lessing: 'Minna von Barnhelm' — HvH: 'Der Schwierige'. *MDU*, XLIV, vi, 257—269, 1952.

105 MAGILL, C. P.: Austrian Comedy. *GLL* (NS), IV, 40 ff. ['Der Schwierige'] 1950/51.

Der Tor und der Tod

106 GILBERT, MARY E. [Ed.]: 'Der Tor und der Tod'. Oxford, *Blackwell's German Texts*, 1942. Reviewed: A. Closs, *MLR*, XXXVII, 526—527, 1942. Reprinted in 1945 by *Blackwell*, also in New York, by *Salloch*.

107 BATT, MAX: 'Death and the Fool'. Translated from 'Der Tor und der Tod'. In: Poet Lore Plays, XXIV, 253—267. Boston, *Badger*, 1913.

108 HEARD, JOHN Jr.: 'Death and the Fool'. Translated. In: The German Classics of the 19th and 20th Centuries. Ed. Kuno Francke and W. G. Howard, XVII, 492—510. New York, *German Publishing Society*, 1913/15. Reprinted in: Representative One-Act Plays by Continental Authors. Ed. M. J. Moses. Boston, *Little*, 1922. Also in: *Poet Lore*, XLV, i, 5—21, 1939.

109 MIEROW, H. E.: 'The Fool and Death', a Metrical Translation of HvH's Poetic Drama 'Der Tor und der Tod'. Including: Introduction on the writings of HvH by Harvey W. Hewett-Thayer, 12 pp. Colorado Springs, *Colorado College Publication. Studies Series*, no. 5. 33 pp., 1930.

110 WALTER, ELISABETH: 'Death and the Fool'. Translated with the consent of the author. Boston, *Badger*, 1914.

133

111 ALEWYN, R.: HvH's 'Der Tor und der Tod' [An article]. *MDU*, XXXVI, viii, 409—424, 1944.

112 ARATA, O. S.: HvH, Lyric Dramatist. [Deals with 'Death and the Fool' with long extracts in translation]. *Open Court*, XXXVII, 551—557, 1923. Chicago.

Der Tod des Tizian

113 HEARD, JOHN Jr.: 'The Death of Titian'. Translated. In: The German Classics of the 19th and 20th Centuries. Ed. Kuno Francke and W. G. Howard. New York, *German Publishing Society*, 1913/15. Reprinted: Boston, *Four seas co.*, 1920.

Der Turm

114 REY, WILLIAM H.: Tragik und Verklärung des Geistes in HvHs 'Der Turm'. *Euph.*, XLVII, 161—172, 1953. Enlarged edition in: Das Deutsche Drama. Ed. Benno von Wiese, II, 265—283. Düsseldorf, *Bagel*, 1958.

115 REY, WILLIAM H.: Selbstopfer des Geistes: Fluch und Verheissung in HvHs 'Der Turm' und Thomas Manns 'Doktor Faustus'. *MDU*, LII, iv, 145—157, 1960.

Über die Pantomime

116 ANON: 'On Pantomime', translated from HvH. *English Review*, XXXVI, 261—264, 1923.

Vor Tag

117 COGHLAN, BRIAN: 'Vor Tag' [An article]. *Babel*, X, 21—24, 28, 1959. Australia.

Der weisse Fächer

118 MAGNUS, MAURICE: 'The White Fan'. An Interlude by HvH. Translated [Incomplete]. *The Mask*, I, xii, 232—234, 1909.

CORRESPONDENCE

a) Translations

119 ENGLAND, PAUL: Correspondence between Richard Strauss and HvH, 1907—1918. Translated. London, *Secker;* New York, *Knopf,* 1927. [Based on first German edition with a Preface by Franz Strauss, 1926.]

134

120 HAMMELMANN, HANNS and OSERS, EWALD: The Correspondence between Richard Strauss and HvH. Translated. Introduced by Edward Sackville-West. London, *Collins*, 1961. [Based on second German edition, Gesamtausgabe, edited by Willi Schuh, 1952 and 1955.] Reviewed *inter alia* by: Donald Mitchell, *Daily Telegraph*, 11 November; Neville Cardus, *The Guardian*, 9 November; Peter Heyworth, *The Observer*, 12 November; Desmond Shaw-Taylor, *The Sunday Times*, 12 November; Music Critic, *The Times*, 6 November (1961).

b) Reviews of German Editions

Eberhard von Bodenhausen

121 ANON: Review of the HvH/Bodenhausen 'Briefe der Freundschaft'. *International PEN Bulletin of Selected Books*, V, i, 1954.

Rudolf Borchardt

122 HAMBURGER, M.: Review of the 'HvH/Borchardt Briefwechsel'. *International PEN Bulletin of Selected Books*, VI, i, 1955.
123 PAULSEN, W.: Review of the 'HvH/Borchardt Briefwechsel'. *Erasmus*, IX, 269—271, 1956.

C. J. Burckhardt

124 WASSERMANN, F. M.: Review of 'Briefwechsel zwischen HvH und C. J. Burckhardt'. *GR*, XXXIII, 75—78, 1958.

Stefan George

125 ANON: Short review of 'Briefwechsel zwischen George und HvH'. Hrsg. von Robert Boehringer. Berlin, 1938. *GLL*, III, 319, 1938/39.

126 BRUNS, FRIEDRICH: Review of 'Briefwechsel zwischen George und HvH'. Berlin, *Georg Bondi*, 1939. *MDU*, XXXII, ii, 92—93, 1940.

127 DUTHIE, ENID L.: Some References to the French Symbolist Movement in the Correspondence of Stefan George and HvH. *Comparative Literature Studies*, III, ix, 15—18, 1943.

128 FEISE, ERNST: Review of 'Briefwechsel zwischen George und HvH'. Berlin, *Georg Bondi*, 1939. *MLN*, LV, 67—68, 1940.

129 GERHARD, MELITTA: Review of 'Briefwechsel zwischen George und HvH'. Berlin, *Georg Bondi*, 1939. *GR*, XV, 226—228, 1940.

130 GODFREY, F. M.: Review of 'Briefwechsel zwischen George und HvH'. *Contemporary Review*, CLXXXV, 316—317, 1954.

131 STEINER, HERBERT: Der Briefwechsel zwischen George und HvH [An article]. *GQ*, XIV, 84—94, 1941.

Claes Lindskog

132 SCHOOLFIELD, GEORGE C.: Two Unpublished Letters of HvH. *MDU*, LI, 337—340, 1959. [To Claes Lindskog, 1921.]

R. A. Schröder

133 STEINER, HERBERT: HvHs Brief an R. A. Schröder. *Mesa*, I, 37 ff., 1945, New York.

Speyer

134 STERN, GUY: HvH and the Speyers. A report on unpublished correspondence. *PMLA*, LXXIII, i, 110—115, 1958.

Richard Strauss

135 ABER, ADOLF: Strauss and HvH; a Revealing Correspondence. [Based on: 'Richard Strauss—HvH Briefwechsel'. Zurich, 1952]. *Musical Times*, XCV, 242—246, 1954.

136 GARTEN, HUGH, F.: The Strauss—HvH Letters. [An article occasioned by their publication by *Atlantis Verlag*, Zurich, 1952]. *Opera*, IV, 274—277, 1953.

137 WOCKE, HELMUT: Review of 'Richard Strauss—HvH Briefwechsel'. Zurich, 1952. *JEGP*, LII, ii, 279—280, 1953.

Anton Wildgans

138 BRADISH, J. A. VON: Der Briefwechsel HvH—Wildgans. *PMLA*, XLIX, 931—953, 1934. 2. erweiterte Ausgabe: Veröffentlichungen d. Verbindung deutscher Schriftsteller und Literaturfreunde in New York. Wissenschaftliche Folge, Heft 3. Zurich, *Franklin Press*, 1935.

HUGO VON HOFMANNSTHAL AND RICHARD STRAUSS

139 CARNER, M.: Strauss Festival at Covent Garden. *Time and Tide*, XXXIV, 1242, 1953.

140 COOPER, MARTIN: The End of the Affair. Comment on HvH, in particular the Strauss Libretti. *Daily Telegraph*, 11 February, 1961.

141 EINSTEIN, ALFRED: Strauss and HvH. *Monthly Musical Record,* LXIV, 99—100, 1934.

142 GARTEN, H. F.: HvH as a Librettist. *Opera,* I, 15—21, 1950.

143 GRAF, MAX: Strauss and his Librettist. *Opera News,* XVII, viii, 4—5, 26—27, 1953.

144 JOUBERT, M.: HvH and his Collaboration with Strauss. *Contemporary Review,* CXXXVI, 632—637, 1929.

145 MANN, WILLIAM; MITCHELL, DONALD; MAR, NORMAN DEL: The Strauss Festival at Covent Garden. Three comments [with illustrations]. *Opera,* IV, 648—664, 1953.

146 SCHARF, URSULA: HvH's Libretti. *GLL* (NS), VIII, 130—136, 1954/55.

147 WELLESZ, EGON: HvH und die Musik. In: HvH. Zum 70. Geburtstag des Dichters. London, *Free Austrian Movement,* 1944. pp. 5—7.

148 WELLESZ, EGON: HvH and Strauss. *Music and Letters,* XXXIII, iii, 239—242, 1952.

MONOGRAPHS

149 HAMMELMANN, HANNS: HvH. London, *Bowes & Bowes,* 1957. Reviewed: M. E. Gilbert, *MLR,* LIII, 286—287, 1958; J. C. Middleton, *GLL* (NS), XI, 152 ff. 1957/58.

CHAPTERS IN WORKS OF LITERARY HISTORY AND CRITICISM

150 BERGEL, LIENHARD: Voraussetzungen und Anfänge der Beziehungen zwischen Stefan George und HvH. New York, *University Press,* 1949.

151 BERGSTRAESSER, ARNOLD: HvH und der europäische Gedanke. Kiel, *Lipsius & Tischer,* 1951. [Lecture given during 'Kieler Woche' on 23 June, 1950.]

152 BITHELL, JETHRO [Ed.]: Germany. A Companion to German Studies. London, *Methuen,* 1955. 5th Edition. HvH: pp. 325—327 and *passim.*

153 BITHELL, JETHRO: Modern German Literature 1880—1950. London, *Methuen,* 1959. 3rd Edition. HvH: Chapter VIII, pp. 210—227.

154 BURNSHAW, STANLEY [Ed.]: The Poem Itself. New York, *Holt, Rinehart and Winston*, 1960. HvH: pp. 134—139. Translation and analysis of 'Die Beiden', 'Ballade des äusseren Lebens' and 'Der Jüngling in der Landschaft' by A. O. Jàszi.

155 CLOSS, AUGUST: The Genius of the German Lyric. An Historic Survey of its Formal and Metaphysical Values. London, *Allen and Unwin*, 1938. HvH: pp. 404—405.

156 CLOSS, AUGUST: Medusa's Mirror. In: Studies in German Literature. London, *The Cresset Press*, 1957. HvH: p. 93.

157 CLOSS, AUGUST: Die neuere deutsche Lyrik vom Barock bis zur Gegenwart. In: Deutsche Philologie im Aufriss. Hrsg. von Wolfgang Stammler. Berlin, Bielefeld, *Erich Schmidt Verlag*, 1960. 2. Ausgabe. HvH: Bd. II, 299—300.

158 CURTIUS, ERNST ROBERT: Europäische Literatur und Lateinisches Mittelalter. Translated by Willard R. Trask. London, *Routledge and Kegan Paul*, 1953. HvH: pp. 142—144 and *passim.*

159 DUKES, ASHLEY: Modern Dramatists. London, *Palmer*, 1911. HvH: pp. 159—180.

160 DUKES, ASHLEY: The Youngest Drama. Studies of Fifty Dramatists. London, *Ernst Benn*, 1923. HvH: pp. 28—30.

161 ELOESSER, ARTHUR: Modern German Literature. With an introduction by Ludwig Lewisohn. Translated from the German for the first time by Catherine Alison Phillips. New York, *Alfred Knopf*, 1933. HvH: pp. 180—189 and *passim.*

162 FRANCKENSTEIN, SIR GEORGE: Facts and Features of my Life. London, *Cassell*, 1939. HvH mentioned throughout: pp. 15, 17—21, 24, 31—32, 38, 39, 58—59, 238—243 [Briefwechsel], 317—321. p. 39: illustration of bust of HvH by Victor Hammer. p. 13: quotes poem with translation: 'Noch spür ich ihren Atem auf den Wangen . . .'.

163 GARTEN, H. F.: Modern German Drama. London, *Methuen*, 1959. HvH: pp. 63—76.

164 HAMBURGER, MICHAEL: Reason and Energy. Studies in German Literature. London, *Routledge and Kegan Paul*, 1957. HvH: pp. 204, 207, 215, 216, 232, 233, 309.

165 HENTSCHEL, CEDRIC: The Byronic Teuton. Aspects of German Pessimism 1800—1933. London, *Methuen*, 1940. HvH: Chapter VIII, Mors, Momus and Mars.

166 KEITH-SMITH, BRIAN: HvH. In: German Men of Letters. Twelve Literary Essays. Ed. by Alex Natan. London, *Oswald Wolff*, 1961. pp. 251—273.

167 KOHN, HANS: The Mind of Germany. London, *Macmillan*, 1961. Includes chapters on Goethe, Wagner, Nietzsche, Spengler, HvH, Rilke and others.

168 KOZIOL, HERBERT: Zu Thomas Otways 'Venice Preserved' und HvHs 'Das gerettete Venedig'. In: Österreich und die angelsächsische Welt. Hrsg. von Otto Hietsch. Wien, Stuttgart, *Wilhelm Braumüller*, 1961. pp. 418—431.

169 LANGE, VICTOR: Modern German Literature 1870—1940. Ithaca, New York, *Cornell University Press*, 1945. HvH: pp. 40—43 and Bibliography: pp. 165—167.

170 MUIR, E.: An Autobiography. London, *Hogarth Press*, 1954. HvH: pp. 219—220. "I thought him then and still think him the greatest German poet of that age...".

171 NICOLL, ALLARDYCE: World Drama. London, *Harrap*, 1949. HvH: pp. 612—613, 614.

172 PEACOCK, R.: The Poet in the Theatre. London, *Routledge*, 1946. HvH: pp. 108—124.

173 PRAWER, S. S.: German Lyric Poetry. A Critical Analysis of Selected Poems from Klopstock to Rilke. London, *Routledge and Kegan Paul*, 1952. HvH: pp. 204—210. 'Manche freilich...' and 'Ballade des äusseren Lebens'.

174 ROBERTSON, J. G.: The Literature of Germany. London, *Thornton Butterworth Ltd.*, 1913. *The Home University Library*. p. 242: "Austria can point to a poetic drama, of which the most distinguished representative at present [1913] is HvH — a drama worthy of a nation amongst whom Grillparzer is still a power".

175 ROBERTSON, J. G.: A History of German Literature. Third revised and enlarged edition by Edna Purdie with the assistance of W. I. Lucas and M. O'C. Walshe. Edinburgh & London, *Blackwood*, 1959. HvH: Part VI: The 20th Century, Chapter I, pp. 534—535.

176 SOMMERFELD, MARTIN [Ed.]: George, HvH, Rilke. New York, *Norton,* 1938. *Gateway Poets Series.*

177 THOMAS, R. HINTON: German Perspectives. Cambridge, *W. Heffer & Sons,* 1940. HvH: p. 6 and 54 and *passim.*

178 WAIDSON, H. M.: The Modern German Novel. A Mid-Twentieth Century Survey. Published for the University of Hull by the *Oxford University Press,* 1959. HvH: pp. 12—13, 75—76, 100.

ENTRIES IN WORKS OF REFERENCE

179 BIBLIOGRAPHY OF GERMAN LITERATURE IN ENGLISH TRANSLATION. [B. Q. Morgan] Madison, *Stanford University Press,* 1938. 2nd edition. HvH: Nos. 4540—4565 and Supplement.

180 CHAMBER'S BIOGRAPHICAL DICTIONARY. Edinburgh, *Chambers,* 1961. HvH: p. 650 (39 ll.) [D. W. Peetz.]

181 CHAMBER'S ENCYCLOPAEDIA. New Edition, 1924. HvH: V, 733 (38 ll.).

182 CHAMBER'S ENCYCLOPAEDIA. New Edition, 1950. HvH: VII, 165 (34 ll.) [W. Rose] This supersedes 1924 entry. Reprinted in 1959 edition.

183 ENCYCLOPAEDIA BRITANNICA. 14th Edition, 1929. HvH: XI, 622—623 (32 ll. inc. bibl.) Reprinted in all subsequent editions.

184 EVERYMAN'S ENCYCLOPAEDIA. 3rd Edition, 1949/50. HvH: VII, 175 (30 ll. inc. bibl.) Reprinted in 4th Edition, 1958: VII, 517.

185 GROVE'S DICTIONARY OF MUSIC AND MUSICIANS. 5th Edition, 1954. HvH: IV, 318, (27 ll.).

186 HUTCHINSON'S TWENTIETH CENTURY ENCYCLOPAEDIA. 3rd Revised Edition, 1957. HvH: p. 325 (7 ll.).

187 THE OXFORD COMPANION TO ENGLISH LITERATURE. Oxford, *Clarendon Press,* 1932. HvH: p. 376 (6 ll.) . . . "a pioneer of the new Romantic Movement in German drama . . .".

188 THE OXFORD COMPANION TO THE THEATRE. *Oxford University Press,* 1951. HvH: pp. 317 and 367. [W. E. Delp.]

189 PEOPLE. [Ed. Geoffrey Grigson and Charles Harvard Gibbs-Smith]. London, *Grosvenor Press,* 1954. HvH: p. 193. [M. Hamburger.]

140

190 ROUTLEDGE'S UNIVERSAL ENCYCLOPAEDIA. London, *Routledge*, 1934. HvH: p. 481 (3 ll.).

GENERAL CRITICISM

a) Articles in Periodicals

191 BAERLEIN, HENRY: HvH [An article, with portrait]. *Bookman*, XLVIII, 238—239, 1925. "This Viennese poet and essayist, writer of mysticism and of libretti, is regarded by many as the greatest imaginative artist now using the German language".

192 BAKER, GEORGE M.: HvH and Greek Tragedy. *JEGP*, XII, 383—406, 1913.

193 BEDNALL, J. B.: The Slav Symbol in HvH's Post-War Comedies. *GLL* (NS), XIV, 34—44, 1960/61.

194 BERGER, DOROTHEA: HvHs Gestalt im Wandel der Jahre. Vortrag gehalten im 'Literarischen Verein' zu New York. *Wort in der Zeit*, II, vii, 1—15, 1956.

195 BLOCK, HASKELL M.: HvH and the Symbolist Drama. *Transactions of the Wisconsin Academy of Sciences, Arts and Letters*, XLVIII, 161—178, 1959.

196 BLUME, B.: A Source of HvH's 'Aufzeichnungen zu Reden in Skandinavien'. *MLN*, LXX, iii, 157—165, 1955.

197 BURGER, HILDE: HvH's Debt to Molière. Monsieur de Pourceaugnac and Baron Ochs von Lerchenau. *ML*, XXXIX, ii, 56—61, 1958.

198 BURGER, HILDE: French Influences on HvH. *Comparative Literature. Proceedings of the Second Congress of the International Comparative Literature Association*. Ed. by Werner P. Friedrich. II, 691—697. Chapel Hill, *University of North Carolina Press*, 1959.

199 COGHLAN, BRIAN: The Cultural-Political Development of HvH during the First World War. *PEGS* (NS), XXVII, 1—32, 1958.

200 COGHLAN, BRIAN: Traditionelle Form und eigener Stil im Spätwerk HvHs. In: Stil- und Formprobleme in der Literatur. *Vorträge des 7. Kongresses der Internationalen Vereinigung für moderne Sprachen und Literatur in Heidelberg*. pp. 492—498. Heidelberg, *Carl Winter Universitätsverlag*, 1959.

201 COHN, HILDE D.: HvHs Gedichte für Schauspieler. *MDU*, XLVI, ii, 85—94, 1954.

202 FEISE, ERNST: Gestalt und Problem des Toren in HvHs Werk. *GR*, III, iii, 218—261, 1928.

203 FEISE, ERNST: Philosophische Motive im Werke des jungen HvH. *MDU*, XXXVII, iv & v, 31—39, 1945. Also in: Xenion. Essays in the History of German Literature. Baltimore, *Johns Hopkins Press*, 1950. pp. 269—278.

204 GILBERT, MARY E.: HvH and England. *GLL*, I, 182—192, 1936/37.

205 GILBERT, MARY E.: Recent Trends in the Criticism of HvH. *GLL* (NS), V, 255—268, 1951/52.

206 GOFF, PENRITH: HvH: The Symbol as Experience. *Kentucky Foreign Language Quarterly*, VII, 196—200, 1960.

207 GOLDSMITH, U. K.: Stefan George and the Theatre. *PMLA*, LXVI, 85—95, 1951. HvH: pp. 91—93.

208 GOLFFING, F.: The Position of HvH. *Partisan Review*, XIX, 711—725, 1952. [Occasioned by the publication of: Selected Prose, translated. London, 1952.]

209 GROSS, F.: HvH. An article. *Contemporary Review*, CXLIX, 709—714, 1936.

210 HILL, CLAUDE: HvH — A Classic of German Poetry in the 20th Century. *Universitas*, IV, i, 63—77, 1961.

211 HOWARTH, H.: T. S. Eliot's Criterion: the Editor and his Contributors. *Comparative Literature*, XI, ii, 97—110, 1959. HvH: pp. 102—104.

212 HOWARTH, H.: Eliot and HvH. *South Atlantic Quarterly*, LIX, 500—509, 1960.

213 JÁSZI, A. O.: Die Idee des Lebens in HvHs Jugendwerk 1890—1900. *GR*, XXIV, 81—107, 1949.

214 KÄSTNER, ERHARDT: HvHs Prosawerk. *Deutsche Beiträge zur geistigen Überlieferung*, III, i, 58—67, Chicago, 1949.

215 LANGE, VICTOR: Forms of Contemporary Poetry. *MDU*, XLVI, 171—180, 1954. [Rilke, HvH, George, Trakl, Benn.]

216 LIPTZIN, S.: Young Vienna. *Poet Lore*, XLVII, iv, 337—346, 1941.

217 MILCH, WERNER: New Forms of German Lyric Poetry [Translated from the German by S. D. Stirk] *GLL*, II, ii, 132—139. 1938.

218 MILNE, H. J. M.: Letters of Rilke, HvH and others to Marie Herzfeld. *British Museum Quarterly*, XIII, 11—13, 1938.

219 NAGLER, A. M.: HvH and Theatre. [An address given at the Plenary Session of the International Federation for Theatre Research in Vienna on 2 July, 1959] *Theatre Research*, II, i, 5—15, 1960.

220 NAUMANN, WALTER: Drei Wege der Erlösung in HvHs Werken. *GR*, XIX, 150—155, 1944.

221 NAUMANN, WALTER: Das Visuelle und das Plastische bei HvH. *MDU*, XXXVII, iii, 159—169, 1945.

222 NAUMANN, WALTER: HvHs Auffassung von seiner Sendung als Dichter. *MDU*, XXXIX, iii, 184—187, 1947.

223 NORTON, R. C.: HvH's Garden Image. *GQ*, XXXI, 94—103, 1958.

224 OSWALD, VICTOR A. Jr.: The Old Age of Young Vienna. *GR*, XXVII, iii, 189—199, 1952.

225 OSWALD, VICTOR A. Jr.: HvH's Collaboration with Molière. *GR*, XXIX, i, 18—30, 1954.

226 POLLARD, P.: Aestheticism of Vienna. *Masks and Minstrels*, 284—289 [About 1912. Unobtainable.]

227 REY, WILLIAM H.: Die Drohung der Zeit in HvHs Frühwerk. *Euph.*, XLVIII, 280—310, 1954.

228 REY, WILLIAM H.: Dichter und Abenteurer bei HvH. *Euph.*, XLIX, 56—70, 1955.

229 REY, WILLIAM H.: Eros und Ethos in HvHs Lustspielen. Eine Studie zur Kunst der Konfiguration in 'Der Abenteurer und die Sängerin', 'Cristinas Heimreise' und 'Der Rosenkavalier'. *DVJS*, XXX, 449—473, 1956.

230 SCHOOLFIELD, GEORGE C.: The Pool, the Bath, the Dive: the Water Image in HvH. *MDU*, XLV, vi, 379—388, 1953.

231 SCHUMANN, D. W.: Ernst Stadler and German Expressionism. *JEGP*, XXIX, 510—534, 1930. HvH: pp. 511—512, 517. ['Manche freilich . . .' and 'Der Jüngling in der Landschaft' quoted.]

232 SCHUMANN, D. W.: Gedanken zu HvHs Begriff der "konservativen Revolution". *PMLA*, LIV, 853—899, 1939.

233 SCHWARZ, ALFRED: The Allegorical Theatre of HvH. *Tulane Drama Review*, IV, iii, 65—76, 1960.

234 SEIDLIN, OSKAR: The Shroud of Silence. *GR*, XXVIII, 254—261, 1953. HvH: p. 255.

235 STEINER, HERBERT: HvHs 'Notizen zu einem Grillparzervortrag'. *MDU*, XXXVII, iii, 170—175, 1945.

236 STEINER, HERBERT: Erinnerungen an HvH. *Deutsche Beiträge zur geistigen Überlieferung.* pp. 203—207. Chicago, 1947.

237 STEINER, HERBERT: Über HvH. *MDU*, XLII, vii, 321—324, 1950. [Concerning the voluminous *Nachlass* publications.]

238 STEINER, HERBERT: A Note on 'Symbolism'. *Yale French Studies,* IX, 36—39, 1952. [HvH and George.]

239 STORK, C. W.: HvH as a Lyric Poet. *The Nation*, CII, 539—540, 1916. New York. [5 poems quoted in translation.] "The name of HvH is fairly well known to those who attempt to follow the course of modern literature in Europe...".

240 VORDTRIEDE, WERNER: Der Tod als ewiger Augenblick. Ein wiederkehrendes Symbol bei Annette von Droste-Hülshoff und HvH. *MLN*, LXIII, 520—525, 1948. [Deals with 'Im Moose' and 'Erlebnis'.]

241 VORDTRIEDE, WERNER: Das schöpferische Auge: Zu HvHs Beschreibung eines Bildes von Giorgione. *MDU*, XLVIII, 161—168, 1956.

242 WALTER, ELISABETH: HvH, Neo-Romanticist. *Poet Lore,* XXVI, 644—648, 1915.

243 WALTER, ELISABETH: HvH — an Exponent of Modern Lyricism. *Colonnade*, XII, 111—112, 1916.

244 WOLF, ALOIS: Weltgeheimnis: Reflections on HvH. *GLL* (NS), XI, 173—181, 1957/58.

245 WOOD, F.: HvH's Aesthetics: A Survey Based on the Prose Works. *PMLA*, LV, 253—265, 1940.

246 WOOD, F.: HvH and Kafka. Two Motifs. *GQ*, XXXI, 104—113, 1958.

b) Dissertations

247 ANDERSON, VERNON L.: HvH and Pedro Calderón de la Barca — A Comparative Study. *Ph. D. Dissertation.* Stanford University, 1954.

248 BARLOW, AUDREY: HvHs Weltanschauung. *M. A. Thesis.* Manchester, 1952.

249 BLOCK, VICTOR RICHARD: Untersuchungen zu HvHs 'Weg' der Lustspiele. *Ph. D. Dissertation.* Cornell, 1958.

250 COGHLAN, BRIAN L. D.: HvH's Three Festspiele and their Place in his Ethical Development. *Ph. D. Thesis.* Birmingham, 1957.

251 DODD, H. R.: A Study of the Dramas of HvH. *D. Phil. Thesis.* Oxford, 1953.

252 EVANS, CALVIN HOROYD: HvH's 'Kleine Dramen' as Seen in the Focus of Maeterlinck's 'Static Drama'. *Ph. D. Dissertation.* Oregon, 1958/59.

253 GRAY, MARY O. R.: HvH and XIXth Century French Symbolism. *Ph. D. Thesis.* Dublin, 1951.

254 GUDDAT, KURT HERBERT: HvH: eine Studie zur dichterischen Schaffungsweise. *Ph. D. Dissertation.* Ohio State University, 1958/59.

255 HALL, DORIS M.: The Venice Legend in German Literature since 1880. *Ph. D. Thesis.* London, 1936. [HvH's 'Andreas', 'Der Abenteurer und die Sängerin', 'Cristinas Heimreise', 'Florindo' and 'Der Tod des Tizian'.]

256 HAUSSMANN-SCHMIDT, ADA: HvH's Lyric Poetry: Interpretation and Critical Analysis. *Ph. D. Dissertation.* University of California, Los Angeles, 1958/59.

257 IVASK, IVAR V.: HvH als Kritiker der deutschen Literatur. *Ph. D. Dissertation.* Minnesota, 1954.

258 LEHN, MARIE THERESE: Tragedy and Comedy in HvH's Dramatic Works. *Ph. D. Dissertation.* Washington, 1960.

259 McGEARTY, LUCY: Stoff, Stimmungen und Form in der Lyrik HvHs. *M. A. Thesis.* University College, Dublin, 1947.

260 MERKEL, GERTRUD: Das Schaffen Georges, HvHs und Rilkes und ihr Verhältnis zur Schönheit. *Ph. D. Dissertation.* Bucknell University, 1951.

261 MOELLER, J. R.: HvH and Romanticism. *Ph. D. Dissertation.* Princeton, 1955.

262 O'SHIEL, EDA: HvHs Verhältnis zur Literatur. *Ph. D. Dissertation.* Vienna, 1957.

REVIEWS IN ENGLISH OF WORKS ON HOFMANNSTHAL
BY GERMAN AUTHORS

Die Erzählungen [Edition], Stockholm, 1945.
263 VORDTRIEDE, WERNER: *GR*, XXI, 235—236, 1946.
264 STEINER, HERBERT: A reply to Dr. Vordtriede. *GR*, XXII, 157—158, 1947.

Alewyn, Richard: HvHs Wandlung. Frankfurt, 1949.
265 ANON: *MLN*, LXV, iv, 291, 1950.

Alewyn, Richard: Über HvH. Göttingen, 1958.
266 BOULBY, M.: *MLR*, LIV, 620 ff., 1959.
267 COHN, HILDE D.: *JEGP*, LIX, 542—545, 1960.
268 LUCAS, W. I.: *GLL* (NS), XII, 145—146, 1958/59.
269 SCHWARZ, E.: *MLN*, LXXV, 540—543, 1960.

Heuschele, Otto: HvH. Dank und Gedächtnis. Freiburg, 1949.
270 ANON: *GLL* (NS), IV, 57, 1950/51.

Jens, W.: HvH und die Griechen.
271 SCHULTZ, H. S.: *JEGP*, LVII, 781—784, 1958.

Metzeler, W.: Ursprung und Krise von HvHs Mystik.
272 COHN, HILDE D.: *JEGP*, LVII, 605—607, 1958.

Pulver, Elsbeth: HvHs Schriften zur Literatur. Bern, 1956.
273 GILBERT, MARY E.: *GLL* (NS), XI, 239—240, 1957/58.

Schaeder, Grete: HvH und Goethe. Hameln, 1947.
274 ANON: *GLL* (NS), III, 238, 1949/50.

MISCELLANEOUS

275 ANON: Obituary: HvH, Poet and Librettist. *The Times*, 17 July, 1929. "In 1925 he visited London, and was entertained by his brother poets and dramatists".
276 ANON: Obituary: HvH. "No better poet has ever written operatic librettos". *London Mercury*, XX, 343, 1929.
277 ANON: The Passion of Acceptance. [An article on HvH.] *Times Literary Supplement*, 19 May, 1950, p. 308.

278 ALKER, ERNST: HvH as the Hero of a Swedish Drama. [Translated by Kenneth Northcott]. *GLL* (NS), IV, 298—300, 1950/51.

279 BRAUN, FELIX: Das Welterlebnis HvHs. In: HvH. Zum 70. Geburtstag des Dichters. London, *Free Austrian Movement*, 1944. pp. 7—15.

280 BRAUN, FELIX: Encounters with HvH. [Translated by Jenny Firth and Gabriele Reichbach.] *GLL* (NS), II, 1—12, 1948/49.

281 ELIOT, T. S.: Obituary: HvH. *Criterion*, IX, 5—6, 1929.

282 FRANCKENSTEIN, SIR GEORGE: Erinnerungen an HvH, meinen besten Freund. In: HvH. Zum 70. Geburtstag des Dichters. London, *Free Austrian Movement*, 1944. pp. 1—5.

283 FRANCKENSTEIN, SIR GEORGE: HvH Address at the Commemorative Festival Held at Salzburg, 20 August, 1948. With bibliographical note by H. F. Garten. *Contemporary Review*, CLXXV, 86—91, 1949.

284 HADAMOWSKY, F.: Ausstellung: HvH. Katalog. Veranstalter der Ausstellung: Österreichisches Kulturinstitut London; University of London, Institute of Germanic Languages and Literatures. London, 1961.

285 HAMBURGER, MICHAEL: HvHs Bibliothek. Ein Bericht. *Euph.* 4. Folge, 55. Band, 1. Heft, 15—76, 1961.

286 KARLWEIS, MARTA (Frau Jakob Wassermann): HvH. A Letter to a Doctor about a Poet. [Translated by M. D. Hottinger]. *Criterion*, XIII, 25—50, 1933.

287 MUELLER, P. W.: Das Oesterreichische Erbe als Grundlage für Stoff und Stil. In: HvH. Zum 70. Geburtstag des Dichters. London, *Free Austrian Movement*, 1944. pp. 20—25.

288 MURRAY, GILBERT: Griechische Elegie. In: Eranos. Festgabe zum 50. Geburtstage HvHs am 1. Februar 1924. München, *Bremer Presse*, 1924. p. 91.

289 REY, WILLIAM H.: Gebet Zeugnis: ich war da. Die Gestalt HvHs in Bericht und Forschung. *Euph.*, L, 443—478, 1956.

290 RYCHNER, M.: Obituary: HvH. [Translated by Marjorie Gabain]. *Criterion*, IX, 710—717, 1930.

291 STEINER, HERBERT: The Harvard Collection of HvH. *Harvard Library Bulletin*, VIII, 54—64, 1954.

292 WALDMANN, ELISABETH: Die Welt des Barock. In: HvH. Zum 70. Geburtstag des Dichters. London, *Free Austrian Movement,* 1944. pp. 16—20.

293 WASSERMANN, JAKOB: Aus: HvH der Freund. In: HvH. Zum 70. Geburtstag des Dichters. London, *Free Austrian Movement,* 1944. pp. 25—30.

WORK IN PROGRESS

294 GILBERT, MARY E.: Study on HvH.

295 GILBERT, MARY E.: HvH and Edgar Freiherr Karg von Beben-burg [An article].

296 HAMBURGER, MICHAEL [Ed.]: Selected Plays and Libretti of HvH. Bilingual Edition. With a Preface by T. S. Eliot. New York, *Pantheon Books* for Bollingen Foundation; London, *Routledge and Kegan Paul,* 1962. [Contains translations of 'Elektra', 'Der Rosen-kavalier', 'Der Schwierige', 'Das Grosse Salzburger Welttheater', 'Der Turm' and 'Arabella'.]

297 HAMBURGER, MICHAEL: A Critical Study of HvH.

298 HAMBURGER, MICHAEL: HvH's Tributes to Actors and Dancers. [Essay to be published in a miscellany, 1962.]

299 KEITH-SMITH, BRIAN: HvH. Eine Bibliographie 1890—1960. Hamburg. *Hauswedell,* 1962?

300 KEITH-SMITH, BRIAN: The Theme of Love in HvH. *Dissertation.* Southampton.

301 LLEWELLYN, R. T.: HvH's Way from the Ideal of 'Pure Poetry' to the Idea of the Writer's Social Responsibility. *M. A. Thesis.* Swansea.

302 PARRY, I. F.: Werther and Lord Chandos [An article].

303 PARRY, I. F.: Letter of Lord Chandos, by HvH [An article]. In: The Concise Encyclopaedia of Modern World Literature. Ed. by G. Grigson, Rainbird, McLean. London.

304 SCHWARZ, ADOLF: Translation of HvH plays. New York, *Bobbs-Merrill,* 1962 or 1963.

305 SOLOMON, R.: HvH and Comedy. *Dissertation.* Manchester.

306 WILLIAMS, J. A.: HvH's Imagery. *B. Litt. Thesis,* Oxford.